D1173946

Text Production

TEXT PRODUCTION

Michael Riffaterre
[*translated by* Terese Lyons]

New York Columbia University Press *1983*

Columbia University Press wishes to acknowledge the generous assistance of the French Ministry of Culture in preparing the translation of the work.

Library of Congress Cataloging in Publication Data

Riffaterre, Michael.
Text production.

Translation of: La production du texte.
Includes bibliographical references and index.
1. Literature. 2. Poetics. 3. French literature—
PN45.R5313 1983 808.1'00141 82-25509
ISBN 0-231-05334-7

Columbia University Press
New York Guildford, Surrey

Printed in the United States of America

Clothbound editions of Columbia University Press books are Smyth-sewn and printed on permanent and durable acid-free paper.

Contents

1. Explaining Literary Phenomena *1*

2. Semantics of the Poem *26*

3. Literary Sentence Models *43*

4. Poetics of Neologisms *62*

5. Paragram and Significance *75*

6. Toward a Formal Approach to Literary History *90*

7. Intertextual Semiosis: Du Bellay's "Songe," VII *109*

8. From Structure to Code: Chateaubriand and the Imaginary Monument *125*

9. Production of the Narrative (I): Balzac's *La Paix du ménage* *157*

10. Production of the Narrative (II): Humor in *Les Misérables* *168*

11. The Poem as Representation: A Reading of Hugo *181*

12. The Extended Metaphor in Surrealist Poetry *202*

13. Semantic Incompatibilities in Automatic Writing *221*

14. Overdetermination in the Prose Poem (I): Julien Gracq *240*

15. Overdetermination in the Prose Poem (II): Francis Ponge *259*

Notes *284*

Index *333*

Text Production

[1]

Explaining Literary Phenomena

I SHOULD like to make a few observations on how the concept of *explanation* should be modified when it is applied to literature. What does it mean to explain a work of literature? How does one go about it? These are the kinds of question I shall be asking.

Since my approach will be a formal one, it would perhaps be of some use to remember that textual analysis has nothing to do with traditional normative stylistics or rhetoric. Rhetoric did no more than generalize an analysis and turn it into a presciptive codification.

It must also be emphasized that analysis does not attempt to form value judgments; it is not literary criticism. It records the existence of something which is then, and only then, appropriated by criticism. Since it simply studies the behavior of words in a work of literature, it is closely related to linguistics. The specific characteristics of the literary work, however, require that textual analysis and linguistics, despite their proximity, continue to be differentiated from each other.

Indeed, it would not be reason enough for the study and teaching of literature to have recourse to linguistics simply because literature is made up of words. The essential problem confronting linguists in a verbal work of art is its *literariness.*[1] Some have tried to solve this problem by generalizing specific textual occurrences and extrapolating a grammer of poetic language from them. They hope, in this way, to find a place for literary expression within the framework of a general theory of signs. Because it is a generalization, this kind of investigation, which belongs to the realm of poetics, cannot account for one particular characteristic of the literary verbal message:[2] its textual nature. This kind of message is known only through texts, which is to say, monuments. Now monuments, unlike informants, cannot be manipulated, tested, and questioned. And a grammar extrapolated from a text, even if it were to produce nothing but idiolectic sentences analogous to those in the text, would nonetheless never produce another literary text.[3]

The text is always one of a kind, unique. And it seems to me that this *uniqueness* is the simplest definition of literariness that we can find. This definition can be quickly confirmed if we remember that the literary experience is characteristically disorienting, an exercise in alienation, a complete disruption of of our usual thoughts, perceptions, and expressions. This is what André Breton meant in his reply to Paul Valéry: "Le poème doit être une débâcle de l'intellect. Il ne peut être autre chose."[4]

The text works like a computer program designed to make us experience the unique. This uniqueness is what we call style. It has long been confused with the hypothetical individual termed the author; but, in point of fact, *style is the text itself.*

The difference between poetics and textual analysis is that poetics generalizes and dissolves a work's uniqueness into poetic language, but analysis, as I see it, attempts to explain the unique.

Now explanation in literature (it would not be too much of a play on words to say that *explication de texte* boils down to just that: it is a literary genre, largely oral, in which the traditional principles that I am examining are systematically applied)—explanation in literature, as it is practiced, has always consisted in generalizing, just like all explanations.[5] The problem here is that a generalization tends to keep the reader from seeing the uniqueness from which it stems. Worse yet, it goes in the same direction as the reader's natural resistance to the text. The reader resists with all the strength of his personal temperament, taboos, and habits. He resists by rationalizing, and his rationalizations reduce everything that is strange in the text to something known and familiar. Explication of texts is really a machine for taming a work, for defusing it by reducing it to habits, to the reigning ideology, to familiar mythology, to something reassuring.

So we have to change our course and head toward the unique, the ineffable, the *je ne sais quoi* that we have been kindly warned is accessible only through some mystical operation. This is where formal analysis proves its utility, if only by enabling us to describe the facts accurately. I would like to propose a definition of the literary phenomenon based on this kind of analysis. It should show just how far off the track traditional explication has been. My definition consists of two essential points.

POINT ONE: *The literary phenomenon is not only the text, but also its reader and all of the reader's possible reactions to the text*—both *énoncé* and *énonciation.*[6] The explanation of an utterance should not, therefore, be a description of its forms, or a grammer, but rather a description of those of its components that prompt rationalizations. The explanation of a rationalization should not consist in confirming or disproving it in terms of the external standards or yardsticks to which critics have traditionally turned: they confirm a rationalization by speaking of "truth," "historical accuracy," and so forth, or deny it by reducing it to an ideology, by seeing it as the reflection of a class- or time-bound mythology, and so forth. A relevant explanation of a rationalization will consist first in accepting the rationalization as a way of perceiving the text and, therefore, in recognizing that it is linguistic in nature. We can confirm it by showing that the words impose it on us, and we can disprove it by showing that the words do not. It matters little that the rationalization may be a mistake in relation to things as long as that mistake is reality in relation to the representation of things.

Let us consider the characteristics of the literary communication act: whereas a normal communication act involves the presence of five elements (to simplify matters, I am not counting the element of *contact*, which I consider to be presupposed by the simultaneity of the other five), literary communication has only two components physically present as things—the message and the reader.[7] The other three exist only as representations. In fact, the linguistic code is represented by the form and within the limits of its realization in the text, a realization that can either conform to or transgress the code. Reality and the author are either verbally present (in which case there is mimesis or simple decoding) or deduced from the utterance and reconstituted by the reader (and then there is rationalization, that is, decoding plus extrapolation from the decoding, based on models—ideologies, for instance—that the reader carries within himself). Contact is assured not by the kind of passive reception involved in normal communication, but by the active performance (in the musical sense of the term) of the score represented by the text.

These particularities of literary communication have three consequences. First, communication is a game, or rather a kind of calisthenics, since it is guided and programmed by the text. An explanation must show how this control is effected by the words. Second, since the game is played according to the rules of language, conforming to or transgressing them, the reader perceives the text in relation to his usual behavior in ordinary communication: a nonfigurative text will be reconstituted and rationalized as figurative. It is, therefore, totally irrelevant to speak of a given text's truth or untruth. We can explain it only by evaluating the degree to which it conforms to the verbal system and by asking ourselves if it obeys the conventions of the code or transgresses them. Third, reality and the author are substitutes for the text. As far as the *author* is concerned, we have one of two possibilities: either he will be represented in the text, or he will not.

In the first case, the author's presence is encoded (in a first person autobiographical narrative, for example), and the author's "I" is merely one particular case of character representation. If the representation of the author takes the form of a statement of intentions, the explanation should not consist in judging the work according to those intentions (in terms, that is, of success or failure). To do so would be to succumb to the error of positivism. Nor should the explanation consist in rejecting the intentions. This would amount to taking the position of the formalists, which is acceptable only when those intentions are expressed outside the text. The explanation should consist in showing the effect of the statement of intention: it directs the reader toward certain interpretations and provides him with a key for decoding the text. For example, the mimesis of intention can be a genre marker. It can also suggest that two simultaneous readings are called for, the interpretation that the metalinguistic statement of intention seems to require and the interpretation indicated by the shape of the utterance, which is the object of this metalanguage. The result of this simultaneity can be a form of irony.

In the second case, the author is not present in the text, but the reader readily imagines him and places him there, after the model of ordinary communication, where an encoder's existence is always evident. This image of an author is, therefore, nothing other than a rationalization. Not that it does not have its use: it serves a purpose to the limited extent that it enables us to complete the title and label and identify the text more quickly than we could by giving a synopsis of it. It is a way of symbolizing the text's characteristics. Consequently, there is nothing wrong with fabricating an author out of his words (which, by the way, is a favorite pastime of traditional criticism), but only on the condition that we fully realize that this author is a by-product of the text. The rationalized author must also not be confused with the historical author, the living writer. If we use the former to improve upon the portrait of the latter, we can prove that the writer-author's only importance is as a represented author, an author in words. In any case, such preoccupations remain outside the literary phenomenon. If, however, we amend the rationalized author's image with the help of the historical author, we destroy the text. We cannot, therefore, invoke the former to explain other texts written by the same person. (This is done all the time, nevertheless, in the two stereotypical and complementary approaches of showing either that the author evolves or that he does not.) To do so would be tantamount to presupposing a stylistic identity between the first text and the others—which is an impossibility. The largest analyzable corpus that we conceive in literature should be the text and not a collection of texts.

POINT TWO: *The text is a limiting and prescriptive code.* Since it is the performance of a score, the text's *énonciation* is not free, or rather, freedom and lack of freedom in interpreting are both encoded in the *énoncé*. In nonliterary communication, because of the grammatical probabilities that every segment of the utterance permits us to evaluate (since the verbal sequence is a stochastic series),[8] considerable latitude in decoding is left to the receiver of the message. If the situation were the same in literary communication, the text would not be a monument, for it would be incapable of enduring. Nor could it function as a program or score. It could not force the reader to experience a feeling of disorientation or strangeness.

We must, therefore, assume that the literary text is constructed in such a way that it can control its own decoding. In other words, its components do not occur according to the same system of probability as in ordinary communication. To describe them, we must have recourse to a different way of segmenting the verbal sequence than the one used by linguistics. We are therefore justified in considering a text's style to be a dialect or subcode. Like all dialects, a text's style takes its syntax, and even its phonology, from language, from the code. But it uses other "words," different lexical and semantic units, and these do not correspond to the words in the dictionary.

By definition, these specifically stylistic units compel the reader's attention. This characteristic requires the analysis to be absolutely obedient to the text, and this obedience should be the cardinal rule of the explication. Not only should it neither emend nor extrapolate from the text, *the explanation should also be based only on those elements that we are obliged to perceive.* Limited in this way, our explanation differs from usual structuralist interpretation, which seeks to integrate everything into its model, but succeeds only in integrating the text qua linguistic material, and not the text qua text.

Once the need for a specific segmentation of the verbal sequence is admitted, it matters little, in view of this discussion, whether or not we know how to put that segmentation into actual practice.

At most, and only because my examples will reflect the model I have adopted, I shall briefly point out that I define a stylistic unit as a dyad made up of inseparable poles, the first of which creates a probability and the second of which frustrates that probability. The contrast between the two results in a stylistic effect. Even if another model seemed preferable, it should still, like the one proposed here, satisfy the following condition: the stylistic unit cannot be confused with the units obtained through normal segmentation, to wit, words and phrases; and, consequently, it must be a group of words (or of sentences) joined together in something other than a syntagmatic relationship. All explanations based on words considered in isolation must therefore be rejected. This type of explanation ultimately leads critics to deny the existence of stylistic features, even though they are clearly perceived, simply because they can be explained only by looking beyond the isolated word.

This is what Antoine Adam does, to give one example, when he discusses the second tercet of Baudelaire's "L'Idéal":

> Ou bien toi, grande Nuit, fille de Michel-Ange,
> Qui tors paisiblement dans une pose étrange
> Tes appas façonnés aux bouches des Titans.

[Or you, great Night, daughter of Michaelangelo, peacefully wringing, in a strange pose, your breasts which were shaped by the mouths of Titans.]

According to Adam,[9] "there is nothing original in the use of the verb *tordre.*" The proof of this, in his opinion, is that Théophile Gautier speaks of women who "tordait leurs membres nus en postures infâmes" [twisted their naked limbs in vile positions], as well as of "corps tordus dans toutes les postures" [bodies twisted in all possible positions]. In point of fact, these texts are not comparable. Gautier is using a cliché in the mimesis of orgies (and metonymically, erotic mimesis): he is describing a frenzied surrender to pleasure. *Tors paisiblement* has exactly the opposite connotation: Night has control over pleasure. An image of the Ideal, as opposed to Gavarni's prostitutes who would behave like the creatures in Gautier, even in the midst of sensual pleasure, it retains the impassive serenity of Beauty in "La Beauté,"[10] the sonnet preceding this one. So, no matter what Adam may think, there is indeed originality here. Be that as it may, what must be stressed is that the commentator's reaction, however negative, proves the efficacy of the very feature whose value he is denying. Adam is blind to the stylistic phenomenon only because he has isolated the word *tordre*, for the stylistic phenomenon lies in the antithetical polarity between *tors* and *paisiblement*. Although mutually exclusive, these words are nonetheless indissolubly linked together by a verbal impossibility of the type found in *merle blanc* [white blackbird], where the signifier *blanc* implies the opposite of the essential characteristic of *merle*'s signified.[11] If Adam, like Vivier, Crépet, and Blin before him, made irrelevant comparisons, it is because they were reacting to a stylistic effect, but resorted to traditional segmentation of the sentence into lexical units to account for it. Now, in normal usage, and in particular if it refers to *corps* or *membres, tordre* excludes *paisiblement* and its synonyms and calls instead for descriptions hyperbolizing the idea of violent effort and convulsive twisting. Gautier has provided us with two examples of precisely this highly predictable sequence. But taking one word at a time keeps us from recognizing that in the text, and only in the text, *tordre* has the opposite property of generating the least predictable sequence. This property can be perceived only if the unit is not the word, but that word associated with another, so that their newly created compatibility, defined by their grouping, is superimposed on their natural incompatibility. It should be noted that the elimination of isolated words necessarily leads to the elimination of the notion of *key words* and to a radical reappraisal of the use of statistics in literature: the hypothesis that a word's high frequency suffices to make it a key word will have to be abandoned. Even if its frequency proves that a word corresponds to an obsession of the writer, that word is merely a stylistic potential. For its potential to be realized in the text, it would seem that the word must be the marked element in a group. Frequency calculations should take into consideration only those groups that are variants of a single structure.

Again, because of the principle of specific segmentation, any explanation based on word groups must be rejected if it fails to show that syntagmatically linked words are also linked together by something else. As an example, let us consider Yves Le Hir's commentary on these two lines from Baudelaire's "Le Balcon":

> Comme montent au ciel les soleils rajeunis
> Après s'être lavés au fond des mers profonds.

[As suns, after cleansing themselves at the depths of the deep seas, climb to the sky.]

Le Hir clearly sensed the importance of the group *au fond des mers profondes*, but since he saw it only as a syntagm, he was forced to try, in vain, to account for its stylistic effect with an unlikely shift in meaning: *profondes*, in his opinion, must mean "extending as far as the eye can see," for it would otherwise "make for a pleonasm with *au fond*."[12] In fact, it is precisely because of this pleonasm that the syntagm is made into a stylistically relevant group. Since repetition would be a transgression of logic or of traditional aesthetics (neither of which have any bearing here), Le Hir claims there is no repetition. But it is precisely repetition that, by violating the law whereby sentences progress from one word to the next by semantic differentiation, creates the stylistic effect. What we have here is an example of hyperbole based on the repetition of a defining semantic feature. Stock epithets and paronomasia such as *dormez votre sommeil* [sleep your sleep] are specific cases of this type of hyperbole. It could even be compared to the *maîtresse des maîtresses* [mistress of mistresses] construction at the beginning of the poem. The hyperbole here is a stylistic form of the mimesis of the extreme: it is the complement of *gouffre interdit à nos sondes* [unfathomable depths].

In accordance with the principle of obedience to the text, any explanation that, when faced with a group of obscure or ambiguous words, would attempt to reduce the ambiguity or explain away the obscurity must be rejected. This, of course, means that we must give up the acrobatic performances of traditional commentaries. The fact is, however, that obscure and ambiguous passages are as much a part of the text's semantic structure as its clearest passages.

The ambiguity, which the explanation must keep from destroying, is not the result of a faulty reading or a lack of understanding that can vary with the readers. It is in the text: it simultaneously encodes the evidence that several interpretations are possible and that making a choice among them is impossible.

The same holds for obscurity. It is usually explained in terms of symbolism or of a word's plurality of meanings. But all words are polysemous.[13] For polysemy to have a role in style, the plural reading must impose itself on the reader. This is why I would see a paragram, in either the limited or the broader sense of the term,[14] only when an element in the text forces me to look for a metatext.

These problems all point to the role of one particular property of stylistic phenomena: we must be able to perceive them. The methodological consequences of this property are very far-reaching: it went unnoticed by the structuralists, who were thus led to introduce the concept of the *latency of structures* into their explanations. This concept seems to me to distort the facts.

The difference between an invariant and the variants that actualize it in a text is translated, by a far from surprising metalinguistic accident, into practical but false images: people speak of a text's surface or literal meaning, and of its deep or true meaning—that is, its structure—and also of reading in depth—in other words, the identification of the structure. So it is easy to posit a contradiction between surface and depth based on the archetypal contradiction between appearances and reality.

This tendency to seek out hidden meanings has, of course, always existed in literary criticism. In the first place, the esoteric concept of the "false bottom" is a universal obsession. Moreover, it places the critic in a flattering light: he can go farther than you or I. It can no longer be said that his vision is inferior to the poet's. But if this hieroglyphic conception of the text has always appealed to critics, it is even more difficult to resist its temptation when we posit a variant/invariant duality.

Barthes writes that "the Racinian theatre finds its coherence only on the level of [the] ancient fable, situated far beyond history or the human psyche: the purity of the language, the grace of the alexandrines . . . are very slight protections; the archaic bedrock is there, close at hand."[15] Quite the contrary is true, however, as a naive reading or checklist of adjectives could show: form in Racine is violent and shocking. His tropes simply translate "the virtually asocial state of humanity" into a conventional language. But translating is not sugar-coating. The convention is a code; it is not censorship. It is precisely because of the restrictions on vocabulary that the notions of "primitive" savagery are so conspicuous. When Barthes contrasts deep-down savageness to surface protections such as euphemism and verse, he is maintaining one of bourgeois mythology's fictions concerning classicism. Other versions of it can be found in the diction of Racinian actors, which Barthes himself has so rightly stigmatized, and also in Leo Spitzer's *klassische Dämpfung*.[16]

The profound violence is not veiled, but rather is expressed through a stylized representation. In the Racinian code itself formal characteristics can be discerned that correspond to the archetypal structures of primitive thought. Now, since this correspondence manifests itself stylistically, it must necessarily be perceived: the structure is not latent. By this I mean that the variants actualizing the invariant must be perceived as variants, and not simply as stylistic phenomena. The difference is the same as in cases of simple stylistic features that are not perceived only as words. The decoding of the text is controlled so that the reader perceives a given segment of the verbal sequence not only as stylistically marked, but also as a variant: it is perceived as the corollary of something else.

If this were not the case, we would be quite incapable of constructing models. Obviously, in each stylistic feature actualizing an invariant, there are formal characteristics that make the reader aware of a similarity between that feature and others elsewhere in the text—different features, but which he feels he can associate with the first despite their difference.

A variant is encoded in such a way that, first, it reveals that it is hiding something and, second, it indicates how we can find that something. In this sense, and only in this sense, can we speak of *latency*. It is *la profondeur de la lettre*, a paradoxical depth of the surface.

The first of these features, the one that points to the structural function of a stylistic fact—I shall call it the deictic feature—is the impossibility of decoding without referring to some external element (external, that is, to a word's meaning, to a group's stylistic effect, to the special code, and so on). In short, it is perceived as a distortion of the mimesis.

The second of these features, the one that shows the reader where to look for the structural relationship and how to interpret it—let us call it the hermeneutic feature—seems to lie in the nature of the mimesis distortion, in the type of distortion (substitution, addition, subtraction, and so forth), which is recognizable as isomorphic with other distortions of other mimeses.

For an example of this, let us look at a poem from Victor Hugo's *Les Rayons et les Ombres*: "Puits de l'Inde! tombeaux! monuments constellés!" The text describes a Piranesian descent into "l'amas tournoyant de marches et de rampes" [the swirling mass of steps and ramps] of an underground temple similar to the one on Elephanta, which so aroused the imagination of the Romantics. At the end of the poem, the narrator gives us to understand that the entire architectural description was only a metaphor:

> O rêves de granit! grottes visionnaires! . . .
> Vous êtes moins brumeux, moins noirs, moins ignorés,
> Vous êtes moins profonds et moins désespérés
> Que le destin, cet antre habité par nos craintes

[O dreams of granite! Visionary grottoes! . . . You are less misty, less black, less unknown, you are less profound and less desperate than destiny, that cave inhabited by our fears]

All the details describing the ruins in the fifty lines preceding this comparison now take on a different kind of a posteriori aptness. While the reader was deciphering them, they seemed realistic because they conformed to the ideal descriptive system of ruins. But a deictic feature, the exoticism so strangely wanting in these Hindu ruins, had put the reader on his guard. Thus alerted, he could not fail to notice one constant: not only are the ruins not Hindu, but the text veers off toward describing a "Gothic" ruin, and the temple looks more and more like a subterranean passageway in Ann Radcliffe or Matthew Gregory Lewis. The metamorphosis of the temple into a scene from a Gothic novel has as its counterpart in the representation of the Cave of Destiny (which gives the meaning of the metaphor) the only word that does not belong in a cave mimesis: the adjective *désespéré.* Of course, the cave and temple images represent destiny as mystery: this is their explicit meaning as stylistic phenomena. But the deviations constitute a hermeneutic feature that forces the reader to decipher them as structural phenomena as well. Whether they are the perfect architectural setting for sadistic confinement or the obscure labyrinth of despair, they actualize the same invariant. The components of this invariant, now translated in terms of destiny, represent destiny as the inevitable—as inescapable Ananke.

This is, however, only the first semantic network in the poem. Another series of deviations from the mimesis of ruins reveals just as clearly that it is hiding another structure: the use of proper names having metaphysical connotations in Romantic mythology (for example, "Effrayantes Babels que rêvait Piranèse" [Frightening Babels dreamed by Piranesi]), adjectives with a similar sense (*grottes visionnaires*), images that do not fit the setting (the depths compared to a *fournaise*, a blazing furnace, turning the viewer into an alchemist), and deviant allegorical attributes. (The ruin is the cell of a *vieillard surhumain*, a superhuman old man, who is meditating over a book—recalling the rabbi in *Melmoth*, who, while hiding from the Inquisition in the underground passages of Toledo, keeps studying the secrets of nature, or the magus in Balzac's *Centenaire*, a kind of Frankenstein in a subterranean laboratory. There is also a cord hanging there and mysteriously offering itself to the hands of passers-by, "corde qui pend" and "s'offre, mystérieuse, à la main du passant," which is an obvious invitation to climb up to the Unknown or the Ideal.) All these elements are foreign to ruins per se, and all are characterized by esoteric symbolism. Furthermore, the ruin's depth is more than dizzying: it opens up on both sides in a manner defying descriptive verisimilitude ("Toits de granit, troués comme une frêle toile / Par où l'on voit briller quelque profonde étoile" [Granite roofs, shot through with holes like a thin canvas through which we see some deep star shining]), or transgressing the confinement mimesis. (The sagging floors give way to reveal spiral staircases descending into a *souterrain sans fond*, a bottomless underground passage, and other spiral staircases *crèvent le plafond*, burst through the ceiling. These torn openings onto the unknown should be stressed: "Où vont-ils? Dieu le sait" [Where do they go to? God knows], and far off in the distant hallways lamps are shining, canceling out the barrier of darkness.)

All this runs counter to the interpretation settled on by the commentators.[17] In their view, the poem is effective because it expresses one of Hugo's main psychological obsessions, his masochistic claustrophobia. This interpretation holds true only if the stylistic phenomena are considered as nothing but stylistic phenomena (that is, as borrowings from the motifs of Gothic novels). If, however, we decode them in relation to the deviations we have noted—in other words, if we decode them as variants—then these "cavernes où l'esprit n'ose aller trop avant" [caves in which the mind dares not go too far] become paths of initiation. These "monuments constellés" [starry monuments] are a variant of an eminently Hugolian structure: a vertical line leading from one infinity to another. (Variations on it abound: dream stairways rising from Death to Life, the metaphysical well into which the poet gazes, the perpendicular path opened up by the buried Titan, an image of the mind seeking Truth all the way to the sky on the other side of the earth, etc.)[18] Consequently, the poem does not symbolize confinement but is, instead, an invitation to escape. The anguish it expresses is merely a stylistic tool emphasizing the anxieties of the esoteric quest. The poem is effective because, while seeming to speak to us of Destiny, it depicts it in terms that, as always in Hugo, turn it into the great adventure of the *anima perambulans in tenebris*, the soul wandering in darkness.

It remains for me to consider the problem of literature as *representation*. In my description of the characteristics specific to literary communication, I remarked that in it, reality is a substitute for the text. This property demands that we drop the traditional viewpoint of the commentators; indeed, it follows that *the referent has no pertinence to the analysis*. No advantage is to be gained by comparing literary expression to reality or by evaluating a work of literature in terms of such a comparison.

Critics have found themselves at an impasse whenever they have turned to an outside norm to define literature. So this leaves us with only signifiers and signifieds. But to begin with the signified would be to adopt a genetic point of view. From my own perspective, which is phenomenological, the signified is deduced from the text. If it is true that every word is attached to a mythology or system of commonplaces, every word combination and, therefore, every stylistic unit will mix those systems and cancel out certain aspects of the mythology. Whether limits are placed on a system or a substitution performed within it, the operation can be defined only by combinations of signifiers. For the reader to perceive these eliminations or substitutions, he must first be able to identify the system and to recognize the mythology involved. Now, this identification is itself possible only if stereotypes are present in the text, which, when read, even if only in fragmentary form, set it in motion: the reading triggers in our minds the development of the system of commonplaces, or at least predisposes us to decipher what follows with full awareness that the system is present as the verbal context.

I must stress one point: the very way in which the score of the text is deciphered totally subordinates the signified to the signifier. Everything happens at the level of the signifier. Everything in what we call the signified is perceived in relation to clichés—in relation, that is, to word combinations, to signifiers. We do not first read words and then form mental images or concepts that constitute their meaning. First come the words that we read, and then come word groups, recorded by the memory, in which the words read appear in different positions and, therefore, with different functions. This explains why literary representations are not affected by modifications in the referent or by the evolution of myths: *white Christmas*[19] retains all its power for an Australian whose Christmas down under has never known snow. He has no trouble deciphering Christmas carols or Thomson's *Seasons*, because *white Christmas* is a stereotype that functions as a hyperbole of *Christmas*. It is a more complete representation of Yuletide, hence a more perfect and a more effective one. And if our Australian's mythology should be an agnostic system, then *white Christmas* becomes the hyperbole of *winter*: it is a particularly expressive element in an ideal verbal model for describing winter as opposed to the seasons without snow. This happens irrespective of the actual patterns of the seaons on the Australian continent.

By contrast, the disintegration of a linguistic code and, therefore, of associations between signifiers can turn a literature into a dead literature. For an example of this, let us consider the *larmes de fiel* [tears of gall] that Baudelaire speaks of in "Réversibilité." To explain this hyperbole of hatred in Baudelaire's text, there is no need to oppose it to its incompatible physiological referents, bile and tears.[20] The reader does not sense such an opposition. He does not imagine eyes crying bile, in a type of extreme term like *sweating blood*. He need not even resort to the mythology inherited from old-fashioned humoral medicine. Quite simply, *tears* is an image of bitterness in the framework of the descriptive system of sorrow, which includes the cliché *larmes amères*, or "bitter tears." And the same holds true for *fiel*—witness the cliché *coupe de fiel* [cup of gall], which is closely related to *lie amère* [bitter dregs]. (This stereotype dates from long before our era: consider the sponge dipped in gall, part of the standard description of the Crucifixion.) In the case of *fiel*, its verbalization was made all the easier by the alliterative opposition: Latin *fel/mel*, French *fiel/miel* [gall/honey], which phonetically actualizes the archetypal simultaneity of opposites. The image of all the ironies of fate, this simultaneity of contraries is evidenced by compound constructions found the world over, such as *bittersweet, doux-amer, bittersüss, agrodolce*, and the like. (Such compounds are variants of a structure defined by the resolution of a polar opposition.) So nothing is left of the referents: we are dealing with two stereotyped signifiers, with two highly effective synonyms of bitterness.

Baudelaire simply joined these two complementary synonyms together. In fact, their very complementarity is a stereotype. For example, the following line from Racine's *Phèdre* is hyperbolic, for it adds synonyms together: "Me nourrissant de fiel, de larmes abreuvée" [Nourished with gall, quenching my thirst with tears].[21] Baudelaire's hemistich, however, renews the cliché by replacing parataxis with hypotaxis, a construction analogous to *au fond des mers profondes*, which we have already discussed.

In any case, the referent here is a rationalization corresponding to nothing encoded and must, consequently, be rejected by the analyst. Because of the referential function's importance in ordinary communication, in everyday, utilitarian usage, this is not easy. The habit of rationalizing by invoking a referent is impossible to uproot.

No doubt everyone will concede that resorting to the referent distorts the facts whenever a text makes it impossible to construct a perceptible reality from its words. But some will still find it valid to resort to the referent where clearly representational texts are concerned—texts, that is, in which reference to reality is itself encoded. Even then, however, it is still to our every advantage to consider references to reality as nothing more than a kind of verbal calisthenics that the text puts the reader through. Anyone who would doubt that literature is a machine for controlling our attention and imagination might reflect that it scarcely matters whether the reference to reality dictated by the text is actually conceivable or not. In either case, the symbols programming our "calisthenics" are the same.

Take a simple case where reference to reality is conspicuously encoded: an explanatory comparison with *comme, semblable à, like*, and so on, or with an adjective followed by *comme*. My example will be the portrait of Quaresmeprenant in Rabelais's *Quart Livre*.

> [Il avait] les jambes, comme un leurre.
> Les genoilz, comme un escabeau.
> Les cuisses, comme un crenequin.
> Les anches, comme un vibrequin. . . .
> La poictrine, comme un jeu de reguales.
> Les mamelles, comme un cornet à bouquin.
> Les aisselles, comme un eschiquier. . . .
> La barbe, comme une lanterne.
> Le menton, comme un potiron.
> Les aureilles, comme deux mitaines.
> Le nez, comme un brodequin anté en escusson. . . .
> Les joues, comme deux sabbotz. . . .
> La peau, comme une gualvardine.
> L'épidermis, comme un beluteau.

> [His legs were like snares. His knees like stools. His thighs like crossbow-string winders. His hips like bit-braces. His chest like a game of nine pins. His tits like a goatherd's horn. His armpits like a chessboard. His beard like a lantern. His chin like a pumpkin. His ears like a pair of mittens. His nose like a buskin turned into an escutcheon. His cheeks like two clogs. His skin like gabardine. His epidermis like cheese-cloth.][22]

What we have here, of course, is a parody of description, a caricature, but one that deprives the text of none of its figurative character. The comic absurdity of the vehicles of comparison is simply a comic transposition of a tautological description. Rabelais is portraying a monster, an Antiphysis.

What we want to know, though, is: how does he do it? With or without reference? Because of their verbal habits, critics have decided in favor of reference: doctors have diagnosed meteorism, decalcification, skin diseases, and perhaps even syphilis. Quaresmeprenant is seen as monstrous because every vehicle of comparison resembles nothing that is human and can, therefore, only be understood as describing a deformity. A learned editor, Robert Marichal, writes: "Through Rabelais's comparisons, Quaresmeprenant appears as a hairless half-giant with twisted legs, his arms thrown back, . . . goitrous, . . . with greasy skin and dilated pores, . . . hollow cheeks, a pug nose, etc." This referential approach does not even respect its own logic, though, and Marichal is forced to put up with a bit of the nonreferential: "Of course, we do not mean to deny Rabelais his knowledge of anatomy, but there is also a good deal of fantasy in this chapter."[23] And what are we to make of his half-giant? Is it not an admission of the impossibility of representing Quaresmeprenant?

There is no problem, though, if we treat the text's comparisons like a verbal calisthenics. Let us look at the psychological portrait that Marichal tries to explain by saying of the monster, "muddled brain, uncertain will":

> [Quaresmeprenant avait] le sens commun, comme un bourdon.
> L'imagination comme un quarillonnement de cloches.
> Les pensées, comme un vol d'estourneaulx.
> La conscience, comme un dénigement de héronneaulx. . . .
> La volunté, comme troys noix en une escuelle.
> Le désir, comme six boteaux de sainct foin.
> Le jugement, comme un chaussepied.
> La discrétion, comme une moufle.

> [His common sense was like a big bell. His imagination like a chiming carillon. His thoughts, like a flight of starlings. His conscience, like an unnestling of young herons. His will like three nuts in a shell. His desire like six bunches of sainfoin. His judgment like a slipper. His discretion like a mitt.][24]

This is a comparative syntagm, *A* is like *B*. The series of *B* slots is filled with a list of the components of a descriptive system: in this particular case, the constitutive elements of the psyche. These components are mentioned in the order of their usual association in the language. In a "normal" comparison—in other words, in utilitarian communication—each slot *B* would be filled in relation to the corresponding slot *A*, with the words b_1, b_2, b_3, and so on, always chosen because of their congruence with the words a_1, a_2, a_3, and so on, within the limits defined by *like* or *comme*. The relations would be established between the *A* series and the *B* series and not from one *b* to another.

But in Rabelais, there is no congruence. If that were the only phenomenon at work, we would have a mark of deformity for every *A*. (Quaresmeprenant's nose and memory would be like things that a nose and a memory do not resemble.) There are, however, relationships between the members of class *B*. These appear as a series of formal paradigms:

> bourdon—quarillonnement de cloches
> vols d'estourneaulx—dénigement de héronneaulx
> troys noix dans une escuelle—six boteaux de sainct foin
> chaussepied—moufle

All of these are either animals or things: the choice of signifieds making up these paradigms was obviously dictated by their common characteristic of nonhumanity. This negates the common characteristic of all the signifieds in class *A*—their belonging to the human. A vestige of reference might still be seen here, but the fact is that animalization and reification are semantic markers of the comic and, in particular, of caricature.

The paradigms are formed by means of a kind of verbal automatism: *bourdon/cloches, vol/dénigement, troys/six*. This is even more evident in instances of phonic analogy such as *estourneaulx* rhyming with *héronneaulx*, or in the passage quoted earlier:

> Les cuisses, comme un crenequin
> Les anches, comme un vibrequin

The text could never more clearly show us that we should not read it in search of a meaning, trying to *see* Quaresmeprenant, but that, instead, we should go with the flow of the words. Quaresmeprenant is a symbol of Antiphysis because the only way of describing him is to say anything whatsoever about him. ("Physis," by contrast, requires a vocabulary set forth, class by class, by the Creator, as Genesis tells us.) Indeed, there is a familiar expression in French for describing an out-of-the-ordinary sight: *ça ne ressemble à rien*, or "that doesn't look like anything at all." Quaresmeprenant is a monster not because he is formless, but because he cannot be expressed, because he is literally unspeakable.[25]

It would be easy to show how the calisthenics of comparison that the text puts Quaresmeprenant through can again be seen in Lautréamont's *beau comme*, or in poems like Breton's "L'Union libre": "Ma femme à la chevelure de feu de bois. . . . Ma femme à la langue d'hostie poignardée. . . . Ma femme aux tempes d'ardoises de toit de serre" [My wife, she of the wood-fire locks. . . . My wife, she of the stabbed-host tongue. . . . My wife, she of the temples the color of the slate on hot-house roofs].[26] The only difference is that a verbal index added to the comparison forces us to decipher it as encomiastic: the adjective *beau* in Lautréamont and, in Breton, a Homeric comparison (*Achille aux pieds rapides* [Achilles of the swift feet]), which, used to glorify heroes as far back as we can remember, has remained an encomiastic marker of that style. In both of these cases, beauty is not defined by the referents, but rather by the marked comparative syntagma. Quaresmeprenant was a monster because he did not look like anything at all. Similarly, it could be said that the woman in "L'Union libre" is as beautiful as can be, or, as they say in French, *belle comme tout*. This comparison is a widely used hyperbole indeed, the absolute compliment in idiomatic French.

It is clear from the preceding examples that whenever the grammatical structure points to a referent, reference is thwarted by the words of the comparative syntagm. But what if this thwarting does not occur? What if the descriptions are clear and intelligible, as in the various styles of Realism? There, too, the notion of verbal calisthenics is all that is needed to account for the phenomena.

For instance, when Balzac writes: "il retourna par un geste inimitable à son client" [with an inimitable gesture, he turned back to his client], he denies us access to the referent. And yet, we think we are seeing reality, since the stereotype used (the adjective *inimitable*; a variant might be "I can't find the words to describe this gesture") belongs to the class of *perceptive observations*. It is all that is needed to create the illusion that not a single detail can escape the narrator's eyes. In accordance with the instructions on the score, we pretend to be seeing through those eyes.[27]

Here is Nerval describing an Orient from his dreams: "Les premières feuilles des sycomores me ravissaient par la vivacité de leurs couleurs, semblables aux panaches des coqs de Pharaon."[28] [The early sycamore leaves delighted me with the brightness of their colors, which resembled the plumes of Pharaoh's roosters.] In spite of the comparison, one reality is not elucidated by another, for we are even less familiar with Pharaoh's roosters than we are with sycamores, which still exist. We nonetheless have the impression that we are now better able to see the sycamore leaves. This can only be a rationalization. It is triggered by nothing other than an accumulation of exotic signifiers, with *Pharaoh* reinforcing *sycamore*. Reference is not from a less-known reality to a more familiar reality, but from one strange-sounding word to another. A description can be false without striking us as wrong or improbable, for the representation does not refer to reality but, instead, replaces it.

Critics have made fun of Hugo for confusing a song (*barcarolle*) with a boat.[29] But all that really matters is that the name have the right look to it. Its rightness does not lie in the signifieds but, rather, in the signifiers. All we need for *barcarolle* to be a convincing boat is to be able to see in it a variation on *barque*, a rowboat.

In "Clair de lune," found in Verlaine's *Fêtes galantes*, a sudden, unexpected evocation of Italy—*masques et bergamasques*—has been unsatisfactorily explained in terms of the importance of carnivals on that peninsula.[30] This is quite pointless: *masques et bergamasques* displays the same relation between signifiers as the one I just mentioned between *barque* and *barcarolle*. It is true, of course, that *bergamasques* predates Verlaine's text; but, stripped of its referent and of all signifieds, it can represent carnivals in the poem only through a kind of morphological derivation. In the context of the poem, *bergamasque* is *masque* enriched with a prefix. It is a true superlative of *masque*.

Even when a text not only seems to resemble reality, but can be checked for accuracy, our perception of its accuracy, whatever part it might play in our reading, is scarcely more than coincidental. We admire Balzac's psychological penetration to the extent

As a result, the critic has the choice of falling into one of two ruts. On the one hand, if the meaning of the words, be it literal or metaphoric, is "normal," if there is resemblance or verisimilitude, the critic underscores the words' aptness and praises the poet for his ability to *donner à voir*, to make us see. On the other hand, if there is dissimilarity, the critic either interprets it, again in terms of reality, as a distortion and attempts to justify it by hypothesizing the author's intentions,[2] or, depending on the reigning aesthetics, admires or condemns "the boldness of method, the daring imagery," and so on. In either case, reality is used to corroborate or even complete the text, or else to measure the discrepancy between the text and the real.

Unfortunately, resorting to reality does not, in the first case, enable us to determine how the semantics of the poem differs from the semantics of the nonpoetic utterance. In the second case, the measuring of discrepancies does not explain why the reader accepts them and tolerates the shift from the usual arbitrariness of the linguistic sign to a different kind of arbitrariness specific to poetry. And finally, in both cases, the recourse to reality isolates meanings from one another, since each meaning is conceived as the relation between one textual component and something outside the text, but is not considered in its intratextual combinations with other meanings.

The more closely a text "resembles" reality the more dangerous this approach becomes, for the conspicuousness of the usual semantic relation distracts our attention from the fact that that relation is subordinate to the intratextual relations. This can lead us to replace what is actually in the poem with a meaning foreign to it and clearly opposed to its structures.

The only example I need of this can be found in the commentaries prompted by the following stanza by Baudelaire:

> Quand la terre est changée en un cageot humide,
> Où l'Espérance, comme une chauve-souris,
> S'en va battant les murs de son aile timide
> Et se cognant la tête à des plafonds pourris.[3]

[When the earth is changed into a dank dungeon, where Hope, like a bat, goes beating the walls with its hesitant wing and hitting its head against rotten ceilings.]

One textbook intended for the use of future teachers invites them to admire the accuracy of the image and the aptness of one descriptive touch in particular: "the bat's seemingly hesitant and zigzagging flight."[4] I shall not dwell on the objection that few texts would survive if their readers needed to have the same experience of reality as their author. Everyone has seen bats. This objection would, however, be valid for more rarely experienced phenomena. But if reality did in fact matter here, the reader would find the inaccuracy of this touch disappointing, for bats have a kind of radar protecting them from just this type of accident.[5] The author of the textbook clearly sensed this, for he excused Baudelaire by saying that the bat's flight was *seemingly* hesitant. Roman Jakobson also reads *chauve-souris* in reference to reality. He claims to hear the murmur of the "chiropter's" wings in the palato-alveolar and sibilant consonants (*changée, cachot, espérance, chauvre-souris*)—the same sounds that Jean Prévost saw as a kind of phonetic trap designed to leave the reader gasping for breath and make his lungs suffer from the oppression of "spleen."[6]

These hypotheses are risky and quite pointless: first, because they bring Baudelaire's intentions into the picture; next and most importantly, because they are concerned with the animal, whereas the pertinent phenomenon is the *word* designating the animal and the symbolism of that word.

What characterizes the stanza is the fact that *chauve-souris* does not represent a chiropter, but a bird, or rather, an antibird, the negative of *bird*. Indeed, the word *bird* corresponds to certain positive semantic features: its descriptive system—a term I shall come back to—includes commonplaces such as an association with daylight and cheerfulness (which, we might note, has nothing to do with ornithological reality, but is simply a rationalization of the *song* of birds). As opposed to *bird, bat* corresponds to negative semantic features, and its descriptive system associates it with obscurity and sadness. In an ode dedicated to this winged symbol, Hugo calls the *bat* a "triste oiseau," a sad bird, speaks of its "vol ténébreux" or gloomy flight, and describes it as he would a nocturnal bird. Moreover, he calls it the "soeur du hibou funèbre et de l'orfraie avide" [sister of the funereal owl and the greedy screech].[7] All too obviously, it would be futile to adopt the point of view of the naturalist, who would see nothing but factual errors here. There is error only in relation to the referent. Within the boundaries of the text, however, such "mistakes" clearly show that meaning results from a relation, or, more precisely, an opposition, between signifiers. Hugo's bat has no meaning except as the antithesis of *bird*. As in any opposition, a polarization is produced: the antithesis of the bat cannot be birds in general, or any kind of bird at all, but only the bird occupying the highest point of the moral scale in literary and mythic traditions, from Noah's ark to the Holy Ghost—the dove. When Hugo contrasts the "Egout de Rome," the sewers of Rome, to the world above, he significantly shows us in the world below:

> les chauves-souris vol[ant] de tous côtés
> Comme au milieu des fleurs s'ébattent les colombes.[8]

[bats flying all around just as doves frolic amidst the flowers]

Baudelaire's stanza, therefore, has no meaning in relation to the referent "chiropter," or even to the isolated signifier. It has meaning only in relation to a stereotyped antithesis, which is only the metaphor of an equally stereotypical, literal antithesis. Since the opposite of *spleen*, the equivalent of *despair*,[9] is *hope*, and since the dove is the bird of hope, the "poetic" significance of the image and its effectiveness are due to the inversion of the stereotype: hope is represented by despair, and the bat is substituted for its opposite. Consequently, the celestial vault, the site par excellence of soaring flights, has first become a *couvercle*, a lid, and then, the *plafonds pourris*, rotting ceilings, of an oubliette. The obstacle to flight could just as well have been represented by an opposition between a *windowpane* and a *fly*, or a *cage* and a *bird*, by virtue of the associative relationship of the signifiers.[10] But *fly* does not belong to a pair of antithetical signifiers, and *cage*, although compatible with *bird*, is not with *bat*. The semantic structure is, thus, a transformation of the binary opposition *bird of flight/bird of non-*

flight into an equation. It would be a mistake to think that reference to reality regains the upper hand by means of an analogy between the heavenly vault and the dungeon vault: Baudelaire ruled out that analogy by choosing *plafonds pourris*. This proves that the word *cachot* was generated by the word *chauve-souris*, and not by a resemblance to the real "sky." Already effective as an antidove, *chauve-souris* totally imposes itself on the imagination thanks to the support of words that surround it with literary clichés. Indeed, if words like *cachot, humide, plafonds pourris*, and later on in the poem *barraux [bars] and araignées* [spiders], do seem to confirm, motivate, and explain the representation, it is not because they are strikingly true, but rather because they belong to the stereotypical setting of Gothic novels.[11]

Now let us suppose that the meaning of the words in a poem is clearly abnormal. The true nature of the phenomenon will escape me if I content myself with explaining it in terms of an alteration of the referential function. This alteration that I perceive is not the cause of the poetic meaning: it is the result of it.

This is what Jean Cohen failed to recognize when he attempted to analyze the semantic anomaly in the group *bleus angélus* [angelus blues][12] in Mallarmé's "L'Azur." He quite rightly sees this anomaly as characteristic of the poetic meaning. But all he sees in it is the substitution of a connotative meaning for the denotative representation of reality: "there is no image in it—in fact, the image is impossible to imagine—but only a device stimulating an emotional response." In his view, the "code of poetic language is based . . . on inner experience," on the emotional and subjective experience of the poet. This experience transgresses the limits of sentences possible in ordinary language, sentences that correspond to the "spatio-temporal contiguities revealed by perception" of the world outside.[13] Unfortunately, this inner experience is still a reality outside the poem. Moreover, affectivity varies with individuals. Like all psychological criticism, therefore, this approach tends to replace the written text, which is always accessible, with hypotheses, which are hard to prove, about mental processes. Cohen nonetheless believes it is possible to assign universally valid emotional "connotations" to the colors. By virtue of this unanimity that he postulates in our experience of reality, he asserts that "the angeluses are blue because the qualitative impression corresponding to that color—let's say calm and quiet—match the impression produced by bells ringing the angelus"[14]—which is obviously an absurdity. Mallarmé's entire poem is devoted to tying the word *azur* and its synonyms to meanings (anxiety, irony, sterility, and so on), that transform its usual value into a negative value. This value reversal is accomplished quite literally with the words of the poem. Similarly, the synesthesia of *bleus angélus*, which Cohen denies on the grounds that the sound of bells does not make us see blue, is actually *stated* by the text:

> l'Azur triomphe, et je l'entends qui chante
> Dans les cloches. Mon âme, il se fait voix pour plus
> Nous faire peur avec sa victoire méchante
> Et du métal vivant sort en bleus angélus!

[Azure is triumphant, and I can hear it ringing in the bells. O my soul, it becomes voice to frighten us even more with its nasty victory and comes out of the living metal in the guise of angelus blues.]

Cohen made the mistake of reading *bleus angélus* in the sense those words would have in the language outside of their context. In the poem, though, the contextual complex immediately replaces the sickly sweetness of *bleus angélus* with the exact opposite of their ordinary meaning.[15] The semantic relationship is contained entirely in the text.

Thus, the meaning of the text can very well be characterized by its "boldness" and "absurdities," but this does not mean that we can content ourselves with seeing those characteristics as distortions of reality. Such an explanation does not account for the semantic structure of the poem as a whole and has no bearing on the question of literariness. We would find ourselves at an impasse even if we were dealing with a "distortion" that has been classified and authorized by rhetoric, as is the case of metaphors that transpose the senses, or seem to.[16] Take this metaphor, which Hugo uses to stigmatize atheists and skeptics:

> Leur âme, en agitant l'immensité profonde
> N'y sent même pas l'être, et dans le grelot monde
> N'entend pas sonner Dieu![17]

[Their soul, while shaking the profound immensity, does not even sense the being in it, and in the little jingle bell that is the world, does not hear God ringing.]

The image is disconcerting; and yet the utterance signifies in a normal way if we isolate the metaphoric vehicle (the presence of a jingling, brass ball in the bell to make it ring). It is also normal in terms of the metaphor's tenor (God's presence in the universe). The anomaly obviously stems from the fact that, in normal usage, it is highly unlikely to find a representation of God in the cosmos and a mimesis of a jingle bell in the same sentence. One critic has attempted to vindicate the image by classifying it with anomalies that have an aesthetic tradition behind them: it has thus been seen as a sound image, the daring transposition of a concept into auditory sensations.[18]

It is nothing of the sort. What we have here is not a metaphor with a metaphysical tenor and a sensory vehicle. The text is not telling us that God makes noise in the world. The image is generated quite simply by the transformation of the phrase preceding it: *n'y sent même pas l'être*. The adverb *y* becomes *dans le monde* and, since *monde* equals *grelot*, the verb *sent* becomes *entend sonner* and, lastly, *l'être* becomes *Dieu*. Consequently, the signs do not represent sounds, but rather a relationship of interiority, a relationship between a contained and its container—*Dieu* is to *monde* what *bille* is to *grelot*.

Are we to conclude that this is an absurdity? Of all the relations of interiority that could illustrate "God's presence in the universe," a little ball in a bell seems inexcusably gratuitous. Shall we admire it out of predisposition? Shall we speak of unbridled imagination? To do so would be an easy way out. It would not tell us if the image is necessary, the form compelling, and the poem successful.

We must demonstrate that it has its own logic and formal imperatives. Why couldn't we just as easily have *dans la cloche monde*, with God being the clapper in a big bell?

In point of fact, the absurdity exists only in the relationship between signifier and signified. Let's give up the criterion that meaning must conform to reality and replace it with the criterion of conformity with words. It happens that there is a necessary relationship between *grelot* and skeptic philosophy. In fact, the metaphor is rigorously deduced from a hyperbole in the preceding phrase, a hyperbole defining the chaotic conception of a cosmos without Providence in terms of madness: "L'univers n'est pour eux qu'une vaste démence" [The universe, to them (the skeptics), is but a vast dementia]. The word *démence* triggers an allegory of the madness of philosophy, all the more convincing since it is deduced from a *coincidentia oppositorum*: astrologers fall into wells and wise men play the fool. This allegory of madness brings with it the attribute of the *fool's bauble* or *scepter*, periphrastically represented by *agiter* [to shake] and *grelot*.[19] In fact, since it is pejorative, the symbol replicates, as it were, the meaning of the word *démence*. Another passage from Hugo confirms the fact that our image is deduced from a word. In *Dieu l'Océan d'en Haut* [God the Ocean Above], a bat symbolizing doubt cries out:

> Rien n'a de sens . . .
> Tout est *insensé*, vide et faux, même la mort;
> L'infini sombre au fond du tombeau *déraisonne*;
> *La bière est un grelot où le cadavre sonne.*[20]

[Nothing has meaning . . . everything is *insane*, empty, and false. Even death. Deep in the grave, dark infinity *raves; The bier is a jingle bell with the corpse ringing in it.*]

Here again, the relation represented is one of a container to a contained. Again, a specific word (the same one as in "Pleurs dans la nuit") triggered the development of the image: the first version of this passage began, in fact, with the phrase *Tout est en démence* [All is demented].

Thus, the interpretation of poetic meaning along the vertical axis leads us astray. The verbal sequence, by contrast, provides us with the pertinent explanation. Might it be that the text is its own referential system?

This suspicion is confirmed in the following poem, "Au vif," by the post-Surrealist poet Michel Leiris:

A cors et à cris
A toutes brides
A ras bord
A tire d'aile

A bouche que veux-tu
A poings fermés
A pierre fendre
A chaudes larmes
A pleines voiles.[21]

The elimination of the verbs in each of these proverbial expressions creates an anaphora equivalent to an inverted rhyme, in that it makes the poem into a whole characterized by a repetition suggesting a similarity among the lines. Without this repetition, the mutilation of each set expression would be an invitation to restore what is missing (Réclamer *à cors et à cris*, Galoper *à toutes brides*, etc.). But the context is comprised of each expression's reflection, so to speak, in similar expressions. They lead nowhere other than to themselves. The missing verbs (*réclamer* [to demand], *galoper* [to gallop], *remplir* [to fill], *s'envoler* [to fly off]) would have had no relationship with one another and no meaning except in the vertical relation in which each, taken separately, would be appropriate. The adverbial phrases modifying them, however, all share the same hyperbolic quality. The accumulation of functionally equivalent expressions and the suppression of whatever differentiates them (the suppression of their respective collocations) eliminate the vertical semantic structures. With their verbs, *à cors et à cris* and *à toutes brides* express fury or momentum; without their verbs, and considered in isolation, these groups evoke the thrill of the chase—a sense that is incompatible with that of *à ras bord*, which evokes the cautious filling of a glass, and not an overflowing goblet at a bacchanal. When these differences disappear, all that remains is a horizontal semiotic structure: the repetition bringing out the isomorphism of the expressions and semanticizing the preposition *à*, raising it from the role of a function word to that of signifier. Corresponding to this signifier, there is not a complex signified, but only a semantic feature, the seme "the highest degree" (or "extreme"—the equivalent of a marker of hyperbole). The repetition of *à* thus indicates that each expression is a variant of the hyperbolic invariant. Consequently, the words that make up each variant are also resemanticized and become symbols of impetuous action. *A pierre fendre* [(freezing) to the point of splitting rock] is closer to Roland cutting through the rock than to the idea of a freeze: it is the symbol par excellence of an obstacle (the rock's hardness) overcome.[22] In like manner, *à poings fermés* [(to sleep) with clenched fists] moves away from *dormir* [to sleep] to signify aggressive effort. This semantic transformation is even more striking when the "freed" expression coincides with the vocabulary of traditional lyricism: in *chaudes larmes* [scalding tears], for instance. But this return to the conventional sense is possible only because the poem, in repeating and mutilating the clichés, has substituted the arbitrariness of its own code for the arbitrariness of the common linguistic code. Finally, the title, "Au vif" [To the quick], retroactively[23] loses its relationship with *toucher* or *piquer* [to move, to sting] and its connotations of offended sensitivity, and henceforth it joins the seme "life" to the semes "fullness," "ardor," "sensitivity," and so on.[24]

These semantic modifications are thus tied to the fact that the verbal sequence alternately has a cumulative and an eliminating effect. It stresses comparable semes and eliminates those that are not comparable, retaining only those semantic features common to all the words. This filtering stems entirely from the relationship of contiguity among the words in the syntagm: it is that relationship which imposes the comparison on the reader.

We can conclude that in the semantics of the poem *the axis of significations is horizontal*. The referential function in poetry is carried out from signifier to signifier: reference consists in the reader's perceiving certain signifiers to be variants of a single structure.

The horizontal axis is represented materially by the syntagm and is organized in a terrace of structures: first, by the *linguistic structure*; then, by the *stylistic structure*, a series of contrasts in relation to the contextual norms that insure the perception of the message qua form; third, by *thematic structures*—that is, structures whose variants are themes; and fourth (and here we touch on something that belongs exclusively to poetry), by the *lexical structure*—in other words, the similarities in form and position among certain words in the text, similarities that are rationalized and interpreted in terms of meaning. Indeed, these words seem to repeat the same message because they resemble one another morphologically or have analogous functions, and because their points of resemblance are stressed.

The first category of these formal and positional similarities involves *parataxis*. The similarities are pointed to, or created, by a simple process of accumulation, such as I have just shown in the Leiris poem and we can also see in this short tercet ("Paille") by Eluard:

Paille mêlée au grain
Fumée mêlée au feu
Pitié mêlée au mal.[25]

[Chaff mixed with wheat. Smoke mixed with fire. Charity mixed with evil.]

The accumulation of three almost identical phrases—all are articulated along the syntagm *X mixed with Z*—transforms all the *X* terms into synonyms and all the *Z* terms into a second sequence of synonyms. Because it is repeated,[26] and since it organizes all the other components, the group *mêlée à* orients the meaning of the entire tercet in relation to its own meaning. This is not simply the all-purpose meaning that *mêler* has in the dictionary: "mixed." The first variant of the group—*paille mêlée au grain*—is the only one of the three that already exists as a set expression in the French language. This formal coincidence with the cliché thus gives *mêlée à* the pejorative value it has in the stereotype of mixture as impurity (and not, for example, mixture as alloy). The relationship expressed by this group, a relationship on which the entire semantic system of the poem hinges, has a negative valorization, which is confirmed by the smoky fire in the second line. Consequently, *pitié mêlée au mal*, which would be a positive expression if it were isolated ("charity lessens evil"), becomes negative ("charity makes evil harder to bear, or more insidious"). Retroactively, the title, which at first glance was not necessarily pejorative,[27] takes on a totally negative value under the influence of the *pitié—fumée—paille* sequence, each element of which repeats the seme "impurity." A semiotic transformation is completed when the meaning of the text's beginning is contaminated by the meaning of the last element in the accumulation.

Accumulation as semiotic transformer does not always have the conspicuous form of rhetorical accumulation. It can just as easily appear as a series of scattered, but formally similar, elements. This is what happens in Rimbaud's "Mouvement":

> Le mouvement de lacet sur la berge des chutes du fleuve,
> Le gouffre à l'étambot,
> La célérité de la rampe,
> L'énorme passade du courant. . . .
> Les voyageurs entourés des trombes du val
> Et du strom.

[The lurching motion of the train on the banks of the river's rapids. The abyss at the stern-post. The celerity of the gradient. The huge passing fancy of the current. . . . The travelers surrounded by the tornadoes in the valley and by the Strom.]

All the lexical anomalies—the Germanicism (*strom*), the improprieties (*célérité, passade, trombes*), the technicisms (*mouvement de lacet* and, later on, the punning *route hydraulique motrice*)[28]—involve signifiers that share the same "motion" or "momentum" seme and, consequently, are a transformation[29] of the title.

The synonymies created in this way are so clearly based on their position that, in order to understand them, there is no need to know the referential meaning of the words expressing them. All that is needed is that the words obviously belong to the paratactic series. We no longer know the meaning of the nineteenth-century railroading term *mouvement de lacet*, "a lurching of a train on its tracks," but our ignorance contributes to the stylistic effectiveness of the word: we cannot help but notice it because of the seeming incompatibility between *mouvement* and *lacet*. Hence the emphasis on motion per se, since we understand *mouvement*, and *de lacet* functions for us only as a call for attention, as an underscoring of the word that it modifies. Moreover, we weaken this emphasis and produce a poetic misinterpretation if we restore the technical meaning, the meaning in relation to things. By subordinating *mouvement* to the reality of the train and its tracks, the technical meaning diminishes the importance of the seme shared by the components of the accumulation: "motion in and of itself."[30]

In "Eviradnus," the setting of which is a medieval castle, Hugo, describing the armory in the castle keep, accumulates long-forgotten technicisms from the art of armor making: "les ardillons d'airain attachent l'éperon, serrent le gorgerin; . . . les genouillères ont leur boutoir meurtrier; . . . chaque heaume est masqué de son crible; . . . la rigidité des pâles morions"[31] [the bronze tongues secure the spur and grip the gorget; . . . the kneepieces have their killing blade; . . . each helmet is masked with its beaver; . . . the stiffness of the pale morions]. The modern reader (today or at the time of the Romantics), either does not understand them or understands them barely at all. And yet, he thinks he can see the ghost-like knights in armor: unfamiliar words are all that is needed, provided they are placed in the appropriate slots of a listing syntagm whose beginning has set up the spatio-temporal coordinates of the scene in clear language. Better yet, the medieval armorers' jargon gives a new meaning to the most common of words: "Les chatons des cuissards sont barrés de leurs clés" [The settings on the cuisses are crossed with their keys].[32] The illusion of reality is complete, and it by no means depends on the reality represented.[33]

To conclude, in all texts belonging to this category, accumulation filters through the semantic features of its words, thereby overdetermining the occurrence of the most widely represented seme and canceling out the semes that appear less frequently. The components of the accumulation become synonyms of one another irrespective of their original meaning in ordinary language.

The second category of formal and positional similarities involves hypotaxis. These similarities are pointed out, or created, between words by their co-occurrence in associative networks: the words forming these networks constitute the *descriptive system* of a nuclear word whose function as such stems from the fact that its signified encompasses and organizes the signifieds of the satellite words.[34] Taken pejoratively, the word *roi* [king] is at the center of a system whose satellites are such words as *courtisan* [courtier] and *bouffon* [jester], stereotypes of the loneliness, boredom, and powerlessness of the all-powerful king. The associative sequences vary depending on the seme or semes of *roi* selected by the context in which the nuclear word appears. The development presents the reader with relations that are familiar to him and give the impression of corresponding to an obvious truth, since they meet his expectations. Hence, some descriptions are convincing because they suggest that their object is exemplary, that it is a type, the raw material of literature. Baudelaire's third "Spleen," for instance, is constructed in its entirety on the actualization of this system of *roi*. The nuclear signified is the ideal model that dictates the arrangement and functions of the system's components (and their function dictated their symbolism). Yet, those components exist in the speaker's mind only in the form of signifiers arranged in clichés. This is because descriptive systems are in no way coextensive with the realities they are supposed to represent. The system of *fenêtre* [window] is limited to *vitre* [pane] (or synonyms such as *carreau*), and to *embrasure* [window recess]. Poetically, it lacks the hinges on which it turns in reality and which, as far as words are concerned, are reserved for doors.[35] But it retains *embrasure* as the literary site for a tête-à-tête, even though window nooks are no longer deeply recessed. Like *vitre*, it is almost exclusively a place of sullen contemplation: "Le front aux vitres comme font les veilleurs de chagrin" [Forehead to the windowpane, as we do when keeping watch in sorrow], as Eluard has written.[36] So words and clichés are valorized by their function in the system.[37] The system thus acts as a code and as a variant of the thematic structures.

A system's signifiers are not synonyms, unlike the signifiers in an accumulation. Subordinate to one another, they are metonyms. Two semantic consequences follow from this.

First, every component in the system can be substituted for that system and can represent it in its entirety, in all the complexity of its associations and, in particular, of its symbolism. A title like René Char's "Le carreau" [The Windowpane] is enough to add to the poem's intimist notes (happiness) a sense stemming exclusively from the *fenêtre* system ("waiting, vainly or not, for happiness").[38]

Second, the system's signifiers play the same role in relation to one another that referents and signifieds play in relation to signifiers in ordinary communication. In fact, because its semantic axis is horizontal, the poetic text cannot be put to the test of resemblance to the real. It avoids gratuitousness only because the descriptive system maintains around a given word a context of commonplaces that conform to the *consensus omnium*, and are, therefore, verisimilar. The word generates the phrase that follows it, developing part of the descriptive system to which it belongs: a stock epithet, for example, or a relative clause expressing in black and white one of the semes implicit in the starting word. Thus, in a previous example, *paille* generates *grain*, and then *feu*, metonyms of two of the descriptive systems to which it is related. (This is combined with semantic relations of the paratactic type.) For instance, Hugo again, dreaming of a nature where "tout vit, tout est plein d'âmes" [life is everywhere, souls are everywhere], wrote: "Les fleurs au cou de cygne ont les lacs pour miroirs"[39] [The swan-necked flowers have the lakes for mirrors]. Despite the "flexibility" seme shared by *tige* [stem] and *col de cygne* [swan's neck], the image would be a bit far-fetched if *cou* did not rid *cygne* of its conventional character in the usual *col de cygne* collocation, if *lac* did not confirm *cygne*, and if *miroir* did not confirm *lac*. Now, the mirror presupposes someone looking into it and a coquettishness, and this animism of the flowers is thereby demonstrated: if flowers have a soul, within the framework of floral commonplaces, that soul can only be feminine.

The utterance verifies, so to speak, the associative probabilities of the system: this is equivalent to resemblance to the real or, at the very least, makes for a convincing extrapolation. When Rimbaud speaks of the "sang rose des arbres verts dans les veines de Pan"[40] [rosy blood of the green trees in Pan's veins], we accept the image, but we do so not because we are pantheists, and only in spite of reality, where sap is not pink. We accept it because *rose* is the complement of *vert*—not in reality (in which case we would have *rouge* [red]), but rather, in a well-known cliché, which is a mawkish variant of the cliché *rouge et vert*. Now, it so happens that this mawkishness is just suited to the meliorative representation of trees in the context of a cosmic *locus amoenus*. Hence, semantic overdetermination displaces the "natural" meaning without the least absurdity.

But if the high probability of the components' occurrence overdetermines the words in the system and makes them convincing because they are convincing and true because they are habitual, the slightest deviation becomes equally significant. It signals the presence of another meaning, a metaphoric one, whenever the system functions as a code for a thematic structure. This overlapping of structures is then the agent of semantic change.[41]

The preceding discussion shows, I believe, that the semantics of the poem is characterized by the *bricolage* that Lévi-Strauss has spoken of: it is based entirely on words arranged in advance, prefabricated groups, whose meaning has to do not with things, but rather with their role in a system of signifiers. Their ambiguity or power of suggestion, far from being an exacerbated polysemy, as traditional interpretations would have it, is a kind of filtering out through structural overlappings. As the reading progresses, word combinations change their appearance, and their meaning undergoes constant modification. Any interpretation tending to immobilize this mechanism by reducing the text to reality and to the static atomism of the dictionary fails to recognize the function of poetry as an experience of alienation.

[3]

Literary Sentence Models

ANY MODEL of the literary sentence should account for the *literariness* of this type of sentence.[1] In other words, it should account for the formal characteristics that result from the peculiarities of linguistic communication in literature. Now these peculiarities can all be traced to the fact that there are only two factors present in the literary communication act: the text and the reader. The latter reconstitutes directly from the text the missing factors: the author, the reality to which the text alludes or seems to allude, and the code used in the message (as a corpus of lexical and semantic reference, which is the verbal representation of the sociocultural corpus, of the mythology comprised of the entire set of commonplaces). The literary sentence should, therefore, allow for these reconstitutions. When uttering a message, telling a story, but also when showing a setting, introducing characters, and explaining their motivations, the literary sentence should, at one and the same time, be action and representation.

Three rules appear to govern the generation of a sentence that satisfies the conditions I have just sketched out: first, the rule of *overdetermination*, whereby the sentence gains the reader's acceptance; second, the rule of *conversion*, which allows us to treat the sentence as a style unit; and third, the rule of *expansion*, which states the transformation from implicit to explicit motivation, from narrative to description.

I shall first consider the workings of *overdetermination*. As in all sentences, the components of the literary sentence are tied together by the syntagm, but these relations are repeated by other, formal or semantic, relations. Each word, therefore, appears to be necessary many times over, and its relations with the other words appear to be multiply imperative.[2] Meaning is not based on the reference of the signifier to the signified but lies, instead, in the signifier's reference to other signifiers. This creates the illusion *that the arbitrariness of the sign has been lessened.* In reality, it has merely been passed from one word to other words; but as the reader sees it, the sentence unfolds like a deduction or derivation from its beginning. A text can, of course, be deciphered in two directions: in that of the initial reading, following the normal progression of the verbal sequence, and in the opposite direction (a retrocactive reading), with the meaning of what we have just read being constantly modified by what we are in the process of reading. In both cases, though, the reader always has the feeling that there has been a reduction in arbitrariness. In the retroactive reading, the initial utterance seems to be confirmed by its derivatives. In the first reading, going from left to right, the derivation is made convincing or verisimilar because, by unfolding in accordance with verbal associations with which we are familiar, it conforms to our expectations.

These associations are well known: formal similarities (including puns), membership in the same paradigm of synonyms or antonyms, in short, all the phenomena capable of transferring similarity onto the plane of contiguity, as theorized by Roman Jakobson.[3] Nonetheless, these phenomena do not necessarily have to do with the sentence, for they can be observed within and without the sentence as well.

I shall, therefore, examine features that are less well known, but that pertain only to the sentence. These will be cases in which overdetermination results from the superimposing of one sentence onto other, pre-existent sentences—sentences that appear in other texts or stereotyped sentences that are already part of the linguistic corpus. The literary sentence is generated from these by hypogrammatization, by polarization, or simply by the actualization of potential sequences. *Hypogrammatization* involves clichés. Take the cliché: "il a passé (il passera) beaucoup d'eau sous le pont depuis que (avant que)" [a lot of water has flowed (will flow) under the bridge since (before)]. From it, Lautréamont derives a sentence whose functions are unquestionably literary. Mervyn, pursued by Maldoror, returns to his father's townhouse, and faints. His father, a sprightly, old English lord, declares that a great deal of water will flow under the bridge before his strength gives out, and that he will avenge his son. This declaration is in English. Or, more precisely, the text reports his words in French and simultaneously provides an indirect representation of the English language:

> Il parle dans une langue étrangère, et chacun l'écoute dans un recueillement respectueux: "Qui a mis le garçon dans cet état? La Tamise brumeuse charriera encore une quantité notable de limon avant que mes forces soient complètement épuisées.
>
> [He speaks in a foreign tongue, and everyone listens to him with respectful reverence: "Who put the boy in this state? The foggy Thames will wash away a considerable amount of silt before my strength will have completely given out.]

There is not a simple, word-for-word, stylistic transposition here, but rather a transformation of a minimal sentence, the cliché, into a sentence that is intelligible on its own through reference to the reality of the River Thames, but whose real meaning (*much time will pass*), is given in reference to time. Not to real time, however, but to certain, already established, familiar signifiers of the signified "time." In context, the literary function of the sentence is precisely the result of this double reading. On the one hand, at the level of the narrative, in the plot, the sentence transcribes the character's words. On the other hand, at the level of representation, the sentence corroborates the "stage directions" (*il parle une langue étrangère*):[5] we thus have a mimesis of British behavior. Furthermore, the hypogrammatization functions metalinguistically, since it parodies the worldly novel in which the hyperbolic variant of the aristocrat is the British gentleman. Thus, the hypogrammatization defines the utterance, on the one hand, as an utterance and, on the other, as wordplay.[6]

Hypogrammatization can also involve proverbs, since these are particular cases, in an archaic and gnomic form, of the cliché. The maxim (a literary genre characterized, as are others, by the fact that the text is coextensive with the sentence), is frequently a transformation of a proverb.[7]

The *quotation* is another partiular case of the cliché. It is nothing other than a signed cliché.[8] I shall take as an example this line used by the Abbé Delille to conclude a moving tale of the September massacres: "Le meurtre insatiable a lassé les bourreaux"[9] [Insatiable murder has worn out the executioners]. The sentence contains a personification of Murder and the metaphor *bourreaux*. Moreover, the syntagm superimposes a relation of equivalence on the predicative relation—the antithesis *insatiable/lassé*—and the actants are synonyms, since *bourreaux* is metonymically linked to *meurtre*. A complex network of relations such as this would be more than sufficient to attract our attention to the shape of the message—which is itself characteristic of literary communication. But along with this linear decoding, the utterance forces us to read, as if a palimpsest or watermark, Juvenal's depiction of Messalina: *lassata necdum satiata*, "tired, but not yet sated." An equation by analogy thus makes Murder into a Messalina, and the bloodthirsty revolutionaries become her lovers, with their thirst for blood thereby translated into erotic terms. The relationship is not exactly the same as in the Latin original; for that, the victims would have to have been Murder's lovers.[10] Be that as it may, Murder-Messalina gives the line an impact totally disproportionate with what the grammatical relations would have had if they had been perceived on a single textual level, rather than on two levels simultaneously. This effectiveness is reinforced by the fact that the hypogrammatization, in keeping with the aesthetics of *imitatio*, gives the reader the pleasant feeling of belonging to the same cultural elite as the author.[11] This is, of course, a rationalization, but one that evidences closer contact with the text.

The literariness of the sentence stems, therefore, from the fact that it is a partial quotation or, to be more precise, a variant of a structure, another famous variant of which already exists in the annals of literature. This type of hypogrammatization is quite common. If we are less aware of it today than readers once were, it is because it is no longer tied to an aesthetic, as it was in classical literature.

The second form of intertextual overdetermination is *polarization*. Of the relations of synonymy, metonymy, and antonymy organizing the universe of meanings, only one—association by contrast—defines a clear-cut structural relation that is immediately perceptible and is perceived without ambiguity. For this reason, the lexicon abounds in binary stereotypes whose poles are in opposition, mutually balancing and complementing each other. This privileged relationship is so powerful that it generates sentences that, quite literally, exist only for the sake of introducing the polar pair. These are teleologically constructed sentences, comparable to certain tales or jokes whose only reason for being is to lead to the punchline or a pun. Binary structure can, therefore, be considered to be a matrix of verbal associations, the mold of an entire system of motivations that is set in motion only to accentuate the polarity of the contrasts. Conversely, constructions that express the contrasts are, in a way, made convincing by that polarization.

This is what happens, for example, with the names of the colors *vert* [green] and *rouge* [red]. They are irresistibly coupled by the fact that green and red are complementary colors. Hence, we find in Baudelaire:

> Delacroix, lac de sang hanté des mauvais anges,
> Ombragé par un bois de sapins toujours vert.[12]

[Delacroix, lake of blood haunted by the fallen angels, darkened by a pine forest, always green.]

It matters little that Baudelaire tried to explain this vision by reducing the sentence to the mold out of which it came: "*lac de sang*: le rouge;—*hanté des mauvais anges*: surnaturalisme;—*un bois toujours vert*: le vert, complémentaire du rouge" [*lake of blood*: red; *haunted by the fallen angels*: supernaturalism; *a forest always green*: green, the complement of red].[13]

The point is that his translation is not literary. What matters is how such a simple and natural opposition could generate so romantic a landscape. A landscape was called for because the context required it, and Delacroix's characteristic green, in a landscape code, could be nothing but vegetation. It is striking, though, that this green generated, rather than any other essence, *sapins*, a hyperbole of greenness. And it is also striking that, of all possible hues of red, this green prompted the most excessive—the dramatic *lac de sang*, a hyperbole of redness.[14] The generation took the path already cleared by the cliché *mare de sang* [pool of blood], for the polarization hyperbolizes *mare* and transforms it into *lac*.[15] The sentence unfolds along the line of least resistance created by the stereotyped associations.[16] The cliché of green as the color of hope is all that is needed for the opposition to dictate to Baudelaire the sentence: "cette sanglante et farouche désolation, à peine compensée par le vert sombre de l'espérance" [this bloody and savage desolation, scarcely compensated for by the dark green of hope].[17] Since the meaning dictates a lessening of the opposition (the representation is suffused with melancholy), the verb expressing the polarity of the colors, *compensée*, is canceled out by its adverb, *à peine*, and this leads to a parallel alteration of the color and, therefore, of its symbolism: the green darkens.[18] The pre-established metaphoric opposition—whether or not it is modified—functions, therefore, as a metaphoric demonstration of the "truth" of the utterance. This demonstration, and nothing else, gives this portrait (in "Spleen III") of a king worn out by his dissolute life, its realism:

. . . ce cadavre hébété
Où coule au lieu de sang l'eau verte du Léthé.

[. . . this stupified, corpse-like prince, in whose veins, instead of blood, Lethe's green water flows.]

The substitution of water for blood is stated grammatically (*au lieu de*), and allegorically (*Léthé*), but the sapping of the blood's life, the transformation of the veins, life-carrying vessels, into "funèbres ruisseaux"[19] [funereal streams] is given the ring of truth, as it were, by this *vert*, which destroys the red of vitality.[20]

It sometimes happens that a lexical pairing is strong enough to be symbolic in and of itself. The semanticized syntagm then becomes capable of generating a "narrative" like André Pieyre de Mandariargues's love story about two schoolchildren: "Lui encre verte, elle encre rouge, ils secouent leurs stylographes" [He green ink, she red ink, they shake their pens].[21]

It remains for us to consider the most important form of overdetermination: the *actualization of descriptive systems*. The ideal model to which our references to a given signified conform (positively or negatively, totally or partially), the descriptive system,[22] in the simplest of cases, resembles a dictionary definition. This is the case with the Romantic theme of the harmonica, whose constants are given to us by the very definition of the word *harmonica*. This word did not refer, as it does for modern readers, to a kind of mouth organ, but rather, to the *Glasharmonika*, which was so popular in the Germany of Werther. It was made of glasses filled with unequal amounts of water, which rang when the performer rubbed their rims with his moistened finger. The definitions of the time always indicate the almost painful effect of the harmonica's vibrations on the nerves. Its music accompanied illuminist rituals, and Madame de Staël noted the "correspondences" between that music and Romantic moods.[23] Thus, the word generates representations of melancholy spirituality.[24] One of many examples of this is the following sentence from the *Vie de Rancé*, in which Chateaubriand discusses the theological disputes in which Rancé, the founder of the Trappist order, indulged before he repented his aggressiveness and resumed his vow of silence:

> Au reste Rancé, tout vieux et tout malade qu'il était, ne déclinait jamais le combat, mais aussitôt qu'il avait repoussé un coup, il plongeait dans la pénitence: *on n'entendait plus qu'une voix au fond des flots, comme ces sons de l'harmonica, produits de l'eau et du cristal, qui font mal.*[25]
>
> [Moreover, Rancé, old and sick as he was, never refused combat, but as soon as he had repulsed a blow, he dived into penitence:

nothing could be heard anymore except for a voice from the depths of the waves, like those harmonica sounds, produced with water and crystal, which make one shudder.]

The sentence repeats the dictionary definition almost verbatim: "produits de l'eau et du cristal, qui font mal," except that *cristal* is a stylistic sublimation of *verre* [glass]. This sublimation is neither gratuitious nor merely ornamental but is, instead, a necessary consequence of the symbolism that the context confers on *harmonica*: as a hyperbole of *verre, cristal* amplifies semes such as *transparence, fragility*, and here, *vibratility*. In the paradigm of possible substitutes for *verre*, the hyperbole is, thus, the *lexical* motivation of the musical vibrations and consequently, in the syntagm, it is the *descriptive* motivation of their effect on the nerves.[26] The relative clause, by actualizing a commonplace in the standard descriptions of the instrument, brings us back to the image's starting point: a melodious voice, but a painful one,[27] and therefore, in this context, a penitent one. Furthermore, the sentence is doubly overdetermined, as it were, for *harmonica* is also tied to *pénitence* by *eau*, since this harmonious water is also the water of repentance. Indeed, the image results from a coincidence or interference between the definition of *harmonica* and the cliché "se plonger dans (la méditation, le désespoir, etc.)" [to immerse oneself in (meditation, despair, etc.)]. Taken literally (as indicated by the elimination of the reflexive pronoun),[28] the cliché turns *pénitence* into a substitute for *eau*. This is a syntagmatic phenomenon, since the two words occupy the same slot in the sentence structure. The sentence then generates *flots*; and *dans*, coinciding with the "retreat" seme contained in *pénitence*, generates the hyperbolic *au fond des*. The metonymic equivalence between the painful waters and the water in the instrument, the source of melancholy harmonies, is easily established.

The actualization of a word's descriptive system is not necessarily dependent on that word's physical presence in the sentence. On the contrary, that actualization can be even better observed if the sentence is literally the transformation of the word—if the sentence is a periphrasis. In fact, *periphrasis* is an extreme case of the overdetermination of grammatical relationships by semantic relationships: whether it is narrative or descriptive, periphrasis simply develops and distributes a given throughout the syntagm. This given is already entirely present in the semes of the word of which it is a transformation, as well as in the functions that that word would have had in the context in which the periphrasis replaces it. For instance, Lamartine writes:

> Tu chantais au berceau l'amoureuse complainte
> Qui le force au sommeil,[29]

[You were singing to the cradle the loving lament that puts it to sleep]

and we have no difficulty understanding that it is a literary equivalent of the sentence "tu chantais une berceuse" [you were singing a cradle song—(to the baby)].

We recognize the literariness because of the conventional nature of the substitution, for, at the same time that we understand the meaning of the utterance, we sense that this way of expressing it inappropriately—*berceau* instead of the baby, and the very fact of the periphrasis—stems from a traditional aesthetic with a well-defined place in the history of literature. Nonetheless, this historical explanation for the literariness does not account for the way in which the reader is conscious of perceiving a phenomenon. The perception itself remains to be explained. First, it is obvious that the substitution functions as a riddle—whereas this nuclear word remains in a sentence generated by a word's descriptive system (*harmonica*, for example), in a periphrasis, the nuclear word disappears. Second, the riddle is perceived to exist because the reader finds himself faced with instances of ungrammaticality. This is the linguistic mechanism of literariness: because these ungrammaticalities keep the reader from understanding, he is forced to resort to hypothesizing a figurative meaning. He understands "tu chantais au berceau" only when he assumes that *berceau* substitutes the container for the contained. From then on, the rule governing the idiolect of the sentence should be formulated as follows: the object of the verb shall designate a melody, since the signifier of the signified "melody" is obtained, to the exclusion of the exact term, by intersecting the semic systems of "melody" and "baby." The first syntagm, an implicitly motivated one, indirectly plays the part that *harmonica* played directly.

Thus determined, the sentence realizes the essential conditions of the potential *berceuse* [lullaby]: namely, a song sung to put a child to sleep, the woman singing the song, the child it is sung to, and the sleep that results. Contrary to what happens with "tu chantais une berceuse" [you were singing a lullaby], a description is added to the utterance. The receiver of the act of singing is represented by *berceau*, thus adding a metonymic link to the syntactic link. (We would have had paronomasia if the word *berceuse* had been made explicit.) This creates a stylistic effect. To this is added *l'amoureuse complainte*, which makes two of the semes of *berceuse* explicit: first, the "motherly love" seme (or, at least, the seme of "love that protects"), which motivates the *berceur–bercé* [luller–lulled] relationship; second, a "melancholy"[30] seme. This explanation is possible, however, only because amoureuse complainte is the direct object of a verb whose meaning is deflected by *berceau*. The equation *amoureuse complainte* = *berceuse* is thus entirely contained within the sentence. Lastly, the relative clause actualizes the "sleep-inducing" seme of the word *berceuse* and, therefore, functions in three different ways. At the level of the sentence, the relative clause ends the transformation and completes the replacement of the nuclear word with its definition: it constitutes a structural style unit by making the reader aware of a pause—there is a clausula. At the level of the representation, it ends the scene and finally presents us with its narrative *telos*: *sommeil*, the teleological justification of *chantais*. At the level of style, *forcer au sommeil* is related to such clichés as *lutter contre le sommeil* [to fight off sleep] and *vaincu par le sommeil* [overcome by sleep]. These clichés are effective because they fuse together contradictory semes: the archetype "faire une douce violence" [to force to a sweet surrender] is, therefore, what is activated by this sentence ending.

Let us now consider the second rule governing the generation of the literary sentence: the rule of *conversion*. It applies to cases in which the sentence is generated by a simultaneous transformation of all of its components—with all the signifying elements (or at least those that actualize a thematic structure) affected by the modification of a single factor. We might note in passing that this overall convertibility allows us to think of the literary sentence as a microidiolect.

For example, Hugo wrote the sentence: "ce livre . . . existe solitairement et forme un tout" [this book . . . exists solitarily and forms a group]. Then he changed the *t* in *solitairement* to a *d*. This modification transformed the components of the rest of the sentence, giving him the following sentence: "[ce livre] existe solidairement et fait partie d'un ensemble" [(this book) exists in solidarity with and is part of a whole]. The matrix and the transformation remain side by side in the text as a statement of the "double caractère," the twofold nature, of *La Légende des siècles*.[31]

As I am about to show, conversion almost always involves relatively extensive sequences, such as a descriptive system or even a more complex intertext. Let us content ourselves for the moment, however, with studying it in a few lines from Baudelaire's second "Spleen," which begins: "J'ai plus de souvenirs que si j'avais mille ans" [I have more memories than if I were a thousand years old]. The literal meaning of each word is diverted by an overriding factor that subordinates the various meanings to a single symbolism. This symbolism results from the pejorative marking of the word *souvenirs*. As we know, the poem actualizes a memory variant of spleen, since it presents as an initial given a memory as dead as the past, and not a normal memory, which would be a surviving past or a past come back to life.[32] It will, therefore, be represented by a series of variations on *la mort dans la vie* [death in life], a Romantic phrase from which Gautier derived two maxims that could well be the matrix of our poem: "Toute âme est un sépulcre où gisent mille choses" [Every soul is a tomb in which a thousand things lie] and "l'homme est . . . une nécropolis" [man is . . . a necropolis].[33] The variations are the images for which Baudelaire's poem is known by every French schoolchild: "Je suis un cimetière" [I am a graveyard], "Je suis un vieux boudoir" [I am an old boudoir], "Un vieux sphinx ignoré du monde insoucieux" [An old sphinx forgotten by an uncaring world]—images in which critics would later discern techniques announcing the writing of the Symbolists. All of them are expansions of the matrix, but what makes them converge on a single significance[34] is the uniformity of the marker, and not equivalences or repetitions directly attributable to the mimesis.

This is particularly apparent when the object of the description is a reality that, like a boudoir, is in no way depressive. That this object is "treated" in terms of sadness does not presuppose a transformation of the object. The details are not selected because they could create a splenetic verisimilitude, so to speak, or because they suggest with their representational content the same feelings as depressing things. These details are merely nouns to which pejorative adjectives have been attached: the mimetic function of the nouns is simply to hide this arbitrariness and to motivate a sequence of predicates that, otherwise, would be nothing more than markers without representational content.

> Je suis un vieux boudoir plein de roses fanées,
> Où gît tout un fouillis de modes surannées,
> Où les pastels plaintifs et les pâles Boucher,
> Seuls, respirent l'odeur d'un flacon débouché.

[I am an old boudoir full of wilted roses, where a whole clutter of outdated fashions lies, where plaintive pastels and pale Bouchers are all that remains to breathe the fragrance of a perfume bottle left open.]

It is easy enough to believe that an old boudoir might have old-fashioned dresses in it, but there is no reason why it should necessarily exclude freshly cut flowers. And there is nothing particularly natural, typical, or characteristic of a boudoir about the pastels and the faded Bouchers. But *modes, pastels*, and *Boucher* do have something in common: in the sociolect, in the intertext, they are positive sememes, and, moreover, sememes representing semes that are easily matched with opposing semes. They are eminently convertible signs, which are capable of turning from white to black in a way that captures the imagination. Fashion itself, *la mode*, is out of fashion, *démodée*, through an exemplary oxymoron; Boucher, who is usually celebrated for his "colorist's palette," "brilliant harmonies," and "color, dazzling with light," is chosen by antiphrasis for faded coloring. And the same hyperbolic bipolarization determines *pastel*, a positive word that the sociolect associates with velvety softness, fine shadings, and brightness, but which here supports *plaintif.*[35]

Might there be some purely visual details that escape this pejorative saturation? The *flacon débouché*, for instance, seems to be simply logical, since one must open a bottle in order to smell the perfume. In fact, it is nothing of the sort, for the prefix *dé-* belongs to the pejorative paradigm as well. Mimetic, it still indicates an opening. Semiotic, it makes *débouché* the pejorative epithet for *flacon*, just as *cassée* [broken] would be the pejorative adjective for *cruche* [jug].

Might there be, by contrast, some intrinsically negative details introducing a pejorative value right at the mimetic level—*fouillis* [clutter], for example? Here again, the thing is transformed into a sign: clutter is already a commonplace in the literary representation of boudoirs; it is the metonymic equivalent of the state of undress of a woman at her toilet. This metonymy presupposes the bedroom, which explains it: it symbolizes an erotic intimacy and a desirable feminity. Clutter is, therefore, a highly positive sign, as we can see in these passages from Balzac: in a countess' boudoir, "Tout était luxe et désordre, beauté sans harmonie" [all was luxury and disorder, beauty without harmony]; in a duchess' boudoir, "Là le désordre était une grâce, là le luxe affectait une espèce de dédain pour la richesse" [There, disorder was graceful; there, luxury affected a kind of disregard for wealth].[36] We must, therefore, give up trying to see in *fouillis* a mimesis rising to significance by the mere fact that it reflects a reality. It is significant only insofar as the word is the aesthetic and moral antonym of a pleasing *désordre.*

These transformations are the result of the simultaneous permutation of an entire set of permutable components, of an overall change in all the markers, and are not generated sequentially by a progression from one word to another. This is demonstrated by the saturation of the mimesis. In the context of descriptions whose main object is itself enough to dictate a negative interpretation, the referent should be sufficiently negative to allow for nuances and contrasts between lights and shadows. And yet, even in such a case, conversion continues its work of unification, of "egalitarianism" in marking, as if the mimesis had not already been marked. In the line "Je suis un cimetière abhorré de la lune" [I am a graveyard despised by the moon], the adjectival use of the participle has troubled the commentators. They have searched in vain for reasons—psychological and other—for what they see as the superfluous painting of *cimetière* in dark colors. The superfluousness and lack of motivation are limited to the mimesis, however: on the semiotic level, just as *fouillis* rewrites *un* (*beau*) *désordre* [a (beautiful) disorder], *abhorré* [despised] transforms *adoré* [beloved]. Indeed, tradition has it that the moon is the sun of ruins and graves. The light it bathes them with is as beneficial, in their inverse system, as sunlight is for the living and their cities. Moonlight is cold, perhaps, but it is also Artemis lovingly caressing Endymion in his sleep. Thus, this line in which Lamartine celebrates the goddess of night, "Froid comme ces tombeaux, objets de son amour" [Cold as these graves, the objects of her love], would seem to be the intertext of Baudelaire's line.[37] No more so than the others, therefore, is that line a sequence of increasingly precise representations; it is, instead, a formal variation. The mimesis merely provides the material of a code, and the components of that code all signify only in relation to their common marker.

Conversion is a paradigmatic transformation. It remains for me to analyze syntagmatic transformations. This type of transformation is subject to the rule of *expansion,* which I shall formulate as follows: given a minimal sentence (a nuclear or matrix sentence), each of its component parts will generate a more complex form.

In most cases, a pronoun will become a noun, a noun a noun phrase, an adjective a relative clause, and so forth, and each of the resulting groups will be capable of generating another group through addition or embedding. The verb is a special case: it is transformed so that the state or process it expresses can be represented dramatically or dynamically, or, at the very least, in a form that can be concretely imagined in terms of sensory perceptions. Thus, in a passage in *L'Eve future*, in which Villiers de l'Isle-Adam has Thomas Edison appear, the inventor turns on his phonograph by pushing a button: "(il) gratifia d'une chiquenaude le pas de vis de la plaque vibrante" [(he) bestowed a flick of his fingers on the vibrating plate].[38] This kind of descriptive mannerism is not gratuitous: it actualizes an antithetical structure—the archetype of the imperceptible gesture that is enough to start the wheels of a complicated piece of machinery turning. Various clichés in the literary mimesis of machines (particularly in science fiction) correspond to this structure.

Expansion is, therefore, the mechanism whereby the sentence goes from narrative to descriptive, from an unmotivated utterance to a verisimilar representation, a representation as capable of arousing emotions as is the thing represented.

To see how expansion establishes a meaning through simple reiteration as well as through the generation of increasingly complex forms, let us consider the following stanzas from Baudelaire's "Flacon":

Parfois on trouve un vieux flacon qui se souvient,
D'où jaillit toute vive une âme qui revient.

Mille pensers dormaient, chrysalides funèbres,
10 Frémissant doucement dans les lourdes ténèbres,
Qui dégagent leur aile et prennent leur essor,
Teintés d'azur, glacés de rose, lamés d'or.

Voilà le souvenir enivrant qui voltige
Dans l'air troublé; les yeux se ferment; le Vertige

15 Saisit l'âme vaincue et la pousse à deux mains
Vers un gouffre obscurci de miasmes humains;

Il la terrasse au bord d'un gouffre séculaire,
Où, Lazare odorant déchirant son suaire,
Se meut dans son réveil le cadavre spectral
20 D'un vieil amour ranci, charmant et sépulcral.[39]

[Sometimes we find an old perfume bottle that remembers, and out of which, full of life, a returning soul springs forth. A thousand thoughts lay asleep, funereal chrysalises, softly shivering in the heavy darkness. They free their wings and take flight, tinted with azure, glazed with rose, laméd with gold. Behold the intoxicating memory flying about in the troubled air. Eyes close. Vertigo seizes the vanquished soul and pushes it with both hands toward an abyss obscured by human miasmas. It knocks it down at the edge of an age-old abyss, where smelly Lazarus, tearing his shroud, moves about in his awakening, the ghostly corpse of a stale, old love, charming and sepulchral.]

In this poem, Baudelaire evokes phenomena of involuntary memory triggered by sensations of smell. This is a frequent enough experience but, transcribed as a literary commonplace, it takes on certain narrative or descriptive characteristics of a *coup de théâtre* or of miracles. On the level of content, this is its poetic potential.

The matrix could not, therefore, simply be "a scent triggers memory," for this would not be sufficient to generate a dramatic text playing on the supernatural—the sudden apparition of a phantom past and the summoning back of the dead. What should be suggested, instead, is a matrix such as: *a scent brings the past back to life.*

In each of the synonymous derivations developed by the expansion, the subject is transformed into descriptive complexes, each of which dramatizes a seme of *parfum*. Those semes are selected that lend themselves to suggesting the fantastic. First, the "volatility" seme. In ordinary usage, it appears in the form of stock epithets: *parfum pénétrant, subtil,* [subtle, penetrating perfume]. Here, however, it generates the statement of an almost magical power:

> Il est de forts parfums pour qui toute matière
> Est poreuse. On dirait qu'ils pénètrent le verre.

[There are some strong perfumes for which all matter is porous. One would think that they could penetrate glass.]

Next comes the "potency" seme, which applies the ambivalence of the word *seduction* to the particular case of perfume: there is no seduction that is not perilous and, conversely, no seduction would be worthy of its name if it were not able to make us forget the danger we are in. Thus, *enivrant* (line 13) is transposed from *parfum* to *souvenir*, because cause and effect, catalyst and catalyzed, have already been confused. This accounts, in particular, for the picture of the intoxicating perfume's pernicious effects, translated into the language of hallucinations or horror stories: "les yeux se ferment; le Vertige / Saisit l'âme vaincue." And in, *l'air troublé*, it also explains the hesitant flight of a memory already closer to a nocturnal vampire than to the butterfly in the preceding stanza. And, lastly, the series beginning with *enivrant* ends, in the final stanza, with the oxymorons: *aimable pestilence, ta force et ta virulence, cher poison, la vie et la mort de mon coeur* [lovable pestilence, your strength and your virulence, dear poison, the life and death of my heart]. These oxymorons are all the more effective because of the perfume-poison motif that was in vogue at the time of the Romantics (Balzac's Ferragus does away with his enemies by giving them gloves saturated with a deadly perfume). This motif seemed so exemplary of the inseparability of Beauty and Evil and so suited to symbolizing Baudelairian inspiration that Mallarmé returned to it in his "Tombeau de Charles Baudelaire": "poison tutélaire / Toujours à respirer si nous en périssons" [beneficent poison, always to be breathed, even if we perish from it].

As far as the verb in the matrix sentence is concerned, it generates a sequence of increasingly long variants that have an increasing effect on the visual imagination (lines 8, 11–12, and 18–20). The first variant transforms *ressusciter* into a ghostly apparition ("flacon . . . D'où jaillit toute vive une âme qui revient"), but this is still a vague and positive touch. The third variant will transform it into the "realistic" vision of a *cadavre spectral.* This realism has two effects: it concretizes the oxymoron that defines the miracle (memory, a past brought back to life, is one of the living dead); it functions as a hyperbole of the first variant (in terms of transformation, that variant is the model for the third; in terms of stylistic structure, it constitutes its microcontext).[40] The expansion of the matrix verb produces, in all, three periphrases actualizing the definition of *ressusciter*, the paradox of a death preceding life. The proof of the miracle (he's moving, he's alive!) is the most fertile component here. (*Jaillit* is picked up and repeated in line 11, "dégagent leur aile et prennent leur essor," and also in the melodramatic climax of "déchirant son suaire / Se meut dans son réveil.")

Since the verb is the main force behind the effectiveness of the matrix, the corollary of *ressusciter* (the presupposition of a prior death) will also be productive: hence, the three metaphors of the *âme qui revient*, the chrysalises, and Lazarus. Once again, a crescendo can be observed as we go from one to the next. It manifests itself by calling on increasingly effective intertexts. The first increase is the selection of *chrysalides*: the image is both a natural miracle, in its entomological aspects, and a stereotype in Christian apologetics representing the temporary death before the soul, transformed into a butterfly, flies off toward eternal life. We should note that the butterfly is not mentioned here. The suppression of the precise term "hymenopter" generates, in compensation, a rhetorical variation actualizing, in three terms borrowed from the vocabulary of painting, the essential seme of *butterfly* (at least as the word is used in poetic discourse)—the dazzling colors of its wings: *teintés d'azur, glacés de rose, lamés d'or.*

The crescendo reaches a climax with Lazarus in his tomb. The image is just as appropriate and pertinent as the chrysalis image, and it carries the weight of scriptural authority as well. The ascending movement characteristic of expansion ends with an apotheosis of significance. Indeed, this variant functions as the text's clausula, not because it comes last, but rather because it brings perfume and memory together in a single symbol. The miracle of Lazarus brought back to life and the proof of that miracle lie in the fact that the dead man really was dead, since he smelled—*jam foetet*. The corpse smell, transposed from the Gospels into the Baudelairian idiolect and positivized,[41] becomes the figurative equivalent of the inseparability and grammatical interdependence of the subject and predicate in the matrix: *Lazare odorant* fuses together scent and revived memory.

Generated from a minimal sentence whose components are given without modification and are acceptable (verisimilar) solely because their motivation remains implicit,[42] the literary sentence tends, therefore, to be a sequence of explanatory and demonstrative syntagms that drive arbitrariness from clause to clause, further and further away. The transformation of simple components into complex representations makes the literary sentence a grammatical equivalent of an allegorical figure rich in symbolic attributes (the vestments, sword, and scales of Justice, the hourglass of Time, and so forth).[43]

[4]

Poetics of Neologisms

LITERARY NEOLOGISMS are profoundly different from neologisms in everyday language. The latter are coined to express a new referent or signified, and their use depends, therefore, on a relation between words and things—which is to say, on nonlinguistic factors. They are, first and foremost, the bearers of a new meaning, and are not necessarily perceived to be unusual forms. A literary neologism, by contrast, is always perceived as an anomaly, and is employed precisely because of that anomaly, sometimes even without regard for its meaning. It never fails to attract attention, for it is perceived as contrasting with its context. Both its use and its effect depend on relationships situated entirely within language. Be it a case of a truly new word, or a new meaning, or the transfer of a word from one grammatical category to another, new coinings suspend the automatism of perception and force the reader to become aware of the form of the message he is deciphering. This awareness is specifically characteristic of literary communication. Precisely because of its unusual form, the neologism ideally fulfills an essential condition of literariness.

It is not surprising, therefore, that scholars have concerned themselves almost exclusively with studying this unusualness. Most think they have explained a neologism when they have described the differences that oppose it to its context, or, one might say, its ungrammaticality within the textual idiolect. But that is only half the battle: such an explanation may account for the neologism's stylistic effectiveness, but it does not tell us what makes it a phenomenon of literary discourse. This literariness can be analyzed only by describing how the neologism functions in the system constituted by the text.[1]

I shall attempt to show how a neologism is integrated into this system of meanings and forms. We can understand its function only if we recognize that the neologism is the result of a derivation from an initial given, as are all the words in a literary sentence.[2] Its very singularity is not due to its isolation, but rather to the rigor of the semantic and morphological sequences in which it is either the end point or the point of conjunction.

This is the case of *Circeto*, a composite creation in Rimbaud's "Dévotion." This prose poem takes the form of a litany addressed to various intercessors: "A ma soeur Louise Vanaen de Voringhem . . . A ma soeur Léonie Aubois d'Ashby . . . A Lulu, —démon . . . A l'adolescent que je fus. A ce saint vieillard . . ." [To my sister Louise Vanaen of Voringhem . . . To my sister Léonie Aubois of Ashby . . . To Lulu—the demon . . . To the adolescent I was. To that holy, old man . . .] etc. The series ends with this stanza:

> Ce soir à Circeto des hautes glaces, grasse comme le poisson, et enluminée comme les dix mois de la nuit rouge, —(son coeur ambre et spunk)—, pour ma seule prière muette comme ces régions de nuit et précédant des bravoures plus violentes que ce chaos polaire.
>
> [Tonight, to Circeto of the lofty icebergs, greasy as a fish, and her face flushed like the ten months of the red night (her heart amber and spunk) for my only prayer, silent as these night regions and preceded by heroic acts more violent than this polar chaos.]

Circeto brings together two names taken from mythology, that of the enchantress Circe and that of a sea goddess, Ceto, the mother of the Gorgons. The portmanteau word is made grammatical by another borrowing from mythology: the hypogrammatical model is the name of the goddess Derceto, a divinity with a body of either a siren or a fish, the mother of Semiramis, and familiar enough to the educated nineteenth-century public for Nerval to place her on the same plane as Astarte.[4]

Circeto thus unites in a single lexeme two groups of semantic components, the combination of which creates the stanza's significance, a final variation on that of the entire poem. Using the litany's "religious" code, the poem lists the characters invoked one after the other, each one the object of a thanksgiving, of a kind of votive offering. Whatever their literal meaning may be, their function is always the same: they all share a common symbolism, that of representing a postulated happiness, either past or yet to come. As in all lyric poetry, the women's names are incarnations of regret or desire.

I scarcely need to point out that Circe is the epitome of the seductress, the *femme fatale*, who is both dangerous and irresistible. The *Circe* component, therefore, makes *Circeto* (because of the hyperbolic character of the Circe sememe, as well as because of its anomalous fusion with Ceto) the culmination of the paradigm of women's names, of feminine symbols of desire, or of a desirable object symbolized by woman.

But the quest for a desirable object, or simply the quest—a commonplace in the Romantic imagination—is also represented in Rimbaud in the code of a voyage to a utopia or to a distant beyond. For him, the equivalent of Baudelaire's departure for "anywhere out of the world" is to seek refuge in the Arctic, to flee mankind in the hyperborean zones, "régions de nuit," "chaos polaire," "aux confins du monde et de la Cimmérie, patrie de l'ombre et des tourbillons" [at the limits of the world and Cimmeria, land of darkness and whirlwinds].[5] *Circeto's* second component, Ceto, is the culmination of the hyporborean paradigm: a feminine allegory, her portrait includes clichés from the conventional description of Eskimo woman (*grasse comme le poisson, enluminée*), from the standard mimesis of the polar regions (*ambre, spunk*), and from the portrait of the goddess herself, who is traditionally associated with images of cetaceans. *Circeto*, a hyperborean idol and a feminine idol, thus integrates woman and the far ends of the earth, the two symbols of the quest.

The dual sign is thus the lexical equivalent (and because of its ungrammaticality, the hyperbolic equivalent) of two simultaneous, synchronized expansions generated parallel to each other, but separately, by a "quest" matrix. Separated in the text, they are again united in the portmanteau word, whose hybrid morphology arouses the reader's curiosity so as to better guide him to the significance.

Thus, the neologism is more motivated than a nonneologism. It reduces the sign's arbitrariness by virtue of its *overdetermination.* Now, literary discourse is characterized by the overdetermination of the words that comprise it: the syntactic relations uniting those words with one another are echoed by other relations, both formal and semantic, for each sentence is derived or deduced, as it were, from one initial given.

Since every given generates its homologue by formal variation either between identical terms or from one opposite to another, the derivation actualizes a paradigm of synonyms (tautological derivation) or of antonyms (oxymoronic derivation) in the text: hence, the favored status of the neologism. In the first place, wherever the limitations of the lexicon make it impossible for the derivation to be carried out, the neologism offers the solution of "ungrammaticality." In the second place, it always presupposes the existence of a paradigm, since it can be neither conceived of nor perceived (and the pertinence of textual phenomena to literariness is defined by the fact that they must be perceived), except in opposition to a nonneological homologue.[6] In the third place, neological derivation always has a maximum of stylistic intensity, because the new coinage is extrapolated from an existing form and can only stand out by altering that form. Lastly, the derivation actualizes a type of "absolute" variation, since the neologism immediately involves the entire semantic structure of the forms it is replacing. By contrast, a variation using existing words and based on partial synomymy can be no more than approximate. The neologism creates a purely verbal opposition that totally confirms or annuls the unmarked utterance, loops the loop, and replaces the referentiality of word to thing with the "verification" of one word by another.

I shall distinguish between implicit derivation, where the opposition's unmarked term is immediately present in the reader's mind but is not actualized in the verbal sequence, and explicit derivation, where it is.

In explicit derivation, the unmarked term is either a word or a phrase, or else a periphrasis corresponding to the same signified as the neologism.

In most cases, a reversal of terms produces a stylistic intensification. By this, I mean that the neologism precedes its unmarked variant. Understanding is consequently suspended until the entire sentence has been deciphered, which explains its unusually strong hold on the reader. Take, for example, Apollinaire's borrowing from the Greek:

> Mort d'immortels *argyraspides*
> La neige aux boucliers d'argent
> Fuit les dendrophores livides
> Du printemps cher aux pauvres gens
> Qui *resourient* les yeux humides.[7]

[Death of undying argyraspids, the silver-shielded snow flees the livid dendrophores of Spring, dear to the poor folk, who smile again with moist eyes.]

The first line is simply the "Greek" variant of the statement: "la neige aux boucliers d'argent fuit." It is the Greek, and therefore hyperbolic, variant, since it is difficult or impossible to decipher until we come to *boucliers d'argent*, the hyperbole of the metaphoric representation of snow as an ephemeral beauty. The *dendrophores*, palm bearers in rites of Spring, metonymically represent the new season. *Argyraspides* functions twice over: as an empty sign, a signal that we are waiting for a meaning, a formal beauty about to be born, and, retroactively, it functions as the equivalent, in loftier style, of the second transposition of *neige* into *boucliers d'argent*. The position of *argyraspides* at the beginning, because it suspends the appearance of the unmarked term that will translate it, enables the neologism to function as a marker, irrespective of its meaning. The cultural prestige of the Greek language makes it an index of poetry, or more precisely, of genre, and momentarily elevates the stanza to the level of the ode. Only momentarily, though, for the stanza's second neologism, *resourient*, brings us back to the style of intimist poetry. It, too, is a genre marker: first because it is intelligible, and next, because its prefix is typical to the ad hoc nonce words found in colloquial conversation. The *printemps cher aux pauvres gens* gives us François Coppée coming on the footsteps of Pindar.[8]

The multiplication of the paradigm's unmarked terms reinforces the neologism's effect, since its contrast with its context becomes all the stonger the better the pattern of that context is established. Thus, in a text by Chateaubriand, the neologism *aphonie* [aphony] is opposed to *silence*. The meaning of the two words is strictly the same,[9] the only difference being that the borrowing from the Greek has an intrinsic appropriateness that *silence* does not. The prefix and root, which are used in the formation of so many common words, make the word, in the eyes of the educated reader, act like a condensation of a descriptive sentence. The effect of this motivation, in contrast to the relative arbitrariness of *silence*, is coupled with the stylistic opposition: Greekness versus non-Greekness. This opposition generates the entire text, for it is so constructed as to lead the reader irresistibly from the unmarked element to the marked element in the *silence* paradigm. This syntactic expansion of a semantic opposition is the equivalent of an overdetermined signification[10] and, on the level of style, of a more and more striking hyperbole.

> Les ordres religieux avaient rebâti dans leur couvent la Thébaïde. . . . Ainsi lorsqu'on . . . était près d'entrer dans Clairvaux, on reconnaissait Dieu de toute part. On trouvait au milieu du jour un silence pareil à celui du milieu de la nuit: le seul bruit qu'on y entendait était le son des différents ouvrages des mains ou celui de la voix des frères lorsqu'ils chantaient les louanges du Seigneur. La renommée seule de cette grande aphonie imprimait une telle révérence que les séculiers craignaient de dire une parole.
>
> [The religious orders had rebuilt the Thebaid in their monastery. . . . Thus, when one was about to enter Clairvaux, one would

feel the presence of God everywhere. At midday, one would find a silence just like that in the middle of the night: the only noise that one heard was the many sounds of the brothers' handiwork or of their voices singing the praises of the Lord. The renown of this great aphony alone imparted such reverence that laymen were afraid to say a word.]

Beneath its seeming variety of details, the description does nothing more than repeat *silence*. Prepared and reinforced by *Thébaïde*, the word *silence* is spelled out, and, by transforming noon into an equivalent of midnight, it reverses the descriptive system in which noise is a metonym of daytime life. By an analogous reversal, those sounds compatible with the anchorites' rule of life become a periphrasis of "monastic silence." Even the allusion to *renommée* [fame], which, ever since Ovid, has been the voice par excellence, is subordinated to the main point of the passage: the only sound was that of their silence. After this paradox, one more step remains before the scale of silences reaches its climax: *aphonie*.[11] The neologism in a case like this is nothing more than the ultimate point of the development. An iconic value is added to its semantic content: it seems to reach beyond the realm of possible signifiers and is a kind of image of limits surmounted. Language—quite literally—outdoes itself.

Of the two possible derivations mentioned above, oxymoronic generation is perhaps the more frequent as far as the particular case of the neologism is concerned. Its frequency, no doubt, is due to the fact that negative and positive prefixes comprise one of the most active forms of new coinings and facilitate antithetical expressions. Similarly, active suffixes such as *-eur* facilitate active–passive oppositions, as in this phrase of Hugo's: "Les extorqués faisant cortège aux extorqueurs" [The extortioned trailing the extortioners].[12] Such oppositions are all the more tempting in that they are based on the rhetorical model of the *figura etymologica* or paronomasia.

Of course, oxymoronic generation is not limited to these mirror effects and to the affixed forms that produce them. But all cases of this second type of derivation are characterized by the fact that, in them, overdetermination takes a polarized form. The neologism-versus-nonneological-homologue pair acts as the matrix of verbal associations, which are consequently so many repetitions and amplifications of each of the poles. They stress their opposition at the same time that they underscore their inseparability. My example here will be a second *aphonie* in Chateaubriand, this time from the "Rêverie au Lido" [Reverie at the Lido], a bravura piece familiar to all Chateaubriand aficionados.

> Il n'était sorti de la mer qu'une aurore ébauchée et sans sourire. La transformation des ténèbres en lumière avec ses changeantes merveilles, son aphonie et sa mélodie, ses étoiles éteintes tour à tour dans l'or et les roses du matin, ne s'est point opérée.[13]
>
> [Nothing had emerged from the sea but a hint of a smileless dawn. The transformation of darkness into light, with its changing wonders, its aphony and its melody, its stars extinguished one by one in the gold and roses of morning, did not occur.]

Here, too, the neologism results from a transcoding from *silence*. But this transcoding occurs only at third hand, as the clausula and the most striking and condensed form of an opposition that has already been firmly established. The text dynamically rewrites a *coincidentia oppositorum* first actualized six lines earlier—the coexistence of contrary feelings: "ma joie et ma tristesse furent grandes quand je découvris la mer . . . à la lueur du crépuscule" [my joy and sadness were great when I discovered the sea . . . in the glow of the morning twilight]. The second variant turns the antithesis into a metamorphosis: "la transformation des ténèbres en lumière, avec ses changeantes merveilles." This utterance is now repeated by *aphonie*, which is opposed to *mélodie*, in a metaphoric and even synesthetic transformation of the opposition of darkness to light according to an analogical model: silence is to sound what darkness is to light.[14] The polarization is further reinforced by the fact that the opposition is, in the end, stated in the paradoxical form of *maxima dissimilitudo in similitudine maxima* by the two words in the text that are most similar, since both are Greek and learned. Opposed to *mélodie*, which is a kind of positive hyperbole of *sound*, there is *aphonie*, the negative hyperbole of *nonsound*.

Now let us consider implicit derivation—those cases, that is, in which the nonneological homologue is not actualized in the text. In them, overdetermination results from the actualization of a descriptive system or from the use of a cliché as a hypogram. Although the unmarked term is absent from the written text, it is nonetheless present in a "mental" text made up of stereotypes.

If the stereotypes are organized in a network of signifiers, which is to say in a descriptive system, the neologism is overdetermined by associative chains existing prior to the text, just as it would be if those chains were present before it in context. In Apollinaire's poem, for example, the *re-* prefix in *resourire* is motivated as a variant of verbal associations such as *retour du printemps* [return of spring], which themselves correspond to a "cyclical" structure in the descriptive system of *season* or *year*. The descriptive system of the signifier *fleur* [flower] includes words that actualize, along with other semes, those of "fragility" and "beauty." The signifiers organized around "beauty" involve, for the most part, sight and smell. The latter, in particular, are so important that *fleur* tautologically generates descriptions of perfumes and, oxymoronically, themes such as that of the hidden flower with no one to smell its perfume,[15] or that of flowers that have no scent. These exist in reality, of course, but what makes them objects of literary mimesis is clearly the lure of antiphrasis, of wordplay similar to the wordplay in the *blason*, which consists in praising the exact opposite of a praiseworthy quality or its lack. The antithesis is so enticing that, at the beginning of the nineteenth century, it generated the neologism *inodore* [scentless].[16] Motivated because it reverses a seme and overdetermined in that it counterbalances, all by itself, all the generally accepted ideas and clichés in the mimesis of flowers, it transforms a positive system, the ideal representation of a flower, into a negative code. In a poem expressing Romantic *tedium vitae*, Gautier wrote:

> Donc, reçois dans tes bras, ô douce Somnolence,
> Vierge aux pâles couleurs, blanche soeur de la Mort,

Un pauvre naufragé des tempêtes du sort!
Exauce un malheureux qui te prie et t'implore
Egrène sur son front le pavot *inodore.*[17]

[So, take into your arms, o sweet Drowsiness, Virgin of the pale colors, Death's white sister, this forlorn survivor of the storms of fate! Answer the prayers of this poor wretch who beseeches and implores you. Put on his forehead the rosary beads of the scentless poppy.]

It is true that poppies have no scent, but that has to do with the referent. At the level of the signifiers, *inodore* is a variant of *pâles couleurs*: here all beauty is an image of death. This is because of the word's exceptional form and because the semic inversion that it represents affects the flower symbolism in its entirety (which is possible only because every component of a descriptive system can be substituted metonymically for the whole of the system). *Inodore* negativizes at once another entire system of representation: the commonplace of symbolic scenes of triumph, of sybaritic or spiritual banquets, of scenes of bliss or sanctification, in which a shower of roses or petals falls on the protagonist.

A neologism is capable of summarizing an entire descriptive system and condensing it into a single sign. Thus the descriptive system of *morale* [ethics] includes metaphors of a path—a steep and thorny one for virtue and an easy one for vice—and of a crossroads (the Pythagorean Y, the crossroads of *choice*, where Hercules proves his virtue by taking virtue's path). The neologism *choisisseur* [chooser], coined by Hugo, acts as a kind of poetic shorthand, referring the reader to the system of metaphors belonging to *morale*: "Ce pâle choisisseur de redoutables routes" [That pale chooser of fearsome routes].[18]

But just as a single symbol can denote a series of equations and allow for the integration of that series into another equation, the neologism permits us to make a group of themes, for instance, function in a new representation. Here, the *-eur* suffix turns the hero of the moral choice into a specialist, a technician,[19] and makes his epic adventure into a habit. The noun is modified, and *pâle*, which for Hugo connotes metaphysical anguish, transforms the entire descriptive system of the moral adventure into a metaphoric code for the gnostic quest. The *choisisseur* is no longer virtuous Hercules, but rather Man, searching for the key to the cosmos, the "buveur de la coupe d'effroi" [drinker from the cup of fright]. By acquiring a self-sustaining meaning as if it were an independent word, the suffix converts the "moral" narrative into a general sign denoting an ethical stance and converts the episode into a sentence laden with symbolism. Similarly, personification is a false portrait in which the attributes (clothing, objects carried, and so on) are explanations. The neologism, then, in the very midst of a mimesis, is the agent or instrument of a semiosis.

The overdetermination of a neologism by hypogrammatization functions in the same way that reference to a descriptive system does. Instead of representing an entire system, however, the neologism appears in a sentence that is superimposed upon a fragment of a system. The fragment is already stereotyped, frozen in a form belonging to the author's (and reader's) mythology, which is a verbal mythology encoded in language. It will be a quotation, a cliché, or a formula.

Hypogrammatization of a cliché (or even of a stereotyped group lacking stylistic effect) is naturally the most frequent kind. Take the stereotype *Assomption de la Vierge* [Assumption of the Virgin], which belongs to two technical languages, those of religion and painting. It determines the transformation of the noun into a verb in the following sentence, in which Chateaubriand describes a famous Titian belonging to a Venetian museum: "La Vierge au-dessus de ce groupe assompte au centre d'un demi-cercle de chérubins; multitude de faces admirables dans cette gloire" [Above this group, the Virgin assumpts in the center of a half-circle of Cherubim; a whirl of wonderful faces in this glory].[20] The neologism is clearly appropriate, since we are dealing with a painting organized along the vertical axis. It is really determined, though, by a pure tautology. Appearing to be a description—that is, a reference—the sentence proposes a lexical circularity very close to that of a *figura etymologica* or paronomasia.[21] A definition or description goes from the word to be described, or defined, to its periphrasis, or equivalent, in another code. Here, however, the word to be described (*assomption*) and its description (*assompter*) are nearly identical. This circularity creates an impression of truth and accuracy; it seems to confirm with the character's actions precisely what the painting's title already announced. By the same token, since the subject of the painting is a variation on the name of a genre, the picture's conformity to its genre appears to be confirmed. We are thus given an outline of a fiction of art criticism, or, if we prefer, its literary mimesis.

It is even possible for a neological hypogrammatization to involve a single word, without, however, being what we would call a pun. Once again, Chateaubriand writes in one of his moonlight scenes that "le jour *céruséen* et velouté de la lune, flottait silencieusement sur la cime des forêts" [the *cerusean* and velvety light of the moon wafted silently over the tops of the trees in the forests].[22] He had earlier written *céruléen* [cerulean]; and, because of that word's exclusively literary character and high "visibility," it is impossible to read *céruséen* in the text without opposing it to *céruléen*.[23] Now, the glaringly obvious hypogrammatization is the very mechanism of overdetermination. First, *céruséen* is doubly neological—both as a formation after *céruse* [ceruse] and as a variation on *céruléen* [cerulean, or sky-blue]. Next, *céruséen* refers to *céruse*, which, in Chateaubriand's time, was the name for the white lead used to make paint. It is, therefore, a realistic expression of lunar whiteness—realistic not necessarily because it is true, but because it refers to a specialized word belonging to the language of paint stores. In this sense, it is generated by a paradigm of *whiteness* synonyms whose vehicles of comparison are all realistic as well.[24] But *céruséen* also refers to *céruléen*—not as a particular color, but as a stereotypical color word in the descriptive system of *sky*. Lastly, *céruséen* is related oxymoronically both to *velouté* [velvety], itself the result of a series of expressions conforming to the norms of literary moonlight,[25] and to *céruléen*, which is tautologically related to *velouté*. The motivation is always double. The neologism is realistic and unconventional because of its root, and conventional and idealizing because it copies a literary model.

It is, therefore, both a genre marker (since a *clair de lune*, or moonlight piece, is a subgenre of the *rêverie*) and an element of "objective" descriptive style (since moonlight functions as a visual vignette). It is the instrument of an aesthetics of tone mixture and stylistic syncretism.

Far from arbitary and anything but a foreign body in the sentence, the literary neologism is the most strongly motivated signifier that can be found in a text. It always belongs to two or more sequences: either it is generated simultaneously by a morphological and semantic sequence, or by two semantic sequences, or even by a more complex combination. This cannot be the case with a pre-existent word (aside from alliterative phenomena). Its function is, thus, to bring together or condense the dominant characteristics of the text. Coined expressly and created to meet specific needs, the neologism is the precise word par excellence.

[5]

Paragram and Significance

MY PURPOSE is twofold: I would like to explore Saussure's concept of the paragram in a direction different from his and, in so doing, I would like to try to come closer to a definition of the significance of a text. Even before we attempt to define significance, it is clear that the word and the notion are necessary. If a literary text is indeed different from a nonliterary text, this difference should first manifest itself semantically and semiotically, since all texts are communication acts. Normal meaning is both referential and discursive—that is, experienced through a linear reading—so significance can be distinguished from meaning only outside of linearity.

Saussure's ultimate problem—and the reason he gave up on the matter—was that he could not be sure that the identification of the paragram's theme-word in the text could be proved. He was unable to show that the presence of the theme-word implies "a larger quantity of coincidence than is the case with the first word to appear."[1] The very fact that this question must be asked, and that the saturation of the text by a phonic paraphrase of a theme-word is not immediately perceived, is hard to reconcile with the reader's natural experience of a literary text. In that experience, the form (the way things are said), captivates the reader, limits his options, and imposes itself on him clearly and inevitably, even if the meaning remains obscure. These problems, it seems to me, can be avoided if the analyst begins with what the surface features of the text—that is, its style—force him to perceive. These features can be seen as variants of a semantic structure that does not need to be actualized in a theme-word (present either intact or as *membra disiecta*, as dispersed elements, in the text), so long as the decoding of stressed elements and other formal distortions sensitizes the reader to their recurrence and, hence, to their equivalence. He then perceives them not only as forms, but as variants of an invariant. This natural reading procedure should obviate the difficulty of proving that a theme-word really exists, because the structure's complex network of relations is self-defining independently of any word that may implement it.

Saussure's stroke of genius, or that of Saussure number one,[2] was to understand that the text's true center is outside the text and not behind it, hidden away, as victims of the intentional fallacy are fond of thinking. The text's true significance lies in its consistent formal reference to and repetition of what it is about, despite continuous variations in the way it goes about saying it. Saussure understood that the truth or depth or real function of the text lies in this system of reference and repetition, and not in the content of what is repeated.

Instead of trying to find a hypogram condensed in one word, only to be spread out again along the sentence in para- or anagrams, I propose to find it in lexical transformations of a semantic given. This distinction allows me to bypass teleology. There is no point of departure preceding other developments of language,[3] but there are, rather, *displacements*: any semantic nucleus functions as if it were a suppressed neurotic symptom. Its very suppression causes it to pop up elsewhere in the text with a flourish of other symptoms, that is, of other synonyms or periphrases.

To arrive at a definition of the semantic paragram, I started from three facts of literary utterance. One, that the literary text is built up by expansion from units of meaning smaller than the text they generate. Two, that such derivations are self-sufficient, since even their referents are verbal. The point on which all the self-reference should focus is then an empty space, and the verbal referent that is the paragram is left unspoken, even as the reader is able to circle around it. Three, that the words actualizing the derivation are never literal statements, but indirect ones—metaphorical or metonymic.

Furthermore, to return to expansion, its point of departure generates derivations only from what is pertinent and significant in it. This generator may not exist lexically; that is, it may exist only in the form of a seme. The significance (the textual relevance), is both what is transformed and the fact of the transformation that represses, displaces, and disguises it. The text functions like a repression, and anomalies in the mimesis and disruptions of apparent referentiality are its symptoms.

The model I propose for the lexical paragram is thus the expansion of a matrix. Since it is lexical, this expansion occurs in the form of words linked together grammatically, and is not phonetic or graphemic, as in Saussure's paragram. Contrary to the verbal sequence that it generates, the matrix is semantic, and not lexical or graphemic, as Saussure conceived the *locus princeps*. Therefore, instead of having fragments of a word scattered along the sentence, each embedded in the body of a word, we get words or groups of words, each embedded in a syntagm whose organization reflects and exteriorizes the inner semantic configuration of the nuclear word or of the semantic given actualized by the word.

The relationships among the paragram's components, aside from fulfilling the needs of the context within grammatical bounds, are so arranged that they duplicate, relation by relation, the structural polar binarities of the semantic given.[4] To put it otherwise, the sentences repeat and develop the components of the nuclear word's meaning: semes are actualized by verbal sequences, by the very words of the text, instead of being represented by abstract words in the analyst's metalanguage.[5]

Consider the following verse of Cocteau's:

> Car votre auberge, ô mort, ne porte aucune enseigne.
> J'y voudrais voir, de loin, un beau cygne qui saigne
> 45 Et chante, cependant que lui tordez le cou.
> Ainsi je connaîtrais ce dont je ne me doute:
> L'endroit où le sommeil interrompra ma route,
> Et s'il me faut marcher beaucoup.

> [For your inn, O Death, bears no signboard. I would like to see it from afar, showing a beautiful swan bleeding and singing, while you wring his neck. Thus I should know what I cannot even guess: the place where sleep will end my road and whether I have a long way to go.]

The semantic given leaves a visible trace: it is *auberge de la mort* [the inn of Death], a familiar image and motif of the literary theme of *life as a road* and, in this version, the road of life, along which the hospitable host, Death, offers the weary traveler his well-earned sleep. For the French reader, an intertext can readily be found in a poem like Baudelaire's "La Mort des pauvres" in *Les Fleurs du Mal*. The group *auberge de la mort* functions as a given because it presupposes another text. But it would still work on a reader ignorant of the tradition, thanks to the very logic of the word group's semantic configuration. In *auberge de la mort*, the relation between the two words is twofold: metonymic and metaphoric. *Auberge* is metonymic of *Death*, in that it complements the metaphor of Death as an innkeeper. But there is also a direct metaphoric relation between *mort* and *auberge*, for the "road of life" theme selects the "weariness" and "longing for rest" semes in *auberge*. Consequently, *auberge* is to the tiring *road* what *death* is to *life. Auberge de la mort* carries the same meaning twice over, and is thus twice appropriate, or may be read in two ways, and is therefore more semantically charged than its context. For the reader unfamiliar with the tradition, but who does know its language, its components replace the intertextual reference with a reciprocal reference, since each of the components is synonymous with the others. The anomaly enabling *auberge de la mort* to generate a text is twofold. It lies both in the paradox of very different components being very closely related and in the equivalence between two forms in spite of the fact that one is subordinated to the other.

The derivation from the semantic given translates into a narrative an actualization of the descriptive system of the word *auberge*, or at least one of its subsystems: that of *enseigne* [signboard].

Now the link between the two is overdetermined four times over. Each link functions as a hypogram of the surface sentence (lines 43–45). This surface sentence states that the speaker would like to be able to tell where the inn is located. Under the pressure of the *road of life* metaphor, the text translates into spatial terms an experience of temporal anxiety, (lines 46–48: "Thus I should know what I cannot even guess: the place where sleep will end my road, and whether I have a long way still to go"). The surface sentence is a transformation of the matrix: *I should like to know when I am going to die.*

The first hypogram is the metonymic derivation from *auberge* to *enseigne*, the latter being the metonym of the former. You lodge at the *White Horse* or the *Singing Swan.* Furthermore, the validity of the *enseigne* mimesis is twice proved, since this kind of sign traditionally bears both animal figures and a redundant caption, such as *Au cheval blanc, Au chien qui fume*, and so forth. This makes the signboard, like its aristocratic counterpart, the *blazon*, a subgenre of the *emblem*. The word *cygne* is modified by two relative clauses, the second of which generates a descriptive rationalization (line 45: "singing while you wring his neck"). Neither of these developments is consistent with the rules of the emblem subgenre, which admits of only one defining adjective or relative clause—the *Singing Swan*, for instance. This ungrammaticality changes the meaning of the phrase from literal—a description—to metaphorical—this sign does more than just name a place of business. The existence of the emblem is negated (line 43: "your inn . . . bears no signboard"), and its description is hypothetical (line 44: "I would like to see it from afar, showing a swan"). This makes the tavern the unnamed and unknown inn, and the unknown inn, the unknown future. One of the variants of *auberge fameuse* [famous inn] in Baudelaire's poem is "le portique ouvert sur les Cieux inconnus" [the gate open onto the unknown Heavens].[6] Unknown or nameless, *auberge* is thus the lexical matrix of line 46, as well as the metaphorical statement of the truism suggested by the whole stanza—that man knows not the hour of his death. But again, what makes for the text's literariness is not that it mouths a truism, but that it does so indirectly.

The second hypogram is the derivation from *death* to *swan*. The descriptive system of the word for *swan* has, ever since Greek and Latin literature, valorized the swan as the bird who sings as he dies. What the text actualizes is the seme common to *cygne* and to the semantic given, *auberge de la mort*. If we see the text as a linearity, the sequence making the signboard a metonym for the inn determines the equivalence of *auberge* and *cygne* with respect to *mort*: they are both variants of a *death* invariant, the first in a *road* code and the second in a *bird* code. But this linear reading would be inaccurate, since the given is a complex network involving the subordination of *mort* to *auberge*. *Cygne* is derived equally from *auberge* and from *mort*, but since *auberge* stands for *death*, *cygne* is twice a sign for *death*: directly, as a symbolic myth, and indirectly, as a mimetic metonym. The acceptability of the representation despite the patent nonexistence of the inn will, at best, make the text seem clever and artful to the reader—which is one more characteristic of literariness.

The third hypogram is the semantic shift that *auberge* undergoes because of the *enseigne* derivation: the inn is less of a stop on the road than it is a symbol. Since it is represented metonymically by its *enseigne*, it is depicted as a sign. The sign being both described and said not to exit, the verbal sequence of images constitutes a "figurative" equivalent of the verbs' conditional mode (line 44: *j'y voudrais voir*; line 46: *je connaîtrais*. The text is a metaphorical representation, but this very representation is so built that it becomes the icon of the sentence's grammatical "geometry": here it is the verbal mode, a mode independent of the verb's meaning. But that is the point of the whole poem: the uncertainty, yet the imminence; in short, the murky expectation of the end. (Compare lines 53–54: "à la longue, il faut, mort, que je m'habitue / A vous recevoir dans mon lit" [in the long run, Death, I shall have to get used to letting you into my bed].) Life is defined in terms of death-to-come, and death is defined in terms of repressed desire. (Compare line 57, addressing Death: "votre amour attire les amants" [your love lures lovers].)

Finally, the fourth hypogram actualizes the semes inherent in *cygne* as the dying bird par excellence: hence the clause "qui saigne et chante" [bleeding and singing]. This double specification makes the relationship between *death* and *swan* doubly explicit (once in *swan* code—*singing*—and once in *fowl* code—*bleeding*). This duplication introduces deictic inconsistencies in the significance: the contradiction between bleeding and strangling and the difficulty of singing while one's neck is being wrung. What is happening, in fact, is that there is no visualization, since the text does not offer a step-by-step description, but simply disposes alternately, along the one line it must limit itself to, elements that belong to two different texts, text and hypotext. If we were to arrange these two texts along two parallel lines, *chante* would be on a level with *cygne*, as the bird of death, and *tordez le cou* would be on a level with the death of farmyard poultry (which brings us back to the inn, the very heart of which is the spit where the victim is roasted). Much more interesting, though, is the relation of *saigne* to *cygne*, for this is obviously not explained by the circumstances of the bird's demise. The relation is one of paronomasia. It would not be enough to see *saigne*, or even both *saigne* and *cygne*, as a paragram of *enseigne*. The paronomasia functions as meaning, because it is by bleeding that the swan becomes a significant sign [c'est en saignant que le cygne est un signe enseignant]. This is so not just because of the literary tradition that makes the wound into a mouth and turns its blood into red ink that writes a plea for vengeance (as in Corneille's *Le Cid*, for instance); nor just because of the pun on *cygne* and *saigne*, of which there are quite a few examples. Rather, it it because its dying is simply the acting out of its symbolism; and above all, because *cygne* and *saigne*, coming after *enseigne*, appear as a circularity, as a closed grammatical declension. *Cygne* modifies the final vowel of *enseigne*, and *saigne* returns it to its original form. This circularity cannot go unnoticed, since no other form in French permits the alternation between [iɲ] and [ɛɲ] in the final position.[7] The swan on the sign is a sign when it bleeds

[Le cygne de l'enseigne est signe quand il saigne]: one cannot avoid perceiving *cygne* as the reverse of *saigne* and *saigne* as the obverse of *cygne*. By modifying the existing semantic relationships, this inversion–reversion variation replaces a rule of language with a rule of the idiolect. Whenever it appears in a text, the primacy of the idiolect over the language is, of course, one of the aspects of the significance.

But it is important to see here that the significance of the text as a whole is constituted by nothing other than the reader's experience of the alternating mechanism I have just described, for that experience establishes the only rule on which the appropriateness of form to content in the poem is based. This rule is unique, for it is to be found nowhere else. It consequently embodies the originality required by the aesthetic presupposed by the conventions of period and genre. It alone structures every representation of the content (that is, of death), in relation to a given subordinating the text's semantic system to a reference to that given. Indeed the reader, entering into this play of alternation, actualizes in the form the literal meaning of the title, the metaphorical meaning of which is actualized in the content.

The title, *L'Endroit et l'envers*[8] [the right side and the wrong side, or: the face and the reverse] is a cliché repeated verbatim by various death images: for example, "mort, à l'envers de nous vivante, / tu composes la trame de notre tissu" [death, living on our inside, you compose the web of our fabric] (lines 5–6), and even the angel of death, Thanatos, transformed into Eros, possessing Death face down—*à l'envers couché* (line 70). This formal back-and-forth sway between contraries comes as a kind of semiotic confirmation—it is almost a grammatical pantomime transferred by reading to the plane of gesture—of the appropriateness of the cliché when applied to a meditation on Death. It replaces a commonplace about death as the great beyond (an all-purpose image) with a representation belonging to this text alone and serving as the earmark of Cocteau's manner: the representation of death as the reverse or the other side of life.

The text's derivation from a semantic given eliminates reference of words to things and replaces it with the reference of the words to a word system or semic system found outside the text. This displacement can be observed on two levels. On one level, even those representations that are incompatible with the code derived from the given are subordinated to that code. And on the other level, the semantic anomalies resulting from the derivation presuppose an implicit intertext. Consider, for example, sonnet 81 in Baudelaire's *Les Fleurs du Mal*:

L'un t'éclaire avec son ardeur,
L'autre en toi met son deuil, Nature!
Ce qui dit à l'un: Sépulture!
Dit à l'autre: Vie et Splendeur!

5 Hermès inconnu qui m'assistes
Et qui toujours m'intimidas,
Tu me rends l'égal de Midas,
Le plus triste des alchimistes;

Par toi je change l'or en fer
10 Et le paradis en enfer;
Dans le suaire des nuages

Je découvre un cadavre cher,
Et sur les célestes rivages
Je bâtis de grands sarcophages.

[One lights you up with his flame, and another puts his mourning in you, o Nature! The same thing is an image of dark Death to the one, and to the other, an image of bright Life. Unknown Hermes, who are my guide and yet frighten me, you make me like Midas, the saddest of alchemists. Thanks to your intercession, I turn gold into iron and heaven into hell. Through the shroud of the clouds, I see a corpse dear to my heart, and on the celestial shores, I erect huge cenotaphs.]

The title, "Alchimie de la douleur" [Alchemy of Sorrow], controls the generation of the entire text. Because of its definite article, *douleur* is an abstract noun with a very general meaning, and it metonymically represents an even more general meaning: man's fate.

The title's syntax forces us to think of *alchimie* as a metaphor. But the choice of a figurative meaning does not carry with it a mimesis of alchemy enabling us to picture Midas as an alchemist in his laboratory surrounded by the picturesque paraphernalia of the arcane science. *Alchimie* is simply the hyperbolic expression of the psychic changes wrought by sorrow. The word enunciates the formal feature common to all the sentences that follow it: each of them describes the transformation of something into its opposite. The word *alchimie* does not refer to its referent. It simply programs the grammar of the text by restricting it to variations on one formula of *change*. It also programs the lexicon of the text by making it into a code: every word will be a statement of transmutation, or of its results—to such an extent that when he finally reaches the second tercet and finds no statement of the kind, the reader is himself programmed to understand *cadavre cher* not as a static representation of a corpse, but rather as the product of the transmutation of a living body.

If *alchimie* is metaphorical, *douleur* must necessarily be literal (with or without metonymy). But its literal meaning (with or without hyperbole resulting from metonymy), instead of giving the text a philosophic or psychological content, as in utilitarian communication, triggers a negative conversion: since the meaning of *douleur* colors all the variants of the *change* structure with its pejorative value, all the transformations go from good to bad. Thus the mythical transmutation of a base metal into gold, for example, is inverted: "changer l'or en fer" (line 9). In this example, conversion also affects the pre-existent, thematically established, lexical sequences. If the inversion involves the opposition between *gold* and *iron*, rather than between *gold* and *lead*, the usual poles of the adynaton defining the miracle of alchemy, this is because it reinforces one of the stereotypes of the theme of humanity's decline: the descent from the golden age to the age of iron.

Both the series of negative variants and the series of metaphors in the *alchemy* code seem to be interrupted with the last four lines. This interruption has been condemned by some as a flaw in the unity of the poem, while others see it and rightly so, as the point where the poem's true originality and most striking images begin. But there is no break other than in the linearity. When the reader, obeying the lexical sequence, stops reading in relation to nonverbal referents and starts reading in relation to the semantic program, the break disappears—or rather the gaps and breaks are perceived as signs that the verbal referents are no longer in the text itself, but in the intertext.

Commentators find themselves quite incapable of relating the sonnet's last four lines to either the title or the topic treated in its first ten lines. At most, they can link them to *douleur*, since the images are of mourning and burial, but this does not explain why these images were selected rather than others. So the critics attribute them to the influence of De Quincey, for whom clouds were the pillows of dying infants, and they never fail to add that at this point in his career, Baudelaire was fond of finding fantastic shapes in the clouds. In fact, the change in register creates the impression of fantasy suddenly let loose or of the mimesis of a dream, or even of an hallucination. This is because *je découvre* suggests an actual vision rather than a verbal image. And yet, this pseudo-quatrain climaxes the derivation from *alchimie*. Parallel to the first quatrain, it suggests a da capo movement and thus points to a clausula. The transmutation no longer leaves its lexical trace, however. The *cadavre* might seem to stem merely from Baudelaire's obsessions or from the death images favored by the extreme votaries of far-out Romanticism. But a nonreferential and ahistorical reading will nonetheless recognize it to be one more variant of the transmutation: *to change an object into its opposite*. In accordance with the conversion rule given by *douleur*, this opposite must be negative, so *cher* is disconcerting. The adjective and noun should be separated, so that instead of there being a transmutation involving an entire group (such as the one whereby André Breton derived *aéré mort* [exhumed dead] from *enterré vif* [buried alive]), *cher* is excluded from the transformation (as are *nuages* and *célestes rivages*, which are also positive, or at the least neutral). The transformation thus involves only one of the group's components (as when Breton forms *clair de terre* [earthlight] from the compound *clair de lune* [moonlight]). The transformed is recognizable by its negative marker: *suaire, cadavre*, and *sarcophages*.

As long as it does not involve *cher*, the transformation process is easily reversed by going back from *cadavre cher* to *cher corps* [beloved (living) body]. Now, *cher corps* is obviously a sensual synonym for "object of desire," and, in fact, appears as such in Baudelaire's love vocabulary (in "Le Balcon"). Thus, the negative transformations of the different means of satisfying desire—*gold, paradise*—are crowned by a negativization of desire itself.

The hypogram that flowed from the negative *alchimie* may explain the transformation of the matrix *corps* into *cadavre*. It does not, however, explain the choice of that matrix in the first place. What did determine that choice was the early model or first example that the text gives us of the effects of the meditating subject's state of mind on the object of his contemplation. That example is the literal statement in line 2 (the tenor preceding the metaphor in line 12): "L'autre en toi met son deuil, Nature!" coupled with the statement of the subject's paranoia: "Ce qui dit à l'un: Sépulture!" Here the statement of sadness (as a psychological state) is transformed into its metonym, *sépulture*, and this metonymic displacement also involves *suaire*, *cadavre*, and *sarcophages*. This last is overdetermined by its synonymous relation with *sépulture*. *Suaire* is not actualized by chance, for it is the site of a coincidence between the burial lexicon and the descriptive system of mist, fog, and clouds: *linceul* [shroud] and *voile* [veil] are cliché metaphors for clouds (compare *un linceul de nuages*), just as, in English, *cloud* metaphorically generates *shroud* and *enshroud*. This type of coincidence works exactly like the paronomasia or paronymy in Saussure's paragram *stricto sensu*.

The *nuages* themselves are invoked because they are a commonplace in literary representations of daydreaming, of nostalgia for the past, and of vague and melancholy yearning for a future that will never be. This theme of the forms seen in clouds is often a narrative depicting a viewer reading his own symbols into them. Clouds are thus the text that the Book of Nature gives to the viewer, who then turns them into his own intertext, as it were.

Here, the conversion triggered by *douleur* transforms them into a *suaire*. The following poem, "Horreur sympathique," presents us with a very similar transformation: "de vastes nuages en deuil / Sont les corbillards de mes rêves" [huge clouds in mourning are hearses for my dreams].[9]

The interpretation of the clouds as fantastic architecture is all the more tempting in that it is overdetermined by an oxymoronic derivation: the most intangible and mutable of objects is described as the most stable, the most solidly tangible, in short, the most monumental of realities. But instead of some other synonym of *tomb*, the word generated is *sarcophage*. It is overdetermined by the combination of the commonplace of the sky as an ocean with the commonplace depicting clouds as seashores. The next poem in *Les Fleurs du Mal* speaks of tormented skies that resemble a rugged shoreline: "cieux déchirés comme des grèves."[10] The clouds are, then, a metaphor for illusion and dreams, a place of desire. And finally, there is a literary allusion or quotation here: in three passages in Vergil, the body of a beloved companion is buried on the beach. In each of these, the strand, sanctified by the funeral pyre, becomes an extension of the monument and is given the name of the *cadavre cher*. The classical word *sarcophage*, rather than *tombeau*, is the trace left on the surface of the text by the Vergilian paragram.[11]

What happens, one may well ask, when a literary tradition is forgotten and cultural changes wash away the paragram? The efficacy of the text is in no way altered, because the text remains unchanged. The text is the starting point of the reader's reactions, not its paragrams. Obviously, the reader who shares the author's culture will have a richer intertext. But he will be able to draw on that wealth only when semantic anomalies in the text's linearity force him to look to nonlinearity for a solution. And the reader who is denied access to the intertextual paragram still sees the distortion, the imprint left upon the verbal sequence by the absent hypogrammatic referent. He does not even have to understand fully: it is quite enough for him to stand before a spectacle, however incomprehensible it may be, in which the inner logic of the hypogram can be seen, provided that spectacle is devoid of internal contradictions. It may be that "je bâtis de grands sarcophages" is clear only to today's handful of remaining classicists. But this obscurity, which is due to the injection of a Vergilian vocabulary into the text, does not alter the "transmutation" invariant. The reader can still sense that the sentence is an equivalent—albeit a disconcerting one—of "je change l'or en fer," and that the second tercet is derived from the matrix, *I substitute death for desire*. The simultaneous perception of the formal differences and their semantic equivalence, of a polarization both opposing and equating the textual sequence and the paragrammatic sequence, explains the efficacy of literary discourse. And this is where linear reading and nonlinear reading can be reconciled: for the result or effect of the nonlinear, paragrammatic reading is perceptible only through the ungrammaticalities or gaps that disrupt the linear sequence.

Whether or not the reader is able to fill in the blanks or gaps is unimportant. In either case, he must accept a verbal detour and perform the ritual of deciphering *a contrario*, just as one has to read Da Vinci's notebooks through a mirror in order to decrypt them. It is in this very game and in our awareness of this artifice that the significance is constituted.

A text proclaiming this kind of artifice differentiates literary discourse from the way utilitarian language carries meaning. In ordinary language, meaning is based on multiple referents, and the truth of a text is established through its contacts with reality. In contrast, the truth test of literary discourse lies in its faithful approximation of the semic configuration of a single given. Starobinski[12] has found fault with Saussure's analysis for retracing backward the itinerary of the poet's creation. If, however, we recognize the semic nature of the paragram, reading itself becomes a practice of analysis. Beneath its discursive appearance (be it a narrative or a description), the text simply spreads out, one after another, in syntagmatic contiguity, the lexical realizations of semes that were present together simultaneously in the given. It demonstrates that given and proves its own truth (its aptness, its appropriateness), in relation to the given, by developing it through successive variants. Each of these is a metonym of the given and corresponds to one of its semes. As in a cubist painting, contiguity and succession generate mimetic anomalies. Yet the text none-theless imposes itself on the reader as a form that is true, necessary, and overdetermined. This is because its obvious infidelity to the referent—the index of literariness—is, in fact, the anamorphosis of the given's network of semes.

[6]

Toward a Formal Approach to Literary History

LITERARY HISTORY tends to interest itself in the genesis of literature, its contents, its relationship to external reality, and in the changes in the text's meanings wrought by time, which are dependent on changes in the reading public's ideology. Formal analysis bears on the text, which is unchanging; on the internal relationships among words; on forms rather than contents, on the literary work as the start of a chain of events, rather than as an end product. The two approaches are thus complementary.

It seems further evident that literary history, ever on the verge of turning into the history of ideas, or sociology, or the historical study of literary matters, should find natural safeguards in these basic assumptions of formal analysis: that literature is made of texts, not intentions; that texts are made of words, not things or ideas; that the literary phenomenon can be defined as the relationship between text and reader, not the relationship between author and text.

Since this ideal complementarity has remained largely unexplored, I would like to examine three areas of literary history wherein analysis of forms is applicable: the assessment of literary influences and the relation of texts to trends and genres; the successive meanings of a text for successive generations of readers; the original significance of a text.

FILIATION AND AFFILIATION

Literary historians do pay close attention to the words themselves when they are trying to ascertain which authors a particular writer was imitating, which influences played a role in the genesis of his text, or to what genre the text belongs. They also rely on external evidence, but they find their ultimate proof of filiation between one work and another in lexical similarities between two or among several texts, or in the identical ordering of their respective components. As proof of generic affinities they take the repeated occurrences in the text of features considered characteristic of the genre. The comparison is regarded as even more convincing if the terms compared are complex, since such complexity appears to exclude random coincidence.

These principles would be unimpeachable were we dealing with things, and not with words, or were words ever independent of one another. But they are not, except in the artificial context of the dictionary. Even before being encoded within a text, words exist in our minds only in groups, in remarkably rigid associative sequences: nouns habitually go with adjectives or verbs that explicitly actualize their implicit semantic features. Entire sentences become clichés because they contain a stylistic feature that is deemed worth preserving. Finally, larger groups develop into descriptive systems.[1]

Thus several systems of commonplaces have crystallized around the word *woman*. One of them, for example, made out of set phrases and sentences, is a list of the beauties of an ideal woman; this system has been widely used in literature—for example as a frame or base for feminine allegories, or as a frame or reference in love poetry. So well constructed are these systems that mention of one characteristic lexical or syntactic component is usually enough to identify the whole and can indeed be substituted for the whole.

Thanks to such groupings, even complex similarities may not prove anything about the relationship between two texts. Many sources have been assigned to texts because of identical wording, when in reality these are ordinary clichés. Baudelaire specialists are convinced that an obscure poem is the source of the words, in "Hymne à la Beauté": "Que tu viennes du ciel ou de l'Enfer, qu'importe, O Beauté." An occasion to marvel that he would stoop so low to borrow an expression of his moral indifference.[2]

In fact the phrase is found all over in the Romantics: "du ciel ou de l'enfer" is a commonplace way of proclaiming that aesthetic value is independent of ethics—rather a cocky repudiation of Classicism, which held the two inseparable. The cliché may be banteringly used of a woman—angel or demon, who cares?—or, in tragic accents, of Byron's Satanism.[3] The tone does not matter: the point is that the statement reflects the spirit of an epoch, that it cannot be used to demonstrate Baudelaire's borrowing habits, and that it simply confirms once again the poet's Romanticism.[4]

Moreover, the fact that the same descriptive system appears in two texts does not prove influence, nor does it prove that any such influence, if real, is of significance, because the system is only prefabricated language, so to speak. What counts is the use to which it is put. Thus, another poem of Baudelaire's, "Bohémiens en voyage," is interpreted by literary historians as a transposition fom the visual arts, the model being an etching by Callot.[5] There are indeed many similarities of detail between the print and the poem, but these could be due simply to a parallel progression of the same system derived in both cases from the word *bohémiens*, or "gypsies." Let us assume that Callot is Baudelaire's proved source.[6] The fact remains that this "influence" is not relevant to literary history.

First, nothing in Baudelaire's description is so precisely oriented as to make the reader connect the poem with Callot; the connection is at best a chance encounter, the lucky find of a scholar,[7] and so an addition to the experience of the poem rather than a deduction from it. On the contrary, there are details in the poem that are not in the etching—a cricket watching the caravan, the goddess Cybele helping the travelers on their way, and so forth.

Second, everything in the poem, including the aberrant details, points to the superposition of two structures. Whereas Callot uses his gypsies as an exercise in the picturesque, Baudelaire makes his description a code into which he translates something else—the theme of the Quest. The gypsies are nomads par excellence. But they are also symbols of man's yearning for esoteric knowledge: not only because of their status as the poor man's prophets, but because nineteenth-century mythology still associates them with Egypt, the land of the Occult. Baudelaire retains the features of the descriptive system that emphasize this symbolism: he calls them a *tribu prophétique* [prophetic tribe]. He shows them dreaming unattainable dreams (*chimères absentes*)—the word *chimera* sums up imagination, yearning for an ideal, and the lure of the impossible. Cybele, *qui les aime* [who loves them], is significantly described in something like a Moses or Sinai code: for them she turns the desert green, for them she strikes a rock and water gushes forth—these gypsies become Hebrews in search of a promised Canaan. Indeed, the Canaan opened up to them in the last line is "L'empire familier des ténèbres futures" [The familiar empire of the future darkness], which we are free to interpret as Death or cosmic mystery.

At this point the reader is compelled to recognize in the poem a variant of the theme of the Human Caravan trudging through the desert of life toward its ultimate destiny—a theme much belabored in Romantic and post-Romantic poetry and one especially important to Baudelaire, who pours forth an endless variety of images of Life as a voyage Thither. The gypsy variant makes it a spiritual quest, and this places the poem squarely in the Orphic tradition.

These are the significant historical relationships. The similarity to Callot is limited to the lexical level. The truly meaningful likeness resides in the arrangement of the words at the higher level of syntax: the words are just "gypsy language"; their ordering is what reveals the underlying structure of the caravan theme, and from this structure, they acquire their significance. Every stylistic stress—every point at which the descriptive system of "gypsy" and the thematic system of "human caravan" coincide—is a key to this significance and a guide to the proper decoding of the poem.

Only by closely scrutinizing the structure of the poem can we arrive at a segmentation of its elements that will characterize this poem alone. Any preconceived segmentation—as by comparing words without regard to their syntax—is doomed to failure.

This is verified when we seek the significance of a text in its relationship to a genre. My example will be "Vénus Anadyomène," a Rimbaud sonnet.[8] The deceptive title invites us to a rather nauseating spectacle: an ugly, misshapen female emerging from a bathtub of dubious cleanliness. On her fat hindquarters are engraved the words *Clara Venus*. Every term used to describe her body is calculated to unsettle the reader yet further with its unappetizing explicitness; all of which terminates with a picture of the hag's backside adorned with an anal ulcer. A sort of aesthetic climax is attained in the last line, which focuses on the ulcer.

Most commentators have had recourse to Rimbaud's biography in their efforts to explain the poem. They seize upon evidence of his homosexuality, although such evidence is foreign and exterior to the text; they find there an explosion of misogyny.[9] Other critics, while not wholly excluding this personal approach, rightly concern themselves with the poem rather than the poet. They interpret it as an exercise in poetic Realism, or even Naturalism. They base their argument, of course, on the many revolting or merely unpleasant details: the assumption is that these details implicitly guarantee the fullness and objectivity of the description, since no prudery has blurred or censored it, and no convention of aesthetic conformism has deflected the indiscreet gaze of the observer. Another supporting argument—a specious one, though it exemplifies a common practice of pseudo-historicism (pseudo because it turns contemporaneity into causality)—is that, although French Naturalism was hardly dawning in 1870, when the poem was written, the Goncourt brothers had already made some literary incursions into the realm of pathology (*Germinie Lacerteux* appeared in 1865), and François Coppée had just published his first collection of poems preoccupied with the lives of the humble and the pathos of poverty and ugliness. In his *Les Soeurs Vatard* (1879), Huysmans was to depict women sweatshop workers in the naturalistic vein tempered with a humor unknown to Zola. Rimbaud's Venus is certainly closer to Huysmans' girls than to the Goddess risen from the sea. To bolster the case for hardcore realism in the poem further, a source is alleged: Glatigny, a minor

Coppée, had published a collection of poems ten years before. Most of them were in the Parnasse manner, but quite a few versified his experience as a vagrant, with glimpses into the special world Toulouse-Lautrec was later to make his domain. This blend was not unlike Rimbaud's early work—which has prompted critics to compare the two. It so happens that Glatigny describes a whore sitting on a patron's lap, and that she is tattooed somewhat like Rimbaud's bather. True, her tattoo is only on her arm, but then the shift downward in the case of his Venus only proves that Rimbaud was going one step further in "emancipation . . . toward an unflinching realism."[10]

At most, such comparisons can account for certain elements of the poem separately, perhaps even within their respective contexts, but they cannot account for their function as components of the overall structure. Only such a structure can give a poem its particular meaning. Hence it is only to such a structure that literary history may hook its chains of causality. The sense of the poem, I believe, is an inverse *laus Veneris*. It reads like a description of a paragon of feminine beauty. The picture unfolds detail by detail in the stereotyped order of nudes in literature (also the order in which the body parts emerge from the water)—except that here each detail is endowed with a minus sign. The grammar of the poem follows its own semantic rule: every salient trait of beauty must be stated negatively. The destructive effect of this consistent reversal is heightened by polarization; the starting point here for the creation of ugliness is not just any canon of feminine beauty, it is a hyperbolic model—to wit, the birth of Aphrodite. The mechanism of this negative permutation is a dual reading: as we decipher the text, we compare it with an implied standard that is nothing less than a Botticelli.

The setting is presented as a word for word inversion as well (instead of rising from the sea, the "goddess" sluggishly emerges from a bathtub explicitly likened to a coffin), and this inversion acts as the initial given establishing the rule for all actualizations of clichés in the poem: each cliché will be transformed into its antiphrasis. A heroine's hair must be blond and soft, fragrant and fluffy, so the cliché generates the greasy stiffness of *cheveux fortement pommadés* [heavily pomaded hair]. Similarly, in a famous phantasmagoria of Théophile Gautier's, a Goldilocks succubus is unmasked as a sorceress with a head of *raides mèches* [straight, stiff locks].[11] The stereotyped white, swanlike neck, sloping shoulders, svelte body, and lithe waist generate, point by point, a *col gras et gris* [fat, gray neck], protruding shoulder blades, a fat back *qui rentre et ressort* [that sticks in and out]. The usual erotic apotheosis—the curve of glorious buttocks, which Rimbaud used elsewhere for a real Aphrodite[12]—turns into its antithesis, a big broad beam, plus this sick detail confirming the polarization: "large croupe / Belle hideusement d'un ulcère à l'anus" [wide rump, hideously beautiful with an ulcer in the anus.]

None of these details has meaning, and none is compelling, except as part of the whole. It is the existence of an established, recognized model that permits a total inversion in one stroke—replacement of plus by minus—without the reader's being allowed to grow confused and forget the positive original. As with any structure, the modification of one component entails modification of the whole system.

This interrelationship of all the parts obviously makes it impossible for any explanation of separate parts to affect our understanding of the text. Thus, even if Rimbaud required the tattooed arm of Glatigny's whore in order to think of decorating his bather's back, that does not mean that her rear end is to the other girl's arm what Naturalism is to Realism.

This detail must be read like all the others in the antiphrastic sequence, *a contrario*: the tattooed behind (no ordinary amorous tattoo,[13] mind you, but an incongruous cliché suggestive of celestial Venus) is an inversion of a well-established literary cliché—the stigmata of election that the chosen one bears on his forehead (inscription, light, or imprint of the kiss of a queen or goddess, as in Nerval's "Desdichado": "Mon front est rouge encore du baiser de la reine" [My forehead is still red from the queen's kiss]. This inversion is all the easier in that it is based on a more general model. From the grotesque medieval sculptures of two-faced de-mons to Rabelais' exuberances to modern (or perennial) vulgar jokes, we have ample proof that the "ass" is the symbolic homologue of the face. And the language of the inscription proves my point. Were the unwholesome bather a naturalistic portrait, every detail being valid only with reference to a real or probable woman, then the learned writing on her rear would be a most gratuitous anomaly. Once you have a wayward detail in any portrait intended to appear real, all its verisimilitude falls quite to pieces. As I read it, on the contrary, *Clara Venus* is altogether natural and consistent within the allegory, even if the image's meaning is upside down.

Once we adopt the structural point of view, we comprehend the poem as an organized whole, wherein all the parts are synonymous. They repeat the significance summed up in the last line: "hideously beautiful." We can now safely return to literary history and assign the poem its true place in the evolution of French poetry. We are not dealing with Realism here, but with a genre developed during the Renaissance and already exhibiting characteristics of the baroque. I am thinking of the monograph-poem celebrating some part or function of the body, discoursing about some disease or deformity or vice: that is, the application of the encomium to some trivial or ugly object—such as Du Bellay's *Hymne à la Surdité* [Hymn to Deafness] (1558). In other words, it is a *contreblason.*[14] Rimbaud is not attacking the modern world, as those would have it who see the sonnet as the counterpart of another poem in praise of Greek beauty. He is not saying, in effect: Look at what our Iron Age has done to classical forms.[15] The *contreblason* does not stand to encomiastic verse in the same relation as satire does; it is a not a moral weapon or a tool of aesthetic controversy. Rimbaud's poem is not against something; it is written upside down.[16] It is not a satire, or a spoof, not even an opposing of themes (such as classicism versus modernity). It is an exercise in grammatical transformation, a clear-cut example of conversion.

And perhaps *contreblason* is too narrow a term to use; perhaps it would be preferable to relate this text to baroque poems on the theme of Topsyturvydom. And perhaps, again, it is wrong to classify the text in relation to the past, since such classification reflects the preoccupation of literary history with cycles. It is tempting indeed to connect the form we are analyzing with something preceding it that may be similarly analyzable, and thus to find in *Venus Anadyomène* the resurrection of a genre—some muscle-flexing of a young man who has just escaped an educational system focusing on French literature of the past. But it will most likely profit us more to classify this *contreblason* as an omen of developments to come. The poem will then take its place alongside Lautréamont's innovations, a trend Jarry, and later the Surrealists, carried forward: that is, the exploitation of the associative potentials of words. It is pure verbal creation; words are arranged *visibly* in relation to a verbal model, and not in relation to reality. The poet draws the mirror image of another text. Just as the physicist deduces antimatter from the known properties of matter, Rimbaud creates an antirepresentation.

What I have said so far makes it clear that any historical comparison carried out word by word, or sentence by sentence, or even system by system, must be an unsophisticated method and a misleading one. Literary influence or classification can be established only by the discovery of structural parallelism. This means that textual components should not be compared but, rather, their functions should be.

THE HISTORY OF SUCCESSIVE READINGS

Important as it may be to find out where a novel, a poem, or a play belongs in the history of literature, what trends it reflects, or what genre it exemplifies, there can be no doubt that these questions remain peripheral to the problem of the literary work's very existence: that is, to the question of whether its mechanisms work and how they work. Aesthetic and sociological definitions must yield here to the test of effectiveness: no text is a work of art if it does not command the response of readers, if it does not provoke a reaction and, to a certain extent, control the behavior of those readers. This response may be delayed or suspended by accidents of history, but it must come some time and it must be such a response as can be explained only by the formal characteristics of the text. The response of the reader to a text is *the* causality pertinent to the explanation of literature.

The effectiveness of a text may be defined as the degree of its perceptibility by the reader: the more it attracts his attention, the better it resists his manipulations and withstands the attrition of his successive readings, the more it is a monument (rather than just an ephemeral act of communication), and therefore the more literary it is. Now, the nature of this perceptibility changes according to whether the reader is a contemporary of the text or comes to it later.

Later generations of readers have more problems to solve than the original readers had. Regrettably, this fact is often used to support the argument that the "first" reading of the text is the standard and later readings must be inferior. This is an error, because successive interpretations of a monument are inherent in its monumentality: it was built to last and to go on eliciting responses. Later readings are as legitimate as the initial ones. Both stem from the same phenomenon.

There is, to be sure, no dearth of *Nachleben* studies. Unfortunately, most of them are devoted to mapping variations in the popularity of a text. These variations are most often explained by the cumulative effect of posterity: an author fades away in the shadow of his followers or else he is praised for an originality that exists only in comparison with his imitators. Such studies also invoke upheavals in literary taste or sociological conditions and the evolution of aesthetics. Meanwhile the most important factor is being neglected or downgraded: that is, the evolution of language. This is where formal analysis must redress the balance.

The two types of perceptibility can be distinguished by the differences between codes. The linguistic code used by the early readers is the same, or almost the same, as that of the text. The linguistic codes used by later readers differ more and more, as time goes by, from the code of the text. The change may be drastic if the text employed a specialized code such as the conventional poetic language of French Classicism. In such cases, an aesthetic revolution means a sudden linguistic break of a kind not observable in the evolution of everyday usage. (Let us add here that these breaks do not coincide with political changes: the French Revolution left untouched the aesthetics and poetic language of French Classicism. Nor do such breaks come simultaneously with the rise of new literary movements: French Romantics went on using much of the Classical language for a long time.) Descriptive systems, clichés, and so forth, offer some resistance to change and may withstand it, but shifts in the meaning of individual words alter the meaning of such systems nonetheless, and their relationships with cultural background also change. All this comes to pass, of course, outside the literary text, for the text does not change and this unchanging form preserves within its structural integrity the code used by the author. A *Nachleben* study, to be relevant, must obviously focus on the widening chasm that time has opened between the immutable code of the text and the codes adopted by successive generations of readers. Formal analysis is the ideal tool for comparing the two readings of the same sentence: one in the code of the context,[17] and one in the code of the later reader.

In some rare cases, the analyst will conclude that the code has so evolved that the gap can no longer be closed. The text is now a dead letter. In one of his early poems—an ode on a naval battle during the Greek War of Independence—Victor Hugo tries to suggest the highly picturesque, intensely Oriental chaos in which the Turkish fleet is wallowing. He gives a long list of boat types, including *yachts* and *jonques*. British pleasure boats and Chinese junks hardly belong in the Ottoman navy; but this incongruity is startling only to the modern French reader.[18] For those who first read *Les Orientales*, all that was needed to create the illusion of Turkish reality was a strange verbal shape. *Yacht* is completely alien to French spelling because it combines the rare initial *y* with the final consonant cluster. *Jonque* has a unique sound: the word does not rhyme with anything if the initial consonant is counted, and if it is not, *jonque* rhymes with and resembles only six other words in the whole French lexicon—two of them obsolete and three others grammatical words not employed, stressed, or connected like full-fledged words. Today's French readers are reluctant to believe in Hugo's Turkish fleet. Their aesthetic rejects this sort of epic anyway, but that might mean only a temporary eclipse. The fact is that the poem is quite extinct, and for an evident stylistic reason. Morphologically and phonetically, *yacht* and *jonque* are as foreign as ever. But the meaning of that foreignness has changed. The French today are more familiar than they were in 1829 with other parts of the world, or rather with assorted representations of those other parts. In consequence, a word's foreignness is semantically more often oriented toward the reality for which the words actually stand. In the case of *yacht* and *jonque*, the foreignness is no longer "free"; it can no longer be used to conjure up any vague exoticism. Those words are now limited to a context-specific foreignness ("technical" uses, for example).

It is even possible for a stylistic effect to disappear entirely, even though its context may offset this disappearance to some extent. Neologisms are especially vulnerable: a new coinage will go unperceived by later readers if, in the meantime, it has been assimilated into common usage. If the stylistic structure of the text is actualized by such neologisms, it is bound to become invisible with time. It may happen that what was once a new coinage will later be interpreted as an archaism: its effect is still visible, but its content (or perhaps orientation would be the better word) is altogether different. Archaisms are also threatened: an archaism in a seventeenth-century text, for instance (let us say a word that was already obsolete or, at least, old-fashioned and that was used at that time to a certain effect—a comic effect, perhaps—precisely because of its obsoleteness), runs the risk of blending into its context, since the other words of that context all seem dated to the modern reader. Literary allusions often suffer the same fate.

But even where shifts in the code have destroyed a component of the stylistic structure, the text still contains the forms corresponding to that structure. Thus some effects can still be felt in most cases, either because these forms are still active, even if they are interpreted differently (or in a way that would have been foreign or incomprehensible to the author or the original readers), or because the context still preserves peripheral evidence of their original power.

The motifs of *basalt* and the *basaltic cave* are a good example of a form that has continued active. Both were frequent in early Romanticism, especially in French literature, although neither had any particular symbolic significance. Baudelaire still uses the basaltic cave as a simile to enhance the magic of another life remembered:

> J'ai longtemps habité sous de vastes portiques
> Que les soleils marins teignaient de mille feux,
> Et que leurs grands piliers, droits et majestueux,
> Rendaient pareils, le soir, aux grottes basaltiques.[19]

> [I long lived under vast gates that the sea suns tinted with a thousand fires, and which their huge, straight, and majestic pillars, in the evening, made just like basaltic caves.]

Footnotes never fail to explain that Baudelaire simply copied two of Hugo's lines,[20] which suggests that the simile evokes nothing more per se. Such an explanation only pushes the problem further back, since in the earlier text the cave is already said to exemplify the motifs of poetic inspiration.

There are many more texts, in fact, that allude to that cave, and all of them depict it as a thing of beauty. Literary history tells us only where the stereotype originated: it started with the Ossian fad that familiarized European readers with Fingal's cave. The underlying assumption is that the image is dead unless you recollect its origin. But experience has shown me that it still stirs the reader. This continuing effect is due to linguistic and semantic features that have survived long after the Staffa cave faded from our memories. First of all, the Staffa cave became poetic material and remained so longer than other Ossianesque paraphernalia, because, I suggest, geology had been fashionable since the eighteenth century. It enriched the literary lexicon with technical words most often used metaphorically. Two of these, *granite* and *basalt*, proved especially successful. *Basalt* (in French, *basalte*) still holds its own, though French readers are now inured to its technical strangeness, because it is such an exceptional word: it rhymes with only seven other words, all of them foreign borrowings.[21] Moreover, *grotte basaltique* survives independent of the Caledonian setting, because its descriptive system is built upon a striking semantic structure, the self-contradictory association between nature and artifice. Clichés like *architecture naturelle* [natural architecture][22] correspond to the peculiar basaltic shapes; these clichés derive their impact from the all-powerful *coincidentia oppositorum*. Here the disappearance of a theme has left behind a semantic structure that remains valid despite our inability to relate it to a forgotten mythology.

Sometimes even the meaning disappears or loses its importance, and yet the literary structure survives, because the emptied words still perform a function very much in the manner of grammatical words. Nineteenth- and early twentieth-century novels, for example, offer details that seem to be there only to establish a setting and add to the verisimilitude of a description: one of these such is *embrasure*—"window recess." The frequency of this word is out of all proportion to its descriptive value. But that recess is a stage set for a passionate exchange of confidences, it is even a trysting place, it is the conventional sign of a paradoxical solitude on the periphery of a group of people, or it may be the vantage point from which a contemplative or satirical observer watches the social drama going on in the drawing room.[23] Today these functions no longer have any connection with reality, but the role of *embrasure* in texts has survived its disappearance from architecture all the same. Walls have grown thinner and rooms so much smaller that it is no longer possible to hold clandestine conferences in window nooks. In common parlance, actually, *embrasure* is used by hardly anyone other than architects; *fenêtre* [window] is quite enough for all practical purposes. Nevertheless *embrasure* lives on in the novel as a convention—it is where you push or pull somebody you want to have to yourself, it is where you withdraw to be by yourself. Its semantic value is all but nil, its reference to reality a thing of the past. But its constant recurrence in contexts where *embrasure* was linked to verbs that singled actors out or set them apart—this was enough to turn it into a kind of linguistic marker. In the narrative sequence, the word (or its periphrastic equivalent) is nothing but a conventional symbol of a situational transition (from several characters to one or two only, the two acting as one), or of a shift in the narrative (a functional shift of the character from actor to observer, and thus a shift from the viewpoint of insider to that of outsider, and so on). This conventional symbolism demands nothing but a written context and is not affected by changes in the code or in the reality it is supposed to represent.

Finally there is the case in which words have completely lost whatever meaning or functional value they had when they were encoded in the text. Textual analysis will still be able to detect secondary structures they have generated within their context. These have remained immune to changes in the language. Thus, in a passage dismissing *Les Fleurs du Mal* as just an extreme case of exaggerated Romantic hysteria, Sainte-Beuve damns Baudelaire by praising him for building at the tip of a deserted peninsula: "ce singulier kiosque, fait en marqueterie, d'une originalité concertée et composite, qui, depuis quelque temps, attire les regards à la pointe extrême du Kamtschatka romantique" [this bizarre kiosk, done in marquetry, with concerted and composite originality, that, for some time now, has been attracting views to the extreme point of the Romantic Kamchatka].[24] In modern French, however, *kiosque* is only an ornate bandstand for open-air concerts in public parks, or else a newsstand. Literary history could account for the discrepancy; it could point out that for the French Romantics, *kiosque* was the epitome of bizarre Oriental architectural forms[25] and that this function was reinforced by the absolutely unique phonetic sequence of the word, to say nothing of its spelling. At that time, it was as typical and representative of exoticism as minaret or mosque. Historians will not fail to stress that kiosks were used as cosy hideaways in seraglio gardens, and that the word thus acquired connotations of refined, clandestine pleasures.[26] Both symbolic values are exploited by Sainte-Beuve—in this particular kiosk, you smoke hashish and read Edgar Allan Poe! But the purely historical explanation misses the point that the image needs no resuscitation. The sentence surrounding *kiosque* still reflects the evocative power that the word alone would no longer possess. It moreover reflects this power precisely because the word is not perceived in isolation, but in its indissoluble relationship to the context. The word is only the kernel of a satellite group of adjectives (*bizarre, fort orné, fort tourmenté, mystérieux, singulier* [bizarre, heavily ornamented, very tortured, mysterious, singular]) which make literally explicit the semantic component of the Romantic kiosk. Moreover, and more importantly, *Kamtschatka* (a common hyperbole for *Siberia* as an image of remoteness or wilderness)[27] graphemically and phonetically takes up and emphasizes the sounds that once made *kiosque* an expressive utterance, an icon in sound of the bizarre. By common reversal of effects, *kiosque* now seems to be present only to reinforce *Kamtschatka* phonetically.

These clusters of concurring devices are a text's best defenses against the growing estrangement between its language and the reader's.[28]

RECONSTRUCTION

Reconstructing the first, original meaning of the text used to be an attempt to restore it to its author. Since my subject here is how formal analysis can contribute to the diachronic study of the literary phenomenon by postulating that the impact of the text on the reader is all that counts, I shall not spend time discussing a method that disregards effects unforeseen by the writer. As I see it, the one and only original meaning of a text is the one given to it by its first readers (whether or not that meaning coincides with the author's intention). It is revealed by the reactions it elicited from those readers. Of course, we cannot hope to reconstruct the code they used, at least not well enough for our purposes, and evidence of their reactions is also fragmentary. But the code changes are mostly of a semantic nature, as was apparent in the examples discussed in the previous section. Our problem is that we have lost contact with the descriptive systems that the text referred to in its early life, and that we no longer know which words generated which system, or which words served as metonymic substitutes for a whole system. We read the same sentence as the first readers, but we have lost its echo. To this problem, literary history provides only a partial solution: thematology. It is incomplete because *Stoffgeschichte* restores only themes and motifs, that is, descriptive or narrative sequences whose literary use is restricted by the fact that they are already stylistically marked (by their symbolism, their connection with a genre, and so on).[29]

Formal analysis should contribute to thematology in the future by including all descriptive systems in these compilations arranged according to type, indicating their generic and chronological distribution.[30] Systems should not be listed in skeletal form, but should be accompanied by their clichés, preferred sentence types, available substitutes, metonymic mechanisms, and so forth. In short, a relevant system of classification should include the structures, the words that actualize them, and the associations that they trigger.

Enlarging the corpus is not enough, however. Ever since its beginnings, thematology has been justly criticized for generalizing. In the process of identifying and classifying themes, it has tended to eliminate everything distinctive and unique in the treatment of these themes. The chain of historical causality stretches from the author (and from the mythology and the languages from which he picked his themes) to the text. The explanation is thus purely genetic. It shows what raw material the text was made of, not the artifact that was made out of it. There is no way to tell what in the general theme is relevant to the text and to that text alone, since the historian has had to cleanse the textual variant of all its peculiarities in order to identify the theme and then to fit it into a general category of thematic models.

With formal analysis, this procedure is reversed. Starting from the text and faithfully retracing the reader's steps, the analyst goes back to the theme—or rather, to the descriptive system—not simply to check the particular case in hand against its composite model, but to sort out and discard all the components of the model that the text has not actualized. The structure of the system, unaffected by the fact that some of its slots remain empty, makes clear the relationships among the slots that are actually filled—and these relationships define their significance. Furthermore, one of the slots may be filled with a word that does not belong to the system. Then that word receives a new meaning from the function that corresponds to the position the word occupies in the system—a mechanism that accounts for much of literary symbolism.

For instance, the first stanza of Baudelaire's sonnet entitled "Obsession" is a complex of three fragmentary systems: forest, cathedral, Man.

> Grands bois, vous m'effrayez comme des cathédrales;
> Vous hurlez comme l'orgue; et dans nos coeurs maudits,
> Chambres d'éternel deuil où vibrent de vieux râles,
> Répondent les échos de nos *De profundis*.[31]

[Great forests, you frighten me like cathedrals. You bellow like organs, and in our cursed hearts—rooms of eternal mourning in which old death rattles are vibrating—the echoes of our *De profundis* are calling back.]

Without reconstruction, the reader has only the written line to guide him. It provides him with a statement with which he is free to agree or disagree. His attitude and his emotive reactions will result from the chance meeting between the experience he has had of forests and of churches, and what the sonnet says about them. The likelihood is that the pathos will repel him as a too obvious prejudice, as too heavily pessimistic. This emotional response will in turn be rationalized into a pseudo-logical decision that Baudelaire's comparisons are gratuitous.

With the help of thematology alone, our reader will learn that there is a Romantic theme that fits in here: the forest as a church

(Nature is God's temple), or in reverse form, the Gothic cathedral as a forest (sacred architecture was born of the effort to imitate the natural temple, whence its authenticity as a monument to faith). Up to a point, of course, this removes the stigma of gratuitousness. The similarity between a Gothic church and the forest is no longer questionable; it is not just one man's opinion. It refers to an accepted code. The *consensus omnium* is guaranteed by the place of this code within the corpus of French myths. In a word, literary history here affords the reader proof that the conventions of the text are acceptable. It informs him of the frequency and distribution of the systems used in the text, of the popularity or prestige they enjoyed. The reader can now restore to these words of the text the valorization conferred on them by membership in a system. He can understand how Baudelaire could be attracted by such a privileged code, and why his choice would appeal to readers in 1860, or at least ring familiar in their ears, or even serve as a marker of a certain type of poetry.

But this reconstruction remains peripheral to the text, for it enables us to understand no more than the potentials and limitations of the material Baudelaire had available. It does not tell us why he actually used that material in this specific instance. All it does is displace the suspicion of gratuitousness, which must now be borne by Romanticism instead of by Baudelaire.

The analysis of forms, however, does address itself to the specificity of the text and to the pertinence of the theme in the context. It permits us to see that both the cathedral and the forest systems are fragmentary, and by identifying what has been left out, it underscores the relevance of what is left of them. The components excluded are the very ones that would be most apt for symbolizing pantheism or animism in the positive form of the theme, or architectural authenticity in the reverse. One component retained is the music: the *organ* is a convincing, or at least acceptable, homologue to the wind in the trees—acceptable because the likeness is a natural one, and because the idea of that likeness has become a cliché. Just as acceptably, music generates a listener. But then, within the *cathedral* system the listener–music relation is either positive (elevation, thoughts soaring) or negative. In this context, the initial postulate (*vous m'effrayez*) entails a negative choice. Such being the case, the heart becomes the fully motivated image of a death chamber, since that is the path along which the clichés of the system lead us. For in this system, the mention of church sounds (bells, organ, choir) is diametrically opposed to mention of the crypt: the symmetry is either that of silence, as in the text of Chateaubriand's that "launched" this theme: "tandis que l'airain se balance avec fracas sur votre tête, les souterrains voûtés de la mort se taisent profondément sous vos pieds" [while the bronze (bell) swings thunderously over your head, Death's vaulted dungeons keep profoundly quiet under your feet].[32] Or else it is that of the echo, as in these lines from Lamartine:

> Le chrétien dans ses basiliques
> Réveillant l'écho souterrain
> Fait gémir ses graves cantiques.[33]

[The Christian in his basilicas, rousing the underground echo, lets his grave canticles moan.]

This second version is the more popular, most likely because it was reinforced by the equally lugubrious clichés of the Gothic novel, wherein dungeons echo to the roll of thunder. In both versions, the response to the plainsong is given by Death. Within the frame of this descriptive structure, the image of the heart as a chamber of death is therefore not gratuitous. The logic of the cathedral image, which is further motivated by an established parallelism with the logic of the forest image, compellingly transforms the listener into a living tomb.[34]

The superimposition of the descriptive system, by eliminating certain elements and emphasizing homologous components, has laid down a sort of filter or grill of actual words on the potential lexicon of the theme, so that the theme's valorizations and connotations (the poem's historical dimension) are limited and focused on words already valorized in context (the stylistic dimension). This sorting out is literally a dual reading, performed simultaneously on the level of the text and on the level of the theme. The resulting stresses—the poetic structure proper—occur at every point at which the historical axis (mythology) and the syntactic axis (sentence) intersect.

I believe the examples given above speak for themselves. It seems to me that they make it quite clear that the stuff literary history works with (and on)—themes, motifs, narratives, descriptions—is first and foremost *language*. Literary history has validity, therefore, only if it is a history of words.

[7]

Intertextual Semiosis: Du Bellay's "Songe," VII

IN HIS "Visions,"[1] Petrarch tells of six mysterious incidents during which an object of beauty, appearing before a viewer, is destroyed. It is left up to the reader to deduce the lesson—*omnia vanitas*, all is vain. He can deduce it without difficulty from the constants he observes from one episode to the next. A laurel wreath struck down by lightning, a sumptuous sailing vessel swallowed up by the sea, Eurydice snatched away by her heel, and so forth: everything that should endure comes to an end. The interpretation is easy, but it must be made. Each episode is an enigma, since each scene can be read only in relation to the neighboring scenes and, after backwards and forwards comparison, must be transposed into an analogical discourse. The obscurity lies less in the difficulty of translating than in the very necessity of doing so: the text conceals only in order to reveal, but we must still go through the ritual lifting of the veil.

Du Bellay's "Songe" is constructed on this model, although its ritual side is even more apparent. The fourteen scenes are much more hermetic than those of Petrarch, but their translation is given in the first sonnet, which explains that the visions come from a dream and deduces the lesson: "Voy comme tout n'est rien que vanité . . . Dieu seul au temps fait résistance" [See how all is vanity . . . God alone withstands time]. The purpose of the obscurity is, therefore, no more to conceal than it was in Petrarch. It is, instead, to reveal. The great error of philological commentary, as it continues to be practiced by many scholars of the sixteenth-century, has been to believe that erudite poetry sets out to hide its idea.[2] It veils it, but it always points to where it is hidden and how it can be revealed. This is, moreover, a general law of all literary discourse, for literary discourse is a locus of semantic indirection. During the Renaissance, this law took the form of indirection in reference to fables, in the use of mythological intertexts. "Songe" forces an exercise in revealing on the reader, by making him symbolically pass through a process of initiation. Its symbolism is underscored by the number of sonnets, which, indeed, can be explained only if each scene corresponds to the beginning lesson. The same relation exists between the fourteen sonnets and the fourteen lines of the first sonnet as between the exempla and the abstract formulation of the law that they illustrate. The title does not indicate the subject (it is a dream, but only as a convention) but, rather, the genre; in other words, how the text is programmed. We know it is programmed for a double reading, since a *songe*, a dream, is defined as a vision to be deciphered, as an exemplum, in which each isolated detail has its own individual meaning but the details taken as a whole partake of the same significance.

This significance, in "Songe," is the same as in Petrarch's "Visions," but with the difference that "Songe" restates in symbolic discourse what is said metaphorically or literally in the *Antiquitez* and the *Regrets*, for which it functions as a conclusion: praise for ancient Rome and satire of modern Rome. Between the lesson ("tout n'est rien que vanité" [all is naught but vanity]) and the exempla, we therefore have the complication of the intermediate code of "Roman" discourse: since the lesson corresponds to a transformation stucture whereby *tout* [everything] becomes *rien* [nothing], its translation into the "Roman" consists in making each scene of unstable, ephemeral beauty into a variant of the constant *grandeur and decadence*. As in Petrarch, therefore, persons and objects are depicted in such a way as to suggest the idea of perfection, and, without fail, they are annihilated by a sudden catastrophe. Each sonnet is a truly exemplary lesson, first of all because the illustration always has qualities of the extreme: no ordinary temple, but one made of crystal; no ordinary obelisk, but a diamond one; no ordinary spring, but a crystalline spring. Moreover, each catastrophe is always particularly appropriate: the temple is toppled by an earthquake, the obelisk is struck down by lightning, and the spring is polluted. Each polarity is a variant of the fundamental structure, and each descriptive system is modified so that it can be used as a code for the Roman mimesis.[3] Read in isolation, each of the texts remains hermetic, or its interpretation is uncertain, or else we cannot go beyond its general meaning, Petrarch's lesson. But when we read the sonnets one after the other, the intratextual, vertical relations of the words to their signifieds intersect with the intertextual relations of the words to their analogues in the neighboring poems.

In sonnet VII, the example of perfection destroyed is the *eagle*, a hyperbolic bird, but also the traditional symbol of Rome:

> Je vy l'Oyseau, qui le Soleil contemple,
> D'un foible vol au ciel s'avanturer,
> Et peu a peu ses ailes asseurer,
> Suivant encor le maternel exemple.
> 5 Je le vy croistre, et d'un voler plus ample
> Des plus hauts monts la hauteur mesurer,
> Percer la nuë, et ses ailes tirer
> Jusques au lieu, où des Dieux est le temple.
> Là se perdit; puis soudain je l'ay veu
> 10 Rouant par l'air un tourbillon de feu,
> Tout enflammé sur la plaine descendre.
> Je vy son corps en poudre tout réduit,
> Et vy l'oyseau, qui la lumière fuit,
> Comme un vermet renaistre de sa cendre.

[I saw the Bird that contemplates the Sun venture toward the sky, flying feebly, and little by little, try his wings, still following his mother's example. I saw him grow, and, flying more broadly, measure the height of the highest moutains, pierce the clouds, and wing his way up to the place where the temple of the Gods is found. There he disappeared. Then suddenly I saw him, beating a whirlwind of fire through the air, all aflame, descend onto the plain. I saw his body reduced totally to dust, and I saw the bird that flees light, rise up, like a little worm, from his ashes.]

Since the literary phenomenon consists in the dialectic between text and reader, it must be explained in two stages. In the first, we describe stylistic features—that is, mechanisms on the surface of the text that impose a uniform perception, whatever the reader's fancy might be, by controlling the decoding and, little by little, by reducing all latitude in interpretation. In the second, we analyze the process whereby representations, mimetic phenomena, come to be perceived as meaning something other than what they seem to mean: this semiotization defines the literariness of the text.[4]

MIMESIS

The narrative goes from an interesting, almost moving sight (lines 1–4) to a miraculous sight (lines 5–8). Two dramatic moments follow (line 9 and line 13), the second of which is the site of the fundamental antithesis opposing two birds to each other point by point: the bird that flies toward the sun and the bird that fears the sun—an "ornithological" variant of the *grandeur and decadence* invariant. The second *coup de théâtre* is the metamorphosis of the bird into its opposite. Each of the spectacular changes is punctuated by the repetition of *je vy*, which might appear awkward or rather facile. But it is not by chance that every new object of wonder or meditation and every turn of events is underscored precisely by the repetition of the specific verb for vision. This derivation is generated directly from the matrix text (the first sonnet, the "program" sonnet). The coincidence at every turning point in the textual space between the visionary[5] and suspense divides the discourse of the *thauma* into segments calling for a separate deciphering, a word-for-word translation changing the miraculous into the symbolic.

Except for this coincidence, the decoding is controlled by the two periphrases designating the birds (lines 1 and 3) and by three series of verbal equivalencies, three tautological sequences.

In these periphrases, the humanist reader would have instantly recognized the eagle and the owl.[6] But the impact of the periphrasis was not lessened; since it takes the form of an enigma, it also has the enigma's delaying effect. Even if it is quickly deciphered, it nonetheless commands our attention by the kind of detour it forces us to take. Moreover, this same periphrasis is also in the form of a definition (even though the word being defined is missing): even if a modern reader can no longer identify the birds, he still notices the definitions and, above all, the exact parallelism between "qui le soleil contemple" and "qui la lumière fuit." The contrast and complementarity between the names of the eagle and the owl stem from mythology and, for that reason, can be lost with the disappearance of myths and become unintelligible, or at least seem far-fetched. The two relative clauses, however, cannot be lost.

Their antithesis is not seen, though, until we reach line 13, for only in the retroactive reading, in the rereading of the text in our memory—a reading that goes hand in hand with the primary reading (which proceeds from beginning to end)—are the parallelisms, series, and repetitions perceived.[7] As long as the parallelism does not enter into it, the periphrasis naturally has its own effect. Of its two mechanisms, the one posing an enigma and the other offering a definition, the latter seems to confer a kind of permanence on what is said about the bird: with the utterance going from descriptive to gnomic, the bird's attitude takes on the role of an allegorical attribute. The eagle, the king of the birds now become the bird of the sun, is bathed in what classical aesthetics called the sublime. This sublime is echoed by the first tautological series, the sequence of words rhyming with *contemple*: *ample* and *temple*, both of which are positve signs (with *ample* in *voler plus ample* suggesting the increasingly daring flight as well as the breadth of the wingspan). This sublimating tautology is the formal expansion of two fundmental antitheses, for it is opposed to the depreciatory sequence in the final two rhymes, in which words with a negative meaning are paired: *descendre/cendre* [to descend/ash] and *réduit/fuit* [reduced/flees].[8]

Foible vol, s'avanturer, and *peu à peu* form a second tautological series derived from the first *oiseau*, since each of these words repeats, in different variants, a "weakness" or "timidity" seme, the meaning of which is clearly indicated by the series' climax—*maternel exemple*. The descriptive sequence, in invading the textual space, compensates for the repression of an unstated[9] *oisillon* [young bird], or even *aiglon* [eaglet], which is all the more visible in that it is not mentioned. In contrast to this image of hesitant weakness, the next tautological series appears all the more heroic. Heroic is, I believe, the right word here, because the contrast between the first flight from the nest, a well-known motif, and the flight to the zenith translates the thematic structure of the hero's childhood (Hercules in his cradle choking snakes to death, the *mocedades* of the Cid, and so forth), into aviary code.

The third tautological series is made up of images of ascent. Their cumulative effect is successively underscored: by the paronomasia *plus hauts/hauteur*, which is further reinforced by the inversion; by *percer la nuë*, which is strictly and literally true, a normal aspect of eagles' behavior that can be observed and verified, but which, literarily, cannot fail to be perceived as a hyperbole (as if the word *nuë*, occupying the highest position in the *nuage/nuée/nuë* paradigm, by that very fact, represented a particularly lofty point in the sky);[10] by the visual symbolism of the last sentence, in which the supreme flight is prolonged by the enjambment and the three hemistiches (as opposed to only one hemistich for the previous stage; *percer la nuë*);[11] and finally, by the semantic climax of *temple*, which is both the zenith in its metaphorical sense and, in its metonymic sense, the top of the world: the eagle touches the highest reaches of both the sky and the heavens.

The three sequences combine to make the eagle mimesis a variant of *grandeur* in the matrix opposition generated by all of "Songe." This is confirmed or continued, paradoxically, by the story of the fall: far from nullifying the effect of the triumphant ascent, the fall has the splendor of a meteor. The tautology of *tourbillon de feu* and *enflammé*; the length of the apodosis in line 11, contrasting with the brief protasis (*je l'ay veu*) and increased by the suspense created by the disjunction in line 10; and, once again, the contrast between this flaming vertical catastrophe and the calm, almost august horizontality of *sur la plaine descendre*—all this goes to make the catastrophe as sublime as the flight. Even as he is punished for his hubris, Jupiter's bird remains majestic.[12] Thus the entire portrait of the eagle, as great in his fall as in his ascent, represents the first pole of the antithesis. The eagle must take on the only one of his meanings that is pertinent to the entire intertext of "Songe": he is the symbol of Rome.

Counterbalancing the weight of the preceding eleven lines, the final tercet forms the other pole of the opposition. The antithesis lies, at first, in this imbalance.[13] The break is all the more striking in that the tercet is constructed symmetrically, since on each side of the second member of the antithesis, the antibird, it has a statement of the destruction of the first member: *poudre* and *cendre*, both of which are variants of the eagle's body destroyed. The entire tercet is, in fact, a negative series corresponding to the three-part positive series of the eagle. *Poudre, tout réduit, fuit*, and *vermet* [dust, totally reduced, flees, little worm] are all variants of the nonsublime and make the owl resulting from the metamorphosis into the exact opposite of aquiline discourse.

In this analysis of the mimesis, I have neglected two details, *rouant* (line 10) and *vermet* (line 14). Because of their precision, they contrast with the other words, which convey meaning in their most general, all-purpose sense. This precision anchors the description in verisimilitude and creates the illusion of a sensory experience. *Rouant* is the exact word for a flight that has been struck by lightning; it is the avian equivalent of the "tailspin" of a crippled airplane. Its appropriateness, however, has nothing to do with experience. It is due, instead, to cratylism: *rouer* seems appropriate because its obvious root, *roue* [wheel] "explains" its meaning and makes it into a particularly vivid symbol. Moreover, it concentrates in a single lexeme a narrative commonplace (Phaethon, Ixion) and a complex mimetic system that normally would require an entire sentence:

> Il tournoie . . . Buvant d'un trait sublime
> La flamme éparse, il plonge au fulgurant abîme.[14]

[He whirls round and round . . . Drinking the scattered flame in a sublime draught, he dives into the blazing abyss.]

As for the second detail, *vermet*, first its diminutive form and then the hyperbole of disgust implied by any synonym of vermin assert the presence of reality. I shall show that the *effet de réel* thus produced is, in both instances, subordinated to a semiotic function.

SEMIOSIS

The displacement of the apparent meanings that follow one another from one sentence to the next toward a significance encompassing the entire sonnet at once and making the text into a unit of poetic meaning—in other words, this move from mimesis to semiosis—results from either the superimposition of one code onto another or the superimposition of a code onto a structure other than its own. The complex networks or, if I may be permitted a play on words, these textile intertwinings, alter the mimesis. This leads to anomalies that are simultaneously the points at which the text has the tightest hold on the reader and markers allowing the reader to discern, through the representations, the outline of the significance.

Their common characteristic is that they all appear either to be *unmotivated* in context or to be *motivated by a nonverbal reference outside the text.* We recognize them, therefore, from the subjective reactions with which the naive reader and the critic (who thinks he is not) try to rationalize their highly unusual motivation: it is said to be an *effet de réel* (the eaglet fluttering his wings, *rouant, vermet*), a point of obscurity (which, in a humanist text, is itself rationalized as the result of mythological erudition), an incompatibility of images, or a lack of unity (which, in a Renaissance poem, would be explained as the *contaminatio* of literary sources or allusions). We must understand that, whatever its rationalization may be,[15] what seems unmotivated on the surface of the text is simply motivated differently: *the unmotivated is the marker of motivation or, rather, of overdetermination on the level of structure.*

This is corroborated by a rereading of all the points in the text where surface analysis makes us aware of these guideposts or markers. I have already mentioned the eagle's "childhood" and the epic quality of the contrast between the eaglet, which, only yesterday, was trying out its wings, and its present ascent to the empyrean. But the commonplace of the first timid steps and hesitant beginnings corresponds, point by point, to a commonplace in the praise of Rome: the motif of the slow, gradual growth of the city that will become the ruler of the world only to fall, and to fall fast. One of the sonnets in the *Antiquitez* expresses this slow growth in a vegetation code (the slow growth of Roman wheat, brutally harvested by the Barbarians), just as our sonnet does in an animal code.[16]

As for *rouant*, its realistic note (revealingly underscored by the tautological *tourbillon*) invites an intertextual reading. It forced the Renaissance reader to identify this eagle as another Phaethon, for he could not fail to draw a parallel between so precise a picture and Ovid's *Metamorphoses*, which at that time were known and read by everyone, and in which two components of our tautology can be found: "At Phaethon, rutilos *flamma* populante capillos *Volvitur. . . .*"[17]

Now, the myth of Phaethon corresponds exactly to the various incarnations of Roman pride: his heavenly course is one of the exempla of the folly of ambition, and his fall is the symbol of ambition punished. In Alciatus' *Emblems*, Phaethon represents political immoderation, greatness, and punishment.[18] The role of the "Phaethon" code is, thus, to guide the reader toward the correct interpretation of the antithesis, to make him feel that even the grandeur symbolized by the eagle carries within itself the seed of its own destruction. Phaethon's name is not mentioned, nor is it defined by periphrasis. Therefore, he does not play the part of a vehicle of comparison, for the eagle is not compared to him, and he is not the metaphor of the bird. The relationship between the primary code ("eagle") and the secondary code ("Phaethon") lies entirely at the level of structure: both codes have the same narrative and descriptive structures. The eagle can be expressed in Phaethonian discourse and Phaethon in aquiline discourse, in a "jeu de l'un dans l'autre," which the Surrealists mistakenly thought they were the first to invent.[19] There are, therefore, words that can be used equally well in either code, since their function is the same in both. If the context lends itself to it, as it does with *rouant*, the words' poetic function is the result of their overdetermination: simultaneously representing two codes and forming a kind of knot with two semantic threads, they have a meaning called for by the primary code or context, and a significance coming from the secondary code. In a way, this secondary code is quoted, since it is possible for us to reconstitute it mentally from the overdetermined word. The efficacy of this phantom quotation is, thus, due to the active participation of the reader, to his rewriting of the unstated. This is none other than the practice of intertextuality. The overdetermined word is a lexicalized text, as it were, a text reduced to one representative lexeme. Moreover, if the lexical overdetermination is double, the first eleven lines weave a threefold network of associations: between Phaethon and the eagle, between Rome and the eagle, and between Rome and Phaethon.

The eagle symbolism commands the reader's immediate acceptance: it is guaranteed by history and, in clichés like *aigles romains* [Roman eagles], by language. The symbolism of the owl, by contrast, has appeared gratuitious: if the eagle has to undergo metamorphosis for the moral lesson to have its impact, why must it be transformed into an owl? Critics have attempted to explain this with a kind of erudite subtlety and taste for complicated allusions.[20] In this specific instance, such value judgments do not reveal the underlying work of the structures. They are simply erroneous, for the critics fail to consider the testimony of language. Let me correct this now, for this symbolism is a case of overdetermination.[21] In the natural history of myth, the eagle, I believe, is the only bird with an antonym. The owl is the eagle's opposite (most likely because of their different attitudes toward light, but their polarity is firmly enough established that this need not be mentioned). They represent the top and bottom of the scale for the feathered race. They are paired together almost everywhere: in the proverb of the "hibou qui se prend pour un aigle" [the owl who thinks he's an eagle][22] in La Fontaine's fable of the eagle and the owl, *L'aigle et le hibou,*[23] and in emblems.[24] It is, therefore, enough that the poem's starting point be Rome and that Rome be symbolized by the eagle for the "Songe" structure—the degradation of all that is great—to produce an owl. The ready-made antithesis in the avian code corresponds to the antithesis of the structural invariant. Of course, the owl can sometimes be a positive sign (the philosopher owl, the owl as a good father, and so on); but when opposed to a symbol of excellence, it can only be negative.[25]

Let us return to those critical reactions that truly reveal the semiotizing functions of the structure. Their usual target is the implicit *phoenix* in the third line.[26] Critics either admire or condemn it as an example of *contaminatio.* With some painstaking marquetry or mosaic work, a transitional bird might have been inserted in between the eagle and the owl, allowing this aviary of symbols to settle, feather by feather, into a well-constructed sentence with a logical conclusion. As for *vermet,* whose contribution to the *effet de réel* I have already mentioned, it seems typical of the obscure details that have been unearthed in the writings of mythographers for no other reason than the Pléiade poets' mania for erudition. It must, of course, be explained to the modern reader: the phoenix did not rise up from its ashes with all its feathers but, rather, was at first nothing more than a little worm.[27] In the sixteenth century, however, there was no obscurity, since the phoenix's *vermet* appeared in many poems. At any rate, far from being a gratuitous detail, the word has a very definite function: it transforms the phoenix into a negative sign.

The commentators are disturbed by line 14 because they read it only in terms of the mimesis. A great deal of artifice must certainly be involved for an eagle, a phoenix, and an owl to come together in the same sentence. This new chimera is irrelevant, however, and there is in fact neither representation nor a complicated *contaminatio* here. There is, instead, a grammaticalization of the myth. Just as *rouant* "lexicalized" the myth of Phaethon, *renaîtra de sa cendre* [will rise up from his ashes] is nothing other than the transformation of an abstract statement of metamorphosis—*will turn into*, for instance—into a kind of figurative syntagm. Since the sonnet's symbolic code is wholly avian, the exact word and the quintessential language of the bird metamorphosis should be "Phoenixian."[28]

Here the semiotic transformation is produced: the borrowing from the phoenix code is accompanied by a reversal of that code's values. Indeed, in normal usage, the phoenix and its miraculous rebirth are positive signs, symbols of the perennial, of the survival of Beauty, and of purification. But the antithetical invariant dictates a rebirth of ugliness and impurity. The reversal takes place in two stages: first, since the positive phoenix is reborn identical to himself, the reverse phoenix is reborn as his opposite—as an owl, since the eagle was in the phoenix position at the beginning. Second, *vermet* replaces *phoenix*, completing the permutation of the markers. Instead of functioning as the metonym of *phoenix, ver* [worm] becomes its metaphor. This word, and its dimunitive *vermet* even more so, is a pejorative sign.[29] Far from being a curiosity of literary archaeology inserted into the text as an ornament, *vermet* belongs to the same negative paradigm as *owl*. Its function is to set up an extraordinary conceit by using an image of Beauty and a myth of purification in the interests of a semiotics of decadence and impurity.

I believe thus far to have shown that the superimposition of codes introduces no incongruity in the text. The sonnet's unity is abundantly clear—which is hardly surprising, since, from the first line to the last, not one of its forms fails to correspond to the fundamental structure of "Songe." My analysis, however, has not yet accounted for the poem's most obvious characteristic, the one that distinguishes it most visibly from the other sonnets—the fact that the symbolic animals are not named, but described. What interests me here are the two periphrases that make the poem into a literary text by giving the discourse both an opening and a clausula, and the implied phoenix, which provides the grammar of the discourse. These are, in short, the very essence of the text. I have already discussed the mechanism and effect of these verbal detours; it remains for me to say *why* these symbols, which give the poem its meaning, are stated only indirectly. I have yet to say why the form was chosen—this will be the key to the poem's significance.

Periphrasis and implication, as well as the fact that something remains unsaid, do not modify the traditional role of each bird. In fact, that role is what enables them to represent the different stages in the history of Rome: grandeur, destruction and rebirth, decadence. Here the unsaid is merely a call for the reader's participation.

There is, however, something constant in the way the periphrasis says what it says and in the circularity of description: a relation is always presented between the symbolic animal and the sun as fire or as light (a positive or negative tropism; combustion). Furthermore, these three relationships are the only ones possible. Witness this sonnet in which Petrarch lists the three attitudes one can take in relation to the sun: either contemplate it, flee from it, or burn up in it:

> Son animali al mondo de si altera
> vista che'ncontra'l sol pur si defende;
> altri, però che'l gran lume gli offende,
> non escon fuor se non verso la sera:
>
> et altri, col desio folle che spera
> gioir forse nel foco, perché splende,
> provan l'altra virtù, quella ch'encende.[30]

[There are animals in the world whose view is so haughty that it even withstands the light of the sun. Others, though, because the strong light hurts them, do not venture out, save toward evening. And others, with a mad desire hoping perhaps to find happiness in the fire because it is shining, experience its other power, the one that burns.]

This ideal paragram—which, since it has three parts, is the very icon of perfection—gives the sonnet's symbolic discourse its formal perfection: the development of the possibilities fills the entire space of the signs.

But what of the significance? We already know the historical meaning of the birds: Rome rising, Rome destroyed, the Rome that survives. We are taught the moral of that history, the birds' philosophical meaning, by their role in relation to fire: the synonyms of flame and light comprise the *interpretant* (in Peirce's sense of the term) for the entire Roman lexicon (the bird lexicon).

The sonnet, therefore, can be a variant of the fundamental structure, and it can condense the lesson of the *Antiquitez–Regrets* diptych and conform to the principles of the genre to which it belongs (the *songe*, or dream, as lesson) only by playing tricks on the reader. At first, it seems to be a bird sonnet, but then its Petrarchism is finally unveiled: we understand the text only when it reveals itself to be a sonnet of fire.

[8]

From Structure to Code: Chateaubriand and the Imaginary Monument

THE GOAL of all criticism is, or should be, to show what characterizes the literary work of art. But critics too often look for this characteristic in the author and in his psychology, which they reconstruct more or less well, and they do not often enough look for it in the work and in its form, which is everything. I propose to define a characteristic aspect of Chateaubriand's work, and I will look for it in the words alone.

One of Chateaubriand's most obvious verbal obsessions is the frequency with which the word *monument* and its synonyms recur in his writings. His books abound in architectural descriptions. Of course, this preoccupation can also be observed in his life: he went bankrupt building a mausoleum for Pauline de Beaumont; he wanted to build one to Tasso; he designed an ostentatiously simple one for himself. What is relevant to literature, however, is that he transposed this obsession into his writing. His *Mémoires* are his real monument: "Mémoires, édifice que je bâtis avec des ossements et des ruines" [Memoirs, edifice that I built with bones and ruins],[1] or even: Memoirs, "temple de la mort" [death's temple] [1.7]. As he wrote them, he compared himself to an architect, and he compared their slow growth to that of a cathedral [1:435]. He readily sees everything that touches him in architectural terms—memories of youthful pleasures, "ruines vues au flambeau" [ruins seen by torchlight];[2] life's illusions, "bâtisses étayées dans le ciel par des arcs-boutants" [fragile buildings propped up in the sky by flying buttresses] [1:599]. He is widely known as a poet of ruins, and he considered himself to be a greater *tombeaux* poet than Young, who launched the genre.

There is no doubt about the obsession, but it explains nothing. What a writer does with his obsessions is what matters in literature. An obsession provides him with a vocabulary. What does he say with it? To what end did Chateaubriand employ "monument vocabulary"? Since such a vocabulary can have either a positive orientation (building and raising up; palaces and such) or a negative one (ruins, tombs), might it offer a solution, at the level of form, to Chateaubriand's fundamental contradiction—on the one hand, his thoughts constantly turned to death, the vanity of all things, the ravages of time, and on the other hand, his continuous creation, which presupposes faith in the victory of art over time and over death? The most important question to be asked is this: what structures does this vocabulary conceal? For an obsessive word does not always have the same meaning or value: its meaning and effect depend on its underlying structures.

Before coming to the structures, which are an abstract geometry, we must examine the function of the architectural representations in the concrete reality of style. The presence of a Chateaubriand-style reverie over monuments is very noticeable in his figures of style. We cannot tell, though, if the monument theme came first or if its development was favored because Chateaubriand had a spatial imagination. Whatever thought or stylistic artifice might be supporting it, the sentence in Chateaubriand often turns to forms that, though not actually spatial images, do momentarily suggest the emptiness of a walled-in space:

> Bonaparte était la *Destinée*; comme elle, il trompait . . . les esprits fascinés; mais au fond de ses impostures, on entendait retentir cette vérité inexorable: "Je suis!" Et l'univers en a senti le poids. [1:564–565]
>
> [Bonaparte was *Destiny*; like Destiny, he deceived . . . fascinated minds; but from the depths of his deceptions, this inexorable truth could be heard resounding: "I am!" And the universe felt its weight.]

Here at least, the allegory does not call for a setting. The preposition *au fond* becomes a cliché as soon as sincerity, the depths of one's heart, is opposed to superficial attiudes. It retains very little of its spatial sense—no more than its opposite, *superficial*, does in my own sentence. This is not the case in Chateaubriand: in his eyes, *au fond* remains sufficiently visual and spatial to awaken the echoes of a palace or temple ("on entendait retentir").

There are many examples of metaphors and similes taken from architecture (for instance, the French spirit after the fall of the Empire is compared to a caryatid freed from the wall that had been weighing it down) [2:8], but I suspect that these are purely ornamental, that they are too visible to be true. For this reason, I preferred the almost invisible image that I quoted above, for it reveals the latent presence of an architectural reverie. This latency is betrayed only by echoes (*retentir*), but the choice of the motif is significant: when Chateaubriand makes use of an explicit monument image, he often suggests the resounding echo of an inner void in order to establish the architecture's tangible presence.

The true stylistic function of the monument theme is its use as a kind of language. Words that would normally describe a monument are used to describe something else. It is not really a question of metaphor: the monument does not replace the object described and the latter is not implied. What we have, instead, is a special code used for description, a code consisting of words marked by an aesthetic index. The reality to be described is congruent with an architectural form, and this conveniently allows the latter to be used to describe the former. The ideas of grandeur, nobility, and harmony that are associated with monuments color the description. We find, for instance, a translation into "cathedral" code: Rancé's confusing treatise on the *Devoirs de la vie monastique* [Obligations of the monastic life] becomes a basilica in which the sounds of an organ can be heard and with stained glass windows illuminated by the sun.[3]

We find another translation, this time of "mountain" reality into "Oriental temple" code: the snowy peaks are described as "pyramides, cônes et obélisques [pyramids, cones, and obelisks]

[*Mémoires* 2:592]. This is an embellishment, a stylization; in reality, the mountains get their "éclat emprunté" from the light of the moon, but stylistically it is the noble, architectural connotations that give them their "borrowed brilliance." This is also a concession on Chateaubriand's part: he grants that the mountains are beautiful, but only by night, and only if they are transformed by the moonlight. Their beauty has neither the balance nor the harmony of Classicism. Classical temples, vaults, and domes could never represent it, but Oriental architecture can.

Here is yet another example: the soul described in a "palace" code. This choice is dictated by two features. Man is one of God's creations, so a palace was required. Man is a web of contradictions, so a hybrid architecture was needed. The obvious advantage here is that the techniques of descriptive style are easily applicable whenever an already structured reality is concerned. To see the soul through a clearly delineated monument is to shed light on it. Hence we are given a word-for-word translation. Wanting to show man denatured by original sin, Chateaubriand says: "c'est un palais écroulé et rebâti avec ses ruines" [he is a palace that has fallen down and been built back up with its ruins].[4] Elsewhere, he wants to show that man is torn in two directions by the double postulation of Good and Evil: in the language of torture, the word to choose would be *écartelé* [quartered], but in monument terms it becomes "on y voit des parties sublimes . . . de hauts portiques" [there one sees parts that are sublime . . . high porticoes]—that is, the soul, man's spiritual side—"et des parties hideuses . . . des voûtes abaissées" [and hideous parts . . . low vaults]—man below the belt, I suppose, the subconscious. Moreover, here we have the id or the superego: "de profondes ténèbres . . . le désordre de toutes parts, surtout au sanctuaire" [profound darkness . . . disorder all around, especially in the sanctuary]. The architectural structure was used, just as shelves or cases in a museum would be, in order to arrange methodically and clearly the characteristic components of the subject being examined. Of course, the ease of the procedure remains a secondary factor. The essential function of this kind of translation is the same as that of noble language in conventional poetry: it raises the subject to a loftier plane. In Classical poetry, the subject is elevated by the elimination of lowly words; with the use of the monument code, by the ideas of grandeur attached to monuments. To analyze the human heart just as we would describe a palace is to analyze it in lofty style indeed.

If the monument used for this stylistic transposition already has its own symbolism in reality, that symbolism then extends to the object being described. If we describe a forest as a cathedral, we not only make it lofty or sublime, but we also express a correspondence and a harmony, in the esoteric sense of the terms, as well, since, according to Chateaubriand's formulation, "les forêts ont été les premiers temples de la Divinité [the forests were the first temples of the Divinity].[5] Even if the monument has no particular symbolism of its own, the description of nature in monument terms—that is to say, in terms of artifice—always presupposes an *artifex*. Hence we have a variant of the Romantic theme of the book of Nature, a book written by the Creator, which the poets alone are privileged to decipher.

The poet who can recognize that one or another aspect of reality is a monument reveals to us, by that very fact, the designs of Providence. Take the motif of the sound of wind in the trees: ever since the time that he was tormented by the Sylphide, René often listened to it. He also often compared it to the noise of waves. At least once, however, he also transformed the parallelism implied by the comparison into a cause-and-effect relationship and rewrote it in monument code: the sound of the wind in the trees is interpreted as the monument (and not as the echo, which has long since ceased) of the sounds of the Deluge. Like a commemorative column on the site of a disaster, this noise serves as a reminder that the ocean once covered the forests:

> Dieu . . . sachant combien l'homme perd aisément la mémoire du malheur . . . en multiplia les souvenirs dans sa demeure. . . . L'Océan sembla avoir laissé ses bruits dans la profondeur des forêts.[6]
>
> [God . . . knowing how very easily man loses his memory of misfortune . . . multiplied the reminders of it in his dwelling. . . . The Ocean seemed to have left its sounds in the depths of the forests.]

Chateaubriand lists many other monuments: some, such as the shells found on mountaintops, would also have been called monuments by Buffon, for the word was the noble equivalent of *vestige*, remains or relics. This is not surprising. If I have preferred to cite the sound monument—the wind memorial—it is because, faced with such an extreme example, one can hardly dispute the diagnosis that there is indeed a monumentalizing tendency or bias. The blowing wind and the sound fading away, signified by motionless architecture and massive stone, are irreconcilable components. They go against all our habits of thought and challenge verisimilitude. In short, they are all that is needed for the poetic tension of the image to be forever preserved. This challenge to normal representations will be found whenever the monument described conceals a structure foreign to it—Chateaubriand's own form, for example, which is hidden, reflected, or better yet repeated in the stones he is contemplating.

It is clear from the preceding examples that the use of the monument quickly goes beyond the level of a simple, straightforward trope, and that the descriptive transposition tends to be much more than a sublimation of style. The passage from one stylistic level to another is accompanied by a change in meaning. The verbal representation of the monument already constituted a special vocabulary: now it becomes a moral structure.

Indeed, the monument in Chateaubriand is always tied to the past. I am not speaking solely of ruins and tombs: architecture is beautiful only in "ses rapports avec les institutions et les habitudes des peuples" [its relationships with the institutions and customs of nations]—in relation, that is, to the past and tradition. To represent the monument will thus be a way to institute the dimension of Time and to give it pride of place in the text, while saving those signs that would otherwise express time, such as verb tenses or the narrative sequence, for other tasks. The "monument" code then becomes a mode of expression presupposing a past and involving the future. On the one hand, the monument is a ruin or relic, something that survives after a disappearance or destruction. On the other hand, it preserves and transmits a future reader's message, lesson, example, or admonition. In both cases, there is a moral anachronism. Thus, the time dimension should be considered a moral dimension in literature. Time will tell. And lastly, as the symbol of absence, especially of absence in time, the monument represents, at one and the same time, death and victory over death. Substituted for that which is absent, it allows the poet to have a face-to-face encounter and emotional contact with something that no longer exists. A structure superimposing two different times on a single point, the monument is the ideal vehicle for those historical comparisons, which readers have laughed at and which often seem gratuitous, but which Chateaubriand is nonetheless constantly making. Now, in such a case, the instrument of verisimilitude is the monument: in the imagination, it is the meeting place of characters and eras that reality keeps apart.

Thus, contemplating Lake Geneva from Madame de Staël's tomb in Coppet, Chateaubriand dreams of Voltaire, Rousseau, and Byron, who had all dwelled along the shore of that very lake, but who were separated by time or enmity. They come: "chercher l'ombre, leur égale, pour s'envoler au ciel avec elle, et lui faire cortège pendant la nuit" [to seek the shade of the one who was their equal, in order to fly off to heaven with her and follow her through the night]. [*Mémoires* 2:606,] The literary comparison, perfectly justified by the many faces of the legendary Corinne, took poetic form in the conventional meeting around a graveyard monument. Chronological impossibility and artificiality as far as tastes and aesthetics are concerned are nonexistent on the plane established by the monument. In the first place, the monument's presence is naturally legitimized by the narrative, in perfect harmony with the almost elegiac tone of this book of the *Mémoires*, which is devoted to Mme. Récamier. Then, and most importantly, we readily accept its function as an imaginary meeting place, because this is nothing more than a variant, in architectural code—the author's personal obsession—of a well-established convention in the fine arts, whereby the glory of a hero is symbolized by the meeting, friendly agreement, and reconciled unanimity of those who preceded him in his career. This is the convention of the

Triumph of the Martyr in Christian painting, where the saints, angels, and recent martyrs can be seen hurrying to heaven's balconies to greet a new victim. We are given a perfect example of the secular version of this convention in *The Apotheosis of Homer*, painted by Ingres in 1827.

As a descriptive frame, the monument allows scenes that were made possible by its symbolism to be organized, dramatized, and fused. The comparison effected through the superimposition of times can, therefore (quite naturally and in keeping with verisimilitude), take the form of a meditation, a pilgrimage, or an intimate conversation with a great man or personage. We thus have in the comparison a highly important instrument for modulating the tone of a style, for making it go from narrative to lyricism, and from lyricism to drama.

Historical meetings, or rather meetings based on the poetry of history (it matters little whether or not Chateaubriand actually met this or that great man, or whether their meeting was of the slightest political importance—the meetings are always with the symbol of an era, with a ruin like George IV—"je l'étudiais, non comme un modèle de bon goût du dernier siècle, mais comme un type de roi qui sera brisé," Chateaubriand tells us [I studied him, not as a model of good taste from the last century, but as a type of king that will be smashed to pieces] [2:980] or else they are with a monument for the future like Washington); meditations in sanctuaries or in front of a landscape that can be read like a book; pilgrimages to landmarks: scenes such as these are repeated over and over in the *Mémoires* and are, therefore, highly characteristic. They come so naturally because the greater part of the work is, after all, nothing but a long travelogue. As an émigré, diplomat, explorer, or lover, Chateaubriand is the epitome of the literary tourist. His political life leads him either to exile or to visits with exiles, which are, as it were, so many pilgrimages to historical monuments. His specifically fictional work takes the form of an itinerary. From *René* to *Le Dernier des Abencérages*, his heroes travel, or else their story is framed by journeys and the experience of a life conditioned by a melancholy yearning for other places.

Now, even more than they are displacements in geography, these peregrinations are displacements in history: searching for the lessons of the past in monuments, Chateaubriand goes from one subject of meditation to another. As he naively formulates it in the *Voyage en Italie*, "Les souvenirs historiques entrent pour beaucoup dans le plaisir ou le déplaisir du voyaguer [Historical recollections contribute much to the traveler's pleasure or displeasure][8]—witness the entire *Voyage*.

This way to explore the world and the importance of the monument as a mental and literary structure is the result of Chateaubriand's classical education. Traditional instruction in Greek and Latin enabled the man of culture to couple his daily experience with visits to an imaginary museum. He learned never to look at anything without combining his own viewpoint with that of a predecessor whose authority was firmly established by history or literature.

This is an extension of the rhetorical doctrine of imitation: one writes according to models, so that one's reader will simultaneously experience the pleasure of discovery and the pleasure of rediscovery. He should be able to read both at the level of the printed line and, by comparing the images and tropes to their ancient models, at the level of allusion. If there are no memories in a setting, there can be no joy. Along with other reasons for not liking mountains, Chateaubriand offers the explanation that they do not encourage parallels with Classical literature. He merely tolerates the mountain herds that his contemporary Senancour could already appreciate, and he maintains that

> couchés dans les herbages du pays de Caux, ces troupeaux offriraient une scène aussi belle, et ils auraient en outre le mérite de rappeler les descriptions des poètes de l'antiquité.[9]
>
> [lying in the pastures of Caux [a limestone plateau in Normandy], these herds would make just as beautiful a scene, and, moreover, they would have the advantage of reminding us of descriptions in the poets of Antiquity.]

In other words, the cows would be a monument with *Mugitusque boum* inscribed at its base. Conversely, as soon as Chateaubriand is moved by a sight, he seeks to endow it with a memorial character and link it with a tradition, with a passage from an ancient historian. In this respect, nothing is more curious than his statement, one day, that he took pleasure in the places he visited in the Orient "indépendamment de l'antiquité, de l'art et de l'histoire" [irrespective of (their) antiquity, art, and history] [*Mémoires* 1:626–627]. Scarcely has he asserted this, however, than he begins to list those monuments that he said he could do without. Moreover, so as better to prove how superfluous they are, he recalls his Plutarch and the historical scenes that were set in these spots. This is tantamount to making the sites into monuments. Lastly, as he meditates on the disappearance of Pompey's tomb, the only way he can represent that absence is by describing the dark grave hollowed out on its former site. It is as if the writing were becoming a monument dedicated to the memory of the monuments that had just been scorned. Every spot in which he stops to linger is both the place he is passing through and the place other men once passed—men whom history has remembered. His great preoccupation, then, is to put himself in the place of those figures, and the spatial coincidence invites him to do just that. He is moved, in short, to become the living monument of their reconstructed emotions. When he is in Rome (the quintessential setting for meditating in front of ruins) and the moon has risen (making the moment archetypal), his first question is: "Que se-passait-il il y a dix-huit siècles à pareille heure et aux mêmes lieux?" [What was happening eighteen centuries ago at this same hour and in these very places?] [*Voyage en Italie* 6:292]. The interval chosen to divide Chateaubriand's own era from the past he is wondering about is itself symbolic: if he could go back eighteen centuries, he would find himself amidst the first witnesses to early Christianity.

What he is searching for, as he reaches out beyond time with his sense of affinity, is not simply the human. It is, first and foremost, *authority* in the classical sense of the term: in other words, the parallel between his own self and that of documented historical figures is the equivalent of the Latin and Greek quotations used by nineteenth-century historians to lend authority to their more daring ideas and help support their arguments.

In its conventional and altogether scholarly form, this manner of seeing led to catalogs of recollected readings, such as the many passages in the *Itinéraire de Paris à Jérusalem* and the *Lettre sur la campagne romaine*, where we find sentences like: "*Baïes, où se sont passées tant de scènes mémorables, mériterait seul un volume*" [Baiae, where so many memorable scenes took place, would deserve a volume all to itself].[10] But whenever circumstances lend themselves to it, Chateaubriand's personality appropriates these remembered common places and subordinates them to his most intimate memories. He strolls through the ruins of Tivoli; the shadows of ancient Tibur rise up before him, but the dreamer greets only those that are in keeping with his own thoughts. On this very spot, he tells himself, Vergil, Horace, and Tibullus, who came before me, felt the same emotions that I am feeling. And long before me, they meditated here on the transience of life [*Voyage en Italie* 6:279–280]. This imaginary communion, to be henceforth memorialized by the ruins, is, of course, the result of an arbitrary selection and is wholly dependent on our poet. Scattered themes in Vergil and Horace are associated with Tibur only because Chateaubriand is there, in Tivoli, copying the inscriptions on the tombs.

There comes a day when Chateaubriand frees himself from this servitude to the Classics. He rephrases the question about what was happening eighteen centuries earlier on that very spot, and asks it this time about his own, personal past. Once again, he is at the foot of a monument, but it is one from his inner world. He writes in 1833 that every year on his saint's day "je me demande où j'étais, ce que je faisais à chaque anniversaire précédent" [I ask myself where I was and what I was doing on each previous anniversary] [*Mémoires* 2:860]. Here the monument is the feast of St. Francis. It is always the same. Nothing about it can be changed. It is a motionless island surrounded by the river of Time, always celebrated on the fourth of October. Those predecessors whose memory he is trying to recapture as they once passed by this anniversary obelisk are other Renés, other versions of himself. He wants to compare his present experience with his past experience. (Let us not forget that it was on the feast of St. Francis that he was "tenté de commencer l'histoire de [s]a vie" [tempted to begin the story of his life] [1:6], and that he began to write his *Mémoires*.) Just like the previous question he asked about other men, illustrious or unknown, this comparison reveals an enduring truth that transcends the individual and is not modified by the vicissitudes of fate. In the example in question, this truth is the idea that man is a traveler on earth, that he is the very image of transition. His one permanent characteristic is impermanence: "cette année 1833, soumis à mes vagabondes destinées, la Saint-François me trouve errant" [In this year, 1833, I am subject to my vagabond destinies, and St. Francis' day finds me wandering] [2:860].

Following this general and universally significant statement, however, a specific memory is aroused. In the chain of his successive St. Francis' days, Chateaubriand suddenly remembers one that he spent in Jerusalem. Of all his saint's days, it is the most exceptional, for it brought the most incomparable of coincidences. This recollection was determined by a crucifix seen along the roadside and which, in the context of his anniversaries, awakens the thought of the first Cross on Golgotha. Time, flying faster than ever, as if impelled by the rush of all his accumulated anniversaries, comes to a stop. The poet gives himself over to a peaceful reverie concerning his love for the humble folk and the joys of charity. Then once again he makes a generalization and compares himself to the archetype of compassion who is his patron saint. In his imagination, Chateaubriand is meditating at the foot of another monument, Golgotha. St. Francis had also made a pilgrimage to Golgotha, so he, consequently, was Chateaubriand's illustrious predecessor there. He was his authority, just as Vergil, Horace, and Tibullus, who came before him at Tivoli, had by their example authorized René's reveries and put the seal of universal truth on the lyric effusions of the as yet unknown Breton communing with them over a distance of two thousand years.

As we can see, this shift from the search for illustrious predecessors to the search for oneself in no way changes the mechanism of the process. (Besides, the search for oneself is perfectly compatible with the search for a predecessor other than oneself, since Chateaubriand moves effortlessly from a comparison of his self of today with his self of yesterday, to a comparison between himself and St. Francis.) The function of the monument is to find the unchanging within universal change and, in the multiplicity of individual experiences, to bring out the great laws or truths common to everyone.

This brings me to a few thoughts on the role of the monument in the workings of memory. An alternation, which I believe is significant, can be observed in the episode of St. Francis' day in 1833. For Chateaubriand, the monument of his feast day is the occasion for discovering a general characteristic of his life. A memory suddenly arises, prompted by the similarity of a cross along the highway to the Cross at Calvary. That memory is unique. It is an irreplaceable sensation and nothing has tarnished its initial joy. Then, concerning another monument, he makes a new generalization, which is also derived from a comparison with the past.

Thus there are two types of remembrance in Chateaubriand: memory opening onto general truths of philosophical meditation and memory turning in on the authenticity of private experience. The latter, which could be termed affective memory, is none other than Proustian memory. Its mechanism is the sudden superimposition of a current feeling on an age-old recollection. The vehicle for meditative memory is the monument.

The only memory critics have seen at work in Chateaubriand is affective memory. This is perhaps because Proust himself recognized Chateaubriand as his precursor. I shall quote a fragment of a passage that Proust cited at greater length. In it Chateaubriand is walking along, thinking about death and the posthumous publication of his *Mémoires*. He is in the park at Montboissier, which he has just described in detail, lingering over its contrasting styles and its charm. Suddenly, he says:

je fus tiré de mes réflexions par le gazouillement d'une grive perchée sur la plus haute branche d'un bouleau. A *l'instant*, ce son *magique* fit reparaître à mes yeux le domaine paternel; *j'oubliai* les catastrophes dont je venais d'être le témoin, et *transporté subitement dans le passé*, je revis ces campagnes où j'entendis si souvent siffler la grive. [1:76]

[I was drawn away from my reflection by the chirping of a thrush perched on the highest branch of a birch tree. *That very instant*, the *magical* sound made my father's estate reappear before my eyes. I forgot the catastrophes I had just witnessed and, *suddenly transported into the past*, I saw once again the countryside where I so often heard the thrush whistling.]

I have underscored the characteristics of the phenomenon. One is the supernatural suddenness and stunning apparition of the resurfacing past. A burst of memory is provoked by the superimposition of a sensation that in itself would be relatively insignificant (like the taste of a madeleine, the scratchy feeling of a starched napkin, an uneven paving stone), did it not correspond to an earlier sensation. But there is something even more important: the present setting disappears. Monuments, if there are any, vanish. And there is no denying that the park, which a moment earlier was so clearly and so architecturally described, was most certainly contemplated just as a monument would be. (Chateaubriand had just stated that "il plaît comme une ruine" [it is pleasing like a ruin].) Even the Montboissier thrush steps aside to make way for the Combourg thrushes, who move in, setting and all. In other words, affective memory lets us relive the past at the expense of destroying the present. This is the meaning of the phrase that Chateaubriand repeated many times over: "ma vie détruit ma vie" [my life destroys my life]. In other words, affective memory destroys reality. While viewing a famous waterfall in the Alps, he sees once again the Niagara Falls, and the remembered sight annihilates the sight before his eyes:

Ma mémoire oppose sans cesse mes voyages à mes voyages, montagnes à montagnes, fleuves à fleuves, forêts à forêts, et *ma vie détruit ma vie*. Même chose m'arrive à l'égard des sociétés at des hommes. [2:585]

> [My memory is constantly opposing my travels to my travels, mountains to mountains, rivers to rivers, forests to forests, and *my life destroys my life*. The same happens to me where societies and people are concerned.]

And this destruction of the present in favor of the past takes place even if the present is buttressed by a monumental framework. Stone monuments vanish away before the landscapes and architecture of his memory. One night this is what happens to the ruins of Tibur—the same ruins that Chateaubriand had used the night before to commune with Vergil over the grief of separation, one of life's laws. At one in the morning, the wind and fog at Tivoli make an electric contact, like the one between the two thrushes or from madeleine to madeleine, with the wind and fog in Brittany:

> Je me croyais transporté au bord des grèves et des bruyères de mon Amorique; . . . les souvenirs du toit paternel effaçaient pour moi ceux des foyers des Césars: chaque homme porte en lui un monde composé de tout ce qu'il a vu et aimé, et où il rentre sans cesse, alors même qu'il parcourt et semble habiter un monde étranger. [*Voyage en Italie* 6:280]

> [I thought I had been transported to the edge of the shores and heaths of my Amorica; . . . memories of my father's home erased those of the Caesars for me. Every man carries a world inside himself made up of everything he has seen and loved. And he is constantly returning to it, even as he travels through and seems to be living in a foreign world.]

Let us again emphasize the mechanism that brings this inner world back to life. It is an echo from the same to the same, a call from one like term to another. A present-day detail evokes its earlier analogue, which destroys it and takes its place (a crucifix recalls Calvary; a thrush recalls a thrush). This echoing or repetition of analogous elements from the present to the past then summons up the unique experience in the past. I shall indicate that this is the opposite of what happens with memory founded on a monument.

The world thus recreated is individual experience at its most intimate and incommunicable, and at its most incurably melancholy, as well. This is, above all, because everything it was made of has also been lost and is no more than a memory ("ce qu'il a vu et aimé" [what he (once) saw and loved]. Everything at this depth is tied to symbols that are unintelligible to anyone who has not *lived* them. They are unintelligible because they are instrinsically insignificant. (A familiar object, scent, or sound of a voice that everyone else has forgotten—they are the chance witnesses to the moment that they restore to life from the mists of time). All they do, therefore, is add to the loneliness of life:

> hélas! ces mondes isolés, chacun de nous les porte en soi; car où sont les personnes faites pour s'aimer qui ont vécu assez longtemps les unes près des autres pour n'avoir pas des souvenirs séparés? [*Mémoires* 2:605–606]
>
> [Alas! Each one of us carries these isolated worlds within him. For where are those persons made to love one another, who have lived near each other for a long enough time so as not to have separate memories?]

Can we not detect in these disillusioned words, which were nonetheless penned with Chateaubriand's beloved Mme. Récamier nearby, a kind of jealousy on being denied access to the innermost secrets of his loved one's heart? What greater cruelty than that of exile or solitude at the very heart of the closest of unions? There is a defense against this sorrow, however: meditative memory with a monument as its vehicle. For affective memory only reinforces the "monde à part" [separate world] that "chaque homme renferme en soi" [every man has hidden within himself], and that world is separate precisely "parce qu'il est étranger aux lois et aux destinées générales des siècles" [because it is foreign to the general laws and destinies of the centuries] [1:519]. Memory aroused by a monument, however, is a memory shared by all mankind. It is the communion of all men with one another in an emotion that reappears from age to age. Affective memory adds the isolation of the former self to the solitude of today's self.

The monument, however, reminds man of what he has in common with others, of those aspects of himself that are generally human, that go beyond the merely individual. The monument remains unique (and for that very reason is the focus of converging attentions and intentions). It enables anyone who contemplates it to find his counterpart, contemplating the same monument, and to find in his counterpart similarities to himself. These form a basis for an affinity and put an end to solitude. At the very moment that Chateaubriand is regretting that his inner world remains separate from Juliette Récamier's, a double monument appears on which their respective meditations converge: Mme. de Staël's empty château and her grave. Thus they can commune in the similarity of their situation in the face of abandonment and death. Henceforth, their "mondes isolés" [isolated worlds] are "liés par une secrète sympathie" [tied together by a secret affinity] [2:605].

It is not enough for us to explain how a structure must have developed in an imaginary universe. Nor is it enough to show what part it plays in the writer's memory system. We still have to understand how that structure functions and how it is actualized in the text, whatever the semantic value ascribed to it by the poet in any given passage might be.

To actualize it—to give it the form that is visible in the text—it is never enough simply to describe a real monument. In the simplest of cases, the monument is arranged and adjusted in such a way as to point out its potential meaning. Now, since the monument concretizes the temporal dimension, it can be reduced to the opposition *before/after*. Chateaubriand stresses this opposition in the *Mémoires* when he comments that

> On voit marcher à la fois Dieu et l'homme. Bonaparte après sa victoire ordonne de bâtir le pont d'Austerlitz à Paris, et le ciel ordonne à Alexandre d'y passer. [1:751][11]
>
> [We see God and Man marching at the same time. After his victory, Bonaparte ordered the building of the Austerlitz bridge in Paris, and heaven ordered Alexander to pass over it.]

If arrangement is too complicated, Chateaubriand invents a monument. He thinks it a pity that the Duc d'Enghien, who was assassinated by Napoleon, was given a proper grave. If his body had been abandoned, it would have allowed for an instructive symmetry:

> Le squelette abandonné du duc d'Enghien et le tombeau désert de Napoléon à Sainte-Hélène feraient pendants: il n'y aurait rien de plus remémoratifs que ces restes en présence aux deux bouts de la terre. [1:571–572]
>
> [The abandoned skeleton of the Duc d'Enghien and Napoleon's deserted grave on Saint Helena would complement each other. Nothing could be more conducive to memory than those two remains facing each other at the two ends of the earth.]

All this is rather heavy-handed. Usually Chateaubriand prefers to let monuments speak for themselves, but here he has tampered with the monument. There is a discrepancy between its representation and what the reader would see, were it possible for him to view the real structure. This discrepancy or difference is the author's voice.

For an example of this, let us return to the *before/after* opposition. When I commented on it just a moment ago, this opposition, expressed in these two terms, represented the revenge of destiny. Now let us eliminate the first term and rearrange our utterance so that *after* presupposes a *before* that has been destroyed. If we then repeat the variants of *after*, we obtain a melancholy symbol of the ineluctable end of all human endeavors. This will be the "empty place" motif, the motif of the *lieu vide* (a *constructed* empty place, that is). Consequently, it is the site of human activities that we know of only because they have ceased. There are countless examples of this motif: an almost abandoned Venice, the empty Escorial in the *Itinéraire*, the return to a deserted Combourg in the *Vie de Rancé* and the transposition of the same story in *René*, and so forth. The sight of emptiness is so traumatic that it produces a new coinage, which, in turn, jolts the reader. The adjective *inhabité* [uninhabited] would denote nothing more than the sight of emptiness, but the neologism *déshabité* [disinhabited] transforms that sight into the "monument" of a departure. Emptiness, the *vide*, becomes viduity. The empty place tends to be the monument of a monument, for desertions follow one on the other. Every departure represents a ruin and every arrival represents a monument to the preceding departure. Before Chateaubriand's very eyes, the setting at Carthage presents, as if in a diorama, first Dido, followed by Hannibal's legions, who make way for Scipio's armies, who make way for the Vandals, who are followed by the Moors, who are followed by St. Louis, the Crusader king, who leaves nothing behind him but the emptiness of his grave.[12] One might say that this is perhaps because the history of Carthage, by its very nature, calls for this kind of accumulation. But Chateaubriand's reaction will be the same in the face of a highly ordinary landscape. On the outskirts of Saarbrücken, he sees superimposed abandoned camps, whose emptiness consists of the tiered deposits of five Barbarian invasions, and the ruins of a monastery. The contrast between peace and war itself appears as a commentary in that monastery, or rather, as a commemorative inscription: "Là furent des passions qui appelèrent le silence et le repos avant le dernier repos et le dernier silence" [there were passions there that called for silence and rest before the final rest and final silence] [*Mémoires* 2:742]. Elsewhere, physical abandonment symbolizes a form of spiritual destruction. Let us listen, for instance, to Chateaubriand as he returns from a visit to the empty home of Mme. d'Houdetot:

> Un âtre abandonné intéresse toujours; mais que disent les foyers . . . dont les cendres, si elles n'étaient dispersées, reporteraient seulement le souvenir vers des jours qui n'ont su que détruire? [1:476]
>
> [An abandoned hearth is always interesting. But what do hearthstones say, whose ashes, were they not scattered, would only carry memory back toward days that could do nothing but destroy?]

Here again, there is a commentary. This example provides me with a transition, however, for it also contains an implicit moral right in the description. The "relentlessness" of the emptiness is indicated by repetitions of the *before/after* opposition on various levels of language: *cendres* restates the hearth's abandonment through the opposition *burning fire/fire gone out.* The hypothetical negative "si elles n'étaient dispersées" intensifies the physical absence by adding to it the grammatical expression of the unreal.

The moral meaning of this monument of emptiness is thus stated twice, once explicitly and once implicitly. In many passages, though, only the implicit moral sense is present, and it is expressed only by the arrangement of the details in the description. The Coliseum in Rome, for instance, is first described as an empty space—as the memorial of its opposite, the crowd that once filled it. Expressed by means of a fullness foreign to things human, this emptiness is somehow intensified: "Le soleil qui se couchait versait des fleuves d'or par toutes ces galeries où roulait jadis le torrent des peuples" [*Lettre*, p. 13] [The setting sun poured golden rivers through all the galleries where long ago a torrent of peoples flowed].

His perception of present details then triggers a new memory relation, which is informed by Classical recollections and transforms the description of the monument into a monument itself. In descriptions of manmade structures, dogs barking are a metonymic expression of abandonment. From his remembered readings about the Roman circus, Chateaubriand selects an analogous detail, a sound that is to man what barking is to a dog:

> Au lieu des cris de joie que des spectateurs féroces poussaient jadis dans cet amphithéâtre, en voyant déchirer des chrétiens par des lions, on n'entendait que des aboiements. [*Ibid.*]
>
> [Instead of the shouts of joy that savage spectators once let out in this amphitheater as they watched Christians being torn to shreds by lions, all one heard was barking.]

The ruin had just been expressed in terms of a *presence/absence* opposition, and here the superimposition of *aboiements* onto *cris* repeats that statement in the form of a value judgment. Life, which was previously represented by men, is now represented only by dogs. Hence the metaphor: in the system of verbal equivalents set up by the "monument" structure, bloodthirsty Romans fill the same slot as a pack of wild dogs.

I just spoke of discrepancies in the monument mimesis. Thus far, these have merely been cases of imbalance: one aspect of the monument was drawn more boldly than the others, and the same idea was stated over and over in different forms. Chateaubriand goes even further, though, and when he does, the description of the monument can turn the laws of nature upside down, or at the very least, contradict what the reader thinks he knows about the reality described.

Consider one particular case of the *monument*—the ruin motif. The average mortal has a static conception of ruins as the end result of a process of disintegration: ruins are the monument to a henceforth complete decay. A more dynamic conception sees ruins in evolution, albeit in evolution toward total disappearance: stones turn to dust. Contrary to these generally accepted ideas, Chateaubriand's ruins have a tendency to reduplicate, or split themselves in two, and even to generate other ruins and live a kind of life in death. Take, for instance, these ruins piling up on the site of ancient Sparta: "un village turc . . . a péri dans ce champ de mort . . . et ce n'est plus qu'une ruine qui annonce des ruines" [a Turkish village . . . perished in this field of death . . . and now it is nothing but a ruin announcing other ruins] [*Itinéraire* 1:231]. Granted: in spite of the verb, this could simply be the observation of an archaeologist. In Rome, however, Chateaubriand sees a correspondence—the term is his—between the ruins of the Coliseum and the *future* ruins of the Vatican. The correspondence between a *ruin* and a building still intact then suggests an alarming affinity: "je songeai que les monuments se succèdent comme les hommes qui les ont élevés" [I reflected that monuments succeed one another like the men who built them] [*Lettre*, p. 14]. A ruin is a process of becoming and not an end product. When the émigrés regain possession of their properties, which had been confiscated during the Revolution, and rebuild their burned-down châteaux, Chateaubriand detects the promise of a coming revolution in the rubble of 1789. Similarly, the remains of churches buried by Vesuvius—their bell towers sticking out of the lava—announce the future burial of their rebuilt sanctuaries [*Mémoires* 1:472].

Generated by the dynamism of the underlying structure, a potential for life is revealed in the ruins motif. During a second visit to the Coliseum, three months after the earlier one, Chateaubriand finds nothing remaining of what he had seen there the first time. The hermit of the ruins has died. The dogs are no longer barking. The impression of nothingness is so great that, in comparison, he says: "j'ai cru voir les décombres d'un édifice que j'avais admiré quelques jours auparavant dans toute son intégrité et dans toute sa fraîcheur" [I thought I saw the rubble of a building that, a few days before, I had admired in all its integrity and all its freshness] [*Lettre*, p. 14]. Yesterday's ruin has now become an unruin, just as Count Dracula becomes undead. Yesterday's ruin was a ruin in the bud, and it has now bloomed into the full-blossomed ruin of today.

From this effort at renewing the mimesis, metaphorical habits develop, giving us phrases like this one on Henri V, who is still a child, but already exiled: "jeune et nouvelle ruine d'un antique édifice" [young and new ruin of an ancient edifice] [*Mémoires* 2:753]. A system of special codes and particular norms is thus created in Chateaubriand's idiolect, a system in which words no longer carry meaning in relation to normal usage, but only in relation to the structure actualized in a given context. Any emphasis is thus subordinated to the structure. Depending on how completely the poet describes his subject, the imbalance or anomaly in the mimesis will be developed to a greater or lesser extent. It is enough for Chateaubriand to dwell on a particular aspect of the ruins theme for that aspect to become the effective vehicle of the structural relationship. We have already noted that the *before/after* opposition with *before* at the zero degree favors the interpretation of ruins as evolution or as life in death. In the description of the remains of Hadrian's villa, a bravura piece in the *Lettre sur la campagne romaine* [*Lettre*, pp. 15–17], Chateaubriand dwells on the motif of the saxatile plants growing among the rocks, and thereby makes it into a hyperbolic expression of the evolution of the ruins. The whole scene is introduced as a variant of the *empty place* or *successive abandonments* invariants:

Il y a même double vanité (des choses humaines) dans les monuments de la villa Adriana. Ils n'étaient, comme on sait, que les imitations d'autres monuments répandus dans les provinces de l'empire romain: le véritable temple de Sérapis à Alexandrie, la véritable Académie à Athènes n'existent plus; vous ne voyez donc dans les copies d'Adrien que des ruines de ruines.

[There is even a twofold vanity [of things human] in the monuments of the Villa Adriana. As we know, they were only imitations of other monuments scattered throughout the provinces of the Roman Empire. The real temple of Serapis in Alexandria and the real Academy in Athens no longer exist, so all you see in Hadrian's copies are *ruins of ruins.*]

The picture of the fallen buildings and the sight of nature invading their rubble alternate in counterpoint. This motif is a frequent one in the representation of ruins. Chateaubriand likes to contrast the mobility of plants with the immobility of stones. In itself, however, the motif is in no way specifically characteristic of Chateaubriand's imaginary landscape. It can be found in any writer who ever looked at ruins. Diderot, it is true, was content merely to note the presence of plants, and Gautier just goes into great detail. Hugo, however, draws the same aesthetic contrasts from the motif as Chateaubriand, and he does so just as frequently.[13] What strikes me as pure Chateaubriand, though, is the fact that the plant motif no longer belongs to picturesque style, but, instead, is articulated on the structure underlying the description of the monument. It acquires its full meaning only in relation to that structure—that is, in relation to the way the monument is represented and not in relation to the monument itself. First of all, there is the telling fact that vegetation is itself described in architectural terms. Stonework is "tapissé de feuilles . . . dont la verdure satinée se dessinait comme un travail en mosaïque, corbeilles et bouquets, guirlandes" [covered with leaves . . . whose satiny green stood out like mosaic work, baskets and bouquets, garlands]. These are not superfluous ornaments. Chateaubriand expressly states that Nature copies Art: "la nature s'était plu à reproduire sur les chefs-d'oeuvre mutilés de l'architecture l'ornement de leur beauté passée" [Nature had taken pleasure in reproducing on architecture's mutilated masterpieces the ornaments of their past beauty]. Thus plants are a living monument to the fallen monument, and nature replacing art is a triumph of Art over Death. These same plants, however, also topple walls, invade interiors, and cancel out the functional character of buildings. Their growth is decomposition in progress. They finish off the work of destruction, and are, therefore, the triumph of Death.

This twofold and contradictory symbolism is summarized in the image of trees replacing fallen columns: "ça et là de hauts cyprès remplaçaient les colonnes tombées dans ces palais de la mort" [here and there tall cypresses replaced the fallen columns in these palaces of Death] [Lettre, p. 16]. On the one hand, the verb expresses the triumph of art (and furthermore, the trees relive the history of art since, according to Chateaubriand, the idea of columns sprang from the contemplation of trees). On the other hand, the choice of the tree of mourning, the cypress, and the substitution of "palais de la mort" for "imperial palace" express the victory of Death. These two parts of the sentence actualize, in turn, two potentials of the "monument" structure: *before* generates *after*, and thus *death* gives *ruin*; and *after* represents *before*, so *ruin* is a monument to *death*. The characteristic strangeness of representing death with a form of life stems, itself, from a semantic property of the structure. This property is roughly analogous to the ambivalence whereby an optimist says that a glass is half full and a pessimist that it is half empty. But instead of being symbolized by an alternative, as in the *optimist/pessimist* case, the ambivalence is represented by a sequence, by succession in time. Realized through a static variant like *être* [to be], the structure is a monument; but realized through a dynamic variant, such as *devenir* [to become], the structure is a ruin. Now, everything indicates that Chateaubriand constantly alternates between the static variant legitimating artistic endeavors and the dynamic variant reflecting his own obsession with death. We just saw this in the case of the ruins of the Coliseum, which became intact once again only to fall back to ruin. We can also see it in genitive constructions such as the already quoted *ruine de ruine*, which corresponds to *monument de monument* in the static code.

If this interpretation is correct, the phenomenon should also appear in cases where the variant is actualized by the *tombeaux* motif. The tombstone is the last monument *par excellence*. It is the concrete expression of all that is final in death. Were ordinary usage to be flouted by attributing the same vitality and reproductive ability to tombs as we just saw distorting the representation of ruins, this would provide even further proof. This is indeed what happens. Chateaubriand's tombstones alternate between their meaning "remains of a destroyed life" and their "monument" meaning; that is their meaning as a future ruin. The following passage corroborates this:

> Les sépulcres dépeuplés offrent le spectacle d'une résurrection et pourtant ils n'attendent qu'une mort plus profonde. . . .C'est le néant qui a rendu ces tombes désertes. [*Mémoires* 2:331]
>
> [Depopulated sepulchers present the sight of a resurrection, yet they are only waiting for a more profound death. . . . What has left these tombs deserted is nothingness.]

Or consider the prophecy that, like a second death, oblivion will soon cover over the memory of the execution of Louis XVI. This is expressed in a sentence in which *échafaud* [scaffold], a metonym of *tombe*, is literally buried under *obélisque* [obelisk], which is a metaphor of *monument funèbre* [burial monument]:

> Et cependant la pierre hiéroglyphique taillée par ordre de Sésostris ensevelit dès aujourd'hui l'échafaud de Louis XVI sous le poids des siècles. [2:911]
>
> [And yet, the hieroglyphic stone cut by order of Sesotris today buries the scaffold of Louis XVI under the weight of centuries.]

It is even possible to find purely lexical variants of the structure that is ordinarily realized by the monument image. In these, the presence of the property revealed by *ruines de ruines* and by the motif of vegetation amongst ruins is confirmed by their synonyms. By lexical variants, I mean words or word groups, whose meaning actualizes the structure without actually constituting a visual image, as in this generalization from the *Voyage en Italie*: "On meurt à chaque moment pur un temps, une chose, une personne qu'on ne reverra jamais: *la vie est une mort successive*" [Every moment we die for a time, a thing, or a person we shall never see again: *life is a successive death*] [6:286]. What is meant by *mort successive*, in an outdated sense of *successif*, is *continual death*. This turn of phrase was so striking that Larousse's *Grand dictionnaire* made special note of it as late as 1875. It is just as boldly revealing as the defiances of normal usage we have already observed. Just as in distortions of reality, the structure's semantic properties help to express a concept of time specific to Chateaubriand. It is not a question of the commonplace of time flying or of universal transitoriness, even though Chateaubriand is also familiar with that commonplace and, to express it, coined the word *fuitif* [fleetive: *fuite* (flight) + the adjectival suffix -if]. Nor is it a case of disintegration or crumbling, or of what Jean-Pierre Richard terms *labilité*. Rather, what we are dealing with here is time measured by the writer's grieving sensibility, a time span made up of abandonments, ruins, and deprivations following one after the other:

> Combien rapidement et que de fois nous changeons d'existence et de chimère! Des amis nous quittent, d'autres leur succèdent . . . il y a tourjours un temps où nous n'avons rien de ce que nous eûmes. L'homme . . . a plusieurs [vies] mises bout à bout. [*Mémoires* 1:103]
>
> [How quickly and how often we change existences and chimeras! Friends leave us. Others take their place. . . there is always a time when we have nothing of what we once had. Man . . . has several [lives] placed end to end.]

It is clear that the same words and the same images can just as well represent life as a monument, for they are arranged by the same structure. Chateaubriand was perfectly aware of this. As early as the *Génie du christianisme*, he said that there was "une conformité secrète entre les monuments détruits et la rapidité de notre existence" [a secret conformity between ruined monuments and the speed of our existence].[14] In point of fact, it is less a matter of conformity than of fusion, for the representation of the monument is also used to represent the author himself.

This fusion is all the easier in that Chateaubriand is loath to represent a monument without bringing a witness into the picture. Perception of the monument, indeed the monument's very existence, is dependent on the eye contemplating it. Architecture is totally vulnerable, for it no longer exists when it no longer has visitors bearing witness to it. It is as if it vanished along with the men and deeds it was supposed to recall: "elles ne sont déjà plus pour moi, ces ruines, puisqu'il est probable que rien ne m'y ramènera" [already these ruins exist no more for me, since it is likely that nothing will bring me back to them] [*Voyage en Italie* 6:286].

The interdependence between the monument and its viewer can no doubt be explained by the attitude of literary tourism which I have discussed. It can also be explained by the fact that the most frequent monuments in Chateaubriand are funerary monuments. Now there is a literary tradition, evidence of which can be found in the *Anthologie grecque*, that originates in the clichés used in epitaphs and is continued with the conventional imitation of the language of epitaphs in elegies. This tradition established a dialectic in poetry between the tombstone and the traveler: *Sta viator*! The traveler stops and reads aloud. Were it not for him, the tomb's message would have been in vain. Without the traveler and without the spectator, the monument cannot create communication beyond absence. This is why Chateaubriand can say that a new death will bury Louis XVI when the obelisk in the Place de la Concorde becomes the center of a new wasteland. When its witnesses disappear, so will the monument.

This is a handy poetic convention, for it provides the outline for meditation scenes. It is, however, much more than a convenient technical device. It actually allows the characteristic successiveness of the structure in question to be represented in the reader of the epitaph or reflected in the viewer of the monument:

> Je lis sur une pierre les regrets qu'un vivant donnait à un mort; ce vivant est mort à son tour, et après deux mille ans je viens, moi

barbare des Gaules, parmi les ruines de Rome, étudier ces épitaphes dans une retraite abandonnée . . . moi qui demain m'éloignerai pour jamais de ces lieux, et qui disparaîtrai bientôt de la terre. [6:279]

[I read on a stone the grief that a living person felt for a dead man. That living man died in his turn, and two thousand years later, I, a Barbarian from Gaul, come into the midst of the ruins of Rome to study these epitaphs in a deserted retreat . . . I, who tomorrow shall leave these places for ever and who shall soon disappear from the earth.]

Here again, we have the *ruine de ruine* type of construction, but it is no longer confined to the description of a monument. For it to be actualized, a mutual relation between the monument and its viewer is needed. The man meditating about the ruins is himself "une ruine encore plus chancelante" [an even more tottering ruin]. Even memory is represented by Chateaubriand as a sanctuary in which monument and viewer are as one. Together they suffer the continuity of death. The heart of a friend, "où s'est gravée notre image, est comme l'objet dont il retient les traits, une argile sujette à se dissoudre" [on which our own image is engraved, is, like the object whose features it preserves, a kind of clay prone to dissolving] [6:313]. There is no lack of variants of this: the image of the river Time watching generations pass by on its banks, with the days of our lives resembling the waves; a dying woman looking at a monument in ruin, the arcades of which seem in turn to be contemplating her: "portiques morts . . . qui avaient tant vu mourir" [dead porticoes . . . that had seen so much dying].[15] We can tell from the strangeness of these images that the pressure of the structure far outweighs the requirements of the representation of reality.

The interdependence between the sight and the person viewing it has generated two families of Chateaubrianesque images in which the poet is observed penetrating the monument. In the first category of these images, the viewer seems to be superimposed on the monument he is contemplating, so that the details that are retained of the architectural whole metaphorically represent the viewer: tell me what you're looking at and I'll tell you who you are. The Coliseum is a monument to the Rome that has disappeared. When Chateaubriand visits it with the dying Mme. de Beaumont [*Mémoires* 1:514], the writer's eyes, and then the eyes of his character, focus on certain details, all of which are synonymous. The universal meaning of this most famous of all ruins is replaced by a meaning determined by the lateness of the hour, the growing shadows, the disappearing sun, and Pauline de Beaumont's gaze as it goes downward from the still sunny rooftops to the gathering darkness in the amphitheater, to the area where the martyrs perished, and to the cross commemorating their sacrifice. Henceforth, the Coliseum is a monument. It is a symbol of Pauline's imminent death, and therefore of Chateaubriand's own feelings. The complexities of reality have been filtered out by the specific concerns of the person viewing it, and what is retained of that reality is the *analogon* of the viewer's thoughts. The viewer has been embodied in the viewed, one might say. On second thought, perhaps the reverse image would be more accurate: the objective, exterior monument, with its well-established, traditional symbolism, has been replaced by another monument, one interiorized in the imagination and whose symbolism is specific to the viewer. In such a case, the monument theme is the specifically Chateaubrianesque form of the Romantic theme of landscape as expression of the soul.

The second group of images in which the fusion of the monument with the poet can be observed is comprised of images of a passerby or traveler carrying out a ritual act that, as did the reading of an epitaph, gives reality to the symbol. Better yet, if the monument disappears, the viewer then assumes its functions, takes its place, and himself becomes the monument to what has disappeared. Mme. Récamier ritually summons up the memory of Mme. de Staël while visiting her late friend's home at Coppet: "Après avoir pieusement suivi les allées qu'elle avait coutume de parcourir avec Mme de Staël, Mme Récamier a voulu saluer ses cendres" [After piously tracing the paths that she had been accustomed to taking with Mme. de Staël, Mme. Récamier wanted to pay her respects to her ashes] [2:606]. The ritual reaches its completion in the celebrant's identification with the object of worship. In reliving the past, the visitor herself becomes the image of death: "pâle et en larmes, [elle] est sortie du bocage funèbre elle-même comme une ombre" [pale and in tears, she came out of the gloomy copse, looking herself like a shadow]. A living monument to the deceased, Pauline in turn has her own viewer. When he sees her, Chateaubriand understands that the faithfulness of her ritual compensates for the ephemeral fragility of the grave. Transposing this to the realm of the literary work, the vanity of all things is compensated for by their representation in art.

In similar ceremonies, veritable liturgies of memory that he summons to "[revenir] en arrière sur la trace des jours" [come back along the trail of days] [2:607], Chateaubriand is able to commune with the great men with whom he feels an affinity:

> J'étais là sur les frontières de l'antiquité grecque, et aux confins de l'antiquité latine. Pythagore, Alcibiade, Scipion, César, Pompée, Cicéron, Auguste, Horace, Virgile, avaient traversé cette mer. Quelles fortunes diverses tous ces personnages célèbres ne livrent-ils point à l'inconstance de ces mêmes flots? Et moi, voyageur obscur, passant sur la *trace effacée* des vaisseaux qui portèrent les grands hommes de la Grèce et de l'Italie, j'allais chercher les muses dans leur patrie; mais je ne suis pas Virgile, et les Dieux n'habitent plus l'Olympe. [*Itinéraire* 1:155]
>
> [There I was on the frontiers of Greek antiquity and the borders of Latin antiquity. Pythagoras, Alcibiades, Scipio, Caesar, Pompey, Cicero, Augustus, Horace, and Vergil had crossed this sea. What diverse fates do these famous personages not hand over to the inconstancy of these same waves? And I, an obscure traveler, passing over the obliterated path of the vessels that once carried the great men of Greece and Italy, I was going in search of the muses in their homeland. But I am not Vergil, and the Gods no longer inhabit Olympus.]

Jean-Pierre Richard contends that at the very heart of their resemblance, an infinite distance is created between Chateaubriand and those who preceded him in crossing the Adriatic and worshiping the muses. For Chateaubriand is obscure; he is not Vergil.

The distance separating ancient and modern times, the departure of the gods, and the vessels' obliterated path "bring us into . . . a universe of desanctification and disenchantment." According to Richard, the journey, for Chateaubriand, is "an imaginary exercise . . . on the echoing of destinies, but also on their distance and their essential non-coincidence."[16] Such a reading is untenable. Passing through the magic gateway where the two cultures he has already united in his heart come together, Chateaubriand celebrates a ritual symbolizing that union. He is a pilgrim following other pilgrims, and his act cancels out the distance separating him from his predecessors. In exactly the same way, from Pythagoras to Caesar and from Horace to Vergil, the diversity of their fortunes, reflected by the inconstancy of the waves, had been annulled because they had made the same pilgrimage. In retracing the footsteps of his predecessors, Chateaubriand revives the cult of the muses. There is a resanctification or reconsecration. He does indeed say that he is not Vergil, but his obscurity in the face of the Vergil's glory gives the pilgrimage its meaning. Like other poets before him, he is following Vergil's example. With a symbolic gesture, he is making two destinies coincide. He does indeed say that the gods have gone away, yet he makes the journey nonetheless. All of the *Itinéraire* is a monument to the muses, an act of faith in the gods, and a celebration of the culture that has been brought back to life by his Adriatic crossing. When he speaks of a *trace effacée*, he is not so much lamenting the loss of the great men as he is bearing witness, albeit by means of a negation, to the permanence of their footprints. When he writes *trace effacée*, it is really the equivalent, in writing, of forging a new path with the prow of the boat carrying him to Greece. In the end, *effacée* is simply the expression of the past, of anteriority, but what commands the reader's attention is *trace*. The *trace* is what remains.[17]

The very words that express ruin, death, and disappearance are thus substituted, in turn, for the viewer of monuments and the celebrant of the liturgy of memory. They relieve him from his vigils. The very act of writing *absence*, *ruin*, or *death* is already the beginning of a monument to them. At every step of the *Itinéraire* and at every stage of his life, Chateaubriand observes the physical destruction of persons and things. But every step marks the *trace effacée* once again, retraces the obliterated path. The story of each step confirms with the presence of words that cannot be obliterated that the absent are present and that the deceased live. The *phenomenon* of writing, even as it is stating a destruction, represents the victory of monuments over ruins.

[9]

Production of the Narrative I: Balzac's *La Paix du ménage*

CURRENT STUDIES on the narrative tend toward an autonomous semiotics that is separate from the semiotics of the different forms actualizing the narrative structure on the text's surface[1] and further still from the particular semantics of a specific narrative—be it a simple tale or a novel. The disadvantages of this tendency should be obvious: at best, it can result in nothing more than a grammar of narrative possibilities and an abstract typology. Now this kind of grammar or typology can describe actantial functions and relationships like those uniting the narrator and his addressee, which must be distinguished from the relations between the narrator and the reader.[2] But such a grammar could never show how these functions are actualized in the words, much less how the reader perceives them (if any latitude is left him, what the threshold of perception is, and so forth). Narrative analysis, therefore, falls short of the literary phenomenon, for that phenomenon consists of an interaction between the text and the reader.

We might seem justified in studying the text as narrative separately from the text as the locus of literariness, as the object of the reader's perception (if only so as better to define problems and separate difficulties, and provided we do not forget that the results thus obtained would remain incomplete and could not be interpreted unless the eliminated factors were taken into account). Unfortunately, this would not solve the real problem, for whatever precautions are taken, "narratology" looks at the narrative from a perspective that does not allow us to perceive its literariness. It gives priority to structures, in accordance with Greimas' postulate that there exists an immanent narrative organization that is anterior to textual realization.[3] From this, Greimas concludes that significance is not generated directly by the text but that it originates, instead, in narrative structures. Of course, it is both true and logical that structure precedes its actualization. The relevance of this approach, however, is questionable, for an analysis founded on Greimas' postulate will consider the text only as the result or end-product of a generative process. But the literary phenomenon is to be found in the dialectical exchange between text and reader. Consequently, the text has no literary existence or function other than as the starting point of the generative process, which takes place in the reader's mind. The reader begins with the text. He tries to adjust or adapt his own contribution, the "input" of his mythology and his sociolect, to the text. He constructs his hermeneutic scaffolding on the text.

No narrative typology can account for these reactions, for they are produced precisely from concrete linguistic forms. If the analysis does not focus on this concrete system and its decoding, it bypasses the intrinsic characteristics of the work of art and misses what is unique in it. I do not mean that we should give up formulating general rules, for all science is based on generalization. I propose, however, to look for them elsewhere. Instead of looking for the rules that govern narrative structures, it seems to me that we should look for the rules that govern their textual actualization and, consequently, those rules that govern the way literary discourse functions as communication. To the minimum conditions for communication, narrativity adds the constraints imposed by the sequence of events (suspense, which may or may not conform to what could be foreseen). But these constraints have no meaning independent of the literal or metaphoric meaning of the events and characters represented. The events are not actual situations, and the characters are not living persons. Both characters and events are words, and those words already had meanings before they entered the text. Communication is dependent both on this meaning and on the semantic transferences or catachreses resulting from the equivalencies established by the narrative among representations or concepts that had no relation to one another in ordinary language. There is another reason for looking for rules of actualization. They alone can account for the fact that the text draws the reader's attention to the features that indicate its significance, which should be distinguished from the meaning of the "story" told to us. They alone can explain how the text guides the reader toward a correct interpretation. Thus, actualization rules should explain how he can remember and retroactively reinterpret details and events that seemed insignificant when he first came across them in the course of his reading, and how he comes to recognize that they are keys to the symbolism or symbolisms of the text.[4]

For my example, I have chosen Balzac's *La Paix du ménage*. Its brevity suits me,[5] for the narrow limits within which the plot must unfold give this little novel a schematic quality emphasizing the way its episodes work together like the parts of a well-oiled machine. The tangled plot is both complicated and easy to untangle. There is a "didactic clarity"[6] to it that has appealed to connoisseurs and appeared to some critics to be a borrowing from the techniques of the stage.[7]

However, if we are to believe the novelist's expressed intention, the work's true importance is moral. According to Balzac it is a novel about morals, a study of French society at the height of the Empire, a time of dissipation and feverish pursuit of pleasure. At that time, he tells us, women would throw themselves at the young heroes of the Imperial Army. The plot and its resolution, conceived according to the boomerang principle, have the tone of light comedy. A rake sets out to seduce a rich man's wife after he has already stolen his mistress, but his wooing only enables the wife to win back her husband by arousing his jealousy, and the mistress leaves the rake for a third party. The wife pretends to encourage the profligate by accepting a diamond he gives in hopes of seducing her. The diamond had, in fact, been hers until her husband claimed to have lost it after giving it to his mistress, who, in turn, gave it as a gift to her other lover, none other than our rake. Having recovered the diamond, the wife forces her husband to confess his wrongdoing, and he comes back to her. Except for this "happy ending," which fittingly takes place in the bedroom, all the events follow one after the other during the course of a ball given by a wealthy senator to celebrate one of Napoleon's victories. The husband had no intention of bringing his wife to the party. She shows up unexpectedly and without an escort, in hopes of catching her husband in the act. She sits down, all alone, in a spot where she can see everything and be seen by everyone. She is beautiful, unknown, and unaccompanied. Naturally the men hover around her, the women are jealous, and her husband, who is convinced she means to get even with him for his unfaithfulness by giving him a taste of his own medicine, is overcome with a powerless rage.

She is quite literally the center of attention. In terms of the narrative, she is the focus of the entire novel, the object of every desire—the desire to win her back, the desire to possess her (or at least the desire to know her). As far as the description is concerned, this focal point coincides with the center of the decor—which is also the point where light is concentrated, the place of maximum visibility, the target on which all eyes are fixed—at the foot of a huge, ornamental candelabrum. In every episode, the most important role is played by the eye. The seducer stares at his victim. She is watched intently by the mistress, the husband, and the rake, who spies on the other two observers and goes on to use the mistress' jealousy to his own advantage. Meanwhile, the wife is keeping an eye on the husband, thereby closing the circle of gazes and desires. This is the mechanism of the suspense and the force behind the reader's interest. All these relations are easy to describe in terms of narrative structures. We could use the model of alternating amelioration and degradation, which Bremond suggests is the fundamental structure of narrativity.[8] What we have here is a perfect example of a balance (the circularity of desires) generating an imbalance. The rake actualizes this transformation by acting (in order to satisfy a new need, his desire to win the wife) according to the rules of his actantial function, and every time the automatic blocking of the ameliorative process triggers a process of degradation (he jeopardizes his conquest by trying to make another one). The narrative dynamic of the novel lies entirely in the balance between the two processes: the rake's self-destructive acts correspond point by point to the acts with which the wife improves her own situation. The proof that the two processes are complementary is that the wife does not do much at all: quite simply, whatever her counterpart does that is negative in his code becomes positive once it is rewritten in her code.

But this model is so simple that it applies to many texts and cannot account for what pertains to our novel and to it alone. At best, it might help to motivate a value judgment, albeit a rather vague one, and offer us some clear-cut reasons for praising the perfect balance between opposing forces and the tension it creates—which is one of the pleasures of reading.

There is, nevertheless, one textual feature pertinent to the specific characteristics of this narrative. It ties together the text's two main characteristics, which, at first glance, seem foreign to each other—the almost mechanical interaction between acts and actors, and the moral intention of the story (or the parody of that intention). It is a formal constant on the surface of the text, and without it the aforementioned structures would have no effect on the reader and could not control the decoding. This constant is the visual detail of the *candelabrum*—the only detail that is mechanically underscored by repetition.[9] In each of the episodes I have reviewed, the candelabrum is alluded to and described in relation to the wife: it is associated with her by a double relationship of physical contiguity with her person and verbal contiguity with the words designating her. This constant contiguity generates a trope. The candelabrum becomes a metonym for the wife, and this metonymy corresponds exactly to the focal point of the narrative and the description: it symbolizes it.

Jakobson has demonstrated the importance of metonymy in mimesis, most especially in Realism. A reader totally ignorant of rhetoric is aware of the importance of the descriptions of settings and decors in novels: they are a kind of periphrasis designating characters, their emotions, their moods, and, above all, their psychological and moral evolution.

It is the text itself that tells the reader how to interpret the metonymies. From the beginning of the novel, as of the second page, an example is given of the way the metonymy carries meaning, and that example will be the model for deciphering the metonymies that follow. At first blush, this metonymy seems to be nothing more than a simile:

> les passions [avaient] des dénouements aussi rapides que les décisions du chef suprême de ces kolbacs, de ces dolmans et de ces aiguillettes qui plurent tant au beau sexe. (p. 993)
>
> [passions came as quickly to an end as the decisions of the commander-in-chief of these busbies, dolmans, and aiglets who so delighted the fair sex.]

But what we have here, in the guise of a simile, is a transcoding that figuratively repeats the abstract statement of one of the laws of the society in question. It had just been formulated in these terms:

> hommes et femmes, tous se précipitaient dans le plaisir avec une intrépidité qui semblait présager la fin du monde. . . . L'engouement des femmes pour les militaires devint comme une frénésie. (pp. 992–993)
>
> [men and women were all rushing headlong into pleasure with a boldness that seemed to foreshadow the end of the world. . . . The women's infatuation with soldiers became a kind of frenzy.]

The hero as object of desire is replaced by his uniform or insignia, and in context this reification has a comical or even satirical effect, since it speaks volumes about the forces motivating the passion[10] and about the essential emptiness of its object.

In itself, however, the substitution indicates the basic postulate of the narrative to the reader—that every object described is the sign of something else. The described object has a threefold meaning. As a description, it implies that the story being told is real and it refers to the paranoia seizing all of the characters. As a symbolic representation, it reveals indirectly what is going on as well as what is happening to the characters to which it belongs. In each case, the metonymic link is not simply the physical contiguity existing between referents (between the soldier and his uniform, for example), but also lexical collocations that already exist as commonplaces. The complex semantic system of a given narrative is not only subject to the lexical and grammatical demands of mimesis, but also depends on a semiotic network, the validity of which is generally limited to the idiolect.

This general rule applies to the candelabrum, and in a way that is relevant to the narrative, since at every turn in the sequence of events the metonymic relation between the wife and the candelabrum is stressed so that it commands the reader's attention. The candelabrum's isolation in the ballroom underscores the fact that the character sitting by it is the center of the action. The light streaming down provides a code for hyperbolically expressing the curiosity or desires of the other characters. And ultimately, the candelabrum symbolizes the heroine. One incident is particularly significant in this regard: the master of the house misunderstands the first question put to him about the lady and thinks he is being asked about the candelbraum (p. 998).

Not only does the candelabrum motivate the events by explaining why everyone is obssessed with the wife, but its description suggests a hermeneutic model. For example, the wife in her role as the focus of desires is presented as an enigma to be solved. Here the reader can make no mistake, for although she is sitting beneath the candelabrum, in its full light, the text shows her "enterrée dans l'obscurité malgré les bougies qui brillent au-dessus de sa tête . . . repoussée de chaise en chaise par chaque nouvelle arrivée jusque dans les ténèbres de ce petit coin" [buried in darkness despite the candles glowing over her head . . . pushed back from chair to chair by every new arrival all the way into the darkness of this little corner]. (p. 996).[11] And the desire to solve the enigma, which is itself metonymic of the desire to win the lady, is expressed in terms of light: "l'homme le plus déterminé à mettre en lumière notre plaintive inconnue [qui] a un peu l'air d'une élégie" [the man most determined to bring to light our doleful mystery woman (who) looks a bit like an elegy]. (p. 996).

I said that jealousy is what makes the characters all move in unison, each trying his or her best to keep the others from discovering what he or she is thinking: the husband would rather kill than admit that the lady is his wife; his mistress cannot bear to hear people talking about her, and so on. This "block" is also represented by a metonymy that functions like a subconscious repression:

> Vous craignez de voir Martial aux pieds. . . . De qui? demande la comtesse en affectant la surprise. . . . De ce candélabre, répondit le colonel en montrant la belle inconnue. (p. 1009)
>
> ["You are afraid of seeing Martial at the feet of. . . ." "Of whom?" the countess asked, affecting surprise. "Of that candelabrum," the colonel replied, pointing to the beautiful stranger.]

Since the candelabrum represses any direct allusion to the wife, the metonymy is transformed into a metaphor. The transformation then generates the main episode and provides the code in which the remainder of the story will be told. And it is because of the nature of that code that the reader can interpret the moral of the novel correctly. When the rake gets ready to attack and invites the wife to dance, it is as if he were getting involved with the candelabrum:

> Au moment où le maître des requêtes s'approchait en papillonnant du candélabre, sous lequel la comtesse . . . semblait ne vivre que des yeux . . . (p. 1019)
>
> [Just when the magistrate, fluttering about like a butterfly, was approaching the candelabrum, beneath which the countess . . . seemed alive only in her eyes . . .]

The reader cannot fail to notice the image of the butterfly, not only because the verb *papillonner* removes any doubt of it, but even more so because the bearing it connotes is perfectly grotesque in a *maître des requêtes.* The reader already vaguely knows that the magistrate's behavior is not the best, but he might forget or disregard this fact if the *maître des requêtes* were designated by name or with a pronoun. His title, however, closely tied to a verb so very incompatible with judicial connotations, forces the reader to "filter" the seducer's image through a metaphor. Now this metaphor implies a moral and that moral is dependent on the candelabrum. Indeed, the butterfly-magistrate would have neither meaning nor significance if he did not presuppose the group "le papillon et la (flamme de la) chandelle" [the moth and the (flame of the) candle],[12] which ever since Petrarch has been an image of love's fatal attraction.

In light of this commonplace, the reader can now see the novel as a comedy about the foolish things that love makes people do. Transformed into a metaphor, the novel's central metonymy controls its interpretation on two levels, both of which are relevant to narrativity.

In the first place, the theme of the moth and the candle lets us foresee what will happen to the seducer. The narrative creates an expectation and suspense, without expressly saying that the man who thought he was about to make a catch has himself been caught. The story unfolds without giving away how it will end; or at least, it does not tell us in its own discourse. But the discourse derived from the *papillon–chandelle* code constitutes a prolepsis.[13] It is obvious that if the analysis were confined to the level of the narrative structures, this prolepsis would escape it completely. Since it is entirely dependent on a metaphor that the reader reconstitutes from a fragment (*papillonnant*), the prolepsis exists only on the semantic level.

Second, this metaphor is not only a deictic device showing the reader how to anticipate what will happen in the story, and it does more than create suspense. It is also a negative marker, for its theme belongs to a cynical or disillusioned version of the mimesis of love. As a marker, it guides the reading, to the extent that the reading is no longer just the simple decoding of the story, but is also interpretive: the metaphor pejoratively marks every description of the relationships between characters. Thus the reader perceives the entire narrative as a single unit of significance: all of its episodes do nothing but repeat the same message, variant after variant. This message or invariant is, of course, love's universal deception and the tricks played on us by the passions. Here again, the message would be perceived only by chance if the metaphor were not clearly derived from the same matrix that, at the beginning of the novel, generated Balzac's first reflection on the morals of the Napoleonic era. This reflection brings together the two driving principles of the novel—the complexity of the plot and the moral intention expressly stated by Balzac:

> Un trait de cette époque unique dans nos annales et qui la caractérise fut une passion effrénée pour tout ce qui brillait. (p. 993)
>
> [One feature of that unprecedented era—and a characteristic one—was an unbridled passion for all that glittered.]

"Tout ce qui brille" [all that glitters] is the model for every metonym of beauty, passion, or simply desire in the narrative: the women, the diamond passing from hand to hand, and above all the candelabrum—as lamp, as woman, and as object of desire. I said that the underscored and repeated *candélabre* metonymy, or rather the "candelabrum" code, gives the narrative its unity and enables it to function as a complex but unique sign. But what gives this sign its meaning is the element that has been repressed and omitted from the matrix sentence. This element is the predicate implied by "tout ce qui brille," which imposes itself all the more forcefully on the reader's mind in that the entire sentence is a well-known proverb: "tout ce qui brille n'est pas or" [all that glitters is not gold].[14]

This is the model for the whole of our story about deceptive appearances and passions. The narrative is, thus, not only a sequence of interconnected functions, but also the textual expansion of a meaning, a melodic variation, or musical exercise, on a semantic theme. The narrative text is produced as a series of sentences that make explicit a fragment censored from the matrix sentence.[15]

The narrative provides the space needed for the series to unfold. The perception of comparable elements in the lexicon, and therefore of the variants of a single invariant, leads to the discovery of the significance. This significance is a two-sided phenomenon: identity within variation and repetition of the invariant in different forms. These forms comprise the corpus of metonymies. By definition, this is a unique complex which is necessarily characteristic of the novel being analyzed, since it is located on the level of discourse. As Balzac himself said: "aujourd'hui que toutes les combinaisons possibles paraissent épuisées . . . les détails seuls constituent désormais le mérite des romans" [nowadays when all possible combinations appear to be exhausted . . . the value of novels will henceforth be comprised only of details].[16] As for the invariant, a change in the semantic structure of the metonymy gives us access to this key to the significance. As we have seen, the metonymy is transformed into a metaphor.

Literary reading is structural reading. In the case of narrative, what enables us to recognize the structure's successive variants is focusing. Over and again this focusing offers the reader, in the simultaneously condensed and stressed form of the matrix, those features that will mark all the textual elements derived from that matrix. Once again, these features all belong to mimetic discourse, to a system for representing the real. The hypograms that they actualize (clichés, proverbs, and so forth) determine the predictability of what follows. Surface features and stylistic characteristics of the text enable the reader to decipher correctly—that is, they enable him to decipher in temporality (in terms of time), and to foresee the succession of events, which is the fundamental factor in the narrative.

[10]

Production of the Narrative II: Humor in *Les Misérables*

SPECIALISTS in literary history and aesthetics find it hard to agree on a definition of humor, or, at least, of its French variety. This is because they try to see it either as a genre (or subgenre) of the comic or as a distinct style system.

But humor has no characteristics, themes, or motifs belonging to it and it alone. It sets down no stylistic or lexical restrictions. It has no particular sequences of events or narrative functions of its own. It is therefore not a genre.

It is not even associated with some genres rather than others, or with particular stylistic phenomena, as is the case of wit, which has a place in any definition of the epigram, the maxim, the *métaphore précieuse*, the witticism, and so on.

Humor is a trope, and nothing else. It is a rerouting of expression, an overall modification of the components of a sentence or text. It is a phenomenon orienting the decoding so as to confuse and amuse the reader. It is a catachresis establishing a discrepancy between a form that is funny and a content that is not (be it neutral, serious, or even tragic), or between a highly unusual form and a content that, in normal usage, would rule out strange ways of expression. Since it is a trope, it can express everything, including the sublime, which alone would be enough to distinguish it from the comic. As a trope, it can fit into every genre and affect all stylistic forms.

It follows that we can hope to resolve the question of literary humor only by analyzing its functions. This analysis should be performed within a single genre, since those functions will inevitably vary from one genre to another.

The nineteenth-century French novel is particularly well suited to such an approach. From what was termed the *roman gai* under the Restoration, to Gautier's *Mademoiselle de Maupin*, and on to Huysmans' *Les Soeurs Vatard*, humor never ceased to play a part in the nineteenth-century novel. And nowhere is its role more obvious than in the Romantic novel, both because its narrative techniques are influenced by the English and German novels and because of the affinities that existed between humor and Romantic sensibility.[1] These affinities are particularly visible in Hugo.[2]

I shall attempt, therefore, to describe the functions of humor in narrative structures by examining *Les Misérables*.[3] These functions fall into three categories: humor in the titles, humor in the digressions (philosophical, historical, and other), and humor in the narrative proper. Two preliminary distinctions must be made. Humor is not satire, since it neither attacks nor destroys stereotypes; and humor is not irony, for although it does present us with a complex semantic network, it does not bring together two simultaneous and contradictory meanings.

HUMOR IN THE TITLES

This type of humor has a structural function in the narrative to the extent that it makes no sense in context. Granted, some titles do indeed correspond to a funny subject. "Quatrevingt-dix ans et trente-deux dents" [Ninety years old and thirty-two teeth] is the title of a chapter about a sprightly, but altogether caricatural, old eccentric. There is also this hyperbole alluding to the astonishment of a concierge who seems to have stepped out of a farce: "Divers coups de foudre tombent sur mame Bougon" [III, VI, I (747), Sundry lightning bolts fall on missus Bougon].[4] But most of the humorous titles designate books or chapters whose content is anything but humorous. These are not cases of what is usually called gratuitous humor, but rather, of a displacement of the semantic relation. This relationship is not established between a signifier, which would be the title, and a signified, which would be the chapter, but is established instead between signifiers, from one title to another. Humor gives a common denominator to the titles it affects and defines them as members of the same paradigm.

For instance, one chapter is a masterpiece of dramatic tension.[5] Thénardier's lies, complicated calumnies, and machinations are incomprehensible to Marius. To him, they are about as clear as mud, or as they say in French, "c'est la bouteille à l'encre" [literally: it's the ink bottle]. All he can understand is that Jean Valjean comes out looking better, rehabilitated, purified, and cleansed of any suspicion in his eyes. This high drama, this turning point, coming right before the mystical elevation at the end of the novel, is topped off with a pun: "Bouteille d'encre qui ne sert qu'à blanchir" [Bottle of ink that does nothing but whiten]. One series of titles—"Commencement d'une énigme," "Suite de l'énigme," "L'énigme redouble" [Beginning of an enigma, Continuation of the enigma, The enigma increases][6]—is obviously a parody of adventure novels or Gothic novels. But the chapters in question contain no parody. Elsewhere, a title seems to satirize a certain social mentality, the attitude of the police toward the rights of a suspect: "On devrait toujours commencer par arrêter les victimes" [One should always begin by arresting the victims]. It so happens that the chapter suggests nothing of the sort. Javert, who has just saved Jean Valjean from an ambush, realizes too late that the victim was bigger game than the gangsters. But that victim is unlike any other, and Javert in no way thinks of generalizing.[7]

We are obliged to see these titles as the expression of an intention that is independent of the story's particulars, the kind of emotions that the story arouses, and the style of the discourse in which it is expressed. In contrast to the variations in the story that we are being told, the humor in the titles is a constant or recurrent element. On the semantic level there is only one permanent element that can correspond to this verbal constant: the presence of the actor or of the author. In short, it is the narrator's voice; and this voice reminds the reader that what he is reading is not a simple chronicle of events, but rather a narrative arranged as a demonstration; not a photograph of reality, but rather a picture composed according to a specific point of view. In short, it is a work of art. Titles like "Le petit qui criait au tome III" [The little boy who was crying in volume III] or "Chapitre où l'on s'adore" [Chapter in which they love each other][8] are clearly humorous, since the child was not crying in volume III itself, but rather in the episode related in that volume, and since the lovers are alone together in a bedroom, and not in the chapter in which they are discussed. The reader perceives the same unvarying message beneath these variants: of course, this is a story taken from reality, but it has been transformed into a verbal object. This is a *text*. Humor in the titles is the sign both of the *montreur* and of his *jeu*, of the showman as well as of his show.

HUMOR IN DIGRESSIONS

Let us take as our example the most criticized and most digressive of the digressions—the long historical monograph on the Paris sewers.[9] At first glance, it is no more than a picturesque compilation. Its ultimate aim—the use of a labyrinth mimesis as a code symbolizing the ordeal of purification and the beginning of a new life[10] (for Jean Valjean as well as for Marius)—does not become apparent until after the six chapters of "L'intestin de Léviathan" [Leviathan's bowel].

Since it is a compilation, this six-chapter-long digression would therefore have remained apart from the literary phenomenon. For this reason it was the role of humor to make it literary by introducing the author, hence an intention, and hence an order other than that of factual contingencies. Humor is not merely *variatio* helping to prevent monotony (although on the surface, on the stylistic level, it is indeed just that), and it is not simply *captatio benevolentiae*, or what is now called contact with the reader, as for example in the following:

> Tel était cet ancien Paris, livré aux querelles, aux indécisions et aux tâtonnements. Il fut longtemps assez bête. Plus tard, 89 montra comment l'esprit vient aux villes.[11]
>
> [Such was that Paris of old, given over to quarreling, indecision, and groping about. For a long time it was pretty stupid. Later on, '89 showed how cities come to their wits.]

Everything here lies in the transformation of the proverbial phrase "comment l'esprit vient aux filles" [how girls come to their wits]. The three sentences in the quotation are teleologically generated and "justified" by the pun they carry with them.[12] Form dictated thought—which is none other than the definition of the literary text's genesis.

In the next paragraph, humor results from the comic conversion of a moral digression.[13] In other words, it allows the novel to moralize without lapsing into an edifying genre such as the moralizing or philosophical essay. Contamination of genres is avoided because the humor eliminates, or more precisely negates seriousness, which is the essential component of the essay.

> Quelquefois, l'égout de Paris se mêlait de déborder, comme si ce Nil méconnu était subitement pris de colère. Il y avait, chose infâme, des inondations d'égout. Par moments, cet estomac de la civilisation digérait mal, le cloaque refluait dans le gosier de la ville, et Paris avait l'arrière-goût de sa fange. Ces ressemblances de l'égout avec le remords avaient du bon; c'étaient des avertissements; fort mal pris du reste; la ville s'indignait que sa boue eût tant d'audace, et n'admettait pas que l'ordure revînt. Chassez-la mieux.[14]
>
> [Sometimes the Paris sewer took it upon itself to overflow, as if that misunderstood Nile were suddenly overcome with rage. There were—horrors—inundations from the sewer. At times, this stomach of civilization digested badly, the cloaca flowed back into the city's throat, and Paris had the aftertaste of its mire. These resemblances between the sewer and remorse had some good points to them. They were warnings—very badly taken, though. The city got indignant that its mud should be so bold and would not stand for the filth's coming back. Drive it out better.]

The description of a problem for city planners is subordinated to the lesson and symbolism, and the whole is subordinated to the narrative. The history and topography of the Paris sewers become tools of verisimilitude, since they anchor the underground epic of Jean Valjean's escape firmly in reality and, thereby, bring that epic back to the novel genre. The part played by the inundation, which on the narrative level is to force the municipal government to improve sanitation, is translated into a moral code: the inundation is described as a belch, and the belch is compared to the soul-searchings of remorse. This identification of mud with remorse, which produces a metaphor of society as a kind of collective body and then soul, is not only a moral view of reality. In Hugolian symbolism, the sewer is the very image of hidden evils, of mankind's criminal and repressed subconscious—witness, in *Les Châtiments*, the poem titled "L'Egout de Rome" [The Roman sewer].[15] Lastly, this entire network of serious meanings is actualized in a funny code: the symbol called for the animation or personification of the sewers, but that personification is produced in the vocabulary of comedy. (The predicate of *égout*, the verb *se mêler*, is normally reserved for intruders, pests, and busybodies: "l'égout se mêlait de déborder." *Méconnu*, a touching adjective normally applied to unrecognized merit, adds the complication of a human parody to the contrast between the sun-drenched glory of *Nil* and the dark filth it conceals.) There is further comedy in the personification of the mud and in the personification of the city in the lofty style reserved for a social superior grown indignant at his inferiors who do not know their place. And one final stroke: "la ville n'admettait pas que l'ordure revînt. Chassez-la mieux"—at first blush, this would seem to be a playful reference to the demands of taxpayers dissatisfied with their public services. In fact, this strange *chassez* in the context of *revenir* inevitably suggests a parallel reading of La Fontaine, as if the following line from the *Fables* were a watermark underneath Hugo's text: "chassez le naturel, il revient au galop" [drive away the natural and it comes galloping back]. But that makes filth the equivalent or substitute of the word *naturel*. Mire therefore belongs to the very nature of society. There is nothing explicitly satirical about any of this. It is nothing more than a manner of speaking that makes use of the pejorative elements of the code used in the description. It brings the poetic symbolism down to the level of a matter-of-fact statement, to the level of the complaints of citizens vituperating their city government. Consequently, it reduces it to a language that is not a mimesis of reality (for the text does not really show us the citizens), but that apes that mimesis and imitates its techniques as they are used in the system of verisimilitude. Since humor results, therefore, from a formal conflict between the two systems of symbolism and verisimilitude, its function is one of integrating the poetic with the novelistic. There is no verisimilitude. (Indeed, there is no need for it here, since the text relates a bit of history that is independent of the plot and foreign to the novel.) Instead, humor helps to maintain unity of tone, a purely formal reminder of the fundamental rule of the novel genre, which is that the story should be told in a plausible fashion. Thus, humor in the digressions serves two purposes: either it makes literary those textual components that would not be literary in themselves, or else it blocks any possibility of slippage from one genre to another and keeps the text from being contaminated by a genre to which it does not belong.

NARRATIVE HUMOR

Since narrative in novels is simply the translation of the characters' actantial characteristics into a temporal sequence, what interests us here is humor in the presentation of characters, their actions, and their reactions.

This humor presupposes an implicit reference to the social hierarchy as it is represented in the *roman gai*[16] at the beginning of the century. In novels of that type, the characters—simple folk of modest means, petty bourgeois—are comic because they seem to be caricatures of a higher society. Sharing their lot are eccentric characters, *originaux* who, although destined to become revealing phenomena worthy of observation, start as curious creatures whose main purpose is to keep the audience entertained. There will be an evolution from the particular to the significant, from the overdone feature to the underscored detail, and from the self-contained detail, so isolated as to be absurd, to the detail that is integrated into relationships and therefore significant. What makes us smile or laugh in the *roman gai* will make us think in the Realist novel. And the characters who once were caricatures of the upper classes with which every reader likes to identify, become the naive and consequently the appealing image of a world parallel to the reader's own, a world both similar and inferior to his and thus capable of arousing his charitable emotions. We will have gone from the comic picturesque to humor as a sign both of realism and of a predisposition to a tender and condescending feeling of sympathy. An analogous development can be found in the novels of Dickens.

Here is an example this move from the comical devaluation of literary burlesque to the humor of sympathy: "L'idylle rue Plumet et l'épopée rue Saint Denis" [An idyll on rue Plumet and an epic on rue Saint Denis].[17] In the classical aesthetic, this transfer of lofty literary genres to a setting of modern, working-class neighborhoods would have been a defining feature of the burlesque. But in the context of Romanticism, the genre of the burlesque, which was born of the violation of a formal restriction, no longer exists, for there are no longer any restrictions. Idyll and epic are henceforth possible in these lowly neighborhoods. Hence, the relation of inequality is reversed. The epic is not debased and made comic by taking place in the rue Saint Denis; instead, the rue Saint Denis rises to epic proportions. Simple folk are also capable of greatness. The human condition is the same in all environments, and it is everywhere to be respected. The stylistic contrast remains, however, and so does its effect. The contrast between the names of the noble genres and the streets that are anything but noble is still comic. But the comic here has lost its meaning and is no longer a formal marker of a generalization about mankind and the rehabilitation of the humble people. Humor is now one of the stylistic markers of the *roman à thèse* or, rather, of the thesis in the novel. Here it is the marker reserved for describing the love of the humble folk for their fellow man. This is confirmed in such characters as Father Fauchelevent and in such episodes as the one in which Gavroche takes in two abandoned children and gives them food and shelter.[18]

By extension, humor becomes the marker of humanity in nonconformists. One of these is Mgr. Bienvenu, since he is a true Christian in the midst of provincial Catholics. When it deals with him, the style of the narrative goes back and forth from a mystic tone to such touches as "il faisait durer trop longtemps ses soutanes" [he made his cassocks last too long].[19] Greatness, virtue, and goodness are thus denoted by the description of socially unacceptable characteristics.[20] The same holds true in this monograph about a good king, Louis-Philippe:

> Il allait peu à la chapelle, point à la chasse, jamais à l'Opéra. Incorruptible aux sacristains, aux valets de chiens et aux danseuses. . . . Il sortait avec son parapluie sous son bras, et ce parapluie a longtemps fait partie de son auréole. Il . . . était un peu médecin; il saignait un postillon tombé de cheval; Louis-Philippe n'allait pas plus sans sa lancette que Henri III sans son poignard. Les royalistes raillaient ce roi ridicule, le premier qui ait versé le sang pour guérir.[21]
>
> [He seldom went to chapel, not at all to the chase, and never to the Opera. He could not be corrupted by sacristans, dog-keepers, and dancing girls. . . . He would go out with his umbrella under his arm, and for a long time that umbrella was part of his glory. He was . . . something of a doctor. He bled a postilion who had fallen from his horse. Louis-Philippe no more went without his lancet than Henri III without his dagger. The royalists scoffed at this ridiculous king, the first who spilled blood in order to heal.]

The narrative is conditioned by the humorous portrait of a character, and the sequence of events flows from it. The hero made humorous is, so to speak, negatively polarized. The narrative sequence that results from this polarization will therefore show how he evolves to a positive pole.

Thus, Marius in love is depicted in the early, naive stage of his passion in a caricatural manner, or in a manner that would be caricatural if the choice of funny details were not offset by a sympathetic warmth. From then on, little by little, Marius is made into a hero and Cosette is, little by little, made into an angel. Through this progressive elevation, the description of their love rises all the way to the heights of the quasi-allegorical scene of a mystical wedding night.[22]

Let us now consider the portrait of M. Mabeuf, a real nonentity of a character, a poor, insignificant fellow, whose foolishness is just barely redeemed by his passion for fine books and gardening, but who is nonetheless good, in a passive sort of way:

> Il allait à la messe plutôt par douceur que par dévotion, et puis parce qu'aimant le visage des hommes, mais haïssant leur bruit, il ne les trouvait qu' à l'église réunis et silencieux. Sentant qu'il fallait être quelque chose dans l'Etat, il avait choisi la carrière de marguillier. Du reste, il n'avait jamais réussi à aimer aucune femme autant qu'un oignon de tulipe ou aucun homme autant qu'un elzévir.[23]

> [He went to Mass more out of meekness than out of devotion, and then too, because he liked people's faces but hated their noise. Only in church did he find them gathered together and silent. Feeling he should fill some public function, he had chosen the career of a churchwarden. Furthermore, he had never succeeded in loving any woman as much as a tulip bulb, or any man as much as an Elzevir.]

So he is an innocent, albeit a rather selfish, sterile, and useless one. This negative polarization is confirmed by a proliferation of characters mirroring his emptiness, characters who are satellites of Mabeuf and no more than variants of the function that he embodies in the syntax of the narrative.

For just as it forms a unique paradigm from all the titles that it modifies, humor also establishes relationships of equivalence between separate objects and characters. M. Mabeuf's maid is thus described as follows:

> La pauvre bonne vieille femme était vierge. Sultan, son matou . . . avait rempli son coeur et suffisait à la quantité de passion qui était

en elle. Aucun de ses rêves n'était allé jusqu'à l'homme. Elle n'avait jamais pu franchir son chat. Elle avait, comme lui, des moustaches.[24]

[The poor, good, old woman was a virgin. Sultan, her tomcat . . . had filled her heart and was quite enough for the amount of passion that was in her. None of her dreams went so far as men. She had never managed to get beyond her cat. Like him, she had whiskers.]

The humor in this portrait is doubly negative. On the one hand, it reverses the cliché "servante au grand coeur" [maid with a big heart].[25] On the other, it repeats and parodies the first mention of shyness ("aucun de ses rêves n'était allé jusqu'à l'homme") in the form of "elle n'avait jamais pu franchir son chat." As with the *Jean Valjean/Fauchelevent* parallel, the impossibility of reading either of these expressions without comparing it to its homologue polarizes their stylistic opposition and reinforces the trope's effect. This negativization is increased by the fact that the theme, on the semantic level, of two creatures who love each other sharing everything in common (or its variant: two creatures who love each other end up looking alike—birds of a feather), is actualized lexically with the selection of a physical detail negating two essential semes of the word *woman* as understood in its positive sense (*beauty* and *feminity*): "elle avait, comme lui, des moustaches" [like him, she had whiskers].

Now this humorous rendering of M. Mabeuf's maid transforms her into one of his attributes—an attribute in the sense of an allegorical attribute; that is, a creature or object belonging to the allegorical figure (like Juno's peacock and the scales of Justice), which identifies that figure, and enables us to translate the allegory by going from the visual to the conceptual (from scales to *equity* or *fairness* and, by metonymy, to *justice*). The servant explains her master. Asexual or sexless, but without any tragedy, she becomes the confirmation, as it were, of the inveterate old bachelor she works for. Not only does she complement his very modest household, she complements and confirms his psychology as well. Humor thus implicitly expresses, at the stylistic level and via the detour of a portrait, something the text expresses explicitly as a conclusion: "Sa servante était, elle aussi, une variété de l'innocence" [His servent was also a variety of innocence].

If this formula, and in particular the word *variété*, were not enough to prove the validity of this reading, another character arrives at just the right moment, for the cat is the maid's attribute just as she herself is M. Mabeuf's. The tomcat does indeed immediately confirm the meaning of the secondary character as well as, by reflection, that of the Mabeuf character. For Sultan has been fixed and is therefore an asexual cat. Once again, the homology is indicated through humor. Instead of the word *coupé* [fixed], we are given its euphemistic expansion and comic conversion into "son matou, qui eût pu miauler le Miserere d'Allegri à la chapelle Sixtine" [her tomcat, which could have meowed Allegri's *Miserere* in the Sistine Chapel].[26]

Humor is the marker showing us that these three contiguous characters, who are metonymically related to one another, are three synonymous metaphors. All three are variants of a single structure, which can be defined as the transformation of a plus sign into a minus sign in the representation of life. Mabeuf, his maid, and her cat are three signs of *life* devoid of such essential semes as *love* (since it has no object) and *desire* (for it is sterile). Beginning with this polarization, the narrative builds a plot, the sole purpose of which is to transform Mabeuf, at all costs, into his opposite. The senile, selfish old man will die a hero out of love for humanity. The *vieux mouton* [(728), the old sheep] will be a sacrificial lamb. His story can be summarized as the passage from emptiness to moral plenitude, from a modest ivory tower to political commitment. Driven by poverty, he commits suicide by braving bullets on the barricades—a suicide calculated to arouse the insurgents. Humor is thus the starting point for a narrative deduction. From a negativized conception of man—old man Mabeuf—the narrative spotlights its positive variant, the hyperbolic concept of *Man*: Mabeuf the martyr.

If we were inclined to see so total a reversal of the character as rather implausible, it would only be all the more revealing, almost the definitive proof, of this function of narrative generation. The relations between humor and the sublime have often been brought to light, but only as they appear simultaneously.[27] It must, therefore, be stressed that with the narrative in novels simultaneity becomes succession, or rather it becomes the transformation of one into the other.

Because it gives assurance of the text's literariness, controls the reader's reactions, and denotes the author's presence, the humor in the titles and digressions is the signifier of intention—whatever that intention may be. Humor in the narrative, by contrast, has a specific orientation. In the particular case of *Les Misérables*, it defines the novel as the epic of a transfiguration of the small into the large, of evil into good, and of a mere character into a hero—just as the Freudian theory of humor would have it. This humor lets us observe, on the verbal level, the way in which semantic structures—here, everything pertaining to Hugo's idealism—on the level of the signifiers and the text, govern the production of the narrative.

[11]

The Poem as Representation: A Reading of Hugo

WHAT IS meant by representation, and in what sense can we speak of description or depiction in a literary text? What is the relationship between mimesis and literariness? Ever since Auerbach, the answers to these questions have been sought above all by studying Realism, and especially realism in the novel. This is quite natural, since one of the criteria of the novel's aesthetic is authenticity, the ability to create the illusion of truth (and, in the case of realism, a truth within the reach of everyone and verifiable in everyday experience). Poetry has been neglected, no doubt because its aesthetic calls for a transmutation—a sublimation or a simple gap in expression. Besides, the alteration of the referential function that is characteristic of all literary expression is more easily demonstrated in poetry than in prose.[1]

Nevertheless readers, and traditional criticism as well, instinctively apply the same criteria to poetic utterances as they apply to normal communication acts, to the utilitarian use of language. They compare poems to reality. They speak of truth, as in the case of mimesis in novels, and of resemblance and striking accuracy, or else they speak of inaccuracy of expression, vagueness in description, the boldness or obscurity of an image, and fantasy. Their reaction to a poem swings back and forth between an account of its faithfulness to reality and an account of its infidelity. Value judgments are based on those assessments according to the reigning aesthetic of the day. At one moment a feature is admired for its faithfulness, and at another, that same feature is seen as nothing but a sterile copy. The same holds true where unfaithful representations are concerned. But whether an unfaithful representation is seen as the free play of fantasy or as imagination run wild, both schools of thought would see it as a case of the text disturbing reality[2] or going beyond the possible, which is analogous to the real. So, whatever the interpretation may be, things are always presumed to be the touchstones of words. The entire thrust of philology has been to reconstruct realities that have disappeared, for fear that poems would die along with their reference.

At first glance, the validity of resorting to reality would seem to be indisputable if the text in question is "figurative"—that is, if it expressly presents itself as a description. And likewise where visual images are concerned: if an image is a partial representation, as in metonymy or synecdoche, the reader must be capable of completing it from a single detail, and he can do so only if there is a consensus about the form of the things alluded to. If the image is a double representation, as in a simile or metaphor, a resemblance must be perceptible between the image's tenor and its vehicle.

All these good reasons notwithstanding, the comparison of a poem to reality is a critical approach of doubtful value: it leads to irrelevant conclusions, for it either falls short of the text or goes beyond it. Nonetheless, even if resorting to reality is simply an inexcusable rationalization on the part of the critic, that very rationalization is one of the modalities of the relation between text and reader that constitutes the literary phenomenon. It must, therefore, be explained.

I shall take my examples from one entire poem and several excerpts from Victor Hugo. They are comparable, for they are variants of a single thematic structure.[3] (In this case, it is one of the structures organizing the theme of time.) The poem is "Ecrit sur la vitre d'une fenêtre flamande" [Written on the pane of a Flemish window]:[4]

J'aime le carillon de tes cités antiques,
O vieux pays gardien de tes moeurs domestiques,

Noble Flandre, où le Nord se réchauffe engourdi
Au soleil de Castille et s'accouple au Midi!
5 Le carillon, c'est l'heure inattendue et folle,
Que l'oeil croit voir, vêtue en danseuse espagnole,
Apparaître soudain par le trou vif et clair
Que ferait en s'ouvrant une porte de l'air.
Elle vient, secouant sur les toits léthargiques
10 Son tablier d'argent plein de notes magiques,
Réveillant sans pitié les dormeurs ennuyeux,
Sautant à petits pas comme un oiseau joyeux,
Vibrant, ainsi qu'un dard qui tremble dans la cible;
Par un frêle escalier de cristal invisible,
15 Effarée et dansante, elle descend des cieux;
Et l'esprit, ce veilleur fait d'oreilles et d'yeux,
Tandis qu'elle va, vient, monte et descende encore,
Entend de marche en marche errer son pied sonore!

[I love the carillon of your ancient towns, o old land, keeper of your domestic customs. O noble Flanders, where the benumbed North warms itself in the sun of Castille and mates with the South! The carillon is the unexpected and mad hour that the eye thinks it sees, dressed as a Spanish dancer, appearing suddenly through the keen, bright hole made by a door of air as it opens. She comes, shaking over the lethargic rooftops her silver apron, full of magical notes, pitilessly waking the wearisome sleepers, taking little jumps, like a merry bird, quivering like a spear trembling in its target. By a fragile stairway of invisible crystal, alarmed and dancing, she descends from the heavens. And as she goes and comes and climbs up and down again, the mind, that watchman made of ears and eyes, hears her resonant foot wandering from step to step.]

A reference to the date and place of composition at the bottom of the text presents the poem as the expression in verse of a travel memory, as the description of something seen and heard. Without exception, all Hugo specialists analyze the poem in relation to reality. They are all in agreement concerning the art with which Hugo was able to turn auditory sensations into visual sensations and to superimpose two different orders of reality. They all admire him for having the imagination to personify the hourly chimes—that is, once again, to describe one reality with another, to describe the inanimate with the animate.[5] Furthermore, they measure his imagination in terms of the distance separating common sense (the thing seen) from poetic representation (the thing "envisioned"), which arises from fragments of the real. We are told that the poem is a perfect example of those "personifications dictated by the poet's fancy, which seizes on a movement, attitude, or formal resemblance in order to create a myth around them, the graceful inspiration of which has a fairy-tale quality."[6] This reasoning, unfortunately, takes us outside the text, since it calls on events in the genesis of the text. In the same way, the commentators attempt to explain the poem by comparing it to the various circumstances in which Hugo had occasion to hear bells chiming the hour in Flanders. But the circumstances of a text's composition could never explain our reactions to that text in its final form. All that matters to us is what is encoded. For external reality is not poetic, but the manner in which it is described and "seen" with words is. The poem is not a destination; it is a starting point. To assume that we must be familiar with other descriptions of the same reality in order to read a descriptive poem correctly is tantamount to assuming that that poem is a failure, since it is incapable of making us see on its own.

As for the transposition from the auditory to the visual, it is indeed a textual phenomenon, one that is entirely encoded in the text. It is, therefore, pertinent to our analysis. Nonetheless, instead of determining how it is encoded in this particular case, critics think only of reducing the phenomenon to a general category. (They classify it among the correspondences and compare it, for example, to "Que la musique date du XVIe siècle" [That music dates from the sixteenth century], which is also part of *Les Rayons et les ombres*.) Then they reconstruct the author's psychology from this generalization, which means that they again leave the poem behind. "This visual transposition of an auditory impression is not surprising in Hugo, whose visual sense is infinitely more developed than his auditory sense strictly speaking. He makes up for this weakness, which he shares with the other French poets of the first two-thirds of the nineteenth century, with a dazzling orgy of imagination," writes Jean-Bertrand Barrère,[7] repeating, with only slight differences, the conclusions drawn by Edmond Huguet concerning all of Hugo's literary production.[8] Even if such characterizations were related to the text, instead of a portrait of the author being deduced from them, they could never be more than the least common denominator of countless stylistic phenomena. They do not inform us about the different functions they fill in the texts in which they appear. They tell us nothing about what gives the poem its unique character; its personality, so to speak. This specificity can be achieved only by describing the verbal combinations that capture the reader's attention and control his decoding of the poem. These combinations are so complex that in every individual case the combination will always be unique—the characteristic form of one and only one poem.

If an analysis is to discover this unique characteristic, it should be based on the fact that the text is a point of departure. Reversing the traditional direction of analyses going from the thing represented to its representation, the analysis should show how the representation creates the thing represented and makes it verisimilar—that is, recognizable and satisfying to the reader. It should show that the reader has no need to refer to his own experience of reality (which may be an inadequate one), because all he needs in order to understand and see is to refer to a linguistic code. (His experience of that code is adequate by definition; if it were not, he would not be a reader.)

I would like, therefore, to propose a reading that is concerned only with the words and their possible collocations, and that shows how they are mutually "triggered" one after the other, resulting in a mimesis that is convincing because each of its components is strongly "motivated" by the combination of verbal sequences that precedes it. This reading will not provide a study of textual genesis: the author and the circumstances of composition will not be invoked. Nor shall I attempt to discover the order in which the poem was written or the modifications it was made to undergo. I am concerned only with observing how the sentences seem, as they are deciphered, to have been generated inevitably. I am concerned with seeing how the utterance, far from being modeled on a nonverbal object, submits to the imperatives of semantic and formal associations among words. These associations severely limit the options offered at each point of the utterance to the further development of the sentence. They are stereotyped and recognizable when read: the description is not true in relation to the geography and sociology of northern France, but rather because it conforms to a mythology that the reader carries within him, a mythology composed of clichés and commonplaces. The poem is poetic not because of a kind of exoticism inherent in Flemish nights, but because of its symbolism, which is the result of the actualization of a thematic structure that is itself combined with lexical structures. The representation is effective not because it is a good "likeness" but because, with every word overdetermined by the combination of structures and perceived in relation to their pre-established models, everything happens as if the sign's arbitrariness had been nullified.

Indeed, everything in the poem stems from the chains of words triggered by *carillon* in the first line. *Carillon* denotes a ringing of bells,[9] a joyous ringing—"L'heure en prenant son vol rit dans les carillons" [The hour, while taking flight, laughs in the carillons].[10] This is because it is defined semantically in opposition to *glas* [knell] and *tocsin*. Its ringing, with its variations and melody, is in contrast to the regularity of a knell or tocsin. It is a sonorous fantasy. The allegorical representation of the carillon results from the convergence between these semes (musicality, merriness, fantasy) and the fact that the word *heure*, which is metonymically related to *carillon*, is a feminine word, as well as the fact that the Hours are conventionally allegorized as young goddesses. The music of the carillon thus becomes that of a *danse de l'Heure*, first because the carillon is a dancing of bells, but above all because the motif of the *ballet des heures* is already a commonplace in the mimesis of Time. (We might recall that "Le Ballet des heures" was the first title of Gérard de Nerval's "Artémis.")[11] This motif itself arises from two transpositions: the transposition of the grammatical feminine into mythological femininity and the transposition of the roundness of the clock's face into the *ronde* danced by the personified Hours. This last transposition is all the more necessary and "true" in that the circle dance is a descriptive stereotype of feminine mythological characters who lack individual identities (like the nymphs), or who appear only as a group (like the Graces). Hugo himself gives us an example of this in a little exercise on the theme "Midi, roi des étés" [Noon, king of summers]: "Les heures, groupe las, ne dansent plus en rond" [The hours, a weary group, no longer dance in their ring].[12] The deviation from a woman dancing a round to simply a woman dancing and her particularization as a Spanish dancer, a *danseuse espagnole*, are dependent on the setting, whose Castilian influence is expressly emphasized in the first lines.[13]

Musical mimesis abounds in metaphors such as *gamme descendante* [descending scale] (which has itself generated a metaphor of moral or physical decline), and *monter la gamme* [to go up the scale].[14] The staircase image is thus a transformation of *scale*—and judging from other texts, it was bound to be generated. For example, the image appears, in a still embryonic stage of development and metonymically suggested by two verbs of motion, in this sentence of Hugo's: "la riche gamme qui descend et remonte sans cesse les sept cloches de Saint-Eustache" [the rich scale ceaselessly climbing up and down the seven bells of St. Eustache].[15] The image appears completely developed, even including a character generated by the verbs of motion, in the following passage in which the deaf hunchback, Quasimodo, is watching "l'octave palpitante monter et descendre sur cette échelle sonore comme un oiseau qui saute de branche en branche" [the quivering octave climb up and down this sonorous scale like a bird hopping from branch to branch].[16] The metaphoric structure of this image is identical to that of the one in our poem:

> . . . l'esprit, ce veilleur fait d'oreilles et d'yeux,
> Tandis qu'elle va, vient, monte et descend encore,
> Entend de marche en marche errer son pied sonore!

The bird and the dancer are interchangeable, and so are their associative systems: if we replace *oiseau* with *danseuse*, we must also replace *branche* with *marche* [step]. The content of the lexical slots of the syntagm changes according to the associative system. The syntagm remains intact, however, for its geometry of syntactic relations corresponds to the geometry of semantic relations postulated by the reduction of *carillon* to its "scale" seme. The verbs *monter* and *descendre* correspond to that seme. They are inseparably united so as to represent, in terms of motion, the totality of the semantic structure of "diatonic scale" (an up-and-down movement). The verbs inevitably generate a subject (the *bird* or *dancing girl* character), as well as predicate complements (the character's setting: *branche* or *marche*). These unchanged functions assure the synonymy of the lexical variants actualizing them. (Whether, for instance, the metaphoric vehicle is *branche* or *marche* in the *X* slot of the construction *de X en X*, the "scale" context indicates that it will correspond to the tenor *musical note*.) What is convincing about the image, and what causes the reader to accept it, is simply the irresistible nature of its verbal "logic." It is nothing other than a sentence unfolding the semantic potentials of an initial word over the length of the text.

As we have just seen, two of these potentials are the *musicality* and *cheerfulness* semes. Their generative capacity is itself oriented, or channeled, by the fact that *carillon* is merely the metonymic vehicle of a tenor that has its own potentials: the Hour. In order to perceive the effect of *carillon*, there is no need to have heard bells chiming, much less to be familiar with the particular case, in certain regions, of carillon melodies played before the striking of the hour. All we need is to be familiar with the code—that is, *carillon*'s semes and how they are valorized. One might raise the objection that the word's independence from things is well nigh unimaginable in this case, since the sound of bells is a fact of everyday experience. But that experience varies with readers, and its perception is dependent on their moods and habits.[17] By contrast, verbal stereotypes involving signifiers grouped around *cloche* [bell] are shared by everyone and hardly vary at all. We need only reflect on more limited experiences to realize to what extent knowledge of reality is simply an illusion where our understanding of words is concerned. A person who has never kept watch at the bedside of someone dying is still sensitive to the evocative power of the word *râle* [death rattle].[18] No experience of an African night is required for us to grasp *rire d'hyène* [hyenalike laughter] in its full force. *D'hyène* is simply perceived as the superlative of one particular sense and negative valorization of *rire*, because it adds a seme of animality to laughter and, above all, because it contaminates *rire* with the strange morphology of *hyène* in relation to the French lexicon. The *hyène* is wild and ferocious for the same reason that the *pterodactyl* is monstrous and prehistoric—to begin with, because of its spelling. Similarly, *carillon flamand* [Flemish carillon] (and *carillon* in the context of the first three lines of our poem) means "Belgian bells" only secondarily: its primary meaning and its function in context is that of a laudatory superlative. On the level of the words, the adjective *flamand* does not situate *carillon* geographically. It hyperbolizes it, just as *pourpre de Tyre* [Tyrian purple] does not solely mean purple imported from Phoenecia, but also the purplest of purples; and just as *tigresse d'Hyrcanie* [Hyrcanian tigress] does not denote a geographically (and historically) limited species (except to lexicographers) but rather, in literary representation from Vergil to Racine, is the hyperbole of feminine cruelty and of aggressively protective motherhood; and just as *froid polaire* [polar cold] is closer to *froid de canard* [freezing cold; literally: duck's cold] than it is to the North or South Pole. There are two reasons for this. The first is a general stylistic law, which I shall formulate as follows: any particularization of a signifier in relation to the other members of a paradigm of synonyms will function, on the syntagmatic axis, as the hyperbole of its metaphoric signified (its tenor).[19] The second is the law of possible collocations: *carillon* acquires its positive valorization from its sterotyped use in contexts in which things Flemish are symbolic of certain virtues.[20] This is because words associated with *Flanders* and the *Netherlands* are usually meliorative in modern French mythology.[21]

Carillon generates a descriptive system consisting of words such as *vibrations sonores* [sonorous vibrations][22] and clichés like *sons argentins* [silvery sounds] and *sonorités cristallines* [crystal-clear tones].[23] Now, the adjectives *argentin* and *cristallin* (or the prepositional phrases *d'argent* and *de cristal*) allow for a positive valorization, since they presuppose a comparison with lofty signifieds in "metal" and "mineral" codes.[24] This is why they are selected by *carillon*'s joyful connotations, as in the following prose passage from Hugo: "un ravissant carillon . . . un carillon fin, léger, cristallin, fantastique, aérien" [a ravishingly beautiful carillon . . . a fine, light, crystal-clear, fantastic, airy carillon], and also: "sonneries . . . ailées, légères et sifflantes de la cloche d'argent" [light, whistling, winged chimes of the silver bell].[25] If the ringing were a tocsin summoning men to arms, the bell's sound would be *bronze* (*de bronze* or *d'airain*), since that is the metal of which poetic weapons are made.[26] If the bell were ringing in the belltower of a village church, it would be *enroué* [hoarse] like the throat of a yokel.[27] If the bell were one of the altogether prosaic variety found on a bourgeois garden gate, then lowly *iron* would do. (Proust lets us hear his little bell "qui étourdissait au passage de son bruit ferrugineux, intarissable et glacé" [which assailed and deafened with its ferruginous, interminable, frozen sound (anyone) who set it off].)[28] But what we have here is a *carillon*, and so, the stairway of a music-hall stage concretizing the rising and falling scale becomes a "frêle escalier de cristal invisible."

The adjectives modifying *escalier* and *cristal* are as rigorously conditioned as the main points of the utterance. In accordance with the rule of stock epithets, whereby such an adjective explicitly repeats a characteristic already implicit in the noun, the staircase is *frêle*, just as Odysseus is resourceful, the sea deep, and streams swift—because *cristal* connotes fragility. Likewise, the crystal is invisible because, in this context, invisibility is the hyperbolic expression of crystal's perfect transparence. (In a different context, that transparence might express the idea of purity in a "mineral" code, but here all it does is confirm and emphasize the crystallineness of the crystal.)

Invisible also functions as an explanation of the vision's imaginary character.[29] It cancels out the visibility seme suggested by all signifiers in an architectural descriptive system.[30] This cancellation phenomenon is the exact reverse of the rule for stock epithets, and is in no way limited to the representation of the imaginary. It is an oxymoron, like *bittersweet* or *black sun. Porte de l'air* [door of air] is another such example. The combination of height (the steeple that the sound is coming from), architecture (resulting from "scale"), and the imaginary causes *porte* to generate *de l'air.* In this way, the metaphoric interpretation of *porte* is assured, since all of *air*'s semes weigh against the semes belonging to the *door* system. Everything airy, breathlike, and mobile excludes the earthbound, mineral motionlessness of architecture.[31]

Critics have always associated stock epithets with the antithetical epithets cultivated by certain literary schools—wrongly so, I believe. We should see them, instead, as two different manifestations of a rule governing the development of descriptive sentences in poetry. After a noun, a descriptive sentence must choose between two opposing semantic extremes.[32] The noun generates an adjective (or adjectival phrase) that is either tautological (as I have just indicated concerning stock epithets) or oxymoronic. (In this case, the adjective cancels out some, if not all, of the noun's semes, and does not spell them out as the tautologically generated adjective does.)

The resulting valorization of the connotations of *carillon* applies to the character as well as to her setting. This is to say that the adjectives *inattendue et folle* [unexpected and mad] have a role analogous to that of *invisible.* They realize metaphorically certain of *carillon*'s semes, specifically the melody's whimsicality and the disconcerting quality of that whimsicality. The comparison with a bird, which reinforces *danseuse* as a representation of the musical scale,[33] also contributes to the valorization. This function is indicated by the fact that it tautologically generates *joyeux.* (Here again the reference is verbal: a real bird is neither happy nor sad, but a represented bird is associated with *song* and *spring*, which are metonyms of *joy*, and it partakes in the conventional innocence of all bucolic mimeses—provided, of course, that it is a little bird, and not a bird of prey.)[34] With both the setting and the character stemming from *carillon*, the separation between the "architecture" code and the "dancing girl" code is not absolute. Indeed, the two codes overlap and intrude on each other. *Vif* in *trou vif et clair* belongs more to the "dancer" series. In that series, it represents a seme of musical fantasy and consequently reinforces *soudain*, which had been generated by *inattendue*. On the other hand, *porte* generates the notion of brightness, for a door must be either open or closed and, if it is open, it must be open onto either light or darkness. Now, in this context, only light is positive, so *clair* is selected. The two sequences thus converge on each other, for there is a cliché *lumière (clarté) vive* [bright light] in which *vif*, which corresponds to the *brightness* or *radiance* seme, is just as meliorative as when it corresponds to *vivacité* [liveliness].[35] Valorization is thus overdetermined by two different codes at once.

Now let us consider the representation of the dancer. This character constitutes a subsystem that the text gives to us only in fragments: its structure is nothing other than what might be called the grammar of the allegory's signifiers. The personified Hour forms the vehicle for a carillon metaphor. Consequently, the words expressing tone, vibrations, musical notes, and the like, which in a literal description would be related only grammatically, here are arranged in accordance with the allegorical character's anatomy: her limbs, body movements, and costume furnish the vocabulary and limit the syntactic possibilities. The divergences from the model are as meaningful as the words themselves: if the verbs of alternating movement correspond to "scale," their accumulation (*va, vient*; *monte et descend encore*; *errer*) once again express "fantasy." *Vibrer* is overdetermined by belonging both to the character's system (nervous vibration) and to the carillon system. The substitution of the vehicle's context for that of the tenor is all that is needed to express the metaphor. The comparison stemming from *vibrer* is a cliché ("comme une flèche dans la cible" [like an arrow in its target]),[36] and, therefore, has as great a hold on the imagination as if it had been generated tautologically. The cliché is transposed into lofty style,[37] and thus continues the sequence of positive valorization.

Now, one amusing detail in this allegory cannot be fully explained either by the metaphorical code or by the imperatives of the *danseuse espagnole* subsystem:

> Elle vient, secouant sur les toits léthargiques
> Son tablier d'argent plein de notes magiques,
> Réveillant sans pitié les dormeurs ennuyeux.

[She comes, shaking out over the lethargic rooftops her silver apron full of magical notes, and pitilessly waking the wearisome sleepers.]

One might see this as nothing more than the visual transposition of a psychological duality: North and South coexist in the Flemish temperament, so there is an inner tension between its phlegmatic nature and its passionate tendencies. This, of course, refers to a mythology, but to a mythology that is already encoded in clichés organized into a narrative or descriptive model. Balzac did no more than realize this same narrative potential when he presented Balthasar Claës as married to a sensual[38] descendant of a line of Spanish grandees. This commonplace is expressed, however, in the first lines of the poem, and it is interpreted there as the harmonious union of two complementary principles ("le Nord se réchauffe engourdi / Au soleil de Castille et s'accouple au Midi"). We are still far from the nasty trick played on the sleepers. Moreover, the choice of a silver apron, the *tablier d'argent*, does not seem as effective for expressing resonant vibrations as silver heels or even silver castanets might have been. Lastly, there is no convergence between the system of the tenor and that of the vehicle that would make the word *argent* necessary and appropriate. Such a convergence can be observed in Proust, though. In describing the little phrase in Vinteuil's sonata, Proust uses none other than the equivalence *silver* = "pleasant sound." He, too, resorts to a dancing girl allegory, but his *danseuse* is "harnachée d'argent, toute ruisselante de sonorités brillantes, légères et douces" [arrayed in silver, glittering with brillant sonorities, light and soft].[39] The adjective *harnachée* [literally: harnessed; rigged out] is overdetermined, for it belongs as much to the descriptive system of a woman in a ball gown (we might recall that the Duchesse de Guermantes is described as being "en cheval de corbillard" [dressed like a funeral horse]), as it does to the descriptive system of bells jingling on a horse's harness.

Overdetermination is not absent from Hugo's poem, however; it just works differently than in Proust. Indeed, the anomaly—of the *apron* as well as of the prank performed with its help—can be explained if we see it as the variant of a structure that is no longer that of a descriptive system and no longer on the level of the lexicon. Instead, it is a thematic structure. Its invariant corresponds to a recurrent symbol in other poems.

If *tablier* was generated by the character's descriptive model, it is because the *notes magiques* are not described as sounds, but rather as tangible, even heavy, things that can be thrown at people's heads in order to wake them up. *Tablier*, therefore, is just the right word: in stereotypical descriptions of women, an *apron* which is pulled up and knotted is used as a pocket for holding things like flowers or fruit.[40] She then shakes it if she wants to drop whatever she is carrying. Here, what she is carrying is noise. It makes for a cruel joke, but one that is well deserved by the sleepers stagnating in their province, for they are *ennuyeux* [wearisome; boring]. The sleep that invades the whole scene (*toits léthargiques*) symbolizes the mind's stagnation, since it is quite literally a waste of time and of life. Indeed, this sudden awakening is nothing other than a humorous version of Horace's *carpe diem* or of Baudelaire's *esto memor.*

This interpretation may seem a bit far-fetched. One might think that the poem simply actualizes a cliché from the mimesis of insomnia—the opposition *sleeper/repeated noise*, with the sleeper's determination to sleep matched only by the noise's determination to wake him up.[41] The comic potential of the rude awakening is obvious; and all the more so if the heaviness of the sleep is pushed toward caricature, which is what happens if the person sleeping is Flemish, for Flemish heaviness is a commonplace. Hugo explicitly refers to precisely that commonplace in his prose commentary on the first impressions that inspired "Ecrit sur la vitre."

But of the original bells, his travel memories have retained only the musical impression: "Ce carillon me faisait l'effet de chanter à cette ville de magots flamands je ne sais quelle chanson chinoise; puis il se taisait et l'heure sonnait gravement" [That carillon seemed to me to be singing some strange Chinese song to that city of Flemish apes; then it would quiet down and the hour would ring out gravely].[42] And the slumbering Belgians (the town in question is Mons) go on slumbering. The chiming of the carillon and the striking of the hour are clearly separate, even in their style: the ambiguity of *gravement* totally removes this "real" hour from the Hour represented in the poem. The deviation of the poetic mimesis from the "realistic" mimesis reveals the presence of the thematic structure. If the hour is mocking and pitiless, *sans pitié*, and if it lets out sounds that are less musical notes than they are comic projectiles, it is because the *carillon* in the text is not the Mons carillon, which has a distinct kind of ringing that accompanies the clock as it strikes the hour. This difference is eliminated by the *carillon* in the poem. That *carillon* is simply the stylistic hyperbole of *hour* (being rung), which is, itself, simply a metonymic representation of Time.

Indeed, the passage of Time can be indirectly represented by the decay of everything it touches: men, their monuments, their loves. If it is represented directly, however, its irresistible advance will be symbolized by the movements or moving parts of the instruments used to measure it: the flow of the sand in an hourglass and of water in a clepsydra, the path traced by the hands of a clock, with variations such as a clock's tick-tock evoking the minutes marching implacably on, [43] the sound of a pendulum beating time to the approach of death, and a ringing announcing to us that another moment has been wasted forever. Hugo's clock far outdoes these other symbols. Its descriptive system is confined to signifiers corresponding literally, metaphorically, or metonymically to the signifieds "hour," "ringing," "clockface," and "hands of a clock." The ravages of Time are represented by characters directly affected by its passage: they are either spectators (they see the face of the clock), or auditors (they listen to the bell striking the hour). Their relationsip with the clock is thus indicated by verbs of perception.

This *clock* lexicon is distributed in accordance with the spatial coordinates of the usual representation of the thing called a clock. But this distribution is modified, indeed disturbed, by the thematic structure defining the relation between Time and human beings as a relation between an executioner and his victim. Victims are characterized by their position of inferiority, which is the lot of the defeated, the oppressed, and the injured: our characters see or hear from beneath the clock that overpowers them—a clock atop a steeple, for example.[44] This *superiority/inferiority* relationship is combined with a note of mobility (*tempus fugit*), a mobility that, as a consequence, is manifested along a vertical axis and is oriented from above to below.

The structural relationship thus generates a meaning that could not have been produced by the development of the clock lexicon alone: Time is a sword suspended over our heads, and its passage is a blow struck from above. On the horizontal plane, the regularity of this motion and of the successive stages of the hours and minutes represents nothing other than itself. Once it is transposed onto the vertical plane, though, it signifies the implacability of an inescapable threat. The mobility is not, therefore, defined in opposition to motionlessness. Instead, by hyperbolizing the *superiority/inferiority* polarization, it gives that polarization the affective value of *conqueror/conquered*.

The variants that actualize the structure express these relations in styles ranging from one extreme to the other on the scale of possible tones. Depending on the metaphoric vehicle, the style can be one of personal lyricism, as much a mimesis of Romantic pessimism as a description of a carillon:

> *De moments en moments*, ce *noir* passant ailé,
> Le temps, ce *sourd tonnerre* à nos rumeurs mêlé,
> D'où les heures s'en vont en sombres étincelles,
> *Ebranlait sur mon front* le beffroi de Bruxelles.[45]

[*From one moment to the next*, that *black*, winged passerby, Time, that *muted thunder* mixed in with our rumblings and from which the hours go off in dark sparks, *over my forehead shook* the Brussels belfry.]

This text is literally a representation of a carillon in *knell* or *tocsin* code. Or we can have melancholy lines such as these:

> Nous entendons sur nous les heures, goutte à goutte,
> Tomber comme l'eau sur les plombs.[46]

[We hear the hours falling on us, drop after drop, like water on the gutters.]

The following passage would seem to be the humorous, or even burlesque, version of the previous one. In it Hugo, who is speaking to mankind (*vos*), describes the clock of life:

> L'aiguille du cadran, lourd cheval hébété,
> Qui tourne, puisant l'heure au puits éternité
> Et qui la vide en bruit sur vos têtes fragiles.[47]

[The hand on the clockface, a heavy, dazed horse that goes round and round, drawing the hour from the well eternity, and that empties it as noise out over your fragile heads.]

The parallelism between these lines and those in "Ecrit sur la vitre . . ." cannot be missed. Indeed, it illuminates the latter. Just as before, Time uses its superiority to unfair advantage, and the hand of the clock plays a trick comparable to the one in which the Spanish dancer had indulged. The joke is even cruder, but the analogy is obvious—the pail is to the well what the apron is to the dancer.

Cheval is generated by *aiguille* as rigorously as was *danseuse* by *carillon*. Imagination is no freer and the invention is in no way more gratuitous. The hand of the clock is captive to the face on which it turns, and this mechanical and circular motion contains a pejorative potential (a potential that can be felt even in the familiar cliché *tourner en rond* [to go round in circles]). It is activated by the negative coloration[48] that the context gives to Time: it is nothingness in the eyes of Eternity. Hence the transposition—always an easy one—of the "mechanical" seme into *hébété* [dazed]. The deadening circular motion becomes a horse-driven mill where the beast of burden turns a machine symbolizing its servitude.[49] At this point, the utterance could branch off in the direction of the millstone or in that of the water wheel. The choice of this second possibility was determined by three factors. First, Hugo's idiolect sets up a semantic equivalence between the synonyms of *infini* [infinity] and those of *puits* [well]. *Puits* may simply be a substitute for *abîme* [abyss] and nothing else, but if the systems of the tenor and the vehicle are in harmony, the word can generate a highly "realistic" representation of a well from which water is drawn. (For example: "Qu'est-ce que ton anneau, Saturne? / Est-ce que . . . / Quelque vaste archange puni . . . / Fait tourner sur cette poulie / La chaîne du puits infini?" [What is your ring, Saturn? Does some vast, punished archangel make the chain of the infinite well turn round on this pully?]).[50] Second, Hugo solves the problem of sound mimesis by describing music as a liquid pouring out over the audience: the bell is a "vase plein de rumeur qui se vide dans l'air" [vase full of noise that empties out into the air].[51] And third, the structure defined above organizes these elements, which are already converging on one another, in a "slapstick" code.[52]

I shall cite yet another variant, because the incompatibility between its descriptive and thematic structures is particularly striking. Its style is that of metaphysical lyricism, and the metaphor is extended at greater length than in the previous passages. The descriptive system of the clock and our thematic structure are easy to spot in it, though:

> En tombant sur nos fronts, la minute nous tue. . . .
> Nous montons à l'assaut du temps comme une armée.
> Sur nos groupes confus que voile la fumée
> Des jours évanouis
> L'énorme éternité luit, splendide et stagnante;
> Le cadran, bouclier de l'heure rayonnante,
> Nous terrasse éblouis![53]

[As it falls on our foreheads, the minute kills us. . . . We storm time like an army. Above our confused groups which are veiled by the smoke of vanished days, eternity shines, splendid and stagnant. The clockface, the shield of the radiant hour, strikes us down, bedazzled!]

The *clock* system is translated by the metaphor into a battle code: Time inflicts a military defeat on man. Thus we have a transposition into lofty style: the shower of noise becomes a rain of death, and the minutes burrow deeper into the wounds, drop by drop. The overlapping of the structures is evident in *bouclier*. As a metaphor for the clock, it is clearly generated by the convergence of its round shape with the roundness of the clock's shape. This formal resemblance is, however, not a reference to things, but to stereotyped signifiers. For example, in his *Epithètes françaises* (1759), the Père Daire recognizes only one stock epithet for *bouclier* and *cadran*: the adjective *rond* [round].[54] Nevertheless, the similarity would no doubt be insufficient to impose the metaphor when other, far more tempting, equivalents exist, such as the one between the minute hand and a lance[55]—especially since the description must violate verisimilitude when it turns a defensive weapon into an offensive one. Now, this deviation from associative probabilities corresponds to the thematic structure: Time is in a position of absolute superiority and its victims in one of absolute inferiority. An evenly matched duel is totally out of the question. Hence the irresistible crushing of and contempt for the adversary implied by the use of a defensive weapon to strike him down. It is again the structure that calls for the motion of the shield to be a falling one. That motion is contrary to the reality of the thing, but it conforms to the structural relation. It is, therefore, synonymous with Time "poured out" in the other poems and with the deadly fall of the minutes in this context. This same anomaly activates a mythologeme in the reader's memory that confirms the interpretation and strengthens the image's effect. This shield is modeled after a prototype: the shields used by the Sabines to crush an enemy who, as a weak woman and a traitor, was doubly worthy of contempt—the vestal Tarpeia.[56]

Three conclusions would seem to follow from this. First, the effectiveness of poetic mimesis has nothing to do with a relationship of appropriateness between signs and things. The analyst should not, therefore, compare the text to reality. Instead, he should replace the criteria of truth and resemblance with the criterion of overdetermination. For every word or phrase, there is overdetermination whenever the possible verbal sequences are restricted by the combined rules of three structures—the linguistic code, the thematic structure, and the structure of the descriptive system.

The rule of the linguistic code needs no comment. However, the way in which the thematic structure is perceived and identified by the reader lets us arrive at a second conclusion. The thematic structure is perceived because of the functional anomalies provoked by its presence in a context.[57] Since the context is generated by one or more descriptive systems, the mechanism of the anomaly is an *interference between structures.* This definition applies to the majority of those phenomena that are usually defined as cases of ungrammaticality. We can speak of ungrammaticality, however, only if we first determine what the pertinent norm is. The notion of overlapping or interference allows us to avoid these hypotheses: since it gives both the rule and its violation, the context, by definition, is pertinent. The shield example shows that interference makes it possible to measure objectively the "boldness" of an image and explain a representation's obscurity by determining which structures are conflicting—without ever abandoning the tangible evidence of the text.

My third conclusion has to do with what I have called a *descriptive system.*[58] Regulating the distribution and functions of its components, it enables us to imagine those components that are not realized in the text by looking at those that are.

Each component can represent and can be substituted for the entire system. (For example, *carillon* is enough to evoke the "clock" system on its own.) This substitutive ability is not altered by the use of the system as a metaphoric code (*carillon* = *tempus fugit*). The components are, as it were, prefabricated syntagms—

that is, syntagms whose lexical slots have already been filled.[59] Once one word in the system has been provided, the words that it generates have a very high likelihood of occurrence. It is further increased by the restrictions on choice that are imposed by the valorization. If the text conforms to this probability (as in a tautological sequence, for instance), it corresponds to the reader's expectations, and the representation is verisimilar and even typical, or rather exemplary. If the text does not conform to this probability (as in an oxymoronic sequence), the representation appears to be fraught with meaning.[60]

In both of these cases, the text is not simply discovered as it is read. It is *recognized*, and it is compared to the stereotyped sentences it reproduces or transforms. The entire mimesis is thus perceived not in relation to referents or signifieds, but rather in relation to verbal forms, to words that are already arranged in texts. Of course, the ideal model for the system as a whole is indeed a signified. But everything happens as if the signified existed in our minds only as groups of signifiers or as ready-made sequences. If the word triggering the system's development were to be replaced by a synonym, that synonym would generate a different model. *Cellule* [cell], unlike *cachot* [dungeon cell], would not generate sequences such as "gémir (pourrir, méditer) sur la paille humide" [to moan (rot, meditate) on the damp straw], or *cruche* [pitcher] and *pain noir* [black bread]. This is because a word's generative power is due, above all, to its stylistic characteristics.

And finally, let us consider the phenomenon of valorization, which replaces the vertical axis of normal signification with the horizontal axis of signification in relation to the word that triggered the whole system. Thus, the adjective *invisible* does not signify a quality of crystal, but rather indicates that the word *cristal* is a hyperbole and a metaphor (required by the symbolism of *carillon*). And by the same token, the three adjectives in *tablier d'argent*, *notes magiques*, and *oiseaux joyeux* refer, in fact, to the carillon. Literary description of reality only gives the appearance of referring to things and signifieds. In point of fact, poetic representation is founded on a reference to signifiers.

[12]

The Extended Metaphor in Surrealist Poetry

SURREALIST IMAGES are, for the most part, obscure and disconcerting—even absurd. Critics are too often content merely to note the existence of this obscurity or to explain it in terms of subconscious inspiration or some other factor outside the poem. It would seem, however, that many of these images appear obscure and gratuitous only if they are viewed in isolation. In context, they are explained by what precedes them. They refer to fragments of the text that are more easily deciphered, and they are attached to those fragments by an uninterrupted chain of verbal associations involving automatic writing. Surrealist images are arbitrary only in relation to our habitual logic and utilitarian attitude toward reality and language.[1] In the reality of the text, they are rigorously determined by the verbal sequence and are, therefore, justified and appropriate within the framework of a given poem. Within this microcosm, a logic of words comes to be, a logic that has nothing to do with normal linguistic communication. This verbal logic creates a special code, a dialect within language, causing the reader to undergo the disorientation of the senses that the Surrealists saw as the essence of the poetic experience.

By its very nature, the extended metaphor constitutes a special code, since the images of which it is composed—taken individually or as a group—have meaning only in relation to the first image. A study of the forms of extended metaphors in poets such as Breton and Eluard should shed some light on the relation between "arbitrary" images and automatic writing.

THE STRUCTURE OF THE EXTENDED METAPHOR

1.1. What is called an extended metaphor[2] is, in fact, a series of metaphors semantically tied together by syntax and meaning. They belong to a single sentence or to a single narrative or descriptive structure. Each expresses a particular aspect of the whole, be it a thing or a concept, represented by the first metaphor in the series. For example:

(I) Tel filet d'idée poétique qui chez André Chénier découlerait en élégie, ou chez Lamartine s'épancherait en méditation, et finirait par devenir fleuve ou lac, se congèle aussitôt chez moi et se cristallise en sonnet.[3]

[A trickle of a poetic idea, which, in André Chénier, would flow into an elegy, or in Lamartine, would pour out into a meditation and ultimately become a river or a lake, immediately freezes in me and crystallizes into a sonnet.][4]

(II) Je veux bastir un temple à ma chaste Déesse:
Mon oeil sera la lampe, et la flamme immortelle
Qui m'ard incessamment, servira de chandelle:
Mon corps sera l'autel, et mes soupirs les voeux.[5]

[I want to build a temple to my chaste Goddess: my eye will be the sanctuary lamp, and the undying flame ceaselessly burning me will be the candle. My body will be the altar, and my sighs the vows.]

(III) La terre promise de la vallée de Provins attirait d'autant plus ces Hébreux, qu'ils avaient . . . traversé, haletants, les déserts sablonneux de la Mercerie.[6]

[The promised land of the Provins valley attracted these Hebrews all the more, since they had . . . crossed, panting for breath, the sandy deserts of Haberdash.]

A comparison of the preceding examples will enable us to identify the components of the extended metaphor. I shall first suggest a general definition of each of those components and then indicate the characteristics specific to the Surrealist variety.

1.2. *Semantics of the metaphoric code.* An immediately acceptable metaphor (which I shall call a *primary* metaphor), sets up the semantic equation $T = V$, tenor equals vehicle.[7] This equation functions as the model for the metaphors that will follow and enables the reader to decode them correctly.

The primary metaphor, M_1, is therefore the key to the special code established by the extended metaphor. Each metaphoric word figuring in the code will be marked as such by its semantic or functional relationship to V_1 of the primary metaphor, and will be translatable in accordance with the general meaning indicated by the model.

In (I), the equation M_1 = *filet d'idée poétique*, where V_1 = *filet* [trickle], marks as metaphoric all the verbs expressing the various states in which water can exist. Within the code established here and by virtue of the translation model proposed by the primary metaphor, each word in the *water* family signifies "form of poetic inspiration." They do not have this meaning in everyday usage.

1.2.1. By *acceptable* metaphor, I mean a metaphor that is intelligible or familiar to the reader, as is the case in (I), since M_1 is traditional or conventional. It "resembles" reality and can be verified by comparing the words to things. It demonstrates the referential function of language.[8]

1.2.2. The *Surrealist primary metaphor* differs from the general type only in that it broadens the notion of acceptability. Three cases can be observed: first, acceptability is determined by the language or a corpus of themes and literary conventions, in accordance with the general rule (1.2.1). Second, acceptability is determined by the context: the reader recognizes in V_1 a word that is identical or related to words used in a previous passage; were it not for this prior use, the choice of the word would seem gratuitous. For example (IV): "Cet instant fait dérailler le train rond des pendules" [This moment derails the clocks' round train].[9]

The meaning is: "a dramatic event is taking place; at moments like this, time seems to stop." Although it is gratuitous in relation to everyday usage, this metaphor seems natural in a context wherein Breton is describing shadows whirling round on the circular walls of a stairway: "ombres de danseurs . . . sur une plaque tournante" [shadows of dancers . . . on a turntable], with *plaque tournante* a borrowing from railroad vocabulary. Third, acceptability is determined by a formal postulate: the primary metaphor is such that the reader recognizes in it the *arbitrary* transformation of familiar forms; this transformation is brought about by so obvious a method that the reader tolerates it in the same way he would tolerate a word game or a paradox. This might be, for instance, the renewal of a cliché, the permutation of the components of a group (**la hache dans la forêt* → *la forêt dans la hache* [*the axe in the forest → the forest in the axe]),[10] syllepsis, and so on.

1.3. *Lexicon of the metaphoric code.* The verbal sequence generated by the primary metaphor contains one or more metaphors derived from it. Each of these derived metaphors returns to the initial equation either by making it more or less precise or by developing it. *Derivation* means that the V slot[11] of each derived metaphor is filled with a word related to the word in slot V_1 of the primary metaphor. The same happens with the words in slots T_2, T_3, and so on.

In other words, the verbal sequence filled by the extended metaphor is formed by the parallel development of two associative systems.[12] One is made up of words related to the primary vehicle: synonyms, words metonymically related to it, words expressing different aspects of its signified. The other is comprised of words similarly related to the primary tenor. Each of these systems uses the word around which it is organized to describe or explain the reality represented. For example, in (I), the system of *filet* [trickle] is: *découle* [flows], *s'épanche* [pours forth, gushes], and so forth. The progressive actualization of the systems is effected, in the simplest cases, by a mere listing of the components, or else by their distribution in a narrative or descriptive structure.

1.3.3. This development, however, is limited and controlled by two requirements. On the one hand, the referential function must be maintained, so the description of the vehicle and tenor should conform to their respective realities, and signifiers should be used only insofar as they represent those realities. On the other hand, the rule of *interaction*[13] must be obeyed: the superimposition of one system onto another emphasizes, by addition, everything they have in common and minimizes their differences. (If *Achilles is a lion*, everything in the lion pertaining exclusively to his "wild beast" side will be eliminated—his coat, for instance. Courage and fierceness will be exaggerated. The use of *lion* as a code word for "man" reorganizes the representation of man so as to focus on his "hero" aspect.) As a result, the vehicle system is developed by using only those of its components that have homologues in the other system. Every component lacking such a homologue either is of no use in establishing the metaphoric relation or is opposed to it and therefore excluded.

1.3.2. In the Surrealist extended metaphor, the factor controlling the development of the two systems is *automatic writing*, a process of formal word association.[14] (Even though it is the dominant factor, it does not absolutely exclude the referential function and interaction.) One word in the system determines the occurrence of the words following it in two ways.

The first is by virtue of a formal similarity, which will outweigh meaning if there is a conflict—for example, spoonerisms such as those in Desnos and Vitrac and, more frequently, phonetic parallelisms (rhymes, assonance) and puns, with or without a narrative rationalization, such as:

(v) une petite *fille* haute comme une *bille*

[a little girl tall as a pearl (literally: marble)]

(vi) les cerfs l'étourdissaient . . . surtout les cerfs blancs dont les *cors* sont d'étranges instruments de musique.[15]

[the stags made his head spin . . . especially the white stags whose *horns* are strange musical instruments.]

The second way one word determines the following words is by virtue of its stereotypical associations (its belonging to a phonetic group, a cliché, a quotation, and so on), whether or not these are acceptable in context:

(VII) le rire de cristal des roches (rire de cristal → cristal de roche)[16]

[the rocks' crystalline laughter (rock crystal → crystalline laughter]

(VIII) métal qui *nuit*, métal de *jour*[17]

[metal that hurts, day metal]

(IX) Ancien acteur qui joue des *pièces d'eau*[18]

[Former actor who plays in water plays]

(X) *Dore* avec l'étincelle *la pilule* sans cela noire de l'enclume.[19]

[Gild with the spark the pill otherwise black from the anvil.]

(XI) j'avais passé la nuit . . . *tapi dans les hautes herbes* d'une place publique, du côté du Pont-Neuf.[20]

[I had spent the night . . . hiding out in the tall grasses of a busy square, near the Pont-Neuf.]

Automatic writing consequently associates signifiers whose signifieds are incompatible, thereby disrupting the representation of reality. This disruption causes the reader to look for various rationalizations. (He tries, for example, to explain the text in terms of oneiric inspiration, as a mimesis of the fantastic, and so on.) The interaction mechanism distorts the systems instead of adjusting them to each other.

1.4. *Syntax of the metaphoric code.* Each derived metaphor consists of one element from the vehicle system joined with its homologue from the tenor system by means of a semantic equivalence. This equivalence is expressed by words that I shall call *connectives.*[21] The most frequent of these connectives are : the copula *être* [to be], as, for example, in (II); a preposition, especially *de* [of, from], introducing a "noun complement," as, for example in (I) *en*, and in (III, IV, VII, X) *de*; apposition (a zero connective); a verb or adjective in the tenor constructed with a noun from the vehicle, as in (III) *ces* and (IV) *rond* (where the tenor distorts the representation of the vehicle); and a word with its full meaning modifying in equal measure, figuratively, the vehicle and, literally, the tenor, as for example in (I) *devenir* and (II) *servir de*. Connectives are found in the ordinary extended metaphor as well as in its Surrealist form. It is, however, fair to say that the last two are more common in the Surrealist form.[22]

1.4.1. These connectives represent real relationships or "resemblances" between the corresponding signifieds: in (I), an effusion common to rivers and Romantic lyricism; in (II), the idea of an offering, amorous or mystical, common to both *body* and *altar*; in (III), the desire to retire to the country is to haberdashers what the desire for Canaan was to the Jews. The succession of derived metaphors confirms, with a repeated exercise of the referential function, the aptness of the primary metaphor. The extended metaphor thus leaves the reader decoding it with an ever increasing impression of its appropriateness.[23]

1.4.2. *Surrealist images*, however, substitute a "structural" meaning for lexical meaning. They do not represent real relationships, and the words they bring together are homologous only because they occupy similar positions in their respective sequences. By grammatically joining the terms of a normal metaphor, connectives symbolize the implicit existence of points common to both the tenor and the vehicle. This symbolism, which is anchored in the reader's habits, withstands the disappearance of similarities justifying any comparison between those terms. Having become the formal substitute for synonymy, a connective metaphorically couples words that have no semantic relationship:

(XII) le crépuscule . . . ce fou qui s'accroche à moi.[24]

[dusk . . . this madman I can't shake off.]

This semantic role of the connective is comparable to the role of grammatical structures in texts like *Jabberwocky*, where the slots reserved for full-fledged words are filled by nonsensical words.[25] The connective function works in lieu of meaning and thereby creates an illusion of metaphor. The reader finds this illusory metaphor all the more compelling since the primary metaphor provides him with a key to its use.

1.5. All the features peculiar to the Surrealist extended metaphor have one point in common. They all replace the referential function of language with a reference to the form of the linguistic message (with what Jakobson termed the *poetic function*). This is precisely the mechanism that gives rise, in literature, to the poetry-creating analogy of which Breton speaks. In his own words, it consists in "making the mind grasp the interdependence of two objects of thought belonging to different planes, [even though] the mind's logical functioning could never bridge the gap between them and would object, as a matter of course, to any kind of bridge whatsoever being built."[26]

DERIVATION

2.1. Surrealist extended metaphors fall into one of two categories depending on the acceptability of their primary metaphor. Whenever acceptability is defined as in (1.2.2, third case), the primary metaphor's arbitrariness adds a restriction to the rules of verbal association. This will be discussed in section 3. Whenever the applicable definition is that of (1.2.2, first and second cases), a special code is set up just as it would be in non-Surrealist writing. The automatic derivation from a primary metaphor is then characterized by a progressive loss or deterioration of meanings. This process results in derived metaphors that are unacceptable and seem close to sheer nonsense from the viewpoint of language. This is because they have meaning only in relation to the primary metaphor.

The derivation of the vehicle and tenor systems will be either simple or multiple.

2.2. *Simple derivation.* Both systems unfold from the primary metaphor without modification. In other words, the verbal associations are limited to the lexicon of words related to the primary tenor and vehicle. For instance:

(XIII) Un bel arbre
Ses branches sont des ruisseaux
Sous les feuilles
Ils boivent aux sources du soleil
Leurs poissons chantent comme des perles[27]

[A fine tree. Its branches are streams. Underneath the leaves, they drink at the springs of the sun. Their fish sing like pearls.]

The primary metaphor does not surprise us: sap flows, and the commonplace of the sun as the source of life, which forms the first derived metaphor, fits in here nicely, since streams have springs.[28] This is a familiar theme of the cycle of universal life. Whereas the "vegetal" tenor should normally block the development of the "aquatic" vehicle here for want of other similarities, the derivation from *stream* continues and produces *fish*[29] according to the analogy:

birds : branches :: fish : streams

The strictness of this analogy leads to the impossible equation *fish* = "*bird.*" This is the maximum arbitrariness André Breton talks about in his definition (see note 1).

Here we can clearly see the radical nature of the Surrealist revolution in literature. This arbitrariness is a rationalization on the reader's part; for, on the level of the words, there is neither fantasy nor gratuitousness but rather the internal logic of a code. Moreover, the creation of this special code has as its corollary the destruction of the linguistic code. The impossible equation is far more than a natural impossibility, and it is far more than an oxymoron bringing together merely contrasting signifiers. By substituting an equivalence for the opposition defined by the poles *water/air, swimming/flying*, and so on,[30] it threatens the very foundation of semantic structure. The equation cancels an essential feature of the semantic definition of its terms. *Chantent* [sing] repeats this process with a cumulative effect. This verb belongs to the tenor system (*branches* → **birds* → *sing*), and is a connective (see 1.4). Thus, in accordance with the terms of the code stipulating that (*stream*, . . . , *fish*, . . .) = (*tree*, . . . , *bird*, . . .), we must accept the grammaticality of the sequence *leurs poissons chantent* [their fish sing]. But once again we are faced with the cancellation of a semantic opposition, *dumbness/voice*, which is sufficient to define fish in relation to the other animals. (Consider such clichés as "muet comme une carpe," "dumb as a fish," or "dumb as an oyster.")[31]

And finally, the hyperbole *comme des perles* [like pearls] increases the impression of arbitrariness by emphasizing *chantent* at the same time that it cancels it out, and *poissons* as well, for neither pearls nor their oysters sing. It increases that impression because a sea pearl is a factual error in a description of fresh water. And, moreover, this meaning of the French *perle* (the equivalent of the English *gem* or *jewel*), applies only to household help. But here, arbitrariness tends to destroy the special code, which is the temporary substitute for momentarily destroyed language, and to deprive the reader of the guidance he had found in the code's substitute grammar. As soon as the possibility arises of our getting used to a certain form of expression and rationalizing it with an explanation—in terms of the fantastic or dreams, for example—automatic associations remind us of the exclusively verbal nature of the phenomenon. For the arbitrariness is merely the result of the meeting of two associative chains. On the one hand, the conventions of the literary representation of nature would require, in the context of *les oiseaux chantent*, that the verb be qualified by a laudatory modifier (such as *à ravir, harmonieusement* [beautifully, harmoniously]). On the other hand, the primary metaphor restricts the choice of the hyperbole to an "aquatic" vocabulary. In the paradigm of metaphors of excellence in French, *perle* is the only aquatic equivalent of *diamant, or en barre* [diamond, pure gold], and so forth. Arbitrariness results, since, with the reference being only to signifiers, *perle* is the appropriate word here, even though a pearl makes utter nonsense. If pearls were found in streams or if underwater images suited the representation of branches, the hyperbole would not have appeared arbitrary, and the special code here would have merged, purely by chance, with everyday language.[32]

2.3. *Multiple derivation.* Derivation from the primary metaphor is complicated by subsystems, with the automatic associations branching off at any point whatsoever in the extended metaphor. The system stemming from the primary metaphor is kept intact. The system derived from the primary vehicle is replaced by a subsystem stemming from the vehicle of one of the derived metaphors. Since the systems stemming from a derived vehicle would by definition be a segment of the system derived from the primary metaphor, the branching off can be caused only by a pun or syllepsis revolving around the derived vehicle in question. For instance:

(XIV) Un coq à la porte de l'aube
Un coq battant de cloche
Brise le temps nocturne sur des galets de promptitude.[33]

[A cock at the door of dawn. A bell-clapper cock shatters nocturnal time on pebbles of promptness.]

The primary metaphor is both very clear (the conventional description of a daybreak scene—the cock's traditional role), and disconcerting. Nothing could be simpler than to compare a rooster to a bell ringer ringing matins,[34] but that comparison is obscured by a double metonymy (the *bell* for the ringer and the *clapper* for the bell).[35] Starting with the first derived metaphor (*brise le temps*), an adventitious vehicle is grafted, so to speak, onto V_1 = *battant de cloche* by means of a derivation analogous to the one in (VI). It is triggered by the double meaning of *battant.* The word is not repeated; instead, there is a syllepsis: two different meanings are successively activated by *battant*'s two functions in the sentence. In apposition with *coq*, the sonorous crower, *battant* is *battant de cloche*, a clapper on a bell. Its role in the group *battant de cloche* revives its etymological meaning: *battant* is also the present participle of the verb *battre* [to beat, to strike]. (We can compare this to the reverse derivation in Michel Leiris: *pioche* [pickaxe] → *battant* → *cloches*, in the context of "des pioches . . . reines d'obscurs travaux battant comme des cloches" [pickaxes . . . queens of dark labors striking like bells].)[36] The vehicle system organizing the extended metaphor begins to unfold only with *brise*.[37]

The general meaning, "a cock promptly puts an end to night with his crowing," is obvious. The continuity of the tenor can be observed all the way to *promptitude*, which literally describes the excessive zeal of dawn's herald.[38] But the last derived metaphor appears grotesque. However much the reader may be used to the concretization of abstractions, he still cannot conceive of any semantic relationship between the object *galet* [pebble] and the concept *promptness*. It would be tempting to conclude that the equation is gratuitous and that *de* is present only as a metaphor of a metaphor (compare 1.4.2.). It is nothing of the sort, though: not even this very extreme case is due to a discontinuity in the special code. The difficulty of this extended metaphor results, doubly, from a shift from one system to the other. It stems from the very fact that there is a deviation—(*un battant de . . .* → *un battant brise*)— and from the fact that the tenor, which itself does not vary, is so far removed from the vehicle when they are brought together one last time at the close of the text. But the verbal chain going from *battant* to *galets* remains as compelling as ever. *Briser*[39] calls for something hard to work against; a hammer calls for an anvil, and the rock, a symbol of hardness, is a variant of the anvil.[40] Now, of all the synonyms of rock, *galet* is a hyperbole of hardness. This is not to say that a real pebble is necessarily so very hard. We are simply dealing here with a stylistic constant, a rule that seems to govern the relative expressiveness of words forming a paradigm of synonyms: the more specific a signifier is in everyday usage, the more it emphasizes the defining features of the class of objects signified by the words in that paradigm. If hardness is one of the defining features of rocks, *granite* (to take one example), or *caillou* [stone], or any other slightly technical rock name will call that hardness to our attention. This is exactly what happens with *galet.*[41]

ARBITRARY FORMS

3.1. The Surrealists use arbitrariness to insure the authenticity of automatic writing. If the automatic sequence is threatened by a lapse into subjectivity that seems to redirect the verbal sequence, the author should intervene by breaking with the context. "After a word whose origin strikes you as suspect, place a letter, any letter, *l* for example, always the letter *l*, and restore arbitrariness by making that letter the initial of the following word."[42] This formula does not seem to have been applied as is to the extended metaphor, but equivalent devices can be observed in it. They affect only the primary metaphor: if they were applied to derived metaphors, they would obliterate the systems' continuity, and all that would remain would be independent metaphors totally unrelated to one another. The only possible exception would be a case in which parallel systems are developed solely by means of rhymes or puns. For example:

(xv) entre les frontières de ton front et le visa de ton visage[43]

[between the borders of your forehead and the visa of your face.]

But this type of development, despite its frequency in the Surrealists' free sentence forms, is overly limited by the syntactic restrictions imposed by the presence of connectives, and scarcely any examples of it are to be found. The primary metaphor, however, can be made arbitrary. All that is required is that it not be interpretable as a representation of reality. It must, on the contrary, seem to be a modification of something real, or at most a purely verbal construction, and its form must clearly indicate that the author's intervention was totally mechanical. An arbitrary primary metaphor has the same functions as a nonarbitrary one, but it also has one characteristic belonging to it alone: it is a kind of marker of nonreference to reality affecting the entire extended metaphor.

3.2. The primary metaphor denotes the absolute nature of expression. As a structure of representation through transposition or substitution, it represents nothing other than itself and makes the reader perform a kind of gymnastics of comparison, a gratuitous exercise. Consider:

(XVI) Et quand tu renais du phénix de ta source[44]

[And when you are reborn from the phoenix of your spring.]

This line seems to be an image illustrating the idea of birth unto a new life and to owe its impact to the superimposing of the vehicle *phoenix* onto the tenor *spring* (which is perhaps itself already metaphoric in the context). A sense of unease on our first reading shows that this meaning is indeed contained in *renaître de* [to be reborn from], but that this construction calls for a complement referring to the death over which the verb triumphs. *Ashes* would be in order in the context of *phoenix*, and *rock* or *parched ground* in the context of *spring*. *Source* and *phénix* should function as subjects, for that is the only function giving these words their requisite symbolism. For example: *"et quand tu renais, phénix, des cendres de ta source" [*and when thou art reborn, o Phoenix, from the ashes of thy spring]. In this hypothetical sentence, *renaître* would be illustrated by referring to *source*, and *source* by referring to *phénix*. Each stage of the utterance would be backed up semantically by a connective. In Breton's text, however, the reference is only apparent. Since it is impossible to make the meaning of the words agree and have the meaning given them by their distribution in the text match their "syntactic meaning" (cf. 1.4.2.), we are left with nothing more than a paradigm of synonyms of "rebirth" (that is, *renaître, source, phénix*, and even *et quand* *tu re* —— *du* ——, which obviously has the same meaning in this context, since *tu* is called *Aube* [Dawn], and *et quand* follows the phrase *quand tu dors* [when you are sleeping]; now, for dawn, the end of night means a return to life). The paradigm does not construct a representation. It is simply a chance accumulation of words waiting for their reality, words that, for want of being directed toward something, merely reflect one another. The construction framing the paradigm "goes through the motions" of organizing it, but all the while blocks any reading in that sense.

In the next example, arbitrariness consists in the mechanical creation by word combination of a pseudo-vehicle that looks as if it were metaphorically representing, as a bird, the concept expressed by those words. A derived metaphor, whose vehicle is also a bird, seems to confirm the real existence of the bird made of words. (Once again, it only *seems* to, for all that is confirmed is a verbal structure. What are compared are not two "birds," but two compound words.)

(XVII) On vient de mourir. . . . Le corps . . . déteste l'âme. . . .
C'est l'heure d'en finir avec la fameuse dualité. . . .
Il n'y a plus ni rouge ni bleu. Le *rouge-bleu* unanime
s'efface à son tour comme un *rouge-gorge* dans les
haies de l'inattention. On vient de mourir.[45]

[Someone just died. . . . The body . . . hates the soul. . . . It's time to put an end to the famous duality. . . . There is neither red nor blue. The unanimous *red-blue* is wiped out in its turn like a *red-breast* in the hedges of inattention. Someone just died.]

At first, the poet offers a discursive explanation of the passage from duality to unity: "Il n'y a plus ni rouge ni bleu."[46] Then he resorts to a "formal" demonstration in the form of a neologism: *rouge-bleu unanime*. (The hyphen topping off the demonstration is explained by the adjective.) And finally, he turns the neologism into an animal and replaces the syntagm indicating the passage from duality to unity (*ni . . . ni . . .*), with a verb giving dramatic expression to that passage, *s'efface*.[47] The primary metaphor is thus obtained by means of a stylistic transposition of the word group from one trope to another. The tenor *rouge bleu* was made into a metaphor by the vehicle *rouge-bleu*.[48]

3.3. The primary metaphor may be perceived as the transposition of a familiar form. Since the primary metaphor provides the key to the special code it generates, this transformation then becomes an index of the permutation similarly affecting all the derivatives. Just as a non-Euclidian geometry can be derived by reversing a postulate, a representation of an unreality can be constructed upon the arbitrariness of a primary metaphor. For example:

(XVIII) Le doux fer rouge de l'aurore
Rend la vue aux aveugles.[49]

[The soft, red-hot iron of dawn restores sight to the blind.]

The meaning is clear: the light of dawn enables men, blinded by night, to regain their sight.[50] Its form is disconcerting nonetheless. If *fer rouge* [red-hot iron] stood alone, critics could marvel at the aptness of the expression.[51] But *fer rouge* represents a dangerous reality: it is even more threatening than a flame. Eluard's final manuscript contains a rough draft in which he shifts from the red-hot iron of sunrise and sunset to torture at the wheel, an image of the pain of living: "Je suis rompu par le fer rouge / De l'aurore et du crépuscule" [I am broken by the red-hot iron of dawn and dusk].[52] But however true the visual impression may be, the incompatibility between *doux* and *fer rouge* remains total. It increases with the second line, for even if the reader focuses on *doux* instead of on the burning metal, this adjective is not enough to erase the iron's aggressiveness and the image of tortures that it suggests. It is hard to believe that this iron could work a healing miracle. The primary metaphor jolts the reader and leaves him unsatisfied. This tension, which is characteristic of the Surrealist image in general[53] and accounts for its effectiveness, takes on a functional role here.

The reader is stopped by the primary metaphor's impossibility. He cannot help but see it as an arbitrary manipulation of reality. He can accept it only in relation to the intact group, as an antithetical statement. At the same time, the truly mechanical simplicity of the passage from antithesis to "thesis" lets the reader interpret it as a minus sign replacing a plus sign. He perceives the two lines as the transformation

> *le fer rouge ôte la vue aux voyants → le doux fer rouge rend la vue aux aveugles
>
> [the red-hot iron deprives the seeing of sight → the soft red-hot iron restores sight to the blind]

In this context, *fer rouge* is an instrument of torture,[54] which accounts for the derivation of *aveugles.* We have here something quite different from the conceit of *doux/fer rouge.* The image's poetry does not stem from the apparent conceit, but rather from the mythical structure it conceals: *weapon that wounds → weapon that heals.* Achilles' spear is one of the most famous variants of this structure.[55]

The effectiveness of this device, enabling an entire sequence to be changed by modifying a single image, is so great that I believe it should be seen as one of the principal stylistic means of representing the surreal. In fact, it is found in forms that are not strictly speaking extended metaphors, for their images have neither the two terms nor the connectives that characterize these metaphors, but instead are narrative or descriptive structures. They are comparable to extended metaphors, however, because they also display a derived associative system. Consequently, they may undergo the same transformations. For instance:

> (XIX) Là des pêcheurs débarquaient des paniers pleins de coquillages terrestres . . . que des étoiles . . . s'appliquaient douloureusement sur le coeur pour entendre le bruit de la terre. C'est ainsi qu'elles avaient pu reconstituer pour leur plaisir le bruit des tramways et des grandes orgues, tout comme nous recherchons dans notre solitude les sonneries des paliers sous-marins, le ronflement des ascenseurs aquatiques.[56]
>
> [There, fishermen unloaded baskets full of earth shells . . . that stars . . . would painfully press to their hearts in order to hear the sound

of the earth. In this way, for their amusement, they had been able to reconstruct the sound of streetcars and church organs, just as we, when we are alone, listen for doorbells ringing in the submarine stairwells and the rumbling of aquatic elevators.]

All that was needed was for the sign of the stock epithet in **co-quillages marins* [sea shells] to be reversed. From its antonym, *ter-restres* [earth], a kind of negative mimesis of the real is obtained—hence, a topsy-turvy world. It is not created by the author's hard-working imagination scrambling reality bit by bit. It is created all at once, and is authentic and plausible; since first, it is lived reality; then it is organized by language; and then it is reversed. The reader rightly recognizes in it—but in a context (by definition unheard of), where all sensations have become primitive again—dreams of an elsewhere, of a complete disorientation.[57] (This archetypal theme, going from myths of submerged cities to Rimbaud's "salon au fond d'un lac" [drawing-room at the bottom of a lake], continues to hold our imagination.) The description does not go so far as to attempt to convince the reader in the way science fiction and fantastic tales do; the text simply makes the reader perform a practical exercise in visionary poetry. The transformation can even affect the very structure of the lexicon—as for instance in another topsy-turvy world wherein, just as in Rimbaud, "le salon central repose tout entier sur une rivière" [the central drawing-room lies entirely on a river] and suddenly tips over and takes the place of its reflection. A clue to the transformation can be found in the neologism *parterre* → *parciel*, giving us:

(xx) Les *parciels* se reflètent légèrement dans la rivière où se désaltèrent les oiseaux.[58]

[The *parciels* are lightly reflected in the river where the birds come to drink.]

This sentence is followed by a world of reflections built entirely upon a formal convention and providing its own justification—compare (XVII). Even the supernatural is in the second degree, as it were, for it is generated entirely by words: "ombre de bêtes charmantes et redoutables, ombre d'idées aussi, sans parler de l'ombre du merveilleux" [the shadow of charming and frightening beasts; the shadow of ideas, too, not to mention the shadow of the fantastic].[59] From the shadows of fantastic animals a commentary is derived.

The importance of the extended metaphor is due to the autonomy of its special code. Thanks to this autonomy, a specific "property of words" can be observed: "the property [enabling] words to come together in singular chains and shine—and this, when we least expect it."[60] Now, as André Breton insisted, this property is the very foundation of Surrealist poetics.

[13]

Semantic Incompatibilities in Automatic Writing

THE SURREALISTS' automatic writing texts have baffled critics only, I believe, because they either resort to psychological considerations without paying attention to the text or, when they do stay close to the text, they are content to analyze its grammar. The former were prompted by André Breton's own definition of the device as a dictation of the unconscious, a definition that in practice has led to an impasse. Once they have catalogued Breton according to psychological categories, it still remains for them to explain how the characteristics common to all mental activity produced a form that is specific to one text. Supposing they arrive at that explanation someday, it would still only account for the genesis of the text, and would have no relevance to the finished product.[1] Grammatical analysis of automatism would seem more promising, since it deals with textual realities. Unfortunately, the syntax of an automatic text is in no way different from that of an ordinary text.[2]

What is different is the automatic text's total departure from logic, temporality, and referentiality. In short, it is different because it violates the rules of verisimilitude and the representation of the real. Although normal syntax is respected, the words make sense only within the limits of relatively short groups, and there are semantic incompatibilities between these groups; or else the semantic consecution of the sentences is normal, but their overall meaning is obscured by smaller nonsensical groups. Because logical discourse, teleological narrative, normal temporality, and descriptive conformity to an accepted idea of reality are rationalized by the reader as proof of the author's conscious control over his text, departures from these are therefore interpreted as the elimination of this control by unconscious impulses. This is precisely what creates the appearance of automatism. This appearance may well be artificial, the product of very conscious work on form.

Whether this appearance is obtained spontaneously or through imitation, I shall call it the *automatism effect*. Any text in which this effect can be observed belongs to the genre labeled "automatic writing." Because the automatism effect results from anomalies of meaning, a semantic rather than a grammatical approach is needed to analyze the textual mechanisms of that genre. I shall attempt to apply this approach to two texts from André Breton's *Poisson soluble*.

Poisson soluble is divided into thirty-two episodes that are unrelated to one another. Each has the semantic autonomy characteristic of a poem, since a poem is a fragment whose temporal, spatial, and logical context—its previous circumstances and long-range motivations—must be reconstituted in the reader's imagination. (This is what enables the reader to integrate it into his own experience, at least in the case of "lyric" poetry.) *Poisson soluble* is therefore a collection of prose poems.

Of the two texts I have chosen, one (poem 29) realizes the model of a typical folktale, and the other (poem 22), the model of an equally common sexual fantasy. Each of them is therefore familiar to the reader and gives him an impression of déjà vu. He recognizes in the different variants the same story going from one tale to another, and thus empirically perceives the existence of a topos. This topos enables him to predict the different stages of the narrative, if not in their detail, at least in their sequence and semantic structure. This predictability then becomes the norm in relation to which the discrepancies creating the automatism effect are perceived.

All texts are produced under semantic, morphological, and grammatical restrictions, and according to the rules of narrative. Once the given has indicated to the reader what can be expected, the text develops in conformity with that expectation, and the sequence of events and their cause-and-effect relationships are then felt to be verisimilar. These events and their reciprocal causality are all the more recognizable when they are expressed by clichés. If a verbal association seems to contradict the expected narrative or deflect its progress, then that association will be perceived as a parenthesis clearly belonging to a different level than that of the narrative. As soon as the parenthesis is closed, the reader returns to the narrative.

At least this is what happens in a normal narrative. In an automatic narrative, however, incompatibilities exist between the narrative and the discourse, and between the narrative consecution and the lexical consecution. These, in turn, generate sequences that appear in context to be aberrant. We thus attempt to explain them in terms of the supernatural or the fantastic, or else as a mimesis of hallucinatory or oneiric perceptions. Furthermore, if the text returns to the norm (which is to say to verisimilitude), this will be compensated for, and the automatism effect will be maintained by a new restriction on lexical choices: only such sentences as do not yield visualizable representations will then be permissible. One of two possible courses will be taken: either the lexical sequence will seem to refer to reality, but that reality will be in conflict with the narrative, or else the lexical sequence will fit the narrative, but will result in an unacceptable representation.

The first possibility is exemplified by the folktale in prose poem 29—a fabulous hunting story. It is a variant of a well-known *topos*. A huntsman encounters a supernatural beast while he is walking or riding through the forest. At once he notices the animal's abnormalities, and reads these as a sign to be interpreted. The hunter's subsequent acts are the result of his interpretation or desire to find one. He may submit to guidance by the beast, or he may pursue the animal. In either case his action makes him the hero of a quest that leads him from trial to trial through the forest or into another world. This is the same sequential pattern as was followed by Flaubert in *La Légende de saint Julien l'Hospitalier*, by Tieck in *Der blonde Eckbert*, and by Victor Hugo in the story of the knight Pécopin and his hundred-year long hunt (*Le Rhin*).[3] Little wonder that the Surrealists favored this type of story. The forest is but a step away from the supernatural. The sylvan setting of the hunt provides a ready-made link between the human and the animal worlds, and makes it plausible that there be a meeting between the two, or between the human and the nonhuman, or between the familiar and the unknown. The forest symbolizes mystery, the invisible world around us, the unconscious itself, and the hunter in pursuit of his prey is pursuing the very object of psychoanalysis.

The narrative sequence cannot be tampered with by automatism, since it is what makes the story identifiable and keeps its strangeness from appearing gratuitous. This sequence is composed of the following stages: preface to the story, announcing that it is mysterious; description of the hunter; depiction of the encounter; the hunter becoming the hero of the quest; tale of the initiatory quest.[4]

> Cette année-là, un chasseur fut témoin d'un étrange phénomène, dont la relation antérieure se perd dans le temps et qui défraya la chronique de longs mois. Le jour de l'ouverture cet homme botté de jaune qui s'avançait dans les plaines de Sologne avec deux grands chiens vit apparaître au-dessus de lui une sorte de lyre à gaz peu éclairante qui palpitait sans cesse et dont l'une des ailes seule était aussi longue qu'un iris tandis que l'autre, atrophiée mais beaucoup plus brillante, ressemblait à un auriculaire de femme auquel serait passé un anneau merveilleux. La fleur se détacha alors et retourna se fixer par l'extrémité de sa tige aérienne, qui était l'oeil du chasseur, sur le rhizome du ciel. Puis le doigt, s'approchant de lui, s'offrit à le conduire en un lieu où aucun homme n'avait jamais été. Il y consent et le voici guidé par l'aile gauche de l'oiseau longtemps, longtemps. L'ongle était fait d'une lumière si fine que nul oeil n'eût pu tout à fait l'endurer; il laissait derrière lui un sillage de sang en vrille comme une coquille de murex adorable. Le chasseur parvint ainsi sans se retourner à la limite de la terre de France et il s'engagea dans une gorge. De tous côtés c'était l'ombre et l'étourderie du doigt lui donnait à craindre pour sa vie. Les précipices étaient dépassés, puisque de temps à autre une fleur tombait à côté de lui et qu'il ne se donnait pas la peine de la ramasser. Le doigt tournait alors sur

lui-même et c'était une étoile rose follement attirante. Le chasseur était un homme d'une vingtaine d'années. Ses chiens rampaient tristement à ses côtés.

[That year a hunter was witness to a strange phenomenon; its previous record is lost in time and it was much talked about for many months. On the opening day of the hunting season this man, who was walking over the plains of Sologne in yellow boots, with two big dogs, saw an apparition over his head, a kind of gas lyre, which gave little light and kept flickering constantly. And only one of its wings was as long as an iris, whereas the other, atrophied but much more brilliant, looked like a woman's little finger with a magic ring on it. Then the flower fell off and went back to fasten with the tip of its aerial stem, which was the eye of the huntsman, to the sky's rhizome. Then the finger came close to him and offered to take him to a place where no man had ever been. He agrees, and now he is being guided by the left wing of the bird for a long, long time. The fingernail was made of a light so subtle that no eye could quite stand it; it left behind a wake of blood spiraling like a shell of enchanting murex. Thus, without looking back, the hunter reached the end of the land of France and made his way into a gorge. All around him was shadow, and the giddiness of the finger made him fear for his life. The precipices had been left behind, for from time to time a flower would fall near him and he would not bother to pick it up. Then the finger was spinning around and it was a madly enticing pink star. The hunter was a man of about twenty. His dogs crept sadly along beside him.]

In the first sentence, the reader recognizes a convention analogous to the "once upon a time" found in fairy tales. This standard narrative device triggers a counteracting ungrammaticality at the lexical level: the two relative clauses, which are mutually exclusive. Both "dont la relation antérieure se perd dans le temps" and "qui défraya la chronique" are clichés frequently found in journalistic accounts of out-of-the-ordinary events. Both are derived by expansion from the past tense of the verb and the adjective "étrange."[5] They are redundant. Both hyperbolically stress the witness' reaction to the strangeness of what he saw. But the statement that all "previous record" has been lost is contradicted by the further comment that "it was much talked about." Moreover, "se perd dans le temps" is twice negated by "recent"-sounding details: the allusions to the opening day of the hunting season and to the custom of hunting in the Sologne region. If this sequence of incompatible elements continues, the cancellation of a distant past by a recent past should generate the reverse cancellation of the recent past by a very remote past. This is precisely what happens with the archaic expression "terre de France," which implies a very distant history.[6]

The description of the hunter is in keeping with the rules of verisimilitude: his reality is confirmed by details associated with country life (boots and dogs). In short, there is nothing here that could not be found in a conventional, author-controlled narrative. But this illusion of reality is simply the context with which the fantastic nature of the apparition is contrasted. The more natural its setting and familiar its circumstances, the more the supernatural will be convincing as well as suprising.

The third stage—the story of the miraculous encounter—flouts the rules of the fantastic genre, since the beast's monstrousness is not acceptable. Even if we do not believe in monsters, they should still respect the conventions of monstrousness. These are usually rules of substitution or negation: for instance, certain physical characteristics will be transferred from one species to another and produce a hybrid (such as Spiderman), or else a symmetrical two-eyed face will be negated by oneness, giving us the Cyclops, or by a mutiplicity of eyes, giving us Argus. But here, where the hunting context calls for an animal, we get a musical instrument. The reader cannot even rationalize Breton's lyre as a metamorphosis, animation, animalization, or personification, which would all be acceptable in traditional mythology. Of course, instruments that play all by themselves can be found in fairy tales. They can also be found throughout literature: for example, the satyr's lyre in Hugo's *La Légende des siècles* and, elsewhere in Hugo, an animated trumpet of Judgment, and in Schiller a bell. But Breton's lyre hardly lends itself to this transformation from inanimate to animate. It is hard to believe that it could conceal a hidden capacity for thought, as do the metal and stone in Nerval's *Vers dorés*, for it is a *gas* lyre. In other words, it is not a real lyre, but rather a lyre metaphor designating a commercial or industrial artifact whose pragmatic and utilitarian uses would seem to keep it at a wide remove from the fantastic and the literary. The *lyre à gaz* was a lyre-shaped fixture used in the 1870s to hold gaslights—a rather popular example of decorators' attempts to combine classical form with the latest in scientific household conveniences.[7] These dubious alliances involved aesthetic contradictions that fascinated writers: Mallarmé, for instance, spoke of such fixtures, if not about the *lyre à gaz* itself.

Even if we do no know the referential meaning of *lyre à gaz*—and our linguistic code and customs have changed enough that indeed we do not know it—it is clear that the stylistic difference is enormous between *lyre*, a word reserved for literary usage by its usual contexts as well as by its spelling, and *gaz*, a word of common usage, scientific at best, but ordinarily quite down-to-earth. What we have here is a gap between signifiers.[8] Although the referential relationship is similar, there would be no such gap with *electric guitar*, since the name of the instrument is stylistically as lowbrow as the adjective; nor with *orgue hydraulique* [hydraulic organ], where the Greek form of the adjective makes up for the nondescript ordinariness of its meaning. In *lyre à gaz*, however, the gap cannot be bridged: in short, the word is a monstrosity indeed—a lexical monstrosity. By having it function differently from the way it is supposed to, the context activates and actualizes an absurdity latent in all compound words.

If the automatism effect is explained by the absurd, it remains for us to explain how the absurd was generated. It is not enough to invoke the *hasard objectif* to which Breton and his friends so often turned in games like *cadavres exquis* or in their forays into the back streets and fleamarkets of Paris in search of unusual or pointless knick-knacks which, removed from their context, could be turned into absolutes they called "objets surréalistes." I suspect, in fact, that the gas lyre in *Poisson soluble* was overdetermined by an intertext: Huysmans' *Les Soeurs Vatard*, a novel much admired by Breton. In it there is a description of a nightclub dominated by a brightly lit sign: "Aux Folies-Bobino . . . elle admira fort l'entrée. . . . Une femme jaune dansant sur le toit retroussé comme celui d'une pagode et tenant à la main un appareil à gaz en forme de lyre la stupéfia" [She marveled at the entrance to the Folies-Bobino. . . . A yellow woman dancing on the roof, which curled up like that of a pagoda, and holding a lyre-shaped gas fixture in her hand left her dumbfounded].[9] Considering the important part played by advertisements and posters in the Surrealist imagination (the Bébé Cadum poster in Desnos' *La Liberté ou l'amour*, for instance, or the Mazda lamp poster in Breton's *Nadja*), Breton could not help but be struck by this passage. All Huysmans did was to provide Breton with an unusually picturesque detail, which could be read in two ways. The conformist reading would evaluate it (and make fun of the bad taste of a low—or popular—art form), and the surrealist reading would focus on its fantastic potential (the other side of its transgression: the gas lyre is a hybrid). Breton comes up with his fantastic bird by combining two aspects of this fantastic put into words: on the one hand, allegorical tradition, which abounds in symbolic objects that fly (a winged hourglass: Time flies), and on the other hand, the compound *oiseau-lyre* [lyrebird] (which would be a fantastic bird if *lyre* were not a metaphor). As a matter of fact, a lyrebird appears twice in *Poisson soluble*.[10]

Oiseau-lyre à gaz [gas lyrebird], patterned after Lewis Carroll's portmanteau words *rocking-horsefly* and *bread and butterfly*, would have done the trick. But such visualizable or overly obvious derivations, which tend to fall prey to rationalization, are blocked. What matters above all is that the derivation is dictated by the narrative structure, which calls for an encounter with a fantastic animal. This is all that is needed for the "monstrousness" seme to eliminate *oiseau* (which would have been an explanation or normalization in *oiseau-lyre*, by restoring *lyre* to its metaphysical function), and for it to add a kind of suffix of anomaly to *lyre* (*à gaz*).

The repression of *oiseau*[11] generates, in compensation, an explanatory text, a periphrasis describing the characteristics of the repressed nuclear word until the reader is able to recognize it. Since this nuclear word is stamped with the seal of the fantastic, each metonymic or synecdochic equivalent entering into the periphrasis automatically undergoes a referential distortion. This distortion symbolizes the "monstrousness" or "supernatural" seme.

In the case of a symmetrical reality, its distortion will automatically be obtained with an asymmetry. In *Poisson soluble*, a dreamed-up dog has one blue eye and one yellow eye, and a character dreams of having two mistresses, one "pourpre qui aurait bien voulu dormir" [crimson, who would have loved to sleep], and the other "blanche qui arrivait sur le toit comme une somnambule" [white, who used to come by way of the roof, like a sleepwalker]. In our poem, since two wings can be either long or short, one wing will be long and the other short. The mimesis underscores the asymmetry and its anomalous nature. The long wing is described in a code that is abnormal for a bird: it is compared to the stem of a flower (or rather to a stem that has been marked as a sign of beauty, a *long stem*, as in *de longs iris*). As for the short wing, it is pathologically short—*atrophiée*. But the moment the mimesis leans toward the pejorative, the compensatory back-and-forth motion is set off and gives us the meliorative description "mais beaucoup plus brillante," and so on.

These formal zigzags in no way hinder the development of the adventure story. However absurd the description may be, the reader cannot fail to follow the narrative thread. The writing follows the logic of the narrative, but it does so mechanically. From among the various representations suitable to a particular episode, it does not choose the one that would go best with the one preceding it. And there is nothing to keep two representations from competing with each other in actualizing the same episode. Deletions and the filtering of reference to reality do not enter into the picture here. The only principle that governs the selection of the successive mimetic codes is the constraint of hypogrammatic derivation,[12] whether the hypogram be a cliché or a descriptive system. For example, the next stage of the hunt is when the animal acts as the hunter's guide. It is represented by two concurrent mimeses: the motif of an index finger pointing in the right direction and the motif of tracks left behind on purpose to show the way.

The first transforms the atrophied wing into a finger (*doigt*), and then into a fingernail (*ongle*), by virtue of the cliché "montrer du doigt" [to point a finger at]. Thus transformed, the wing is luminous because light is at the meliorative extreme of various paradigms of positive signs: a blazing beacon, a pillar of fire—like those that guided the Hebrews through the desert—the star of Bethlehem, and so forth. Now, in the descriptive system of *doigt*, the nail is expected to shine, as can be judged from fashionable cosmetic practice, or from the literary representations transmuting it into *onyx*. Witness Mallarmé's "Ses purs ongles très haut dédiant leur onyx" [Her pure nails raising high their onyx].[13] Since a miraculous or even divine light is always too strong for human eyes to bear, the cliché "une lumière si forte que nul oeil ne peut l'endurer" [so strong a light that no eyes could withstand it] would be a normal derivation. But the meliorative adjective used to modify *doigt* and *ongle* is *fin*. And in a feminine context (here the finger is a woman's finger and takes on feminine characteristics such as its *étourderie* [giddiness]), *fin* is the antonym of *fort* [thick, heavy—when speaking of a woman's waist or figure]: for example, *taille fine* [a tiny waist] is opposed to *taille forte*. The praise of the finger calls for *fin*, and the praise of the light maintains the stereotype, which leads to an internal contradiction: "si fine que nul oeil ne peut l'endurer." This contradiction does, however, allow the positive markers required by the narrative to subsist. They will be repeated a little later in another positive transcoding: "le doigt . . . était une étoile rose follement attirante." It is a *pink* star because pink is a positive adjective when applied to fingers and nails.[14] *Attirante* continues the motif of the star that must be followed. All together, though, *rose, follement*, and *attirante* exteriorize a femininity that, when the "digital" sequence began, was nothing more (or so it seems) than a relatively minor comparison (the wing "ressemblait à une auriculaire de femme" [resembled a woman's little finger]).

The second motif is that of a trail left by a guide who has gone ahead—broken twigs left behind by Leatherstocking and pebbles scattered by Tom Thumb, for example. Here it appears as drops of blood leading to the wounded animal, which fits a hunting story perfectly. But since automatism has removed all restrictions, *ongle* continues to function as a metonym of the animal. This is not entirely contradictory, since the rosy glow of blood seen through a fingernail is a mark of beauty. (For instance, Germain Nouveau writes: "Et le *sang* de la *rose* est sous leurs ongles fines" [And the blood of the rose is underneath their *fine* nails].)[15] In any case, blood is now the stressed element. *Pourpre* [crimson] would be the most appropriate and the most hyperbolic epithet, but it is suppressed just as *oiseau* was earlier, and its repression has the same effect. A periphrasis is generated wherein *murex*, the shell from which ancient cultures extracted purple dye (and one of the Latin synonyms for "crimson" as well), replaces the color with its origin. This would be quite in keeping with traditional rhetoric if only automatism did not usher in a whole conchological series that we do not know how to understand: hence we have *coquille* [shell] and *en vrille* [spiraling], which actualizes the shell's helical shape. (I have no idea if murex has this kind of shell, but it is commonplace to admire enthusiastically the perfect spiral shape of shells. This, of course, is a variant of the theme of nature as a geometrician, which can be seen in the stereotypes about spiders' webs, the hexagonal beeswax cells of honeycombs, and so forth.) An uncontrolled expansion of "sang pourpre beau comme le murex" [crimson blood beautiful as murex] gives "sang en vrille comme une coquille de murex" [blood spiraling like a murex shell], and every unacceptable detail in the "murex" descriptive system represses the one word that would justify the comparison of blood to the mollusk. The blood immediately reappears, though—clothed, so to speak, in its cliché epithet from mystic texts: *sang adorable* [precious blood]. This underscores the tie between automatism and embedding: the derivation from *en vrille* to *murex* mechanically reviewed the associative possibilities of a simile that would have required but one word in controlled writing. The embedding is the result of a pathological expansion replacing the word with its definition or descriptive system, all the while remaining subordinate to the sentence dictated by the narrative structure. Automatism opens wide the associative lock: whereas controlled writing aims for the one appropriate word, subordinates inappropriate words to a context in which they can be assimilated, and favors semantic and stylistic harmony and a unity of tone going from word to word, automatic writing by contrast replaces a word with its satellites and tonal unity with continuous transcoding.

The second type of derivation creating an automatism effect is that in which the narrative includes sentences that are simultaneously compatible and incomprehensible. These sentences are semantically and syntactically grammatical, but they are unmotivated in context and consequently, either they are contrary to verisimilitude or they may even be nonsense. We are dealing here with a phenomenon of intertextuality: these sentences contain dispersed fragments of a pre-existent verbal sequence that has been borrowed from another text. With few exceptions, readers are not able to recognize the source, even if they do realize that the dispersed fragments once belonged to a different whole.

My example, prose poem 22, is the story of an erotic pursuit through city streets. Any reader familiar with such texts will at once recognize a recurrent Surrealist theme: a passerby chances upon a mysterious woman; he tells of his desire for her and follows her through the city by night. Sometimes the chase leads him from streets and squares into parks and gardens, and even into the country. Sometimes the unknown woman, still keeping her distance, will shed her clothes as she walks, stripteasing from block to block: this is what happens in Robert Desnos' *La Liberté ou l'amour*. Sometimes the climax of the pursuit comes when she suddenly exposes her naked body under her coat. The climax, but not the end of the chase—for this last sexual enticement is only a new beginning. It confirms that this pursuit resembles the never-ending quest for the beyond. This is the case here. The adventure is an expansion of a Romantic theme that is particularly well exemplified by Baudelaire's "A une passante": a chance meeting with an unknown woman in the street. An exchange of glances is enough to reveal strange affinities and to establish a mystical bond between two souls that have never encountered each other before, and no doubt will never meet again.

> Car j'ignore où tu fuis, tu ne sais où je vais,
> O toi que j'eusse aimée, ô toi qui le savais.

[For I know not where you are fleeing, and you know not where I am going. Oh, I would have loved you, and you knew it.]

This theme is also exemplified by Breton's "Tournesol" and by his own commentary on it in *L'Amour fou*. Since the theme is a common erotic fantasy, even a reader unfamiliar with its literary variants will recognize its narrative structure and will as a consequence be particularly aware of the anomalies in the *Poisson soluble* text. Together, these anomalies multiply semantic impasses and emphasize the symbolic mysteriousness of the narrative, without ever explaining matters at all:

> Cette femme, je l'ai connue dans une *vigne immense*, quelques jours avant la vendange et je l'ai suivie un soir autour du mur d'un couvent. Elle était *en grand deuil* et je me sentais incapable de résister à *ce nid de corbeaux* que m'avait figuré l'éclair de son visage, tout à l'heure, alors que je tentais derrière elle *l'ascension* des *vêtements de feuilles rouges* dans lesquels brimbalaient des *grelots de nuit*. D'où venait-elle et *que me rappelait cette vigne s'elevant au centre d'une ville*, à l'emplacement du théâtre, pensais-je? Elle ne s'était plus retournée sur moi, et, sans le brusque luisant de son mollet qui me montrait par instants la route, j'eusse désepéré de la toucher jamais. Je me disposais pourtant à la rejoindre quand elle fit volte-face et, entrouvrant son manteau, me découvrit sa nudité plus ensorcelante que les oiseaux. Elle s'était arrêtée et m'éloignait de la main, comme s'il se fût agi pour moi de gagner des cimes inconnues, des neiges trop hautes.

[This woman, I met her in an immense vineyard, a few days before harvest time. And one evening I followed her around a convent wall. She was in deep mourning. I felt incapable of resisting the crow's nest, of which, to me, the lightning of her face was the image. This happened while I was trying to climb garments of red leaves with night bells dangling in them. Where did she come from? And what did this vine remind me of, rising up in the middle of the city, where the theater used to be—such were my thoughts. She had stopped looking back at me. Without the sudden glimmer of her leg that now and then showed me the way, I should have despaired of ever touching her. I made up my mind, however, to catch up with her, when she did an about-face and opened her coat, revealing to me a nudity more bewitching than the birds. She had stopped and was pushing me away with her hand, as if it were a matter of my reaching unknown summits and inaccessible snows.]

I have italicized the unintelligible details. None can be explained by the incidents of the pursuit. They are quite different from a detail like the glimmer of flesh under the dress, which is perfectly appropriate within the context as a sexual symbol. Some of them (*le couvent, en grand deuil*) are simply unexplained givens, as are found in all narratives, but with a difference producing the automatism effect. Because they are left dangling in the air, the details hold out the lure of correspondences and vague memories from which, sooner or later, the spark of intertextual contact will arise: this is the case of *couvent*. Or else a detail, which was unexplained only in terms of the sequence of events, generates an obscure lexical derivation. This is what happens with *en grand deuil*, which leads to the image of the crows' nest, the "nid de corbeaux que m'avait figuré l'éclair de son visage." This derivation falls within the province of the extended metaphor as described in my last chapter, so I shall touch upon it here only briefly. The passage contains its own metalanguage, since the verb *m'avait figuré* makes it clear that these crows are simply the metaphorical vehicle for a predictable development in a love story: the sudden glimpse of her face stirs up a surge of emotion, shatters his will, and changes his life. What we have here is an ornithological metaphor in which *birds* are equated with inspiration, élan, and promise, as in Rimbaud's line: "Million d'oiseaux d'or, ô future vigueur" [A million golden birds, o future vigor]. Continuing along the path of least resistance for superstitious stereotypes associating death with crows, *oiseau* becomes *corbeau*, for this flight is inspired by a woman in black. The discourse of the follower is affected by the descriptive system of the woman he is following. It is the lexical icon of love at first sight.[16] The difficulty of the image is due to an automatic transcoding. It escapes the constraints of referentiality and acceptability, but it is still merely a transcoding.

The unintelligible passages characterizing the second type of automatic derivation fall into two categories: those that, at first, seem to present no problem and only on second thought are found to be hiding their real meaning, and those that block the reader from the very start.

The *vineyard* belongs in the first category: at first glance, it looks like a typical realistic or picturesque detail. Since it is specific and yet has nothing to do with the plot or with the characterization of its personae, the reader concludes that its sole purpose is to reflect outside reality objectively. In the context of an urban setting, however, a *vineyard* is much less acceptable than a convent. The second instance of *vigne* effects an almost imperceptible shift from *vineyard* as a place to *vine* as a high-climbing plant. This reduces the possibility of visualization, so that the reader will see the detail merely as a sign, an index for him to interpret, or an enigma for him to solve. Moreover, the question asked by the narrator contributes to this impression. The question mark will remain until the intertext provides us with an answer.

The woman's black attire is an erotic commonplace. The following passage underscores this point when it describes the troubling contrast between the black, filmy clothing and the color of her flesh: "les mailles extérieures étaient noires, tandis que les mailles qui avaient été tournées vers la chair en avaient gardé la couleur" [the outside stitches were black, but the stitches turned toward her flesh had kept its color]. Mourning dress also denotes her widowhood and suggests that she is easier prey because she is lonely, a potential object of interested compassion, receptive to an invitation to start living again. Besides this eroticism, her mourning implies a whole past that must be known by anyone wishing to possess the mysterious woman. This less and less latent sexuality only underscores the function of her mourning attire as a sign referring to the unknown (woman) and emphasizes its role as a question mark. In real life, chance may or may not bring the answer. In a text controlled by its author's intention, that answer will come in a final episode. In automatic writing texts, it will be found in an intertext, which will be relevant only for its homophonic similarities and lexical collocations.

In the second category, there is a total block from the very first reading on. Nothing at all is to be made of the *climbing*, especially since the street setting would suggest a horizontal pursuit. And what of the red-leaf garment? And the little bells? The only conceivable explanation (that these allude to the cap-bells and wand of a court jester, a conventional symbol of madness) is struck down by *de nuit*.

It so happens that these unintelligible details were borrowed from Hugo's *Les Misérables*. They all mark stages in the manhunt during which Hugo's hero, the escaped convict Jean Valjean, flees the Paris police with the little orphan girl he has adopted. Both of them elude their pursuers by taking refuge in a convent. Cosette, the child, is *tout en deuil*, as the novel insistently declares.[17] The place in which she was hiding before the chase began is on the rue des Vignes-Saint-Marcel, a picturesque name for some outlying district, obviously the relic of a long-gone vineyard. The street name is all the more striking in that the address looks itself like a metaphor for a woman in mourning: "petite porte noire et en deuil" [little black door in mourning].[18] What is even more significant, when the fugitives are trapped in a dead-end street, the convict first thinks of climbing the waterspouts on the face of the building. These are elaborately described as resembling vine stalks clinging to the wall:

> les embranchements variés des conduits qui allaient d'un conduit central aboutir à toutes ces cuvettes dessinaient sur la façade une espèce d'*arbre*. Ces ramifications de tuyaux avec leurs cent coudes *imitaient ces vieux ceps de vigne dépouillés qui se tordent* sur les devantures des anciennes fermes.[19]

[the different junctions of the pipes going from a central pipe and ending up in all those basins pictured a kind of *tree* on the facade. These pipe branchings with their hundred elbows *imitated those old, bare vine stocks twisting* in front of former farms.]

Jean Valjean climbs to the top and pulls the little girl in mourning up the "vine" after him. This epic ascent is referred to repeatedly as a feat possible only for experienced convicts, and we know that such convicts used to wear the red uniform of repeat offenders.[20] And then, behind the wall—this final bizarre detail must be the clincher—the fugitives find a convent garden, and in that garden a gardener (despite the fact that all this is happening in the dead of night), and that gardener, being the only man in the nunnery, wears a little bell on his leg like a leper, to warn the nuns of his approach.[21]

Hugo's manhunt is thus clearly the intertext of Breton's prose poem. The reader can read *Les Misérables* through the lines of the automatic sequences, as if it were present as a watermark beneath the text. He is able to do so and to recognize in one page of *Poisson soluble* details spread over some fifty pages of *Les Misérables* because their strangeness in the poem attracts his attention and gives his memory a jolt, and perhaps also because of the similar settings in which the two pursuits take place. Above all, he is able to make the connection because both texts actualize the same narrative structure. One text is not the intertext of another simply because their surface elements are the same or similar. For intertextuality to exist, an interpretant must be present to tie the two texts together. This interpretant can be a structure.

Now let us examine more closely the impact of the text on the reader. First comes the fundamental mechanism of the automatism effect: as I have already said, the reader reacts to the incomprehensibility of an image by attributing it to an uncontrollable upsurge from the depths of the author's psyche. Second, an unintelligible image or detail is always believed to be intelligible elsewhere, on another level of meaning or in the context of another text. Because he is accustomed to normal communication, where details refer to a significant whole, the reader reads as if these details were fragments of a code. No decoding is needed, though. Indeed, decoding would be impossible, since the details taken from Hugo have no meaning in Breton. In their new context, they function neither as quotations, nor as allusions, nor even as metaphors. (We cannot say, for instance, that the climbing and the vine illustrate a theme, or that they are vehicles referring to a tenor that would be "woman pursued.") These details have no structural significance in Hugo's narrative: they are simply picturesque or realistic elements in the mimesis. A conventional imitation, giving the appearance of being intentional, would have gotten rid of them, since they have meaning only in relation to Hugo's setting and characters, and are incompatible with Breton's. Automatic texts, however, retain such details for precisely the same reasons. Their meaninglessness within the narrative is the index of their meaning in a discourse outside the narrative, so we read them in the same way that we would read hieroglyphs. We understand them neither as an isolated language nor even as isolated symbols, but rather as the representation of a language, the key to which is hidden somewhere else. In Breton's mind, they were evidently synecdochic for the whole Hugo chase, its *restes visuels*, visual remnants residing in unconscious memory—a term Breton borrows from Freud.[22] Or, to use Saussure's felicitous image, these visual remnants were accessories, or theatrical props: "The poet who gathers and organizes legend only recovers, for any particular scene, those things which are *properties* in the most exact, theatrical sense. When the actors have left the stage, a few objects remain: a flower on the floor, which lingers in the memory."[23] Even though the reader cannot explain what these visual remants or props remind him of, what matters is that he knows they would remind him of something if only he could crack the code. The text's grip on the reader is exactly that of unconscious memory.

Thus it does not really matter whether automatic texts are genuine or not.[24] Their literariness does not reside in their recording of unconscious thought, but rather in their appearance of doing so. The incompatibilities that create this impression are true semantic ungrammaticalities at the level of the text. At the structural level, however, they are grammatical. Precisely because they pose obstacles to decoding, the absurd and the nonsensical force the reader to go straight to a reading of the structures.

[14]

Overdetermination in the Prose Poem (I): Julien Gracq

THE PROSE POEMS that Julien Gracq published under the title *Liberté grande*[1] have either a narrative or a descriptive structure. Whether they are attempts to grasp the physical world or imaginary constructions, they all shatter the semantic system of the French language. And yet the inaccuracies, divergences from the commonly accepted relations between signifers and signifieds, difficult images, and sequences defying accepted logic—all these challenges to the referential function of language do not impress us as being the products of gratuitous imagination or of an entirely chance arrangement. On the contrary, these poems display a kind of coherence and exercise a hold on the imagination that can be explained only by the existence of a strict system of expression. This system, which makes an irregular use of language appear necessary and compelling, seems to be based on the power of words to generate associative sequences that are relatively independent from reality. The mechanism behind this "dynamisme explosif du mot" [explosive dynamism of words]—the expression is Gracq's—is what I would now like to analyze.[2]

I shall begin with the text that appears to be the most arbitrary: "Salon meublé" [furnished living room].[3] It is a perfectly clear poem, but description in it systematically violates the law of the real. No emotion or obsession in the observer can account for the distortion of reality. Representation is "normal" only in the first sentence, in which the uncomfortable and even morbid impression left by the room endows it with the real presence and aura of familiar places. But the effect of this initial note of reality is dissipated by the details that follow—water streaming down the walls and disconcerting furniture:

> dans une grande cage de Faraday à l'épreuve des coups de foudre, jetée négligemment sur le bras d'une chaise curule comme au retour d'une promenade matinale, la toge ensanglantée de César, reconnaissable a son étiquette de musée.
>
> [in a big, lightning-proof faraday cage, carelessly tossed over the arm of a curule chair, as upon one's return from a morning stroll, Caesar's bloody toga, identifiable by its museum label.]

The reader thinks this is a dream or a foray into the genre of the fantastic. But this is immediately followed by a series of satirical allusions to the bad taste of petty bourgeois furniture and, concluding it all, there is a touch of pure whimsy: at the far end of the room, a freight car is dozing on its siding. This whole ending seems too "self-conscious," too calculated, for an oneiric interpretation to be possible, and it succeeds all the more in destroying the impression of reality of the beginning.

And yet, despite this game of now you have it, now you don't, the text is not zigzagging haphazardly along. The seeming gratuitousness of the pseudo-living room is, in fact, a strict application of one of the poem's own rules of "grammar." Everything happens as if each utterance were supposed to generate its opposite, each definition to self-destruct in a point-by-point contradiction, and each description to produce an incompatibility with itself. The series of these utterances triggering their opposites is no less determined, but it exists prior to the poem: it is the descriptive system of the word *salon*.

Whenever a text partially actualizes a descriptive system, it invariably stresses one of the semes of the nuclear word. Here, the emotional note I pointed out at the beginning of the poem emphasizes the "insideness" implicit in *salon*:

très sombre—de cette nuance spécialement sinistre que laissent filtrer par un après-midi d'août torride les persiennes rabattues d'une chambre mortuaire.

[. . . very dark—in that especially sinister tone which, on a scorching August afternoon, manages to filter through the closed blinds of a death chamber.]

The room is not simply closed. Its closure is underlined by its opposition to an outside world, whose outsideness is further emphasized by its intense light. And the closure is itself reinforced by the strongest emotional associations that can be found in the lexical field of *house*.[4] In this framework the living room is, of course, already more representative of the house as an *interior* than is any other room.[5]

Now, scarcely has the living room been presented as a symbol of the inside than this given generates its negation. Interiority is contradicted by a stream of water:

sur les murs peints de cet enduit translucide . . . qui tapisse les cavernes à stalactites, une légère écharpe d'eau sans bruit, comme sur les ardoises des vespasiennes, frissonnante, moirée, douce comme de la soie.

[on the walls painted with that translucent coating . . . which covers stalactite caves, [there is] a light scarf of noiseless water, like on the slate tiles of urinals, rippling and shimmering and soft as silk.]

We are given no latitude for seeing this as a realistic detail—this is not the kind of little leak found even in the best of houses whether or not the climate is rainy or the heating adequate. This water is right at home where it is, and it is flowing freely, since it waters a *cressonière*, a bed of watercress, in a corner of the room. It would be hard to imagine a better way to dissolve everything that protects the home from outside threats. And stylistically, the unseemly *vespasienne* [urinal] destroys *salon*'s associations even more violently.

The freight car at the end of the poem, "sur sa voie de garage légèrement persillée de paquerettes et d'ombellifères" [on its siding lightly sprinkled with daisies and umbelliferae], right where a piano or sofa would be expected, clearly has the same effect. It, too, is a denial of the interior.

The rule of opposites canceling each other out is also applied to the furniture. Only the faraday cage and the curule chair might perhaps be no more astounding than an armillary sphere in the window or any other example of the studied mixtures of styles invented by modern decorators. The addition of the stabbed toga, with its "déchirures particulièrement authentiques" [particularly authentic tears], would suggest, instead, an application of the haphazard aesthetics of the umbrella and sewing machine on an operating table. But, in fact, these details go together and, as a group, form an image that is incompatible with the typical furnishings of an ideal living room. They have to be read in opposition to the other descriptive pole—the usual knickknacks, packs of cigarettes, and:

> la photographie en premier communiant (carton fort, angles abattus, tranche épaisse et dorée, travail sérieux pour familles catholiques, avec la signature du photographe) du président Sadi Carnot.
>
> [the first communion photograph (heavy cardboard, worn-out corners, thick, gilded edge, good, solid workmanship for Catholic families, with the photographer's signature) of President Sadi Carnot.]

The person in the photo is himself atypical, but that only makes for stylistic emphasis or parody. If a first communion picture is an indication of respect for the family, and a picture of the president one of patriotic respect for country, their superimposition functions as a hyperbole: this living room is truer than nature. The superimposition is, therefore, a way of stressing the extent to which this living room is the very epitome of what a living room should be. Hence the increasing distance between this model (which is all the more real for being ridiculous) and its negation—the delirious furniture (the faraday cage, and the like).

The same holds for the clock that rounds out the ordinary furnishings of a real living room. On the one hand, it is as conventional as can be: "horloge suisse, à deux tons, avec caille et coucou" [Swiss clock, with two tones, a quail and a cuckoo]. But the end of the sentence quickly destroys this reality: "sonnant les demies et les quarts pour le silence d'aquarium" [striking the half and quarter hours for the aquarium silence]. In other words, it does not strike the hour and is nullified in its very function. The same also happens in this ideal apartment that Giraudoux decorates with "glaces où l'on ne se voit pas . . . , pendules qui sonneront à la fois, pour s'en débarrasser, toutes les heures, puis, en règle avec le temps pour la journée s'attarderont à ces quarts et à ces demies qui festonnent l'après-midi" [mirrors you can't see yourself in . . . , clocks that, in order to get it all over with, will strike all the hours at once, and then, in keeping with the tempo for the day, will linger over the quarter- and half-hours that festoon the afternoon].[6]

Even the freight car, which cancels out the living room as an interior, is itself canceled out: "il laisse suinter par la porte entrebaillée l'étincellement d'un service en porcelaine de Sèvres, et le bel arrangement des petits verres à liqueur" [through the half-open door, it lets the gleam of a set of Sèvres porcelain and the lovely arrangement of little liqueur glasses ooze out]. There is no question that this china and crystal correspond to the semantic feature "luxury" in the descriptive system of a bourgeois interior. But in what is now a railroad context, they are also the hyperbole of fragility and, as such, act as a counterpoise to faulty switching, rammed buffers, and bumpy tracks—in short, to all the connotations of a real railway car. The *wagon* exists only as a word. Its sole function is to be the exact opposite of *salon*.[7]

We can interpret this self-destruction of meanings as the verbal equivalent of some of the Surrealists' "symbolically functioning objects," or else, as analogous to their attempts to find a verbal absolute in which semantic incompatibilities would deny words any relationship with their signifieds. Here I am thinking of phrases like Breton's "poisson soluble" [dissolving fish], or Leiris' "nuits sans nuit" [nightless nights]. Or it can even be interpreted as an *a contrario* representation in which contemplation of the most everyday images serves precisely as an opening onto everything that those familiar images exclude:

> Souvent je fuis les traits familiers
> du monde étroit qui nous est assigné
> et hors des mains des grands meubles je passe
> du songe épais de ma solidité
> à l'autre rêve à celui de l'espace.[8]

[I often flee the familiar features of the narrow world that is assigned to us, and away from the hands of the big pieces of furniture, I go from the thick dream of my solidity to the other dream, to the one of space.]

Whichever interpretation we pick, the poem's significance is dependent on a structural constant that reorganizes strict verbal associations: there is nothing gratuitous about it.

Since "Salon meublé" brings imcompatible images together, its negative representations cancel out its positive ones; but each representation, taken separately, is written in a prose that is not at all alarming. Now let us consider a case in which language seems to deviate within the very limits of the sentence. In it understanding becomes difficult, and the images become obscure.

In the poem entitled "L'Averse" [The Downpour],[9] the initial metaphor is prolonged by subsidiary images all the way to the end of the poem. The development of this extended metaphor is modeled exactly after that of the descriptive system of *rain* (in the sense of "summer rain").[10] This system comprises: visual and auditory effects, heat before and during the shower, suddenness of the rain, freshening and purification of the air, calm. The extended metaphor is triggered by the semantic feature "damp heat," which is simultaneously expressed literally and translated metaphorically:

> Voici le monde couvé sous la pluie, la chaleur moite, le toit des gouttes et des brindilles, et les molles couvertures d'air aux mille piqûres d'éclaboussements.

[Here is the world hatched under the rain, the damp heat, the roof made of the raindrops and twigs, and the soft blankets of air with their thousand pinpoints of splashes].

What is evoked by the cliché "chaleur de serre" [hothouse heat]—an oppressive atmosphere "negating" open spaces and turning the sky into the lid of a stewing pot à la Baudelaire[11]—is restated by Gracq in terms of an incubator and then in terms of the suffocating covers on a bed. In the cliché "molles couvertures" [soft covers], the adjective is not merely descriptive: it reinforces the "warmth" seme implicit in the noun. The transference of these characteristics onto *air*, a vital and freely circulating element, has the same canceling-out effect as the incompatibilities in "Salon meublé," for it is the equivalent of groups such as *thick air* or *unbreathable air*. The hyperbole results from a function reversal: what once brought comfort now oppresses.[12] However paradoxical *couverture* may be in an "air" context, it generates *piqûres*, "pinpoints." Here there is, in fact, a crisscrossing of two descriptive systems. The word is just the right one for describing the splashing of raindrops, but this appropriateness is not immediately apparent. Only after our reading do we notice it. What directed the sequence toward this possibility was the association (via *couverture piquée*, "quilt") with a quilted bedspread.

Reinforced in this way, the metaphor *couvertures* generates a metaphor of a bed, and the bed generates one of a sleeping woman:

> Voici la belle sur son lit d'eau, toute éveillée par la soudaine transparence fraîche, toute coïncidante à une pure idée d'elle-même, toute dessinée comme l'eau par le verre.
>
> [Here is the beauty asleep on her bed of water, wide awake from the sudden fresh transparence, coinciding totally with a pure idea of herself, drawn entirely like water through glass.]

Couvertures was still justified by reality. But now that the extended metaphor is developing as a *bed* image, the resemblance ceases to exist, and the equivalence between bed terms and rain terms becomes a mere convention specific to this poem. The reader, therefore, needs a formal indication reminding him how to translate: whence the arbitrary "explanation": *lit d'eau* [bed of water], which is inconceivable in reality. A traditional extended metaphor would respect that reality: it would generate only those signifiers whose meaning would not conflict with its literal meaning. But this metaphor has no rule other than that of associating words; so that *couvertures*, which goes with *air*, generates *bed*, even though this last word is incompatible with the reality of a downpour.[13] This would be an instance of automatic writing, except that *d'eau* is not only an arbitrary justification, but a clearly conscious one as well, of the derivation from the "resembling" image at the beginning.[14]

As for the sleeping woman, she arises from the fact that the word *averse* is feminine. She is beautiful because the tenor is positive (the downpour is beneficial). And she awakens—in a transmutation of the *belle matineuse*, so dear to the *précieux* poets—because the suddenness of the shower and change in the air, translated in a bed code, are the equivalents of waking up with a start. Here again, we are dealing with a logic of words and not with reference to things: we could do away with the bed and still express suddenness, in accordance with the same system, with a paradoxical "Cette averse est un feu de paille" [this downpour is a flash fire]. This is no exaggeration. The line was, in fact, penned by Eluard, and it was deemed sufficiently representative of these mechanisms to be included in the *Dictionnaire abrégé du surréalisme.*[15]

The end of the poem returns to the reality of the downpour, but that reality is subordinated to the words and not vice versa. An *alcôve* [bedroom alcove] is derived from *lit* by a kind of stylistic ennoblement, since an *alcôve* is to a bed what the *belle matineuse* is to an ordinary sleeping woman. Each fragment of reality is distributed into the empty slots provided by the allegorical structure in the form both of adjectives (*verdissant* [turning green], *emperlées* [pearly]) and of prepositional phrases (*d'air* [of air], *d'herbe* [of grass], *de lianes* [of creeping vines]),[16] serving in either case as a reminder of how the *alcôve* code is to be translated:

> Dans l'air où nagent les balbutiantes étoiles de l'eau, une main d'air sort de l'alcôve verdissante aux parfums d'herbe et suspend à l'embrasse de lianes les courtines emperlées et l'arithmetique crépitante du boulier de cristal.[17]
>
> [In the air where the faltering water stars are swimming, a hand of air emerges from the alcove that is turning green with its scents of grass, and hangs in loops of creeping vines the pearly curtains and the rattling arithmetic of the crystal abacus.]

The generating power of associative series is thus so great that any system whatsoever can serve as a code for translating any other system. Metaphor no longer requires a constant resemblance between two orders of reality. All that is needed is an initial equation. There is, however, in "L'Averse" a continuity that keeps the metaphoric code from admitting of any internal contradictions and canceling out the starting equation. But the formal relationships between words so completely outweigh the relation of words to things that sometimes the verbal derivation can cancel out the initial given. In "Paysage,"[18] for instance, a meditation at sunset in a large Parisian necropolis, the narrator evokes the profusion of funeral chapels in a mishmash of styles, and continues: "il n'était pas défendu, sans doute, de fourrager dans l'imprévu de ces curieuses poubelles" [of course it was not prohibited to dig about in the unexpectedness of these curious garbage cans]. There are no trash cans in the cemetery, as we well know, but in the description the word *poubelles* represents an architectural catch-all, a hodgepodge of monuments. It is derived from the abstract *imprévu*, and is metaphorically synonymous with it. It is a synonym, however, that adds a pejorative note: the stroller rummaging through the graves is a kind of ragpicker trading in the crazy bric-à-brac of posthumous vanity (bric-à-brac is the initial metaphor in the series). The associative chain keeps on generating new links: "on s'étonnait même de l'absence frétillante autour des boîtes à ordures du caniche matinal" [one was even surprised by the frisky absence around the garbage cans of the early-morning poodle]. This is a true derangement in relation to reality as it is described to us, for the poem has twice already mentioned that the walk takes place at dusk and that the lighting is that of sunset. But the poodle is only *matinal*, an early-morning poodle, because morning is the time *par excellence* for garbage cans. The poodle is a component of the descriptive system of garbage can. It metonymically confirms *poubelle*, even though the same "natural" metaphoric relationship does not exist between *caniche* and *imprévu* as exists between *imprévu* and *poubelle*, and even though the noun cannot represent an animal without upsetting the entire scene.[19]

Moreover, even if the words appear to resemble reality, or even if they do indeed resemble it in a strikingly apt way (to use the words of another aesthetic), their poetic function may nevertheless have no relation to their truth. That function depends not on their relation to things, but rather on their relations to each other in context. Here is a phrase whose impact would seem to stem from the image's aptness: "La main qui tisonne le loquet de fer" [the hand poking the iron latch].[20] The sound of a hand rattling a rustic door is indeed the same as that of a poker in a wood-burning stove, but the number of readers who know what it is to try to lift a rebellious latch grows smaller and smaller everyday. Would the text no longer have an effect if latches were to join the *chevillette* [latch] in oblivion, or if radiators eliminated all live fires? Not in the least: for there to be contact, there is no need for a shared experience between author and reader. All that is needed is that the minimum condition of any reading be fulfilled: the text's linguistic code must be identical to the reader's. And if this is the case, if the the reader knows his French, consciously or unconsciously he senses among the words in this phrase a kinship causing them to converge on the same symbolism. First there is *la main* [the hand], a synecdoche of an as yet invisible somebody: it is the sudden movement of the latch, a start, the suspense of a still anonymous presence behind the door. This intruder or visitor thus, by way of contrast, defines the home and its shelter. Next, *tisonner* and *loquet* both belong to an archaic way of life: the poem extracts them from an age-old layer of the vocabulary in which words like *rouet* [spinning wheel] and *bougeoir* [candlestick] also lie dormant. *Fer* [iron] is more a confirmation of this archaism than a description of the latch (basically, it is a tautology rather than an explanation), since modern homes have done away with latches and replaced them with copper, bronze, or glass doorknobs, and steel or chrome gadgets. Consequently, these three words (which are synonymous from this point of view) represent the atmosphere of another age, the indissoluble link, in our memories and in our readings (motifs of evening gatherings, cozy cottages, and so forth) between archaisms and a quiet life far from the cares of the world. In short, the phrase is poetic because the words in it—regardless of the image's aptness—are all suggestive of "Intimité" [Intimacy], which is the poem's title.

Still other verbal sequences intervene between words and reality—pre-existing texts to which the poem refers us in such an obvious way that we cannot fail to read on two levels at one time. We simultaneously decipher the text that is before our eyes and the one that comes back to our memory. This double reading is a comparison and acts as a kind of guarantee of artistic value. It is as if the poem that we are reading had already been tested and approved since we can recognize another poem in it. (This supplementary structuring is not without analogy to that provided by versification.) As far as this goes, the process is not new: the doctrine of *imitatio* is, after all, one of the foundations of classical style. And the imitated poem underscores, if only by reduplication, the effects of the poem imitating it. The subject of the poem entitled "Le vent froid de la nuit" [The cold night wind][21] is loneliness; its successive symbols are clear, especially since they form a sequence of synonyms running from the beginning to the end of the text. But the significance of the whole is reinforced when we compare it in our minds to a poem with the same title by Leconte de Lisle, the leader of the Parnassians. Granted, this poem is a meditation on death; but that meditation valorizes certain words that reappear in Gracq's prose poem. They would be merely descriptive were it not for this valorization, which fills them with symbolism. In the hunting lodge in which Gracq's character is awaiting his ghosts, suddenly

> sur les steppes de neige des nappes blanches, à perte de vue, comme des feux se décollent des étangs gelés, se levait la lumière mystique des bougies.
>
> [on the snowy steppes of the white tablecloths, as far as the eye could see, just as fires rise up from frozen ponds, mystical candlelight was rising.]

To a reader reading on a single level, these objects, which seem to extend the cold of the night onto the inside, constitute a haughty and frigid luxury decor: they suit the proud solitude of a moody, melancholy lord. (Besides, the hero is dressed *en habit de soirée* [in evening attire], and this is reflected, conversely, by the night "doublée de gel comme le satin blanc sous un habit de soirée" [lined with frost like the white satin underneath evening dress].) But when the reader reads on two levels as the title tells him to, beneath the tablecloth he can detect Leconte de Lisle's metaphoric cloths: "La neige, sur la plaine où les morts sont couchés, Comme un suaire étend au loin ses nappes blanches" [The snow, on the plain where the dead are asleep, like a shroud, stretches its white cloths out into the distance]. The atmosphere goes from chilly to funereal: not only does it reflect the snow outside, but that snow is a shroud. The setting becomes an emblem of melancholy.

The double reading also enables us to make predictions: the text remembered by the reader warns him in advance of what he will find in the text that he is deciphering. When his expectations are confirmed, he feels the same sense of harmony and certainty that might elsewhere have been inspired by a close relationship between words and reality. The imitated poem acts, therefore, like a particular case of a descriptive system.

But for this to occur, the double reading cannot be left to the reader's own initiative. It must be a formal imperative. There must be more than simple allusion, for the success of allusion is dependent on the level of our education and culture.[22] There must be a signal alerting us to the intertextuality. Sometimes this signal is obvious from the very first. One such instance, in "Paris à l'aube," is the use of the adjective *baudelairien* and of a passage in quotation marks.[23] If, however, the signal is at first obscure, its meaning becomes clearer as we read the text, and the comparison suddenly comes to us like a revelation.

This is the case in "Bonne promenade du matin" [Good walk of the morning].[24] At first glance, the title hardly gives us pause. At the very most, we might sense a slight awkwardness about it: the adjective *matinale* would be more natural than the genitive construction *du matin*. And as soon as we read *promenade matinale* in the third line, its visual contrast with the title adds to our first impression. In the absence of the adjective *matinale, le matin*, with the definite article, would have been preferable to the genitive we are given. Had there been a possessive adjective, but no *bonne*, everything would have been just fine: *ma promenade du matin* [my morning walk]. But none of this enters our consciousness until we discover that the poem is an ode to dawn, that dawn is rising over a large city, and that the main symbol of the new day are workers celebrating dawn—"choeur rafraîchi de rosée" [choir refreshed by dew]—by returning to work. At that moment, a connection is made with a summer daybreak in Rimbaud:

> Là-bas, dans leur vaste chantier
> Au soleil des Hespérides,
> Déjà s'agitent—en bras de chemise—
> Les Charpentiers.[25]

[There, on their vast construction site in the sun of the Hesperides, the Carpenters—in shirtsleeves—are already stirring.]

"Bonne promenade du matin" was hiding "Bonne pensée du matin" [Good thought of the morning]! In fact, right before our eyes, Gracq's workers are transformed into stagehands in a theater, and the city is their stage. This metamorphosis was predetermined by Rimbaud's lines, for the stagehands removing the nighttime scenery and creating the morning city are synonymous with the carpenters, who are also building an artificial world.

> Dans leurs Déserts de mousse, tranquilles,
> Ils préparent les lambris précieux

Où la ville
Peindra de faux cieux.

[In their mossy deserts, calmly they ready the precious panels, on which the city will paint false skies.]

Rimbaud's text, however, is but one of the sequences structuring this complex poem. "Bonne promenade du matin" is built on two images: the image of the stagehands, which is a daydream, and a phantasmagoria—the dance of the street lights, which ceases when the first passerby of the morning appears. A text like this must be closely guarded against any appearance of gratuitousness. Every one of its images must be compelling, and their common meaning—daybreak over Paris—must always be evident.

The second sequence of images is the simpler case. It closes the poem:

> Déjà la rue m'appelait accueillante; les pavés en grand arroi reprenaient leur place dans leurs alvéoles—rien, n'est-ce pas, ne s'était passé—et comme un loup sur le visage le plus troublant d'une femme aux débauches folâtres, après leur entrechat matinal les réverbères et les poubelles branlantes avaient repris leur faction de conserve sous l'oeil militaire des balayeurs municipaux.
>
> [The street was already calling to me welcomingly; the paving stones, which were scattered all about, returned to their places in their grooves—nothing had happened, had it? And like an eye mask over the most disturbing face of a woman at a wild orgy, after their morning entrechat, the swaying street lamps and garbage cans had all returned to their guard duty under the military eye of the municipal street sweepers.]

No sooner do we read this than we have a feeling of déjà vu. We are not tempted to ask the poet for a justification of his boldness, for the motif is the well-known myth of the nightly dance of familiar objects that is interrupted by a visitor or the return of daylight. More generally speaking, it is the stereotypical representation of the secret life of things: marionettes dancing a jig while the puppeteer sleeps, a motif exploited in ballet and film; the dance of the Lilliputians in "Le Meuble" by Charles Cros;[26]

a statue that could be seen moving if only we turned around fast enough (child's play, but poets from Hugo to Cocteau take it quite literally); or in another poem by Gracq: "ces beaux pylônes électriques entre lesquels les anges font de la corde raide chaque fois que le coup de canon du départ fait tourner la tête du spectateur. C'est du joli." [those beautiful electric pylons, between which angels go tightrope walking whenever the starting cannonblast makes the spectator's head turn. It's a fine sight.].[27] The myth is itself language, and the reader readily accepts these clichés because they are all variations on an opposition as tempting in its polarity as were the antitheses in "Salon meublé." Every statement of immobility irresistibly summons up a statement of mobility, and the more natural and permanent the immobility is made to seem, the more dramatic or suggestive of the fantastic is its transformation. If the immobility comes *before*, the image is a hyperbole of that which is imminent. (This motif enables Gracq to give his landscapes and settings the suspense of a drama.)[28] If the immobility comes *after*, it is the *a contrario* proof of invisible life. This creates the effective simplicity of a descriptive style in which one negation added to a statement of reality suffices to create the unreal or the surreal.[29] As for the stagehand image, it is an even more frequent myth. The variant representing it in our poem is overdetermined by a combination of sequences.

The myth is the representation of the world as a theater, which moralists have put to such wide use that it would be pointless even to attempt to quote them. But the myth is not always subordinated to ethics. In a much more general sense, it exploits the potentials of *a contrario* description. What is perhaps the most powerful of semantic oppositions—reality versus appearances—structures it, along with the corollary of that opposition: the postulate that all visible existence is accompanied by a hidden existence. This postulate is expressed by clichés such as "les coulisses de la politique, du Vatican, de la ville" [behind the political scenes, behind the scenes at the Vatican, in the city]. Thanks to this postulate, the word *façade* immediately generates questions pertaining to what lies behind the facade. Texts abound describing nature as a stage on which life is played—in Hugo, for instance, and Rimbaud.[30] But more often the stage set is a city. Here again, Rimbaud supplies Gracq with a model for a city rigged with stage effects like the stage of the Châtelet theater.[31]

The fundamental semantic structure, actualized as a description, would be sufficient to establish the myth and impose it on the reader. But the details of the description introduce their natural context into the poem—in other words, they generate clichés. Surrounded by representatives of their lexical family, the words seem to be confirmed and verified, as if we had compared them to reality. The stagehands are not comdemned to just any kind of hiding, but rather to a "dissimulation d'apaches dans les coulisses les plus poussiérieuses" [dissimulation of Apaches in the dustiest of wings]—which of course does not mean that the crew is behaving like Indians or toughs (another sense of the French term *apache*), or even that the backstage has not been swept; but rather, that they have concealed themselves particularly well. (The narrator alone was able to detect their existence; anyone else would have thought the stage set was reality.) Moreover, the backstage is the epitome of a backstage—in other words, it cannot be seen. This amounts to saying twice over that the stagehands have hidden themselves very well. They are invisible in the invisible. Thus, these groups are in fact superlatives, and more effective ones than *très* or *le plus* [*very* or *the most*], since they make use of words with full meanings, words that "donnent à voir" [that make us *see*].

Nor is this all. The myth of the stage set is reinforced by another myth: that of ruins as the scene of some mysterious goings-on. This myth not only repeats the first one on the semantic level, but integrates it on the narrative level into a system of *verisimilitude*:

> j'étais parfois surpris, à peine entamée ma promenade matinale, par des éclats dissonants de cuivre provenant d'une gracieuse maisonnette de briques en démolition. Sur les thèmes choisis de ce mystérieux orphéon des ruines, j'imaginais derrière cette façade de plâtras tristes toute une théorie de tonnelles ingénues et matinales, où des électriciens en cotte rouge, de blondes marcheuses des trottoirs de l'aube, des cortèges au sérieux travesti professionnel face au soleil

levant dissipaient à part soi leurs brumes nocturnes dans quelques-unes de ces chopes d'étain ouvragées qui font si belle figure au premier plan d'une bacchanale d'opéra-comique.

[sometimes, when I had scarcely begun my morning stroll, I would be surprised by dissonant clashes of brass coming from a charming little brick house that was being torn down. To the carefully chosen tunes of this mysterious band of the ruins, I imagined that behind the facade of sad, crumbling plaster there was a whole procession of artless morning arbors, where electricians in red overalls, blond walkers of the dawn streets, and processions in serious professional disguises, facing the rising sun, were privately dissipating their nocturnal fogs in some of those finely tooled pewter tankards that look so nice on center stage in a comic opera bacchanalia.]

We can see how the music episode prepares the way for the metaphor of the city's backstage. The reader might reject that metaphor if it were submitted to him right at the outset, but he cannot refuse the music episode since, within the descriptive system of a stroll, the motif of these particular incidents can be expected. If a stroller is going to stop and stare, his surroundings had better give him something worth staring at. Nor can we question *j'imaginais*, which subordinates the image to the morning saunterer's experience.[32] As for the myth that ruins are the site of clandestine activities, it is a particular version of the theme of life in death. This is why it is so frequent with the Romantics. Here, it hyperbolizes the "deceptive appearances" seme implicit in *décor*. Moreover, the text is constructed so as to make the equation *stage set = ruins* explicit, since the last allusion to the little house describes it in a theatrical code:

minuscule enceinte dissimulée aux arpenteurs de bitume par la retombée conventionnelle d'une courtine de plâtres promise aux trois coups du démolisseur.

[miniscule enclosure hidden from the asphalt surveyors by a conventional curtainfall of plaster that was promised to the demolition worker's three blows.]

The circle of the words' logic thus closes on the reader.[33]

Now all this powerful machinery designed to convince us of the city's secret life is subordinate to the theme of morning. All these accumulated systems are not developed for their own sake, but appear in the text only as codes, as hyperbolic language, for describing dawn. How does this subordination occur? Once again, not by reference to reality, but by the linkage of words.

As in "L'Averse," a series of formal indicators reminds the reader that the images have no value of their own, but only as synonyms of dawn. The adjective *matinal* and its synonyms modify not only words that suit them, but also nouns that cannot be modified by a temporal sign: "trottoirs de l'aube," "tonnelles ingénues et matinales," and "s'ouvrent les élytres matinales des joyeuses bestioles des jardins" [the morning elytra of the merry garden beasties open up]. In other words, these nouns are merely substitutes for *morning*. Moreover, in contact with *matinal, ingénu* comes to designate the new day's innocence: whence *machinistes ingénus*. Better yet, the diminutive *bestiole* is to *bête* what *machiniste ingénu* is to *machiniste*,[34] and this analogy is confirmed by *joyeuse* and the positive connotations of *jardins*. Everything—morphologically the diminutive, syntactically the stock epithet and comparison, and semantically the value of *joyeuses, jardin*, and *s'ouvrent*—repeat what Eluard called "la naissance du jour tendre" [the birth of a new day].

The very unfolding of the sentences is occasionally diverted by the underlying presence of the thematic structure. *Cortèges* [processions] in the passage I just cited are disconcerting in a sentence describing workers sitting at tables under arbors. But their drinking bout, which looks like a realistic detail, is in fact generated by the tenor of the metaphor. The drinkers "dissipent leurs brumes nocturnes" [dissipate their nighttime fogs] in tankards only because one of the clichés entailed by sunrise is the sentence: "le soleil levant (les premiers rayons du soleil) dissipe(nt) les brumes nocturnes (de l'aube)" [the rising sun (the first rays of the sun) dissipate(s) the night's fogs (of dawn)]. The sunrise is told of in the code of *workers leaving for work*, but the workers are represented in terms of a rising sun.[35] In Gracq's own words: "it is important that we let the essential driving elements of the *potential* sentence [*la phrase en puissance*] subsist, like joining-marks, beneath the written sentence."[36]

All these examples clearly show that in order to evaluate these literary forms, we must stop calling on reality and speaking of truth or aptness. We must speak, instead, of efficacy, for what we are dealing with is an *energetics of words.*[37] Even if we cannot prove that its verbal sequences are coherent and that the images they generate are natural and plausible, we shall always judge this poetry, made of lexical linkages rigorously *deduced* from an initial given, to be a success.[38]

[15]

Overdetermination in the Prose Poem (II): Francis Ponge

A PROSE POEM by Ponge is never anything more than the textual expansion of a nuclear word. The text's formal and semantic characteristics are derived directly or indirectly from that word. Ponge is perfectly aware of this, and has offered his "Huître" [Oyster] as an example of direct derivation:

> It is obvious that if words like *blanchâtre* [whitish], *opiniâtre* [stubborn], *verdâtre* [greenish], or God knows what appear in my text, it is also because I am determined by the word "huître" [oyster], by the fact that there is a circumflex in it, over the vowel (or diphthong) *t, r, e*. . . . Furthermore, given the fact that an oyster is hard to open, I find it hard to express it other than by pronouncing the word *opiniâtre*.[1]

In the case of indirect derivation, the text is an expansion of a matrix sentence that is itself generated by the nuclear word. It actualizes syntagmatically, in the form of a predicate relationship, one or more of that word's essential semes. The text is produced through a series of variations on this matrix invariant. Ponge again finds an example of this, in a sonnet by Malherbe to Calixte:

> Calixte already means, etymologically, the most beautiful one. Now, to say: "Il n'est rien de si beau comme Calixte est belle" [There is nothing as beautiful as Calixte is beautiful], well, it's a pure tautology! And the whole poem is a pure tautology. Beauty

is beauty. It's nothing but beauty. And what has to be done is simply to develop and structure this tautology, which, after all, is contained in the name alone. It is a matter of developing it joyfully, jubilantly.[2]

These derivations, however, are characteristic of literary discourse in general when it is realized within the limits of a text. Associative chains (including secondary sequences stemming from words that are themselves derived from the matrix) unfurl, and these chains crisscross each other at every point at which one of the text's components is pertinent to two descriptive systems at once. The sequences are reinforced by a continual reference to stereotypes. Thus the text is not to be verified in terms of reality but, rather, in conformity with commonplaces and with a "bonheur d'expression," a felicity of expression, going back to the sources of everyday usage. All of this comprises a network of overdetermination that is superimposed on grammatical relations, on the logic of the narrative, and on the system of verisimilitude. This network thereby transforms the entire textual complex into a single unit of significance and gives it its character as a verbal monument and, hence, its "literariness."[3]

Since it is one of the universals of the literary work, overdetermination could not on its own account for what belongs to Ponge alone. Wanting to demonstrate the workings of overdetermination, which he perceives empirically, Ponge readily finds an example of it in this distich by Malherbe: "Je veux croire que la Seine / Aura des cygnes alors" [I want to believe that the Seine will then have swans]. Ponge writes:

> This, to me, displays the most glorious and surest kind of invention. It is easy to see the reason why (but we only see it if we look for it): *Seine, cygne, aura, alors*. And I can't ignore the *Je veux croire*, which sets in motion a truly glorious movement and expresses in a nutshell the gliding of the bird with its wings spread wide. I mean, it expresses, through the expansion of the diphthong, the quivering optimism of the sentence as it moves forward.[4]

It is possible to reformulate this analysis less impressionistically, albeit a bit more pedantically. The distich is overdetermined in that it twice states the promise of swans. It states it semantically with a verb in the future tense that expresses belonging (*aura*) and another in the present tense that expresses certainty (*je veux croire*), and it states it semiotically by translating the statement of belonging into a figurative style. (We go from the abstract *aura* to the subject's interiorization of the predicate: the word *cygne* is already contained in *Seine*.)

It goes without saying that many examples are to be found in Ponge of overdetermination in which the textual practice in no way diverges from the rules applying to all literary discourse. In this way, he depicts himself searching through the Littré for just the right word to designate a particular precious stone. Having found it, he calls the dictionary "ce coffre merveilleux d'expressions anciennes" [that wonderful treasure chest of age-old expressions].[5] This word grouping is motivated three times over: by the metaphor (this goes without saying), by the cliché (*cet ouvrage est*) *une mine inépuisable* or (*il est*) *riche en* [this book is a goldmine; it is rich in, it is a treasure house of], and so on, and by a play on words. This wordplay causes the conversion of *riche mine* into *trésor* [treasure] and of *trésor* into a synonym of *dictionary—thesaurus*—to coincide with the conversion of *expressions anciennes* into an object kept in a thesaurus. From this he obtains the matrix tautology: "j'ai trouvé un trésor dans ce trésor" [I found a treasure in this treasury].[6] I shall not dwell any longer on these universals of poetic language, especially since excellent studies of them in Ponge (albeit using a different terminology), have already been made by Marcel Spada and, more recently, by Gérard Genette.[7]

It seems to me that what characterizes Ponge's writing and defines his specific mode of text production is the *visibility* of overdetermination. To repeat the statement I just quoted, Malherbe's reader sees only if he is looking for something. Ponge's reader, however, has no need to look, for the text marks out the path of the derivation for him. Whether the initial given—the nuclear word or matrix sentence (for a word's semic configuration can always be rewritten as a sentence)—provides the model for a tautological series of variants, or whether that model is provided by those variants themselves or by words that are the points of intersection or climax of the various derivations, certain formal characteristics are always present which force the reader to recognize their overdetermination. This is what Ponge terms the text's *functioning*, which he is careful to distinguish from what traditional aesthetics would call harmony and from the organization of words resulting from the use of rhetorical tropes. The existence of a series of variants on the initial model and the very fact of that model's transcoding into successive vocabularies compel the reader's attention (the structure "se déclare hautement pour ce qu'elle est" [loudly proclaims itself for what it is]). This gives the reader, so Ponge tells us, a feeling of jubilation, which he calls *objoie*, "objoy."[8]

Visibility, deconventionalization, and pleasure—I propose to explain these three aspects of a single phenomenon in terms of one formal constant: humor.[9] It is, of course, not a question here of either irony or the comic, but rather of a kind of discourse, a playful use of language (most often, in fact, in the form of plays on words or outright puns). The incongruity of this special kind of discourse is amusing and, therefore, a way to control the reader's attention. But this very incongruity is the mark of overdetermination: it is the result of word relationships foreign to their grammatical relations and to the narrative or descriptive sequence of meanings; in short, to everything related to the mimesis. It results from the incompatibility between the logic of the derivation, which is serial, linear, and syntagmatic, and the requirements of referentiality.

The derivation always gains the upper hand, and this imbalance is nowhere more evident than in actual puns. If language does not provide him with an appropriate derivation then Ponge, rather like those poets who alter words so as to make them rhyme,[10] resorts to the most conspicuous approximations. For example, at the end of "Prose à l'éloge d'Aix," we read that the cultural traditions of Aix-en-Provence allow us "d'y accueillir, à deux pas seulement de Pourrières et du triomphe de Marius, les services de l'amadoué Mozart" [just two steps away from Pourrières and the triumph of Marius, to welcome the services of the mollified Mozart].[11] *Amadoué* is a rather heavy-handed play on Wolfgang Amadeus, but its very heaviness underscores the fact that it is the antithetical transformation of a sentence that appeared eight paragraphs earlier: "trois cent mille Teutons, exterminés par Marius, y furent laissés sans sépulture à Pourrières" [three hundred thousand Teutons, exterminated by Marius, were left there graveless at Pourrières]. The artful adaptation of the Latin first name polarizes its opposition to *Teutons*, and this polarization is made complete by the censoring of the German first name, which is expelled from the text and itself exterminated. It is as if an initial sentence, "barbares, Aix les arrêta" [barbarians, Aix stopped them], were matched with a final sentence, "une fois civilisé, elle accueille l'un d'entre eux" [once he has been civilized, she welcomes one of their number]. Without this derivation in spite of the language, the text would be nothing more than a blurb from the local tourist board.[12] This polarization is not my own invention: I have deduced it from other derivations. The *A* in *Aix* represents the mountain upon which Marius' victory took place, and the final *X* symbolizes "la croix mise en ce lieu sur certaine entreprise barbare" [the cross placed on this site on a certain barbarous undertaking]. A remark like that would be a touch of prosaic picturesqueness if it were not the expansion of the *X*: Mozart is welcomed by the arts of Aix, forming a procession with their "palettes et pinceaux, archets et violons croisés" [palettes and paintbrushes, bows and violins crossed].

To return to *amadoué*, it is obvious that this sense of the word would be unintelligible and gratuitous on the level of everyday language. A new "Mozartian" sense (the compact equivalent of a common opposition concerning Germans in the nationalistic French sociolect: *Barbarian versus la musique adoucit les moeurs*, "music soothes the savage soul"), a new meaning perceptible only in context, arises out of the two-page-long derivation from two letters. It is quite impossible to perceive this derivation without having the annoying feeling that it is a rather heavy-handed joke or, at the very least, that it subverts the unity of tone required in traditional literature. Nevertheless, not only does Ponge do nothing to lessen this impression, but the verbal humor leads, in its turn, to new expansions, which perpetuate it and aggravate the author's case. These expansions are triggered solely by humor: a taboo is lifted, authorizing associations that are subordinate to the first one. This is similar to the case of the extended metaphor, in which only the primary metaphor need be acceptable in normal usage and the secondary metaphors need merely be possible derivations or lexical analogues of the primary one. This is what happens in the following piece, which is dedicated to the mouth as the seat of taste:

> La bouche en son palais—c'est le temple du goût—procède à ses appréciations particulières. Elle s'y fait son opinion elle-même, puis la communique au cerveau, siégeant en chambre du conseil, par l'intermédiaire de l'arrière-nez, chargé de l'odorat, avec lequel tout au long de vestibules et d'escaliers intérieurs elle se concerte.[13]
>
> [The mouth in its palace (palate)—it's the temple of taste—proceeds with its individual appraisals. It forms its own opinion there, and then passes it on to the brain, holding court in the council chamber, by the intermediary of the rear-nose, which is in charge of smell and with which, up and down vestibules and inner stairways, the mouth consults.]

If all we had here were two allegorical characters taken from a personification of the Five Senses, the piece would fit perfectly into the kinds of amusing popularizations that were still published around the turn of the century. What makes it different, though, is that the reader is forced to give in to the obvious and recognize—a bit late, however—that the allegory comes straight from the ambiguity of *palais*, which must be taken in both its palatial and its palatal sense. Except for the construction *en son palais*, which is permitted by the palatial sense, the palatal *palais* could never produce the carbon copy of judicial jargon, *siégeant en chambre*. Nor could it produce the comic allusion to Voltaire's *Temple du Goût* or the extended metaphor of an architectural space going from the neologism *arrière-nez* (modeled after *arrière-plan* [background] or *arrière-boutique* [rooms behind a shop]) to *Vestibule* and *escalier*.

It nonetheless remains that the construction *en son palais*, whereby the palatial comes to outweigh the palatal, is incompatible with the mouth, be it a real mouth, a referent, or a signified: the mouth contains the palate, and not vice versa. Furthermore, the Voltaire quotation, in this context, seems to be an embellishment conforming to the rules of this prose poem's genre: the *blason*. The quotation functions, therefore, as the encomiastic conversion of a matrix: "la bouche est le siège du goût" [the mouth is the seat of taste]. In an actual natural science textbook "written for young ladies," the tongue or, more likely, the taste buds, would be the organ of taste. Here, however, the description is tampered with to the detriment of physiology, because the verbal associations outweigh reality and clichés are more plausible than truth. And such clichés make the *palais* the site of taste, understood both as the sense of taste and as the refinement of that sense. Do we not speak in French of a *palais blasé* [indifferent palate] or a *palais délicat* [delicate palate]? This play on words, which theoretically should establish verbal inappropriateness or, at least, an amphibology, has the paradoxical result of giving new vitality to the mimesis. Indeed, it is highly doubtful that any reader is actually aware of the representation's lack of fidelity to reality. All he sees is the happy encounter that by means of a displacement of meaning, a catachresis, rediscovers the aptness of words. What the double derivation from *palais* generates is a metaphor, if you will. But just when the figurative sense turns its back on reality (since, by definition, it takes over from the literal meaning), it returns to the literal by means of one of the metaphor's vehicles, the architectural *palais*. The selection of this vehicle is motivated by the fact that it is already a metonym (in the oral sense of *palais*) of the metaphor's tenor, the mouth. The model according to which the mimesis is generated is neither the referent nor even the semantic field in which the signified is inscribed, but rather the descriptive system of the word *bouche*. Unfolding as a periphrasis of that word, that descriptive system is a tautology *par excellence.* The "parti pris des choses" [taking the side of things]—in other words, the choice of the descriptive genre as the rule for poetic writing—is truly subordinate to Ponge's corrective: "compte tenu des mots" [bearing in mind the words]. The description is not true in relation to its non-verbal object, but rather in relation to the possible collocations required by the signifier. It is true not because of its fidelity to reality, but because of its grammaticality.[14]

It must be stressed that the overdetermination of the mimesis cannot be separated from a challenge to referentiality. Puns, or at least the membership of one word in two incompatible codes, insure the coexistence of representation and verbalism, of a supposed reference to the things hidden beneath the words and the words' obvious reference to a verbal given. The text's poeticity lies in the double meaning—in the coincidence, at the same point, between a proper sense and a contextual sense that are mutually exclusive. Ponge's textual practice puts this maximum oxymoron to the test by taking it to the point of absurdity: the more the text claims to be turned toward the real, the more explosive is its scandalous derivation from words. This is what happens in the poem "Des Cristaux naturels,"[15] which by virtue of both the meaning and the syntax of its title belongs to the genre of didactic poetry. That genre's very ethos is an oxymoron, since it is built on the principle of praising the miracles of nature, which is to say of representing the natural as supernatural. One common way to actualize this paradox is metaphorically to cross the borders separating the different natural kingdoms. Minerals, for example, are described in a vegetal code, and a crystal traditionally becomes a stone flower. Speaking in the first person in the text, Ponge spurns this stereotype and proposes a more exact image, one cleansed of the lyricism of miracles. The reader expects a clear-cut example of an image modeled on reality. He even expects a technical vocabulary, that hyperbole of reality. And in fact, Ponge very scientifically opposes crystals, which are defined, predictable, and calculable shapes, to amorphous rocks [*roches amorphes*]. But no sooner does the word *amorphe* affirm the principle of scientific precision than a derivation nullifies that principle with a play on words—and an especially disconcerting one at that, since its figurative sense is complicated by a marker quite incompatible with the genre. The wordplay involves a familiar expression which is already comic. *Amorphe* generates a fairly humorous humanization of rocks, since the word applies to a person who is *veule, passive,* and *indifférente* [spineless, passive, and indifferent] (here I am simply repeating the adjectives listed by Ponge), and who seems to *tourner le dos* [turn his back] (once again, the expression is Ponge's). Hence, this excessive enthusiasm for crystals: "Enfin des pierres tournées vers nous et qui ont déclos leurs paupières, des pierres qui disent oui! Et quels signes d'intelligence, quels clins d'oeil!" [At last, rocks turned toward us and that have opened their eyes, rocks that say yes! And what signs of intelligence, what winks of the eye!].[16] The sole raison d'être for this entire exclamation is the expansion of the opposition between *amorphe* and *the opposite of amorphe.* Since it is the opposite of an amorphous mineral, crystal is a mineral with lots of get-up-and-go. And, as if the first pun were not enough, a second play on words comes to complicate text production within the genre by presenting a further incompatibility with that genre. In the context of the derivation from *amorphe,* the group "pierres . . . qui ont déclos leurs paupières" [rocks that have opened their eyes] is truly ungrammatical, since it is foreign to that opposition. The corrected crystal mimesis is contaminated by the metaphor that Ponge had supposedly rejected, for the relatively rare verb *déclore* inevitably reminds the reader of Ronsard's rose: "Qui ce matin avait déclose / Sa robe de pourpre au soleil" [Which this morning had opened its crimson gown to the sun]. In short, *déclore leurs paupières* is *open their eyes* in floral code, since the rose is the queen of flowers. This *open their eyes* matrix is no doubt another variation on the *amorphe* antithesis, but the very form and manner of this variant, the choice of which appears to be most unusual and unmotivated, is nonetheless derived from the initial given. *Open their eyes* is based on an original variation on the equation *crystal* = *flower,* which the text had rejected when it proclaimed "le parti pris des choses."

This variant, which accompanies the title as an epigraph, is a quotation from Rimbaud's "Après le déluge": "Oh! les pierres précieuses qui se cachaient, les fleurs qui regardaient déjà" [Oh! the precious stones that were hiding, the flowers that were already looking]. These two examples show how the play on words also acts as an index of literariness: its incompatibility with the context negates the paragram.[17] The second example (the reappearance of the floral vocabulary), differs from the first in that it also functions as an icon of circularity and demonstrates that, by closing in on itself to form a unit of significance, the text is behaving like a poem. And since the play on words indicates circularity, it is also an icon of tautology itself.

Lastly, my two examples illustrate another function of verbal humor as a factor in overdetermination: borrowed from a code that its context negates (*déclos*), or sitting astride two different codes (*amorphe*), humor is the instrument of the transcoding. In the continuous series of variations on the initial model forming the text, a word with a double meaning, "le mot du jeu," forms the transition from one variant to another. It puts the text back in motion. This is best seen in metaphors and similes: these two figures usually presuppose the maintenance or accentuation of the difference or distance that separates the two codes and which the text momentarily postulates as equivalent. The symbolization of that equivalence is left to a function word or to an entirely abstract grammatical relation. These grammatical words are all-purpose words immune to the lexical influence of their context and therefore to overdetermination. In Ponge, these words tend to disappear and are replaced by a contamination or even a mutual saturation of the vocabularies of the tenor and the vehicle. Instead of vehicle and tenor being two mutually exclusive variants of the matrix that are linked by a purely formal equation, the vehicle seems to be a direct variant of the tenor. Take the series of comparisons at the beginning of the prose poem about the asparagus fern, "Asparagus":

> Plus divisément encore que chez le cèdre, admiré-je peut-être chez l'asparagus cette façon de plafonner par chacun de ses hauts étages,

de ne présenter au salut de la lumière (ou mettons à l'atterrissage en douce des avions de la lumière) que le dos de ses mains à hauteur de lèvres suspendues; d'étendre aussi largement ses générosités, ses libéralités, ses largesses—c'est-à-dire non seulement l'ombre qu'il procure, mais ses pluies: pluies fines, non seulement d'ombres mais de graines . . . car chacune de ses branches est un long nuage effilé, un large nuage profilé—comme ceux qui s'étirent à l'horizon sur les plaines aux heures des crépuscules, crépuscules d'orient comme d'occident, lorsque s'apaisent les vents. Ainsi s'immobilisent de longues rames de wagons violets abandonnées par leurs locomotives quand celles-ci sont rentrées dans leurs rotondes, leurs rosaces en verrières, qui s'empourprent et s'enfument: vraiment la rosace des vents, bouquet de larges anémones vues à travers des branches de cèdres.[18]

[Even more dividedly than in the cedar, I perhaps admire in the asparagus fern its way of spreading out with each of its high levels and of offering to the salvation of light (or shall we say the smooth landing of the light's airplanes) nothing but the back of its hands at the height of suspended lips; its way of so widely extending its generosities, its liberalities, its largesses—in other words, not only the shade that it provides, but its rains: fine rains, not only of shade, but of seeds . . . for each of its branches is a long, tapered cloud, a wide streamlined cloud—like those that stretch out on the horizon over the plains at the twilight hours, both the Eastern and Western twilights, when the winds die down. Thus, long trains of violet cars stand still, abandoned by their locomotives when the latter returned to their roundhouses, their glass-roofed rose windows, which turn crimson and smoky: truly the rose window of the winds, a bouquet of wide anemones seen through cedar branches.]

The paradoxical comparison of a potted plant to the huge cedar—a bit of playfulness very close to the garden baobab in Daudet's *Tartarin de Tarascon*—is rationalized by the horizontality common to both. The first comparison is: "car chacune de ses branches est un long nuage effilé, un large nuage profilé." The second comparison is: "Ainsi s'immobilisent de longues rames de wagons violets." The third, the sentence "nuages . . . qui s'étirent à l'horizon . . . lorsque s'apaisent les vents," generates, in turn, a secondary comparison of the winds to locomotives: "rames . . . abandonnées par leurs locomotives quand celles-ci sont rentrées dans leurs rotondes." This last detail generates a synecdoche replacing *rotonde*, which is too exclusively a railway term and has no conceivable referent in the sky, with its *verrières*, which at the least are a concession to mimetic verisimilitude, since they permit an allusion to the twilight colors and vapors: "leurs rotondes, leurs rosaces en verrières, qui s'empourprent et s'enfument." These *rosaces* are a metaphor grafted onto the synecdoche, and this metaphor acts as a springboard for another, which is helped along by the play on *rosace* and *rose*. This metaphor develops into one final comparison: "bouquet de larges anémones vues à travers des branches de cèdres."

The incongruity of the color violet or purple in a railroad descriptive system is a good example of how the sign of the image-producing equation is replaced by the overlapping of two lexical codes: instead of simply saying that the clouds resemble trains on their siding (in this particular case, instead of simply saying *ainsi*), the text attributes to the railway cars a twilight color belonging only to the clouds. This overlapping is constant, though: all the metaphoric or comparative vehicles—*cèdre, nuage, rames*—are derived from one essential seme of the word *asparagus*, which is the tenor of all these metaphors. That seme is *horizontality*. The codes of the vehicles are saturated by the very tenor that they would normally replace. The passage untiringly repeats the matrix: *the asparagus fern is the plant of horizontality*. The horizontality of its branches is both its characteristic shape and the principle of its aesthetic use, since the fern's horizontal planes are used to contrast with the vertical thrust of flower stems. The poem's second paragraph demonstrates the existence of the matrix by spelling it out: the derivation (carried forward by the transition "Voyons maintenant l'asparagus dans un bouquet" [Now let's see the asparagus fern in a bouquet]) culminates as follows: "c'est l'asparaqus, par le contraste de ses tranquilles horizontales largesses, qui fait goûter au maximum la prodigieuse ressource hélicoïdale des roses" [the asparagus fern, by the contrast of its tranquil, horizontal liberalities, lets the prodigious, helical resources of roses be enjoyed to the utmost].[19]

Lexical overlapping is therefore simply a variety of tautology. The more it affects the codes of the vehicles, and thereby threatens or compensates for the difference and distance between the figurative and the literal, the more it compels our attention. And in each case it is because of a strangeness of form or an ambiguity, either immediately evident or suspected after the fact, that it catches the reader's attention. The transformation from one variant of the matrix sentence to another is effected by plays on words that are all generated by another essential seme of *asparagus*, the seme of *vegetality*. That seme maintains the plant's literal presence in the midst of transformations presupposing the elimination of the botanical code. The double meaning of *rame* corresponds to this seme, for not only is it the appropriate term in a railroad context, but it is also a gardening term—a stake—and furthermore it is closely related to *ramée* [leafy boughs] and *rameau* [branch]. If I, too, were to engage in some wordplay, I would say that the text speaks the language of the rails, but with a vegetal accent. With the next transition comes another play on words, this time an etymological one. *Anémone* belongs to the vegetal vocabulary, but when it is overdetermined by the cloud trains, the word returns to the image of the locomotive wind, for *anémone* also means the wind, *anémos* (not to mention yet another association involving the signified: the color of the flower is also that of the evening clouds). However vaguely it may be perceived, this play on words forces the reader to decode *bouquet de larges anémones* in terms of the group *rosace des vents*. The former is a word-for-word conversion of the latter, for despite their semantic incompatibilities, *bouquet* and *rosace* are related, just as *anémones* and *vents* are.

Rosace des vents is the most important transition: it begins the circularity of the text. From this point on the deviation retraces its steps, as it were. The passage quoted above begins by comparing the asparagus fern to the cedar; and its ending, together with the beginning of the following paragraph, form through repetition the equivalent of a comparison: "des branches de cèdres. Ainsi des branches de l'asparagus" [cedar branches. So too the branches of the asparagus fern]. Revealingly, this is precisely where the play on words becomes explicit. The previous ambiguities were latent, insofar as they are perceived only retroactively, when the course of the reading lets us sense to what extent words read with one meaning were preparing a different meaning, which their context would seem to exclude. But it is impossible not to see that *rosace des vents*, although fully justified by the image preceding it, is a parody of the compound *rose des vents* [wind rose]; and at the same time it becomes literal again by virtue of its generating seme, for a *rosace* is also a big rose.[20] And, as always in the workings of style, a corrective, excuse, or precaution—*vraiment* [really]—serves only to underscore the approximation and accentuate the humor. This adverb asserts the threefold appropriateness of *rosace* in the three codes of wind, rails, and flowers, at the same time that the word's form—nowadays almost always pejorative—makes it look like a grammatical error.

Equally strong puns can be found almost everywhere in Ponge. Although a pun conceived as an independent genre is by definition its own end, Ponge's puns are never gratuitous. The genre's characteristic artifice becomes in his work a marker of overdetermination and the icon of its mechanicalness. This is why the humor in these texts is dispensed with a heavier hand the more strongly they are determined. For instance, expressing questions about death sparked in him by a newspaper survey (Is cremation preferable to burial? Should we risk the wrath of the Church in order to escape graveyard worms?) Ponge risks the outrageous: *vous m'asticotez* [you bug me].[21] He then underscores this with a *je parle très sérieusement* [I'm speaking very seriously], which is analogous to the *vraiment* in "Asparagus." This coincidence is revealing: correctives are invariably found in humor for the simple reason that they state exactly what the function of humor is. It is mockery without mockery, empty play—*the absurdity of language*, as Ponge says concerning the *objeu*. It is therefore a purely linguistic phenomenon, independent of mimesis and referentiality and, consequently, a sign whose sole relevance is to the internal system of the text.

This relevance lies in the part this sign plays in the text's *functioning*: puns and plays on words mark out the stages of overdetermination and guide us toward the key to the significance. Because of its obviousness, humor draws circles around the latency of the matrix: it dictates an associative exercise to the reader and makes him go through a kind of linguistic calisthenics and review—just as we can review a lesson—the various meanings of a single word. Ponge terms these different meanings the *semantic thickness* of words. He seems to believe that they are "l'histoire des significations variées qu'un mot a pu prendre au cours de son histoire" [the history of the various meanings that a word managed to acquire in the course of its history].[22] But they really are simultaneous meanings, present together at the same moment in the word's history, but which in purely utilitarian language use are mutually exclusive in a single context. Poetry, however, invites the reader to recognize their coexistence in a single context and explore the lexicon's *family tree*, its "*arbre généologique*" as Ponge called it, thereby defining the play on words with a play on words.

Writing such as this displaces the site of the literary phenomenon. Its most perfect state and most finished version are no longer the text, but rather the work complementing it (the practice of comparison), which the reader performs on the text as he goes from the actual words to associations of ideas, from the explicit to the implicit, from what is written in black and white to presuppositions.

Under these conditions, the phenomenon of perception through humor, which is the meeting place of text and reader and is usually defined by a signal preceding the interpretive activity, is interiorized by the reader. The matrix itself is a pun—an invisible one that the reader must recreate. Here, once again, is Ponge on Malherbe:

> C'est en tout, à mon sens, montrer la seule imagination qui vaille, que d'inventer les séquences verbales (littérales, syllabiques), c'est-à-dire à la fois significatives et sonores, qui permettent d'installer cette image inoubliablement dans la mémoire:

> Et des perles sans nombre
> Germeront dans la Seine au milieu des graviers.
>
> Notons bien que Malherbe n'écrit pas: "que des *gemmes* sans nombre" comme sans doute l'aurait fait un artisan plus grossier. Il se borne, par le seul *germer*, à évoquer secrètement, discrètement l'association. Voilà la poésie! le langage remis en son état naissant.[23]

> [All in all, as I see it, the only worthwhile kind of imagination is shown by inventing verbal sequences (of letters, of syllables)—that is, both meaningful and sonorous sequences—enabling this image to be unforgettably fixed in our memory:
> And countless pearls
> will germinate in the Seine amidst the gravel.
>
> Let's clearly point out that Malherbe does not write: "that countless *gems*," as no doubt a coarser artisan would have done. He restricts himself to evoking the association secretly and discreetly, using *germer* alone. This is poetry! Language restored to its nascent state.]

Or rather, the text restored to its nascent state. Insofar as it is a body of lexical collocations, clichés, and stereotypes established by years of usage, language provides the *tertium comparationis*, the meeting point, the verbal association that would be a pun if it appeared in the text. But since it does not appear in the text, it is the matrix, the key to the enigma that the formal strangeness of the verbal sequence (its "trouvailles de style" or stylistic strokes of genius, as critics used to say) would pose, if only the latent association did not reveal the logic behind that sequence. Those forms in the text compelling the reader's attention indicate possible chains of associations, which will intersect in his mind. The reading works like a kind of geometry pointing to the locus of overdetermination outside the text.[24]

The prose poem entitled "Les *Illuminations* à l'Opéra-Comique" [The *Illuminations* at the Comic Opera] posits its rules of overdetermination right in its title.[25] In the guise of announcing a musical adaptation—just as we might have "*Mignon* à l'Opéra-Comique" or "*Fantasio* à l'Opèra-Comique"—the title is really announcing a pseudo-report on the modernization of the stage lighting. This report is the metaphor for a meditation about the updating of an old fashioned genre—the tricks of the fairy Electricity (light as spectacle), replace the outmoded fairies of the Comic Opera (light as a prop). Of course, this meditation is nothing but a verbal exercise, a long derivation based on the play on the plural *illuminations*, out of which the text produces *mise en scène* [staging], *éclairages de fête* [party lights], *éclairage comme forme artistique* [lighting as a form of art], and even *révélation esthétique* [aesthetic revelation]. It then closes the circle with a quotation from Rimbaud's *Les Illuminations* on the very subject of the Opéra-Comique. By virtue of this generator, all representations of electricity are valorized, and they in turn generate various figures. Electricity as danger, for instance (but from which we can protect ourselves), translates the description of the installation of a high-tension wire into a metaphor: the image "d'une sorte de fauve (invisible), ou de tigre du Bengale (abstrait)" [of a kind of (invisible) wild animal, or of an (abstract) Bengal tiger]. Electricity domesticated—a tamed tiger, voltage turned into light—becomes a metaphor in the shape of brightly colored birds: "le tigre formidable . . . s'y trouvait . . . transformé en une multitude d'oiseaux multicolores . . . transformé, ce tigre du Bengale, en une profusion de bengalis" [the fearsome tiger . . . was . . . transformed into a multitude of multicolored birds . . . transformed, that Bengal tiger, into a profusion of waxbills].[26]

The first of these metaphors presents no problems. The descriptive given of the *grille* [electric grid] generates two derivations, one of which is literal (the grid protecting a transformer box), and the other metaphoric: caged danger, that is, a wild beast, a *fauve*. *Tiger* is simply the hyperbole of *fauve*. Buffon tells us that tigers are more dangerous than lions, and the sociolect classifies them with the killer beasts. (Ponge himself produces a variation on this point in reference to wasps when he asks: "Pourquoi aussi les animaux tigrés sont-ils les plus méchants?" [Why then are tiger-striped animals the meanest?].)[27] So what we have here is a derivation pushed to the climax of a danger paradigm. And *du Bengale* further hyperbolizes *tiger*, in the same way that *lion de l'Atlas* would be a hyperbole of *lion*.

The second metaphor—that of the birds as footlights—is just as strongly overdetermined. The theme of brightly colored birds can be found everywhere. (And here there are even "multitudes d'oiseaux multicolores," with the added derivation from the prefix.) Birds and fire are traditionally associated. Larousse's *Grand dictionnaire universel du XIXe siècle* lists at least one *oiseau de feu*, or firebird, and Michelet produced this paraphrase of Ponge's lights in the mid-nineteenth century:

> ces flammes ailées que vous nommez oiseaux, flamboyants . . . de couleur. De la main brûlante de Dieu échappe incessamment cet évantail immense de diversité foudroyante . . . où tout m'inonde d'harmonie, de lumière. . . . Mélodieuses étincelles du feu d'en haut.[28]
>
> [these winged flames, which you call birds, ablaze with color. From the burning hand of God there escapes continuously this huge fan of lightning diversity . . . where everything drowns me in harmony and light. . . . Melodious sparks from the fire on high.]

Along the path from Michelet to Ponge, there can be no question of any recollected reading. Their parallel derivations simply demonstrate how narrow are the limits that language imposes on text production. As soon as one component of a descriptive system has been activated by a semic coincidence—*saisir le noeud* [grasping the knot], as Ponge says[29]—the same stereotyped complexes belonging to the system will unfold, always in the same direction, and more or less completely.

But none of this explains the most visible textual component: the translation of the literal *transformé*, a technicism belonging to the vocabulary of electronics, into a barely tolerable pun on *Bengale* and *bengali*. The question might even arise when we first come on *Bengale*, since there was nothing, after all, to keep Ponge from writing *tigre royal* instead. And nothing prevented him from starting out with *aras multicolores* [multi-colored macaws], since, in this same passage, macaws close the paradigm that was begun with *bengalis* [waxbills].

If the *before* and *after* states of the metaphor have *Bengale* in common, or rather if they are a formal variation on *Bengale*, or even if they continue to be *bengalis* in spite of the change, it is because those two states are metaphors for *illuminations*. Indeed, one member of the paradigm of words sharing a common connection with Bengal is not mentioned here. It just happens that it is a metonym (or synecdoche) of *illuminations* in the sense of "brightly lit festivities," and is therefore a metaphor for dramatic, theatrical lighting (rather than for lighting in a theater). It is, of course, none other than *feux de Bengale* [Bengal lights]. This missing compound is the matrix of the repetition. The obvious wordplay (the humorous paronomasia *Bengale/bengali*), is overdetermined by a latent (that is, present, but outside the text—in language), play on *feu*. Provided that *feu* is *de Bengale* [that *fire* is *Bengal fire*], and this is stipulated by the rule of the title,[30] *feu* can be translated as "wild beast" if it burns and as "little bird" if it glows brightly.

Fully aware of tautological and circular overdetermination, Ponge has said that "the poet [is a moralist] who dissociates an object's *qualities* from one another and then puts them back together again, just as a painter dissociates colors and light and recomposes them on his canvas."[31] The problem with this formula is that *object* and *qualities* seem to refer directly to things, to the referent. Such an interpretation excludes humor—be it an innuendo perceived on reflection or the immediate scandal of a pun. Let's replace object with *word* and qualities with semes. And since the reader's knowledge of reality is so imperfect and fragmentary that any reading in terms of reality would be left up to chance, let's replace reference to reality with reference to language. This kind of reference asks no more of the reader deciphering the text than his linguistic competence, total and indispensable. Language: that is to say a *pre-text*[32] (to use another of Ponge's revealing puns), whose text appears only by negating it.

Even the mechanism of circular "reference" ends up as the ghost or abstract image of itself. Such is the case in this piece, "Le

Quartier des affaires," about the monotonous routine of office workers:[33]

> Le temps s'assombrit encore. Un maçon poudreux gravit son échelle: il va pleuvoir.
> A plusieurs milliers nous habitons dans le quartier de la Bourse un groupe de vieilles maisons qu'une administration prospère fait rajeunir. Elle dispose de beaucoup d'employés à son occupation sordide.
> Ils manipulent un grand nombre de feuilles de papier, de la ficelle; tandis que le téléphone et les machines à écrire fonctionnent; huit heures par jour.
> Le reste de leur temps, il le dorment, ailleurs, ou s'acheminent.
> A la fin du mois ils reçoivent un petit nombre de francs.
> Il ne pleut jamais très fort dans ce quartier, et cette maison malheureusement n'est pas en sucre.
>
> [The weather gets overcast again. A dusty bricklayer climbs his ladder: it's going to rain. Several thousand of us in the Stock Exchange district inhabit a group of old houses that a prosperous management is having spruced up. It has lots of employees doing its sordid business. They handle a great many sheets of paper and string; while the phone and typewriters are going; eight hours a day. The rest of their time—they sleep it away, elsewhere, or go on their way. At the end of the month, they get a small number of francs. It never rains very hard in this district, and, unfortunately, this house is not made of sugar.]

The piece seems to correspond to a thematics of mediocre life that goes back to *Bouvard et Pécuchet* and to short stories like those by Henry Céard and Maupassant. It contains the same touches of pessimistic atmosphere ("Le temps s'assombrit encore," "occupation sordide"), and shows the same bias of summing up an entire existence with inglorious activities ("ils manipulent . . . de la ficelle," and even "le reste de leur temps, ils le dorment"). There is even the same disillusioned humor in the "petit nombre de francs" echoing the "grand nombre de feuilles de papier," which we would not be surprised to find on a page of the early Huysmans.

The humor in the last paragraph is altogether different. Thoughts on starvation wages belong in a Naturalist depiction of the life of the lowly, and the expression *petit nombre* is funny only because it is a lexical transposition of the more usual understatement, *quelques sous* [a few cents]. So, transposition notwithstanding, this still corresponds to a realistic system of representation. But the rain falling at the end could never be real. At the beginning, it could have been, but the final sentence violates the rules of verisimilitude. We can speak of droughts in a country or an entire region, and we can speak of valleys or even cities where it rarely rains, but no micro-climate exists that is so limited that it does not extend beyond a *quartier*. Moreover, in realist discourse, one would expect to find a sentence like "there is never much sun in this district," since that would presuppose narrow alleyways and courtyards without light, which are obligatory motifs in the mimesis of the sordid. None of these features of urban squalor rule out rain. Indeed, they demand it, and we have seen how the beginning of the text conformed to that stylistic demand. But this apparent contradiction in terms of the mimesis is not a contradiction in terms of humor: the rain in the district imitates the shower of gold in the preceding paragraph. Everything is reduced and skimpy, including the negation that seems to be modeled after a favorite understatement of superstitious pessimists: "ça ne va pas fort" [things aren't going so well]. Instead of going from one realistic detail to another, the verbal sequence is a scale of negative signs. It is as if, by repeating the commonplace about the miserly sun in slums, the sentence were negating the model's only remaining positive connotation—turning *sun* into its antonym, *rain*. If there were realism or at least description here, an augmentative predicate would reinforce the negative aspects of the subject *rain*: it would rain a lot. Since all we have is a continuous variation on words that have been reduced to the state of dark touches, the predicate is as negative as the subject: the grammatical distinction between subject and predicate no longer serves any purpose. All that counts is contiguity. Despite their functional differences, the words are mutually equivalent members of the same pejorative paradigm. The word in the predicate position should be as negative as the word in the subject position: *it rains little.* All the reader anchored onto reality can see in this value reversal—rain as an inverse function of sadness—is a funny paradox, a joking comment on the motif of extremes. The height of mediocrity is reached when its symbol is also mediocre. This play on words is immediately confirmed when the text slides into an even more obvious joke, which, however, is not without an impeccable verbal logic: even a little rain would free the workers if their prison were soluble. This brings us back to a Naturalist theme: there's no escaping poverty. But the proof depends on the absurd, and this is incompatible with Naturalist (or realist) style.

The rain's only reality is verbal, and its only function is playful. No sooner does the reader sense this than his understanding of the beginning suddenly changes. A potential absurdity, which he sensed at the beginning, but suppressed while reading the text, is let loose by the humor in the conclusion. This absurdity was the temptation to relate the ladder to the forecast of bad weather. The context and functional similarity turn the realistic detail of the bricklayer climbing the scaffolding into a parody of the frog in those children's barometers that are made of a jar in which a captive amphibian climbs up a little ladder when it is going to rain. Of course, this absurdity is neutralized until it is revealed by its homologue at the end. In a retroactive reading, however, it is obvious. Besides, it is confirmed by the colon, the punctuation mark that symbolizes a causal or explanatory relation, joining "Un maçon poudreux gravit son échelle" to "il va pleuvoir." The only function of this causal punctuation, and the only way it can be understood, is in relation to the hypogram *a frog climbs its ladder.* It does not follow, however, that the worker is assimilated into the amphibian. The second reading—the absurd one—simply keeps us from interpreting the piece as a realistic slice of life. The first shift in perspective, whereby the clausula draws out the still latent words from the text's beginning (or makes our formerly optional perception of them obligatory), entails a drastic upheaval in our reading of the whole. The text, which at first seemed to be oriented toward a content and a referent, and based on an aesthetics of descriptive exactness, now appears to be a fantasy on a realistic motif, a variation on a formal given. In short, it no longer appears to be a piece of descriptive prose, but a poem. Far from pledging his allegiance to the daguerreotype school, the narrator is challenging the entire genre. And since his challenge is repeated at the end of the text, realism itself is represented, commented on, and negated in its intention (for realism is a serious genre) by the utterance. Conversely, realism is used on the surface to destroy the lyricism that Ponge is trying to eliminate from poetic writing. This realism, in turn, is destroyed, allowing only a kind of verbal revolving door or coming-and-going motion to subsist. The discourse is both a narrative description conforming to a genre and a commentary eliminating the goals of that genre. In other words, it is a formal exercise, the realization of a form for its own sake, the practice or calisthenic-like exercise of that form. Here again, we find textual referents made of prefabricated utterances. And what the homologues point to, again, is one of those latent texts. Since it exists prior to the text we have before our eyes, it designates that text as a parody. This hypogram is not an implicit text with which we are already familiar. It is, instead, the presupposition of a text that should exist, for Ponge's realistic picture would be its parody. That text would complete the linking together of the end homologues through satirical continuity. Something remarkable occurs: the linking text—the periphrasis in realist style surrounded by the two parodic homologues—is itself transformed into material for parody, into a text to be destroyed. This effect is based on a paradoxical exchange of functions: the printed poem appears to be a hypogram, and its invisible side appears to have been displaced and transferred to the future text that will negate it. It is almost as if the poem, as a reverse actualization of the relation of the signified to the signifier, were the parodied text of a potential parodying text.

Although a literary text always carries meaning in relation to texts that it presupposes, Ponge's poems tend toward a kind of circularity in which, since the hypogram and text are reflections of each other, all that is left of the literary phenomenon is a metalinguistic activity directly concerned with the status of writing and not with what the poem seems to represent. All that remains of the text is the very practice of its production.

NOTES

1. Explaining Literary Phenomena

1. Russian linguists working in the 1920s were the first to define clearly the concept of *literariness*: see Victor Erlich, *Russian Formalism* (The Hague: Mouton, 1955), pp. 146ff.

2. This terminology, used by linguists to describe the communication act, is necessary if we are to distinguish, as we do here, between the utterance as verbal sequence and the utterance as text.

3. See W. O. Hendricks, "Three Models for the Description of Poetry," *Journal of Linguistics* (1969), 5:1–22. He offers a judicious analysis of failed attempts to apply grammar to poetic language (in particular, J. P. Thorne's study of E. E. Cummings's poetry and R. Ohmann's work on George Bernard Shaw).

4. [A poem routs the intellect. It can do nothing else.] André Breton and Paul Eluard, *Notes sur la poésie*, in Eluard, *Oeuvres complètes* (Paris: Pléiade, 1968), 1:474; see also 2:1469.

5. The French word used here, *explication*, has the very general sense of the English *explanation*, as well as the more specific sense of *explication* in English, which is very close to the meaning of its cognate in the well-known *explication de texte*. Since the word here covers both these senses at once, suggesting both the analytic and synthetic traditions they represent, its translation alternates between the two possibilities in English.—TRANSLATOR.

6. The usual practice of translating both these terms into English as "utterance" obliterates their essential difference. The *énoncé* is the something that is uttered, (spoken or written), whereas the *énonciation* is the act (and the conditions of the act) whereby the *énoncé* is produced. The French has been retained here so as not to lose this distinction. Henceforth, when the term *énoncé* appears in isolation, it will be translated most often as "utterance" and, occasionally, as "statement."—TRANSLATOR.

7. Leaving aside the element of *contact*, the elements comprising the communication act are: the encoder (the author in the case of literary communication), message (text), decoder (reader), code (language), and context (reality).

8. A Markovian chain, to be precise. Chomsky's reservations in *Syntactic Structures* (The Hague: Mouton, 1965), section 3.1, do not apply to the observation of texts as "monuments."

9. Baudelaire, *Les Fleurs du Mal*, Antoine Adam, ed. (Paris: Garnier, 1961), p. 298, n. 7. See also J. Crépet and G. Blin, eds., *Les Fleurs du Mal* (Paris: Corti, 1942), p. 328.

10. This poem, the seventeenth in *Les Fleurs du Mal*, is a particularly famous expression of one aspect of the Baudelairian aesthetic. In it, Beauty describes herself as motionless, silent, and cold.—TRANSLATOR.

11. It should be noted that the expression *merle blanc*, unlike its literal equivalent in English, is used in various set phrases referring to something that is so very rare that it is impossible: *chercher le merle blanc*, for example, has the meaning of "looking for the impossible."—TRANSLATOR.

12. Yves Le Hir, *Analyses stylistiques* (Paris: Colin, 1965), p. 201.

13. Roland Barthes, *Critique et Vérité* (Paris: Seuil, 1966), p. 40.

14. The limited sense, as Saussure conceived of it; the broader sense, as Starobinski and, especially, Julia Kristeva have proposed. See chapter 5.

15. Roland Barthes, *On Racine*, Richard Howard, trans. (New York: Hill and Wang, 1964; Octagon Books, 1977), p. 9.

16. Barthes, *On Racine*, pp. 141–149. Leo Spitzer, *Romanische Stil- und Literaturstudien* (Marburg: N. G. Elwert'sche Verlag, 1931), 1:135–269.

17. For example, Pierre Albouy in Victor Hugo, *Oeuvres poétiques*, P. Albouy, ed. (Paris: Pléiade, 1964), 1:1550; J. Gaudon, *Le Temps de la contemplation* (Paris: Flammarion, 1969), pp. 86–88, 409–410.

18. For instance, in *Les Contemplations*; "Pleurs dans la nuit," lines 505ff.; *La Légende des Siècles*, "Le titan"; and *Dieu, l'Océan d'en haut*, line 257, among other examples.

19. In English in the original—TRANSLATOR.

20. See Julia Kristeva's explanation of this in Σημειοτκη: *Recherches pour une sémanalyse* (Paris: Seuil, 1969), pp. 266–267.

21. Jean Racine, *Phèdre*, line 1245.

22. François Rabelais, *Le Quart Livre*, ch. XXXI. In none of my translations of the literary texts quoted here do I pretend to do justice to the original, and this is more than ever the case with Rabelais. His texts give particularly clear evidence to the true impossibility of adequately translating a work of literature. In choosing to approximate the meaning of these texts, I have had to forgo any attempt at rendering the play of their signifiers, which is their very essence. The Samuel Putnam translation in *The Portable Rabelais* (New York: Viking, 1946) was consulted.—TRANSLATOR.

23. Robert Marichal, ed., *Le Quart Livre* (Lille and Geneva: Giard, Droz, 1947), p. 332 and ch. XXXII, n. 3.

24. Rabelais, *Le Quart Livre*, ch. XXX.

25. We might note in passing that this approach formally corroborates the synonymy between the portrait of Quaresmeprenant and the Ennasin Island episode which Michel Beaujour has so clearly demonstrated in his fine book, *Le Jeu de Rabelais* (Paris: L'Herne, 1969), pp. 137–139. See pp. 126ff.: on Ennasin, words make love; here, they play the fool. In both cases, verbalism attacks the real.

26. Lautréamont, *Les Chants de Maldoror*, canto VI, stanza 4; André Breton, "L'Union libre," in *Clair de terre* (Paris: Gallimard, 1966), pp. 93–95.

27. Honoré de Balzac, *Les Comédiens sans le savoir*, in *La Comédie humaine*, 2d ed. (Paris: Pléiade, n.d.), 7:41.

28. Gérard de Nerval, *Aurélia*, part I, ch. 7, in *Oeuvres* (Paris: Pléiade, 1952), 1:379.

29. See Elisabeth Barineau's comments in her edition of Victor Hugo, *Les Orientales* (Paris: Didier, 1952–1954), 1:84, 98, and n. 3.

30. This explanation is offered by Jacques Henry Bornecque in *Lumières sur les "Fêtes galantes"* (Paris: Nizet, 1959), pp. 150–151.

31. Emile Zola, *Les Rougon-Macquart*, Armand Lanoux and Henri Mitterand, eds. (Paris: Pléiade, 1960–1967), 5:623.

32. In their order of appearance, the original place names are: Donchery, Briancourt, Marancourt, Vrignes-aux-Bois, Douzy, Sarignan, Rubécourt, Pouru-aux-Bois, Francheval, Villers-Cernay, Saint-Monges, Villers-Cernay.

2. Semantics of the Poem

1. The verticality of the axis is a convention, but not a gratuitous one. It graphically represents the fact that the sign "covers" the thing and that there is a relation of simultaneity between the signifier and the signified. However, since the signifiers are tied together in a relationship of contiguity materialized in the syntagm, it is natural for that relationship to be represented by a horizontal axis.

2. Anyway, these intentions are wholly irrelevant to an analysis of the effectiveness of communication and of the effects of a poem.

3. Charles Baudelaire, *Les Fleurs du Mal*, "Spleen," IV, lines 5–8.

4. Marcel Galliot, *Commentaires de textes français modernes* (Paris: Didier, 1965), p. 248.

5. This radar was well known before Baudelaire's time. Sainte-Beuve, for instance, wrote in 1830 that: "les hommes doués d'une seconde vue sont assez semblables à ces chauves-souris en qui le savant anatomiste Spallanzani a découvert un sixième sens plus accompli à lui seul que tous les autres" [men endowed with a second sight are quite similar to the bats in which the learned anatomist Spallanzini discovered a sixth sense, which by itself is more accomplished than all the others]. *Premiers lundis*, "Hoffmann" (Paris: Pléiade, 1950), 1:382.

6. Roman Jakobson, *Questions de poétique* (Paris: Seuil, 1973), p. 426. Note the revealing concern for exactness in the learned terminology. Jean Prévost, *Baudelaire* (Paris: Mercure de France, 1953), p. 296.

7. Hugo, *Odes*, V, v (Paris: Pléiade, 1964), 1:456–457, 1269. Lefèvre-Deumier, in *Vespres de l'Abbaye du Val* (G. Brunet, ed., pp. 94–95), refers to his bats as *faux oiseaux*, false birds.

8. Hugo, *Les Châtiments*, VII, iv (Paris: Pléiade, 1967), 2:190). See *La Fin de Satan* (Paris: Pléiade, 1950, p. 900): "les hiboux se changent en colombes" [owls turn into doves], meaning "the evil are forgiven."

9. See the article on *spleen* in the *Grand dictionnaire du dix-neuvième siècle* by Pierre Larousse (vol. 14, 1875), in which Musset, Nerval, and Baudelaire are cited: "Nous avons en France une variété du spleen, la désespérance. Le spleen anglais est plus inconscient, moins douleureux que la désepérance française" [In France, we have a variety of spleen: despair. English spleen is more unconscious and less painful than French despair]. [The French word for *hope* is *espérance*. The opposition between *hope* and *despair* is therefore particularly striking in French in that it is marked by the presence or absence of the privitive prefix: *espérance/désespérance*—TRANSLATOR.]

10. In Hugo, for example: "frappant . . . du front l'infini, / Ainsi qu'un moucheron heurte une vitre sombre" [hitting his forehead against the infinite, just like a gnat striking a dark window pane] (*La Fin de Satan*, p. 912); "Nous sentons, dans la nuit mortelle, / La cage en même temps que l'aile" [In the deadly night, we feel the cage at the same time as the wing] (*Les Contemplations*, VI, xxiii, lines 335–336); by contrast, there is a mixture in *La Fin de Satan*, p. 828: "La mouche humaine allant heurter aux cieux son aile" [The human fly going to hit his wing on the heavens].

11. All the details of this setting are affected by a negative index. This reversal of signs explains why flight, normally swift and light, becomes what Heredia called *le vol des vampires* [the flight of vampires] (*Les Trophées*, "Les Conquérants de l'Or," part II). Hitting against the ceiling is a cliché for the frustrated desire to escape: in Hugo, Satan after the fall is *Cette chauve-souris du cachot éternel* [That bat in the eternal dungeon cell], striking his wings against the vault. The line demonstrates the interdependence between *cachot* and *chauve-souris*. Hugo, *La Fin de Satan*, p. 771; also see pp. 807, 829–830, 916.

12. The angelus, church bells rung morning, noon, and night summoning the faithful to stop work and pray, is perhaps most familiar to us today from Millet's painting of peasants praying in the fields, "L'Angélus." In the translation, the word *blues* should under no circumstances be confused with a type of music unknown to Mallarmé. It is simply the plural of the noun for the color blue.—TRANSLATOR.

13. Jean Cohen, *Structure du langage poétique* (Paris: Flammarion, 1966), pp. 210–216.

14. *Ibid.*, p. 212.

15. On the meaning of *azur* in its various contexts in Mallarmé, see Pierre Guiraud, *Essais de stylistique* (Paris: Klincksieck, 1969), pp. 109–120.

16. That is, metaphors of sight, hearing, smell, and touch, whenever they represent invisible objects in terms of seeing (in a sight code), silence or inaudible sounds in terms of hearing, and so forth.

17. Hugo, *Les Contemplations*, "Pleurs dans la nuit," VI, vi, lines 130–132.

18. Léon Cellier, ed., *Les Contemplations* (Paris: Garnier, 1969), p. 708, n. 17.

19. The fool's bauble, we might recall, is traditionally represented as having little, jingling bells dangling from its tip.—TRANSLATOR.

20. Hugo, *Dieu, l'Océan d'en haut*, René Journet and Guy Robert, eds. (Paris: Nizet, 1960), lines 133–136.

21. Michel Leiris, "Vivantes cendres, innommées" (1957–1958), in *Haut mal* (Paris: Gallimard/"Poésie," 1969), p. 219. [This poem truly defies translation. The following is meant as no more than a rough, line-by-line approximation: "To the quick. With horns and hollers. With free rein. To the brim. In full flight. Lickerishly. With clenched fists. To split rocks. Hot tears. At full sail."—TRANSLATOR.]

22. *A pierre fendre*, the title of a collection of poems by the Belgian Surrealist Achille Chavée (Mons, 1952), has a similar effect. The phrase, instead of being isolated (in the chemical sense of the word), by the anaphora, is isolated in a privileged position by its zero microcontext.

23. The act of reading goes from the beginning to the end of the text, but this reading is accompanied by a turning backwards. The meaning and value of elements in the text that have already been deciphered are modified retrospectively by what the reader discovers as he progresses in his reading. See my *Essais de stylistique structurale* (Paris: Flammarion, 1971), pp. 58–59.

24. A complete analysis would also mention the secondary parallelism between the last line of stanza 1 and the last line of stanza 2: *à tire d'ailes* and *à pleines voiles* subordinate the life-force semes to a symbol of departure or of a Baudelairian voyage. My interpretation is confirmed by the title of another version of this poem (*Très*) and by its variants: *A tire d'ailes / A coeur battant* [With a beating heart] / *A bride abattue* [At a full gallop] / *A bouche que veux-tu / A corps et à cris* [With bodies and cries] / *A en veux-tu en voilà* [All you could ever ask for] / *A boire et à manger* [A bit of everything].

25. Paul Eluard, *Le Livre ouvert* I, in *Oeuvres complètes* (Paris: Pléiade, 1968), 1:1025.

26. *Repetition* is a particular instance of *accumulation*: it accumulates components that are identical. In relation to simple accumulation, repetition is, therefore, a hyperbolic form of the figure. My formalism here might perhaps appear pointless, but it is quite necessary if we wish to delimit our categories clearly and to keep the rules defining them as simple and general as they should be.

27. Along with *paille* meaning "chaff," as opposed to "grain," and *paille* meaning a flaw in metal, *paille*, in the sense of "straw," is commonly used as a symbol of lightness and vulnerability (cf. *fétu* [wisp of straw], *Jouet des vents* [the winds' plaything], and so on). This last sense is only passively pejorative.

28. Combining two fixed collocations: *roue hydraulique motrice* [water wheel (driving something)] and *route hydraulique* [waterway].—TRANSLATOR.

29. I use the terms *transformation* and *generation* in their linguistic sense.

30. An error confined to the level of the words does not lead us as completely astray as do attempts to explain the words through the author. Suzanne Bernard, for example, thought the term had to do with the meanders of the Escaut, which Rimbaud and Verlaine traveled down on their way to London. Arthur Rimbaud, *Oeuvres*, Suzanne Bernard, ed. (Paris: Garnier, 1960), p. 532.

31. Hugo, *La Légende des Siècles*, Jacques Truchet, ed. (Paris: Pléiade, 1950), pp. 243–246.

32. The *chatons*, which in a nonarchaic context would refer to settings on a piece of jewelry, here are understood to be those of clasps on the *cuissards*, thigh-

coverings. When they are "crossed with their keys," we then understand that their clasps have been fastened, holding the armor in place.—TRANSLATOR.

33. From here to creating the illusion of a nonexistent reality is but one step: see the chapters on imaginary natural history in the poetry of Henri Michaux. (But in them, as soon as the illusion is created, stylistic markers of parody indicate that the representation is imaginary.)

34. On how descriptive systems are actualized, see chapter 3.

35. And certain words characterizing windows belong to other systems as far as literature is concerned. In prose, *espagnolette* [latch] appears in the system of *suicide* (by hanging), a thematic variant (the theme of despair) of a dramatic structure (or narrative structure) related to the cliché *faire flèche de tout bois* [to use whatever means available]. Also, on the theme of the humble life, it is a detail that creates verisimilitude in the system of the *toilette matinale*, [morning toilet] (a shaving mirror hung on the window latch, and so on). [We should recall that the windows, and systems, in question here are French, not American.—TRANSLATOR.]

36. Eluard, *L'Amour la poésie*, I, xxii, in *Oeuvres complètes*, Marcelle Dumas and Lucien Scheler, eds. (Paris: Pléiade, 1968), 1:238. These functions are oriented along the plane of the signified: someone is looking out the window from the inside, or in from the outside. Transposed onto the plane of the signifier, the orientation becomes a sign and, possibly, a symbol: the window gazed at from without is the literary site of longing or solitude, and of exclusion. On *embrasure*, see chapter 6.

37. An entire system may acquire an overall valorization. For instance, the system of *maison* [house] has a positive (meliorative) valorization.

38. See Georges Mounin, *La Communication poétique* (Paris: NRF, 1969), pp. 246–254.

39. Hugo, *Les Voix intérieures*, "A Albert Dürer," in *Oeuvres poétiques* 1:964.

40. Rimbaud, *Poésies*, Louis Forestier, ed. (Paris: Gallimard, 1973), "Soleil et chair," lines 15–16.

41. On the overlapping or interference of structures, see chapter 11 in its entirety.

3. Literary Sentence Models

1. Studies of the literary sentence all neglect literariness: if they deal with an author's style, they lapse either into statistics or into grammar, or else they look only for characteristics of that style (rhyme, word order, etc.), and not for characteristics of the sentence. If they do deal with the sentence itself, they vainly attempt to exhaust the list of possible word combinations or else establish facts about the words that remain the same within or without the sentence.

2. On these multiple relationships (in particular, the interferences among the linguistic and thematic structures and the descriptive system), which, it seems to me, comprise overdetermination, see also chapter 11.

3. See, for example, the associations listed in J. Dubois, F. Edeline, J. M. Klinkenberg, et al., *Rhétorique genérale* (Paris: Larousse, 1970), pp. 118–119.

4. Lautréamont, *Les Chants de Maldoror*, Pierre-Olivier Walzer, ed. (Paris: Pléiade, 1970), canto VI, ii, p. 227.

5. These stage directions are corroborated later on with the words *commodore*, designating the father, and *la sensible Londonienne* [the sensitive lady from London], designating the mother. *Le garçon* should perhaps be read as an anglicism (*the boy*).

6. On the role of the cliché in the literary phenomenon, see my *Essais de stylistique structurale* (Paris: Flammarion, 1971), pp. 161–181.

7. On the functioning of maxims in general, see S. Meleuc, "Structure de la maxime," *Langages* (1969), 13:69–99.

8. It is quite enough that the reader recognize that a quote is a quote: it is not necessary for him to identify its author. Cf. Julia Kristeva's concept of *prélèvement* in *Semeiotikè* (Paris: Seuil, 1969), pp. 332–334.

9. Jacques Delille, *L'imagination*, canto III, in *Oeuvres complètes*, 6th ed. (Paris: Didot, 1840), p. 132, col. 2. [These massacres, which marked the beginning of the Reign of Terror in the French Revolution (1793), are perhaps best known to the English-speaking reader from Dickens' *A Tale of Two Cities*.—TRANSLATOR.]

10. This obscene variant of the *executioner–victim* relationship is found in the metaphor *la veuve* [the widow], used in French slang to refer to the guillotine, and in literary versions of the myth of the devouring woman who kills her lovers, such as Queen Margot in *La Tour de Nesle* (1832) by Alexandre Dumas *père*.

11. Recognition of this is made easier for readers familiar with Baudelaire because of the poem "*Sed non satiata*" in *Les Fleurs du Mal*. It posed no problems for Delille's contemporaries, but Baudelaire, coming later, felt the need to replace Juvenal's *necdum* with the more widely accessible *sed non*.

12. Baudelaire, *Les Fleurs du Mal*, VI, "Les Phares," lines 29–30.

13. Baudelaire, *Exposition universelle de 1855*, in *Oeuvres complètes*, Y.-G. Le Dantec and Claude Pichois, eds. (Paris: Pléiade, 1961), p. 973. Cf. "si l'ombre est verte et une lumière rouge, trouver du premier coup une harmonie de vert et de rouge, l'un obscur, l'autre lumineux" [if the shadow is green and a light red, immediately find a green and red harmony, one being obscure and the other luminous], (*Salon de 1845, p. 817); "pondération du vert et du rouge" [balancing of green and red] (p. 816); "un cabaret mi-parti de vert et de rouge crus, qui étaient pour mes yeux une douleur délicieuse"* [a tavern half in harsh green and half in harsh red, which were delightfully painful to my eyes] (*Salon de 1846*, p. 883).

14. One might object that, at the level of the signifieds, there is a natural contiguity between pines and mountain lakes. Real pine trees, however, do not bleed into the lakes that they surround. When Baudelaire speaks of this kind of lake without mentioning pine trees, the water is *noire* [black] or *sombre* [dark] (*Petits poèmes en prose*, XV, "Le gâteau," and in his early poems, "Incompatibilité"). There is no longer a polarization based on *vert*, and the water is not transformed into blood.

15. *Sang* has contaminated *anges*, making them into *mauvais anges*. In "Incompatibilté," there is no blood, and the angel of the lake remains benevolent.

16. Here is a case of the cliché structuring the sentence on the syntactic level and, on the graphemic level (italics), giving it a humorous valorization (a painter is being torn to pieces by the critics): "Ah! les chevaux *roses*, ah! les paysans *lilas*, ah! les fumées *rouges* (quelle audace, une fumée rouge!), ont été traités d'une *verte* façon" [Ooh! the *pink* horses, ooh! the *lilac* peasants, ooh! the *red* smoke (such daring, red smoke!) were treated harshly]. Baudelaire, *Salon de 1859*, in *Oeuvres complètes*, p. 1049. [Placed before the noun it modifies in *une verte façon*, the adjective *vert* (green) takes on the sense of *severe, sharp, harsh*.—TRANSLATOR.]

17. Baudelaire, *Salon de 1846*, 4:894.

18. A similar change takes place in Baudelaire's "La muse malade": "Le succube verdâtre et le rose lutin" [The greenish succubus and the pink imp]. The word *lutin*, because it is positively charged, transforms *rouge*, with its ambiguous symbolism, into a meliorative *rose*. Conversely, the *vert* of the succubus (a negative index) acquires a pejorative suffix. See Théophile Gautier, "La Comédie de la Mort," lines 97–98: "Le flot a . . . couvert de son linceul *verdâtre . . . les rougeurs de rose*" [The waves have covered the *rosy* blushes with their *greenish* shroud], he says of young people who have drowned. This interpretation strikes me as more sound than Michel Butor's commentary on Baudelaire's *vert* and *rose* in *Histoire extraordinaire* (Paris: Gallimard, 1961), pp. 144–148.

19. Baudelaire, *Les Fleurs du Mal*, "A Théodore de Banville."

20. Blood changed into water is also modeled after a familiar cliché. The *red/green* opposition can even create an ad hoc reality for itself: a "natural" green can generate a "verbal" red, as in Gautier, *Poésies diverses 1838–1845*, "A trois paysagistes": "artistes souverains / Amants des chênes verts et des rouges terrains" ["To Three Landscape Painters": Sovereign artists, lovers of the green oaks and the red earth].

21. Mandariargues, "Les yeux gelés," *Dans les Années sordides*, in *L'Age de craie* (Paris: Gallimard/"Poésie," 1967), p. 94.

22. I examine various applications (and implications) of the concept of the descriptive system in chapter 2. In a study dating from 1966, to which I returned in my *Essais de stylistique structurale*, pp. 213–222, I spoke of a *code*. It now seems to me that this term should be reserved for a descriptive system already encoded (actualized) in a text as a metaphoric vehicle.

23. Mme. de Staël, *De la littérature*, I, xi, Paul Van Tieghem, ed. (Geneva: Droz, 1959), 1:185: "Le frémissement que produisent dans tout notre être de certaines beautés de la nature, . . .l'émotion que nous causent les vers qui nous retracent cette sensation, [ont] beaucoup d'analogie avec l'effet de l'harmonica. L'âme, doucement ébranlée, se plaît dans la prolongation de cet état, aussi longtemps qu'il lui est possible de le supporter" [The shudder certain beauties of nature produce in our whole being, . . . the emotion caused us by verses tracing this sensation for us are very much like the effect of the harmonica. The soul, gently shaken, takes pleasure in prolonging this state, as long as it is possible for it to endure it]. Cf. George Sand, *La Comtesse de Rudolstadt*, IV, x (Paris: De

Potter, 1844), 4:263, n. 1: "Les imaginations poétiques voulurent y voir l'audition des voix surnaturelles. . . . Les néophytes des sociétés secrètes . . . en étaient si fortement impressionnés que plusieurs tombaient en extase" [Poetic imaginations tried to see in them the sound of supernatural voices. . . . Neophytes in secret societies . . . were so impressed by them that many fell into raptures].

24. Elsewhere Chateaubriand speaks of the "plaintes d'une harmonica divine, ces vibrations qui n'ont rien de terrestre" [laments of a divine harmonica, those vibrations which have nothing earthly about them]. *Les Natchez*, IV, Gilbert Chinard, ed. (Berkeley: University of California Press, 1919), p. 174.

25. Chateaubriand, *Vie de Rancé*, Fernand Letissier, ed. (Paris: Didier, 1955), p. 338.

26. Cf. Baudelaire, *Choix de maximes consolantes sur l'amour* (1846), in *Oeuvres complètes*, p. 471: "poètes hoffmaniques que l'harmonica fait danser dans les régions du cristal, et que le violon déchire comme une lame qui cherche le coeur" [Hoffmanic poets that the harmonica sets to dancing in the regions of crystal and that the violin tears open like a blade searching for the heart].

27. Failing to recognize the pleasure-pain ambivalence associated with the glass harmonica and confusing it with the *mouth organ* of today, Jean-Pierre Richard misses the fundamental unity of these seemingly contradictory semes and resorts to futile hypotheses about Chateaubriand's sensitivity. *Paysage de Chateaubriand* (Paris: Seuil, 1967), pp. 79–80. Everything is in the descriptive system, and that entire system is in the sentence.

28. Chateaubriand does not use the formula that would be expected here, "il *se* plongeait dans la pénitence" [he immersed himself in penitence]. [Instead, he eliminates the reflexive pronoun *se* and writes, "il plongeait dans la pénitence," which is quite literally: "he *dived* into penitence." This transformation from the abstract to the concrete cannot be so economically performed in English.—TRANSLATOR.]

29. Lamartine, *Recueillements poétiques*, XXVIII, "A Mlle Delphine Gay," in *Oeuvres poétiques complètes*, Marius-François Guyard, ed. (Paris: Pléiade, 1963), p. 253.

30. This seme can already be observed in the Latin *nenia*, which was both a "lullaby" and a "dirge." If Apollinaire was able to use the French *nénie* with its double meaning, it is not only because *nénie* has these two meanings in the dictionary, but also because *berceuse* [lullaby], for which *nénie* can substitute, retains something of this ambivalence: "La mer et ses nénies dorlotent tes noyés" [The sea and her lullabies pamper your drowned] (*Le guetteur mélancolique*, "Au prolétaire"). This comparison was suggested to me by Jean-Claude Chevalier's subtle commentary on "Le larron" in his *"Alcools" d'Apollinaire: Essai d'analyse des formes poétiques* (Paris: Lettres modernes, 1970), p. 53, n. 19.

31. *Double caractère* is the expression that introduces the twofold sentence, before and after conversion. Preface to *La Légende des Siècles*, Jacques Truchet, ed. (Paris: Pléiade, 1950), p. 3.

32. The most complete analysis of "Spleen II" can be found in Sebastian Neumeister, "Baudelaire, *Spleen*. Ein Beitrag zur Theorie und Praxis der Interpretation," *Poetica* (1970), 3:439–454.

33. Gautier, *Comédie de la mort*, lines 571 and 575–576. (The part in which these lines appear is entitled nothing other than "La mort dans la vie" [Death in life].)

34. In other words, the poem seems to progress in the way a piece of object-laden, realistic fiction would; but in so doing, it constructs a unique allegory. See Leo Bersani, *Baudelaire and Freud* (Berkeley: University of California Press, 1977), p. 111, on Baudelaire's "Cygne."

35. I have taken these stereotypes from the articles on "Boucher" (1867) and "pastel" (1874) in Pierre Larousse's *Grand dictionnaire universel du dix-neuvième siècle* (Paris: Larousse et Broyer, 1866–1890). Of course, sounds are also an overdetermining factor in the lexical selection (the rhyme for *Boucher*, the repetition of /*p*/ and /*t*/ in *pastels plaintifs*). This factor clears the way for and facilitates the generation of the text; it is also an imperative of reading, as far as the decoding is concerned. But it would not explain why, from among so many possible negative adjectives, the ones retained were *pâles* and *plaintifs*. The rule of conversion alone can account for their specificity: each of them reverses a seme of its intertextual homologue.

36. Balzac, *Gobseck*, in *La Comédie humaine*, Marcel Bouteron, ed. (Paris: Pléiade, 1951), 2:632; *La maison du chat-qui-pelote, ibid.*, 1:62. In *Gobseck*, Balzac begins by listing the equivalencies I have just summarized which make the boudoir a periphrasis for woman. The word *volupté* [sensual pleasure] precedes these two quotations, implicitly in *Gobseck* and explicitly in *La maison*: we can therefore consider the intertext to be Baudelaire's "Luxe, calme et volupté" [Luxury, calm and voluptuousness] ("Le voyage" in *Les Fleurs du Mal*). The same demonstration could be made for the Egyptian landscape at the end of the poem when the speaker compares himself to

> Un vieux sphinx ignoré du monde insoucieux,
> Oublié sur la carte, et dont l'humeur farouche
> Ne chante qu'aux rayons du soleil qui se couche.

[An old Sphinx unknown to the uncaring world, forgotten on the map, and whose sullen temper sings only to the rays of the setting sun.]

The ungrammaticality here lies in the contamination (in the philological sense of the term) of the Sphinx with the colossus of Memnon at Thebes. We can clearly see that the Sphinx is the viewer and that he had to sing because the viewer represents the poet; hence the fusion of the Sphinx with the nearby colossus which, as Herodotus tells us, sang to the rays of the rising sun. But only the tendency toward conversion can explain the exemplary reversal here causing an image traditionally tied to dawn to introduce the opposite of dawn. As with semic inversion, the polarity existing between dawn and dusk lets a morning twilight be used to symbolize an evening twilight.

37. Lamartine, *Harmonies poétiques et religieuses*, X, in *Oeuvres poétiques complètes* (Paris: Pléiade, 1964), p. 325. Two prose poems by Baudelaire also develop this motif of the beneficial moon: "Les bienfaits de la lune" and "Le désir de peindre."

38. Lisle-Adam, *L'Eve future*, I, vii (Paris: Pauvert, 1960), p. 27.

39. Baudelaire, "Le Flacon," in *Les Fleurs du Mal.*

40. See my *Essais de stylistique structurale*, pp. 68–80.

41. *Odorant* is still a dual sign: taken negatively, it reflects its intertext; taken positively, it conforms to its context.

42. On motivation in narrative, and zero-motivation as motivation, see Gérard Genette, *Figures II* (Paris: Seuil, 1969), pp. 96–99.

43. Of course, this equivalence goes beyond the case of a poem that develops its matrix through an allegory in the strict, rhetorical sense of the term. Allegory is, in fact, a "visual" form of expansion. Whereas tropes are generally limited to short syntagms, allegory extends to complex sentences. In the eighteenth century, the rhetorician Dumarsais was already suggesting that "allegory is closely related to metaphor, indeed, allegory is nothing but a prolonged metaphor." Dumarsais, *Traité des Tropes* (Paris: Le Nouveau Commerce, 1977), II, xii, p. 129.

4. Poetics of Neologisms

1. On the various possible ways neologisms are formed, see H. Marchand, *The Categories and Types of Present-Day English Word-Formation, A Synchronic–Diachronic Approach*, 2d ed. (Munich: C. H. Beck, 1969). The hunt for literary neologisms is not easy. The existing concordances do not give separate lists for neologisms, except for a very few, such as Journet and Robert's listing for Hugo. The lists in *L'Histoire de la langue française* by Brunot and Bruneau are merely polls, and even at that they include words that appeared neological only by virtue of aesthetic and normative exclusion. For the modern era, we have the *Dictionnaire des mots sauvages* (Paris: Larousse, 1969) by Maurice Rheims, a collection of one cultivated reader's discoveries giving special attention to the most highly unusual forms and to funny or parodying neologisms. On the theory of neologisms, see especially: E. Souriau, "Sur l'esthétique des mots et des langues forgés," *Revue d'esthétique* (1965), 18:19–48. P. Guiraud ("Néologismes littéraires," *La Banque des mots* [1971], 1:23–28), tries to distinguish between cognitive neologisms and expressive neologisms, which alone are literary in his opinion. Both categories, however, can be found in literature, so the distinction lies elsewhere: it should be made between these categories in literary discourse and these same categories in nonliterary discourse.

2. My conclusions apply just as well to neologisms that are misunderstood and perceived as archaisms by readers who are too far removed from the time of the text. See chapter 6.

3. Arthur Rimbaud, "Dévotion," in *Les Illuminations.*

4. Gérard de Nerval, *Voyage en Orient*, appendix 2, iv, in *Oeuvres* (Paris: Pléiade, 1961), 2:688. Whenever a poet sees a goddess as woman and sexuality reappears in the monstrous, the Circe association becomes irresistibly tempting. In turn, Circe becomes the hypogram of a revealing variation on the name of Derceto: Paul Valéry, in *Sémiramis*, evokes a "déesse *Derceto*, figure du style le plus barbare, visage de femme et corps de poisson" [goddess Derceto, a figure

of the most barbarous style, the face of a woman and body of a fish]. *Oeuvres complètes*, Jean Hytier, ed. (Paris: Pléiade, 1957–1960), 1:182. The same hybrid and the same bodily components are found as in Rimbaud.

5. Rimbaud, *Une Saison en enfer*, "Délires II." We find the Arctic as a place of spiritual escape in the *Illuminations*: the entire text of "Barbare" and the final stanzas of "Métropolitain" and Génie." In "Mouvement," the voyage takes on the same symbolism as in Baudelaire, but without going so far as Death, the ultimate escape in *Les Fleurs du Mal*.

6. It is based on the same system of reference as the archaism: the relationship between a marked element and an unmarked element in an opposition of a *form pre-existing the text* to a *form not pre-exiting the text*. (In relation to the archaism, the marker is displaced from the first to the second term of the opposition.) This formulation repeats— but, I believe, more accurately and as a generalization— the definition offered by the Groupe μ (Dubois et al.) in *Rhétorique générale* (Paris: Larousse, 1970), pp. 60–61.

7. *Alcools*, "La Chanson du Mal-Aimé," stanza 39. See the close commentary on this stanza by Claude Morhange-Bégué in "*La Chanson du Mal-Aimé": Essai d'analyse structurale et stylistique* (Paris: Minard, 1970), pp. 151–154. I differ with her on a few points, but she demonstrates admirably well that there is no representation of Greek antiquity in the poem, but rather a metaphoric discourse hyperbolized by the adynaton *mort d'immortels* and by the Greek forms.

8. Coppée (1842–1908), known as the "*poète des humbles*," wrote popular poetry celebrating the lives of the lower classes.—TRANSLATOR.

9. Chateaubriand, *Vie de Rancé*, Fernand Letissier, ed. (Paris: Didier, 1955), p. 251. Chateaubriand was inspired by a text of Rancé's in which *grand silence* was replaced with *grande aphonie*. What is important, though, is that we can reach our conclusion from Chateaubriand's text alone. In fact, it would not allow for any other. There is no metaphor between *aphonie* and *silence*. Instead, there is simple synonymy, for *silence* is translated into Greek by means of a borrowing from technical language. Letissier tries hard to prove that *aphonie* is indeed, in terms of chronology, a new coinage. Like so many other philological commentaries, his attempt has no pertinence to the literary phenomenon. Even though *aphonie* was used in the medical vocabulary of the time, it was a neologism in meaning nonetheless, for Chateaubriand was not talking about a pathological accident, but rather about a voluntary and entirely spiritual renunciation of speech.

10. Or cumulative signification: see my discussion of Eluard's "Paille" and Rimbaud's "Mouvement" in chapter 2; also see M.-N. Gary-Prieur, "La Notion de connotation(s)," *Littérature* (1971), 4:96–107.

11. Not only because *aphonie* is polarized with *silence*, but also because any morphological particularization of one of the signifiers in a paradigm of synonyms makes that signifier a hyperbole of the signified. Here the particularization is the Greek form. That this form coincides with the final position in the paradigm provides further reinforcement.

12. Quoted by E. Huguet, "Notes sur le néologisme chez Victor Hugo," *Revue de philologie française* (1898), 12:198.

13. Chateaubriand, *Mémoires d'outre-tombe*, IV, vii, xviii, Maurice Levaillant, ed. (Paris: Flammarion, 1948–1950), 4:402–403. In the version of this text published in the *Essai sur la littérature anglaise*, Chateaubriand is content to use *silence* in the place of *aphonie*.

14. We can also read this metonymically, since the passage from night to day is described by the passage from silence (which is nocturnal) to noise (which is diurnal).

15. Cf. Baudelaire, *Les Fleurs du Mal*, "Le Guignon": "Mainte fleur épanche à regret / Son parfum doux comme un secret / Dans les solitudes profondes" [Many a flower reluctantly pours forth its perfume, sweet as a secret, in deep solitudes]. In his edition of *Les Fleurs du Mal* (Paris: Garnier, 1961), Antoine Adam traces these lines to Gray's "Elegy Written in a Country Churchyard": "Full many a flower is born to blush unseen, / And waste its sweetness on the desert air" (p. 288, n. 3).

16. This neologism has since become a technicism used to advertise products that have had their bad odor removed. This diachronic accident makes it hard for us to appreciate texts, going from Rousseau to Roucher and even Baour-Lormian, where we come across a *tulipe inodore* [scentless tulip). In 1872, Larousse's *Grand dictionnaire universel* still classified *inodore* as a stock epithet belonging to *fleur*.

17. Théophile Gautier, *Poésies diverses*, "Thébaïde" in *Poésies* (Paris: Lemerre, 1890), 1:215.

18. Hugo, *Dieu, l'Océan d'en haut*, René Journet and Guy Robert, eds. (Paris: Nizet, 1960), line 1519.

19. On this suffix, see J. Dubois, *Etude sur la dérivation suffixale en français moderne et contemporain* (Paris: Larousse, 1961), pp. 40–41.

20. Chateaubriand, *Mémoires d'outre-tombe*, IV, vii, iv: 4:346. The potential humor of all new coinages is almost irresistible here, since *-pte* is verging on parody. Added to this comic playfulness is the transgression of a mythological taboo, for this banter threatens two different orders of the sacred, that of religion and that of Titian devotees. Since nothing allows the reader to give in to the temptation here, the suppression of humor acts as a supplementary factor in controlling the decoding. The reading is total, so it is conscious of this play on forms.

21. The Virgin assumpts in the *Assumption*, just as Christ "ascends" in an *Ascension*. Compare paronomasia in Rabelais, such as "les moines . . . toussoient aux toussoirs, resvoient aux resvoirs" [the monks . . . coughed in the coughatories, dreamed in dreamatories] or "Dieu vous le rendra en son grand rendoir" [God will get back at you in his great get-backery]. See Leo Spitzer, *Die Wortbildung als stilistisches Mittel* (Halle: Niemayer, 1910), pp. 47ff.

22. Chateaubriand, *Essai sur les Révolutions* (1826 edition), *Oeuvres complètes*, 2:423. The 1797 edition gives *céruléen*.

23. To such an extent that some critics have tried, in vain, to see *céruséen* as a misprint, even though Chateaubriand uses the word *céruse* elsewhere in speaking of the moon; see Jean Mourot, *Etudes sur les premières oeuvres de Chateaubriand*

(Paris: Nizet, 1962), pp. 77–82. This controversy reflects the impact of the *dissimilitudo in similitudine* (which is based on only one letter), and the contrast with *velouté*.

24. And in the same fashion there is *blanc de craie* [chalk white], the moon sleeping *étendue comme des toiles*, in other words, spread out like sheets bleaching on the grass, following a now-forgotten artisanal practice.

25. The idealizing series referring to the clouds bathed in moonlight: *zones diaphanes, flocons [de] troupeaux errants, mollesse et élasticité* [diaphanous and wavy zones, flakes of roaming flocks, softness and buoyancy].

5. Paragram and Significance

1. Saussure's manuscript notes quoted in Jean Starobinski, *Les Mots sous les mots* (Paris: NRF, 1971), p. 132 [trans. Olivia Emmet, *Words Upon Words: The Anagrams of Ferdinand de Saussure* (New Haven and London: Yale University Press, 1979), p. 100]. On this reasoning of his, see Sylvère Lotringer, "Le Dernier mot de Saussure," *L'Arc* (1973), 54:80.

2. That is, the Saussure who has not yet escaped nonlinearity and renounced the *cahiers* for the *Cours*, "a pyramid erected on a fundamental repression" (Sylvère Lotringer, "The Game of the Name," *Diacritics [Summer 1973], p. 8).*

3. Compare "Notes inédites de Saussure," *Cahiers F. de Saussure* (1948), 8:56: "One must never consider one side of language as anterior and superior to the others, nor as being their starting point. One could do so if there existed a side that was given . . . apart from any operation of abstraction or generalization on our part." See also Lotringer, "Le Dernier mot de Saussure," p. 75.

4. Saussure came close to the concept of a semantic paragram à propos of such Latin habitual collocations as *Xerxes* and *exercitus*: "the name itself makes one think . . . readily of a 'grande armée'" (*Les Mots sous les mots*, p. 118; [*Words Upon Words*, p. 89]). But he considered them only in the case of clichés, where overdetermination results from semantic derivation plus paronomasia (otherwise, why not *Xerxes* and *agmen*?). And he was kept blind to the phenomenon by his intent, which was to prove something else. Julia Kristeva has pointed to the significance of this mistake: *Semeiotikè* (Paris: Seuil, 1969), pp. 292–293.

5. The starting point is the seme or a complex of semes; the end product is the text, the reading of which indicates which semes are involved and how they are mobilized. The fact of such a selection and of its being perceived through reading the text seems to me to solve the problem that structural semantics could not deal with when it attempted to derive the text from the totality of the nuclear word's semes, a problem discerned by Kristeva, *Semeiotikè*, p. 319. This conception of the paragram also provides a solution for the question she raises about the semantic nature of what she calls *mots pivots*, in *La Révolution du langage poétique* (Paris: Seuil, 1974), p. 268: I interpret these as the lexical variants of the nuclear word.

6. A verification of my neurosis simile, above. If *unknown* is the death (as unforeseeable, or mystery) element in *auberge*, its displacement or repression for

contextual reasons in Baudelaire entails its reappearance elsewhere, here in the metaphorical apposition derived from *auberge*: "portique ouvert sur des Cieux inconnus."

7. Except for two unlikely couplings: *beigne–bigne* and *daigne (daigner)–digne*.

8. Jean Cocteau, *Vocabulaire* (1922), in *Poésie, 1916–1923* (Paris: Gallimard, 1925), pp. 430–433.

9. Baudelaire, *Les Fleurs du Mal*, "Horreur sympathique" comes directly after "Alchimie de la douleur" in the collection.

10. It is quite possible that some wordplay between the two official languages of nineteenth-century French culture is contributing an added determination here. A cliché in Latin poetry calls the expanse of the sky the *caeli plaga*, or, in Vergil, *aetheria plaga* (*Aeneid*, I, 394). From the Latin *plaga* to the French *plage* [beach] is but a short step. Paronymy astraddle the frontiers of two languages was easy—so easy, in fact, that it was used by schoolchildren to parody their Latin translations: instead of picking French words semantically equivalent to the Latin original, they would produce a pseudo-translation through paronymy. Vergil's *rari nantes in gurgite vasto*, "a few swimmers in the boundless swirling gulf," became *de rares Nantais ingurgitent*, or "unusual people from Nantes ingurgitate."

11. These Vergilian episodes are all famous quotations, parts of the corpus of passages French children were to learn by heart: *Aeneid*, VI, 105ff., 149ff., 365ff.

12. *Les Mots sous les mots*, p. 152 [*Words Upon Words*, p. 129].

6. Toward a Formal Approach to Literary History

1. On the notion of the descriptive system, see chapters 2, 3, 4, and 11.

2. See Antoine Adam's critical edition of *Les Fleurs du Mal* (Paris: Garnier, 1961), pp. 301–302.

3. The woman is Herodias in Heine's *Atta Troll* (chapter 19). Byron's devotee is Lamartine, *Méditations*, II, ii: "Esprit mystérieux, mortel, ange ou démon, / Qui que tu sois, Byron, bon ou fatal génie, / J'aime de tes concerts la sauvage harmonie" [Mysterious spirit—mortal, angel, or demon—whoever you may be, Byron, a good or evil genius, I love the savage harmony of your concerts]. See Balzac, *Modeste Mignon*, Marcel Bouteron, ed. (Paris: Pléiade, 1951) 1:483; Gautier, *Le Capitaine Francasse* (Paris: Garnier, 1962) p. 194; *Mademoiselle de Maupin* (Paris: Charpentier, 1880) p. 59.

4. It has been proved a thousandfold. But the detail is still important: the same cliché, mistakenly believed to be Baudelaire's own coinage, is regarded by some as an indication of his Augustinian ethics: M. A. Ruff, *L'Esprit du mal et l'esthétique baudelairienne* (Paris: Armand Colin, 1955), p. 335.

5. See M. Menemencioglu, "Le Thème des Bohémiens en voyage dans la peinture et la poésie de Cervantès à Baudelaire," *Cahiers de l'Association des Etudes françaises* (1966), 18:227–238; R. L. Füglister, "Baudelaire et le thème des Bohémiens," *Etudes Baudelairiennes* (1971), 2:99–143.

6. This is likely, since Baudelaire's gypsies, like Callot's, carry weapons. From what we can deduce from the various texts on the tribe, this is not a feature of the descriptive system.

7. Jean Pommier, *Dans les chemins de Baudelaire* (Paris: Corti, 1945), p. 293.

8. Dated July 27, 1870. At this period Rimbaud had not yet developed the aesthetics he practices in *Une Saison en Enfer* and *Les Illuminations.*

9. See, for example, Jacques Plessen, *Promenade et poésie* (The Hague: Mouton/De Gruyter, 1967), pp. 37, 121, 158.

10. Suzanne Bernard, in her critical edition of Rimbaud's *Oeuvres* (Paris: Garnier, 1960), p. 373. Glatigny's poem (*Les Vignes folles* [1860], "Les Antres malsains," ii–iii) was unearthed by Jacques Gengoux in *La Pensée poétique de Rimbaud* (Paris: Nizet, 1950), p. 18: "Son bras, qui dans le vide au hasard se ballotte, / Merveille de blancheur et de force, est orné / De ces mots au poinçon gravés: PIERRE ET LOLOTTE, / Et d'un coeur d'un foyer éternel couronné" [Her arm, which tossed about haphazardly in the air, a wonder of whiteness and strength, is adorned with these words, engraved with a hallmark: PIERRE AND LOLOTTE, and crowned with a heart of eternal flame].

11. Gautier, *Albertus* (1832), stanza cv. *Fortement pommadés* appears in Glatigny's naturalistic tableau (*Les Vignes folles*, p. 78), and this coincidence naturally suggests that it is, in fact, Rimbaud's source. But this is a point of history, and not a fact for literary history. It is likely that what we have here is a cliché and that our two authors used it separately from each other: see Rimbaud, *Un Coeur sous une soutane*, (which has nothing to do with Glatigny), June 16: "une mèche de cheveux raides et *fort pommadés* lui cinglant la face comme une balafre" [a lock of straight and heavily pomaded hair lashing across his face like a scar]. It matters little whether Rimbaud came across the cliché directly in everyday usage or via Glatigny's intercession, since he does not actualize the same structure as Glatigny, and the cliché's function is entirely different. Word borrowings are of interest to history (and minor history, at that). Literary history is concerned only with the borrowing of functions.

12. *Poésies*, "Soleil et Chair" (written only a few months before, on April 29, 1870): "Cypris . . . cambrant les rondeurs de ses reins" [Cypris arching the curves of her back].

13. Compare the sodomite tattooing in Jacques Prévert's *La Pluie et le beau temps*, in the poem titled "Sceaux d'hommes égaux morts," p. 36.

14. It existed before the Renaissance under other names, the *sotte chanson*, for example: see P. Bec, *La Lyrique française au Moyen Age: Contribution à une typologie des genres poétiques médiévaux* (Paris: Picard, 1977), 1:158–162. The word *contreblason* suits my purposes particularly well, however, since it implies the permutation of the markers of the *blason*.

15. This interpretation was skillfully argued by W. M. Frohock, *Rimbaud's Poetic Practice* (Cambridge: Harvard University Press, 1963), pp. 52–53. There is such a motif: it was found in Coppée [see Rimbaud, *Oeuvres complètes*, Antoine Adam, ed. (Paris: Pléiade, 1972), p. 657], and I also see it in Baudelaire's "J'aime le souvenir de ses époques nues."

16. Just as the Baroque themes of the "topsy-turvy" world are written upside down or inside out; see Gérard Genette, *Figures* (Paris: Seuil, 1969), pp. 9ff. On conversion, see my chapter 3.

17. I use the term *context* in the strict sense of verbal sequences preceding and following the sentences in the text. I never use it in the looser sense of the nonverbal environment of the linguistic or textual phenomenon.

18. Hugo, *Les Orientales* (1829), "Navarin," lines 175 and 181. The commentators—for example, E. Barineau in her critical edition (Paris: Didier, 1952), 1:97–98—never fail to stress that Hugo does not know what he is saying or that he does not care, and that his scene is a failure. In their opinion, the evocation is unsuccessful because it is inexact, and the *effet de réel*, the realistic effect, presupposes faithfulness to reality.

19. *Les Fleurs du Mal*, "La vie antérieure" (1855).

20. Hugo, *Odes et Ballades*, "La Fée et la péri" (1824). Says the fairy personifying the poetry of the Occident: "J'ai la grotte enchantée aux piliers basaltiques, / Où la mer de Staffa brise un flot inégal" [I have the enchanted cave with basalt pillars on which the Staffa sea breaks its uneven waves]. All editors find it necessary to explain where Staffa is and why the cave is later called Fingal's palace.

21. They are foreign, and (except for *halte*) they are perceived as such.

22. And its descriptive variants, the many descriptions of nature (strange rock formations, clouds, and so on) in a human architecture code, which is rationalized as "fantastic architecture."

23. The only examples lexicographers have been able to unearth for *embrasure* are, significantly: *Dictionnaire de l'Académie* (1835), "il m'a parlé dans l'embrasure" [he spoke to me in the window nook]; *Grand dictionnaire du XIX*[e] *siècle* (1870), "causer à voix basse dans l'embrasure" [to chat softly in the window nook]. Balzac uses *embrasure* in this sense very often; one example has been commented on by Roland Barthes, *S/Z* (Paris: Seuil, 1970), pp. 28–35 [New York: Hill and Wang, 1974, pp. 21–28]. Barthes, however, does not see the stereotypical nature of the device. A good illustration of the complex sort of intrigue carried on in window recesses can be found in Zola, *Son Excellence Eugène Rougon*, in *Les Rougon-Macquart* (Paris: Pléiade, 1962), 2:33, 49–51.

24. Charles-Auguste Sainte-Beuve, *Nouveaux Lundis* (Paris: Lévy, 1863), 1:398.

25. In fact, this literary fashion was preceded in the eighteenth century by a specifically architectural fashion: see, for instance, F. Baldensperger, "Le kiosque de Stanislas à Lunéville: Décor et suggestion d'Orient," *Revue de littérature comparée* (1934), 14:183–189. The word very quickly became metonymic of the typical Oriental landscape: for example, Delille, *Les Trois Règnes*, II: "[Les simouns] Des déserts africains . . . enterrent en grondant les kiosques, / . . . La riche caravane et ses nombreux chameaux" [The simooms in the African deserts roaringly bury the kiosks, the rich caravan, and its many camels]. Then, by extension, it became the setting for dreams, from the kiosk in Nerval's *Aurélia* (1855), II, vi, to Claudel's kiosk: "En ce lieu fictif le spectateur devient roman lui-même" [In this fictive place, the viewer himself becomes a novel]. *Jules ou l'homme-aux-deux-cravates, Oeuvres en prose* (Paris: Pléiade, 1965), p. 857.

26. As Flaubert tells us in his *Dictionnaire des idées reçues*: "Kiosque. Lieu de délices dans un jardin" [Kiosk. Place of delights in a garden].

27. See, for example, Balzac, *Autre étude de femme*, Marcel Bouteron, ed. (Paris: Pléiade, 1951–65), 7:228.

28. I myself have tried to analyze the mechanisms whereby the effect of a neologism is maintained in literary texts even after it has been assimilated into common usage. *Romanic Review* (1953), 44:282–289.

29. The solution is also incomplete in that thematology summarizes themes without regard to their structures. This could be corrected by setting up typologies after the model of Vladimir Propp's pioneering *Morphology of the Folktale* (Austin and London: University of Texas Press, 1968).

30. This task is less formidable than it appears, since it could consist in a simple reordering of the dictionary. We do have usable evidence in the examples compiled by lexicographers (such as the *Grand dictionnaire du XIXe siècle*, a veritable compendium of French myths) and in Renaissance compilations of exempla (such as those by Ravisius Textor, Rhodiginus, and others).

31. *Les Fleurs du Mal*, LXXIX (1860).

32. *Le Génie du christianisme*, III, I, ch. viii, "Des églises gothiques."

33. Lamartine, *Harmonies*, "La Prière de femme," in *Oeuvres poetiques complètes* (Paris: Pléiade, 1963), p. 1230. In another poem, Lamartine describes the Gothic cathedral, literally, as a resonance or echo chamber, built like a machine to amplify the voices of prayer (*ibid.*, "Hymne du soir dans les temples," pp. 317ff.). Cf. Delille, *L'Imagination* (1806), ch. 7, and the vestiges of the theme in Jules Laforgue, *L'Imitation de Notre-Dame de la Lune*, "Climat, faune et flore de la lune," (lines 8–9): "climat de silence, écho de l'hypogée d'un ciel atone" [climate of silence, the echo of the subterranean vaults of an atonal sky].

34. This effect is even more compelling because the poet makes the forest noises into symbols of his own memories and also uses death images to evoke painful memories (in "Le Cygne," I, line 50; "Spleen," II, lines 5–10, etc.).

7. Intertextual Semiosis: Du Bellay's "Songe," VII

1. This title comes from Clément Marot's sixteenth-century French translation. The poem in question is the canzone XLII in the *Rime sparse*.

2. In the words of J. Jolloffe and M. A. Screech, the editors of Joachim Du Bellay, *Regrets et autres oeuvres poétiques* (Geneva: Droz, 1966), p. 35: "It is poetically valid to hide truths beneath fables . . . if doing so truly adds something to the naked idea, but it does present some dangers, [among them] the pursuit of obscurity for its own sake."

3. What I mean by *code* is that the system is used to designate something other than what is represented by its nuclear word. The modification of the systems in "Songe" is either contextual (the temple and obelisk are described from the perspective of a viewer who dreams that he is standing on the banks of the Tiber), or determined by the fact that its nuclear word is already a symbol or a metonym of Rome (the she-wolf in sonnet VI, for instance).

4. My analysis of the text's surface is based on the concept of the stylistic feature, which creates a contrast in relation to its context (and not in relation to the norm, as certain theories would have it). I have defined this concept in my *Essais de stylistique structurale* (Paris: Flammarion, 1971), pp. 50–94. For the theory of semiosis, see my *Semiotics of Poetry* (Bloomington: Indiana University Press, 1978).

5. This word is no exaggeration: See G. Gadoffre, "Structures des mythes de Du Bellay," *Bibliothèque d'humanisme et renaissance* (1974), 36:285–286 and 288.

6. The bird that flees light could be understood by Du Bellay's contemporaries only as an owl. The function of this periphrasis is not altered, however, if the modern reader is unable to find any other solution to the enigma than a compound such as *oiseau de nuit* (night bird). This is because no matter what ornithological reality they represent, all the names of the nocturnal birds are pejorative; hence, the nucleus of the periphrasis must be a negative index.

7. On the two possible ways in which a descriptive sentence can be generated in poetic discourse—from like term to like term, or from opposite to opposite—see chapter 11.

8. This semantic opposition is reinforced by the fact that it coincides with a phonetic contrast between the /ãpl/ series and the /i/ series. This coincidence seems to actualize the symbolism that is traditionally attributed to these sounds (for example, vastness versus smallness). But even if this were not the case, the phonetic opposition could not be stronger.

9. The unstated or the unsaid [non-dit] should not be confused with the implied [sous-entendu]. The latter is usually a hypothesis on the part of the analyst: it is used to complete forms that are incomplete only in relation to an arbitrary norm (the nominal sentence, for instance, which is termed nominal only in relation to an ideal model of the sentence as containing a verb). *Sous-entendu* is usually proof that an analysis is faulty. The unsaid or unstated, however, is a necessary presupposition of a concrete text. It is the lexical or semantic component that is repressed and thereby generates the text.

10. This is all the more so since *nuë* is singular here, and not the plural *nues*, which is more commonly used in representations of the sky. This seems to transform it into the vapory equivalent of the *heavenly vault*.

11. We could take our study of syntactic masses still further: the entire description of the soaring flight is in sharp contrast with the brief transition ("je le vy croistre" for the transition versus three and a half lines for his flight). This makes for a kind of secondary climax: we do not go from the little bird to just any winged creature, but straight to the king of birds, the eagle.

12. See Gérard de Nerval's variation on a similar actant in his "Le Christ aux Oliviers" (part V, lines 1–4): "C'était bien lui ce fou, cet insensé sublime . . . / Cet Icare oublié qui remontait les cieux, / Ce Phaéton perdu sous la foudre des dieux, / Ce bel Atys meurtri que Cybèle ranime!" [He was that madman, sublimely insane . . . that forgotten Icarus going back up to the heavens. Phaethon lost in the lightning of the gods, that handsome, wounded Athys, brought back to life by Cybele!]

13. This imbalance is similar to the imbalance provoked by *là se perdit,* which abruptly interrupts the ascending series (growth, soaring flight) of the first eight lines, only it is even more marked.

14. Heredia, *Les Trophées,* "La mort de l'aigle." Cf. Apollinaire, *Alcools,* "Le brasier": "Descendant des hauteurs où pense la lumière / Jardins *rouant* plus hauts que tous les ciels mobiles / L'avenir masqué flambe en traversant les cieux" [Descending from the heights where light thinks. Gardens whirling round higher than all the moving skies. The masked future flames as it crosses the heavens]. See also Lautréamont, *Les Chants de Maldoror,* I, xi, in *Oeuvres complètes* (Paris: Pléiade, 1970), p. 69.

15. See my *Essais de stylistique structurale,* pp. 42–50.

16. Du Bellay, *Les Antiquitez de Rome,* XXX: "Comme le champ semé en verdure foisonne, / *De* verdure se haulse *en* tuyau verdissant, / *Du* tuyau se herisse *en* epic florissant, / D'epic jaunit *en* grain . . . / Ainsi *de peu à peu* creut l'empire Romain, / Tant qu'il fut despouillé par la Barbare main" [As the seeded field abounds in greenery and *from* greenery rises *into* green-growing stalks, and *from* stalks bristles *into* flowering ears, and *from* ears turns *into* golden grain . . . so did the Roman Empire *little by little* grow, until it was sacked by a Barbarian hand].

17. Ovid, *Metamorphoses,* II, lines 319–320: "But Phaethon, with flames searing his glowing locks, was flung headlong, and went hurtling down through the air, leaving a long trail behind" [. . . in praeceps longoque per aera tractu/Fertur]: Mary M. Innes, trans. (Harmondsworth: Penguin, 1955), p. 58. The verb translated by Du Bellay's *rouant* is also stressed in Ovid—by its position.

18. *Alciati Emblematum Flumen Abundans* (Lyons, 1551), p. 65. The emblem ("sic plerique rotis Fortunae ad sidera Reges Evecti ambitio quos juvenilis agit") is in the chapter *Stultitia,* "In temerarios." Also cf. the Humanist interpretations of Phaethon collected by G. Demerson in *La Mythologie dans l'oeuvre de la Pléiade* (Geneva: Droz, 1972), in particular, Barthélémy Aneau's 1555 commentary on Ovid (p. 500), Baïf's *Hymme de la paix* (1572; p. 578), as well as the discussion of mythological discourse in considerations on the morality of political events (pp. 277ff.). One constant theme in the Renaissance was the representation of the growth of the Roman Empire as a sacrilegious assault on the heavens (although the most frequent code was the myth of the Giants, which Du Bellay also uses in "Songe," xv).

19. "Le jeu de l'un dans l'autre," the game of the one in the other, was a favorite verbal guessing game of the Surrealists. It consisted precisely in representing something, which remained unnamed, in the code of something else. André Breton, for instance, represents a child being born as an hourglass, and Michel Zimbacca represents a wooden leg in monocle code.—TRANSLATOR.

20. V. L. Saulnier, for example, thinks that the owl was chosen because the Germans who were threatening Rome in her decadence had the owl as their totem. Since the ancient naturalists thought that the owl and the crow were enemies, it follows that the owl should be Rome ("Commentaires sur les *Antiquitez de Rome,*" *Humanisme et Renaissance* (1950), 12:114ff. and, in particular, p. 125, on the owl).

21. The text does not mention the owl by name, but again, no one at the time of Du Bellay would have failed to identify it.

22. This has become the model for scenes in comedies, as we can see from the Voltaire and Fénelon quotes under the *aigle* entry in the *Littré*.

23. This, in fact, is an ancient proverb, patterned after Abstemius. (The owl simply represents the blindness of people who cannot see themselves as they really are. There is no particular reason why the eagle should be the one to open the owl's eyes, except for the fact that they are traditionally paired.)

24. For example, the eagle surrounded by lesser birds who are trying to pick a fight with him, in Arthur Henkel and Albrecht Schoene, eds., *Emblemata. Handbuch zur Sinnbildkunst des 16. und 17. Jahrhunderts* (Stuttgart: Metzler, 1967), col. 766: the legend speaks only of crows, but the engraver could not resist adding an owl.

25. This is true not only in Du Bellay. One emblem, after saying that the owl, who flees the light (*lucifuga*), cannot pretend he is an eagle, then adds: "Sors, Virtus, Natura ducum contraria vulgo est" (Henkel and Schoene, *Emblemata*, cols. 764–765).

26. Let me stress that it is impossible to separate the words *renaître de sa cendre* from the myth of the phoenix and read them as the innocuous metaphor they are today. The *vermet* and the fire consuming the eagle prevent us from doing so.

27. This was probably a rationalization patterned after the model of the caterpillar who becomes a butterfly and having the further advantage of actualizing a structure establishing an opposition between *earthworm/star*, *snake/bird*, and so on.

28. It is not a question of a mistaken confusion or "coarse analogy" between the myth of the eagle and the myth of the phoenix, as Saulnier would have it ("Commentaires," pp. 124–125). What we have here is, instead, an adaptation of a figurative metamorphosis grammar to the lexicon required by the context. Similarly, in the interests of imperial propaganda, the account of Augustus' funeral tells us that an eagle rose from the ashes of the emperor's funeral pyre. See J. Hubaux and M. Leroy, *Les Mythes du phénix* (Liège and Paris: Droz, 1939), pp. 239 and 246–247.

29. This negativization is especially exemplary because of the fact that any kind of crawling animal is the exact antithesis of a flying animal in mythic discourse. If the context lends itself to such a manipulation, even *ver* [worm] can be valorized. This happens in the "Stances sur les amours de Desportes" by the Cardinal du Perron, who plays on the homophony of the Phoenix's *ver* and poetic *vers* [verse]: out of the ashes of Desportes' loves rise the *vers* inspired by his passion. The end of mimesis.

30. *Rime sparse*, p. 19. We have already seen the first two animals. The third, in Petrarch, is the moth, which flies into the flame. Another version of this would be Hercules on Oeta, and yet another would be our phoenix, which so many Christian apologists in the Renaissance used to represent the resurrected Christ.

8. From Structure to Code: Chateaubriand and the Imaginary Monument

1. François-René de Chateaubriand, *Les Mémoires d'outre-tombe* (Paris: Pléiade, 1958), 1:197.

2. *Ibid.*, 1:424 (and repeated in the *Essai sur la littérature anglaise*).

3. Chateaubriand, *Vie de Rancé*, Fernand Letissier, ed. (Paris: Didier, 1955), p. 253.

4. Chateaubriand, *Le Génie du christianisme*, I, III, iii (Paris: Flammarion, 1910, 1:71).

5. *Ibid.*, III, I, viii, Flammarion, I, pp. 299–300.

6. *Ibid.*, I, IV, iv, Flammarion, I, p. 86.

7. Quoted in Alice Poirier, *Les Idées artistiques de Chateaubriand* (Paris: Presses Universitaires de France, 1930), p. 48.

8. Chateaubriand, *Voyage en Italie, Oeuvres complètes* (Paris: Garnier, 1932?), 6:570.

9. *Voyage au Mont-Blanc, Oeuvres complètes*, 6:347.

10. *Lettre à M. de Fontanes sur la campagne romaine*, J.-M. Gautier, ed. (Geneva: Droz, 1961), p. 25.

11. The Alexander in question is Czar Alexander I, whose armies were defeated by the French at Austerlitz in 1805. He led the allied invasion of France in 1812, and became famous as the man who defeated Napoleon.—TRANSLATOR.

12. *Itinéraire de Paris à Jérusalem*, Emile Malakis, ed. (Baltimore: Johns Hopkins University Press, 1946), 2:292.

13. See Jean-Bertrand Barrère, *La Fantaisie de Victor Hugo* (Paris: Corti, 1949–1960), 3:165–172.

14. *Le Génie du christianisme*, III, v, iii (Flammarion, 2:45).

15. *Voyage en Italie*, 6:278–279; *Mémoires*, 1:514.

16. Jean-Pierre Richard, *Paysage de Chateaubriand* (Paris: Seuil, 1967), pp. 125–126.

17. Cf. the first version of this image—"les tombeaux ont été effacés par les pas de la joie" [the graves were worn away by the footsteps of joy]—which is repeated in the *Vie de Rancé* without any change in meaning, in the following form: "les tombeaux poussent sous les pas de la joie" [graves grow under the footsteps of joy] (p. 54, n. 1; p. 55).

9. Production of the Narrative (I): Balzac's *La Paix du ménage*

1. In other words, lexical, syntactic, and stylistic features. See Claude Bremond, *Logique du récit* (Paris: Seuil, 1973), p. 46. The first part of the work stresses the disadvantages of the kind of narrative typology that was first conceived of by Propp and that, today, is represented first and foremost in the work of Greimas. On the drawbacks of Bremond's own approach, see W. O. Hendricks, "The Work and Play Structures of Narrative," *Semiotica* (1975), 13:281–328.

2. The addressee as he is presupposed by the narrative text: see Gérard Genette, *Figures III* (Paris: Seuil, 1972), p. 265. On the relations with the reader, see Tzvetan Todorov, "Reading as Construction," in *The Reader in the Text: Essays on Audience and Interpretation*, S. R. Suleiman and I. Crosman, eds. (Princeton: Princeton University Press, 1980), pp. 67–82.

3. A. J. Greimas, *Du Sens: essais sémiotiques* (Paris: Seuil, 1970), pp. 158–159. Greimas' *Maupassant: la sémiotique du texte* (Paris: Seuil, 1976), a work in which he tries to bridge the gap between narrative structures and surface structures, is also based on this postulate.

4. On identifying these strategic points in a narrative text, see Roland Barthes, "Introduction to the Structural Analysis of Narratives," in *Image—Music—Text*, Stephen Heath, trans. (New York: Hill and Wang, 1977), pp. 79–124; and Philippe Hamon, "Clausules," *Poétique* (1975), 21:495–526.

5. Published in 1830 along with five other novels in the *Scènes de la vie privée*, *La Paix du ménage* takes up approximately sixty pages and, in the typography of the Pléiade edition, thirty-five. My citations are from the Marcel Bouteron edition of *La Comédie humaine* (Paris: Pléiade, 1951). [*Domestic Peace*, in *La Comédie humaine of Honoré de Balzac* (New York: Century, 1908), 2:289–327, was consulted, but in all cases the translations have been considerably modified—TRANSLATOR.]

6. This expression is taken from an introduction inspired by Balzac himself (*Oeuvres complètes*, Pléiade edition, 11:164).

7. Comparisons with theatrical techniques are a constant in Balzac criticism. See, for instance, H. J. Hunt, *Balzac's Comédie humaine* (London: Athlone, 1964), p. 25; M. Bardèche, *Balzac romancier* (Paris: Plon, 1940), pp. 176–203 on the *Scènes de la vie privée*.

8. Bremond, *Logique du récit*, pp. 162–173 and 282–308; on motifs, see pp. 187–188.

9. Dazzling and luxurious lighting is a commonplace in descriptions of balls and formal gatherings in the nineteenth century: cf. the cliché *éclairer a giorno* [to light up as bright as day] (for example, in Balzac, *Sarrasine*, in the *Oeuvres complètes*, Pléiade edition, 6:79; Flaubert, *Madame Bovary*, I, viii). The difference here is that, concerning the same lighting, there is a detailed description and focusing.

10. The satire is more clearly sketched out on a second level of comprehension. If *aiguillettes* are the insignia of a regiment, they are also, in their archaic sense, synecdochic of men's leg coverings, and even of the codpiece or fly. This last is metonymic in its own turn. This wordplay is not possible in the context of *kolbacs* and *dolmans*, but "qui plurent tant . . ." is sensed retroactively to be a transformation of "le beau sexe courait l'aiguillette" [the fair sex were aiglet-chasers].

11. Let me emphasize that the *corner* is at the foot of the highly visible candelabrum. The darkness in the midst of the bright light is metaphoric: it refers to the ignorance to which the men on the dance floor are condemned, since they are kept away from the beautiful stranger by the rows of chairs on which the jealous ladies are seated.

12. The French *papillon* covers a wider semantic field than the English *butterfly*. When specified as a *papillon de nuit* [night butterfly] or, as here, appearing in a flame context, *papillon* should be translated as *moth*. The English-speaking reader should bear in mind that the *papillon*-moth flying up to the flame retains all the fluttering characteristics of the *papillon*-butterfly.—TRANSLATOR.

13. "Any narrative maneuver consisting in telling of or evoking beforehand a subsequent event" (Genette, *Figures III*, p. 82).

14. The proverb, or the truism that it expresses, is so well established that under the entry *brillant* some dictionaries list the figurative antonym *solide* [solid] before the literal antonym *terne* [dull].

15. On the suppression or making implicit of the matrix sentence, see chapter 6.

16. *Scènes de la vie privée*, "Note de la première édition," 11:165.

10. Production of the Narrative (II): Humor in *Les Misérables*

1. This is not the place for a bibliography of works on humor in French literature. On Romantic humor, I must at least mention Claude Pichois, *L'Image de Jean Paul Richter dans les lettres françaises* (Paris: Corti, 1963), pp. 198–229. He arbitrarily excludes Hugo, however (p. 212), and does so without a shadow of demonstration.

2. This should come as a surprise only to biased readers. Hugo's humor was denied in the years when right-thinking critics in France were proclaiming that the most thoughtful poet of the French nineteenth century was simply stupid. A certain Auguste Rochette devoted a book to *L'Esprit dans les oeuvres poétiques de Hugo* [Wit in Hugo's poetic works] in 1911. In it he explained that the writer made a mockery of things that should be respected, that he did so heavy-handedly, and that his wit was vulgar. This prejudice was so strong that even an objective scholar such as W. Gottschalk forgot to include Hugo when he examined modern humor *Die humoristische Gestalt in der französischen Literatur*, (Heidelberg: Winter, 1928), pp. 197ff. Today's reading public is better prepared to accept Hugolian humor, thanks in the first place to J.-B. Barrère, whose *Fantaisie de V. Hugo*, 3 vols. (Paris: Corti, 1949–1950), opened the critics' eyes. Barrère is interested above all in Hugolian thematology, however, and does not distinguish between humor and the comic and other forms of "fantasy." Moreover, he uses the word too frequently as if it only meant playful, amusing jest. Henri Guillemin's opuscule titled *L'Humour de V. Hugo* (Neuchâtel: Baconnière, 1951) is merely a collection of the poet's better strokes of wit, his polemical ones in particular, and Guillemin mixes up the comic, wit, irony, and humor.

3. My choice is explained by the novel's variety as well as by its central place among Hugo's works. It combines characteristics that would have to be sought separately in the novels written before 1851 and the other novels written in exile (aside from *Quatrevingt-treize*, which is a later work). My references give the part, book, and chapter numbers, in that order. The numbers in parentheses refer to the pages of M. Allem's edition of *Les Misérables* (Paris: Pléiade, 1956).

[Charles E. Wilbour's translation (New York: Modern Library, 1931), was consulted in the preparation of the English texts. In all cases, the Wilbour translations have been reworked.—TRANSLATOR.]

4. *Les Misérables*, III, II, i (p. 636) and III, VI, v (p. 747).
5. *Ibid.*, V, IX, iv (pp. 1482–1500).
6. *Ibid.*, II, v, vi-viii (pp. 500–504).
7. *Ibid.*, III, VIII, xxi (pp. 854–857).
8. *Ibid.*, III, VIII, xxii (p. 858; see p. 416); III, vi (p. 164).
9. *Ibid.*: the entire second book of the fifth part (pp. 1305–1324).
10. Cf. the title of the third book: "La boue, mais l'âme" [Mud, but the soul] (p. 1325).
11. *Les Misérables*, V, II, iii (p. 112).
12. This construction is similar to that of jokes or funny stories that end with a punchline, which often consists of a pun, as here. (Hugo's notes contain such constructions: see, for example, Guillemin, *L'Humour de V. Hugo*, pp. 33–34.) On this type of story, see V. Morin, L'Histoire drôle," *Communications* (1967), 8:102ff., in particular pp. 109–112.
13. On conversion, see chapter 3.
14. *Les Misérables*, V, II, iii (pp. 1312–1313).
15. On the function of this symbolism in *Les Misérables*, see R. B. Grant, *The Perilous Quest* (Durham: Duke University Press, 1968), pp. 170ff.
16. As defined by M. Bardèche in *Balzac romancier* (Paris: Plon, 1940), p. 22. This same hierarchy is found in novels with romantic plots, but there it is not exploited, since such novels are confined to a single social class, without outside contacts.
17. The title of the fourth Part (p. 861).
18. Fauchelevent returns Jean Valjean's good deed with another (pp. 506ff.). The fatherly Gavroche was once a foundling, but becomes the father of two abandoned children (pp. 989–1010). The thesis is expressed by the repetition of a situation on different "social" levels. Humor is what establishes the distance between these parallel levels. It points out their parallelism (their homologous situations) by making the second episode into the formal (distorted) reminder of the first (Jean Valjean as benefactor) or of the model (normal paternity).
19. *Les Misérables*, I, I, v (p. 43).
20. Acceptability is defined in terms of conformity to the social norms of the novel with aristocratic characters and a love plot. The prototypes of that novel include *Amélie Mansfield* by Mme. Cottin and *Valérie* by Mme. de Krüdener, not to mention Mme. de Staël's *Corinne* and even Stendhal's *Armance*.
21. *Les Misérables*, IV, I, iii (pp. 872–873.)
22. It goes from Marius courting Cosette: "Je viens de rencontrer le chapeau neuf et l'habit neuf de Marius, et Marius dedans" [I just met Marius' new hat and new suit, and Marius inside them] (p. 744); cf. his meditations on the initials on a handkerchief: "aventures de la lettre *U* livrée aux conjectures" [adventures of the letter *U* abandoned to conjecture] (p. 751) to the wedding night: "dans leur chambre un bruissement d'ailes confuses . . . au-dessus de ce baiser ineffable

. . . un tressaillement dans l'immense mystère des étoiles" [in their chamber a rustling of confused wings . . . above that ineffable kiss . . . a thrill in the immense mystery of the stars] (p. 1429). The transformation model is given in sentences such as "la maison Gillenormand devint un temple" [the Gillenormand house became a temple] (p. 1428).

23. *Les Misérables*, III, V, iv (p. 727).

24. *Ibid.*, III, v, iv (p. 728). The only words that are favorable to Mère Plutarque—"pauvre bonne vieille femme"—are not enough to counterbalance the negative polarization, since they make her inferior in relation to the witness (the narrator and the reader). Not enough, though, for the humor to degenerate into satire, especially since the condescension is balanced with this mention of lowly merit: "Sa gloire était dans ses bonnets, toujours blancs" [Her glory lay in her bonnets, which were always white]. Here the mechanism of humor is comparable to the *parapluie-auréole* of Louis-Philippe above; also cf. Cosette's park bench as seen by Marius: "ce banc qu'une auréole entourait" [that bench which was surrounded by a halo] (p. 746.) In contrast, another character is similar to Mère Plutarque, but is treated satirically: "elle avait une amie de chapelle, vieille vierge comme elle . . . absolument hébétée, et près de laquelle Mlle Gillenormand avait le plaisir d'être une aigle" [she had a friend from chapel, an old maid like her . . . (who was) absolutely stupid, and beside whom Mlle. Gillenormand had the pleasure of being an eagle] (p. 646).

25. The maid in Flaubert's *Un Coeur simple* also makes do with an animal, but Félicité, at least, once loved someone higher on the scale of beings. Besides, Flaubert's humor is less polarizing than Hugo's. Félicité's parrot, after all, is only named Loulou, but the name of Mère Plutarque's cat is laden with caricature—his name is Sultan.

26. The image's impact is all the greater in that the theme of Allegri's *Miserere* belongs to the register of the sublime in nineteenth-century literature (in Goethe, Chateaubriand, and Mme. de Staël, for example); see R. Lebègue, "Le thème du *Miserere* de la Sixtine," *Revue d'histoire littéraire* (March–April 1972), (pp. 246–263). The theme functions as the metonymic hyperbole of the theme (which is generally comic) of the Sistine Chapel's *castrati*.

27. Among others, by André Breton, who more than anyone else sensed the romanticism specific to humor. See the introduction to his *Anthologie de l'humour noir* (Paris: Pauvert, 1966).

11. The Poem as Representation: A Reading of Hugo

1. On the relation of the referential function to the poetic function (which would perhaps be better termed the formal function), see Roman Jakobson's 1958 discussion, published in his *Essais de linguistique générale* (Paris: Minuit, 1963), pp. 209ff., in particular p. 218. I have attempted to refine his views: see the first part of my *Essais de stylistique structurale* (Paris: Flammarion, 1971).

2. This is because reality is conceived of as having a logic. This myth is reflected in the cliché *fait probant* [a convincing fact] as opposed to all the com-

monplaces about words "that can be used however we like." It is also reflected in the logic/a-logic opposition used to rationalize the opposition between natural language and figurative language, as Tzvetan Todorov has shown in *Littérature et signification* (Paris: Larousse, 1967), pp. 99–100.

3. By "thematic structure," I mean any structure having one or more themes as variants. In contrast, a theme can correspond to different structures depending on the texts in which it appears.

4. Victor Hugo, *Les Rayons et les Ombres*, poem XVIII, Ed. Pierre Albouy, ed. (Paris: Pléiade, 1964), 1:1062–1063.

5. At least this is the explicit reasoning. But an admiring value judgment is also an arbitrary superimposition of the observation of a complex stylistic phenomenon upon the fact that the poem is signed by Victor Hugo. It was demonstrated long ago, however that it is advantageous for the analyst to disregard the author's name, since it can prompt stereotypical reactions of admiration or distrust, depending on the aesthetics of the moment. See I. A. Richards, *Practical Criticism: A Study of Literary Judgment* (New York: Harcourt Brace, 1929). Traditional criticism claims to base its evaluations on descriptions and to motivate the former by the latter. In most cases, though, all it does is add laudatory adjectives to the nouns in descriptive sentences, or even more simply to subordinate the descriptive sentence to an utterance like: "We have to admire the way in which this passage (. . .)." The link between the description and the evaluation is not a causal relationship, but simply the grammatical binding of a metalinguistic utterance (seasoned with textual features) and quotations taken from a "mythological" or "ideological" corpus (the stereotypes of a generation of readers or of the group with which the critic wants to be identified, regarding a particular author).

6. M. E. I. Robertson, *L'Epithète dans les oeuvres lyriques de Victor Hugo* (Paris: Jouve, 1926), p. 419.

7. Barrère, *La Fantaisie de Victor Hugo* (Paris: Corti, 1949), 1:248.

8. The other critics are more or less in agreement with Barrère. See the comments of M. Levaillant, *L'Oeuvre de Victor Hugo* (Paris: Delagrave, 1938), p. 356, and P. Moreau and J. Boudout, *Oeuvres choisies* (Paris: Hatier, 1950), 1:857. The most recent editor, Pierre Albouy, *Oeuvres poétiques* (Paris: Pléiade, 1964), 1:1552–1553 (see also 1:1574), simply repeats M. E. I. Robertson's commentary of forty-three years before. Of course, I do not believe that a textual commentary is of value only if it departs drastically from all previous ones. In the case with which I am concerned, however, the commentaries do nothing but repeat two very general features that are indifferently applicable to many texts. No one attempts to account for the role played by these factors in the complex system of the text.

9. The other meaning of the word *carillon*, "a group or set of bells," is immediately ruled out by the fact that it is singular and, therefore, in opposition with the explicit plural in "tes cités antiques" and the implicit plural in "plus qu'une église par cité," can refer only to the sound. If the slightest ambiguity remained, it would disappear with line 5.

10. Hugo, *Dernière gerbe*, poem XXIII (Paris: Imprimerie nationale, 1941), p. 320. Joyful, or at least positively valorized. (See Baudelaire, "La cloche fêlée": "Au bruit des carillons qui chantent dans la brume" [To the sound of the carillons singing in the fog]. Here the positive valorization is actualized by *chanter* [to sing]. There is a parallelism with *cloche au gosier vigoureux* [strong-throated bell] and an opposition to the cracked bell, the *cloche fêlée*.) See also the famous "éveil des carillons" [awakening of the bells] in Hugo's *Notre-Dame de Paris*, book III, ch. ii, Marius-François Guyard, ed. (Paris: Garnier, 1976), pp. 162–164, where we are told that there is nothing "de plus riche, de plus joyeux, de plus doré, de plus éblouissant" [richer, more joyful, more golden, more dazzling], and that Quasimodo's "ardeur carillonneuse" [carilloning ardor] puts the cathedral "dans une perpétuelle joie de cloches" [into a perpetual joy of bells]. *Ibid.*, book VII, ch. iii, p. 300.

11. Nerval and Méry had thought of realizing this ballet in the staging of *L'Imagier de Harlem*, in the sixth tableau, scene 2, where the hours are dancers led by the god Pan in a circle around the protagonist. See Jean Richer, *Nerval, Expérience et création* (Paris: Hachette, 1971), pp. 590, 602–603. There is a similar ballet in Jules Janin, *Contes fantastiques* (1832), "La vallée de Bièvre."

12. Hugo, *Dernière Gerbe*, poem XV(p. 310). Barrère, *La Fantaisie*, 1:250 n. 2, believes a ballet of the Hours can be see in *Dernière Gerbe*, poem XIII (p. 308). This is not quite the case, though. What we can see is a round of witches at their sabbath, which is evoked by the twelve strokes of midnight. Proust made use of another possibility: noon wearing a crown with twelve jewels. *A la Recherche du temps perdu* (Paris: Pléiade, 1954), 1:70–71.

13. Barrère, *La Fantaisie*, p. 248, thinks that the dancer is Spanish because of Hugo's interest in the traces of the Spanish baroque in the architecture of Flanders. But it is not even necessary to invoke a personal curiosity of the tourist-poet: the oxymoron *flamand-espagnol* [Flemish-Spanish] was a commonplace in the literary mimesis of Flanders in the nineteenth century. Furthermore, Barrère does not account for the *danseuse* component. He speaks of the poet's fantasy (which is precisely what remains to be explained), and of a *correspondence* expressing "the age-old lightness, the gracefulness, the strangeness of these hours dancing on tiptoe in the unbroken silence of the night." The cleverness and subjectivity of Barrère's image are typical of traditional criticism, which thinks the way to explain a poem is to "rival" it in prose. Clearly, what we have here is an a posteriori rationalization of the text's effect, a rationalization that, in fact, distorts the text (the tiptoeing dancers on *pointes* cancel out the Spanishness of the dance). It does so by substituting the reality "danseuse" for the verbal chain *heure qui tourne → ronde → danseuse*.

14. The rich wordplay in the French cannot be carried over into the English, which has only one word for *scale*. The usual French *gamme* has a synonym in the *échelle*, which can be either a *scale* or a *ladder*, and it is but a step from the *échelle musicale* [musical ladder] to Hugo's staircase.—TRANSLATOR.

15. *Notre-Dame de Paris*, book III, ch. ii (p. 163).

16. *Ibid.*, book VII, ch. iii (p. 301). The novel predates the poem by only five years.

same time that it unites them in a simultaneity represented by the watchman character: the transposition of the auditory to the visual is therefore not represented as synesthesia, but as hallucination. The hallucination is poetically effective; but from the perspective of literary mimesis this is just another excuse, an admission of the necessity of referring to a rational context.

30. See Saint-John Perse, *Oiseaux* (Paris: Gallimard, 1963), ch. 9, p. 25: "l'oiseau, créateur de son vol, monte aux rampes invisibles et gagne sa hauteur" [the bird, creating its flight, climbs to the invisible runways and reaches its altitude], and ch. 11, p. 29: the birds "tiennent aux strates invisibles du ciel . . . la longue modulation d'un vol [are keeping the long modulations of a flight to the invisible strata of the sky]. *Invisible* is obviously a key word in the mimesis of the abnormal, the supernatural, and so forth. In a more general way, as an index of "convention" and of a "postulate," it enables any concrete, visual descriptive system whatsoever to be transformed so as to be applicable to the representation of the abstract, the immaterial, and so forth.

31. See Hugo, *Album*, no. 13.350, in *Dieu, Le Seuil du gouffre*, René Journet and Guy Robert, eds. (Paris: Nizet, 1961), p. 199: "effet de soleil merveilleux, un rayon perce la voûte de brume comme par une fenêtre aérienne" [a wonderful effect of the sun—a ray of light pierces the misty vault as if through an ethereal window]. Also see Michel Leiris, *Haut mal*, p. 47, and René Char, *Seuls demeurent*, "Carte du 8 novembre": "vous occupez moins de place . . . que le trait d'un oiseau sur la corniche de l'air" [you take up less space . . . than the outline of a bird on the cornice of the air].

32. Everything takes place as if the representation of nuances were confined to prose mimesis, as the use of the detail—and especially the unmotivated detail—in Realist style would seem to indicate. This is not to say that poetry does not express nuances. It represents them, however, in their perfect or complete form—in short, as exemplary and general.

33. I have already observed the isomorphism of the *bird* and *dancer* representations in comparable texts. Here their synonymy is exploited within the same poem; but instead of developing in a syntagm, the *bird* mimesis is summed up by *comme* [like], which is a reminder of its equivalence with the *dancer* mimesis.

34. This distinction does not take us back to winged animals, but instead is dependent on the opposition *big/little*. In an animal context, *big* (in human terms) has threatening qualities, whereas *little* is positive (since it functions as a term of endearment, permits us to express a *protector/protected* relationship, and so on). The word *oiseau* need not be modified by *petit*. Substitutions such as (voler, sauter) → (voleter, votiger, sautiller) [to fly, to jump → to flit about, to flutter about, to hop] will do the trick, just as *sautant à petits pas* [taking little jumps] does in our poem.

35. See Baudelaire, "Chant d'automne": "Adieu! *vive clarté* de nos étés trop courts" [Farewell, *bright light* of our all-too-short summers!]. It is even possible that the effect of the group *vif et clair*, which is a transformation of *vive clarté*, might be reinforced by the phonic ambiguity whereby it could be read *vif éclair* [a sudden flash]. [The pronunciation of the two word groups is identical.—

TRANSLATOR.] This would give us a translation of *sudden* in terms of light, which would still be compatible with the door being opened. Cf. André Breton, *Le Revolver à cheveux blancs*, "Toutes les écolières ensemble": "après une dictée où *le coeur m'en dit* s'écrivait peut-être *le coeur mendie*" [after a spelling class where *le coeur m'en dit* (the heart tells me of it) was perhaps written *le coeur mendie* (the heart begs)] [both groups again are pronounced the same.—TRANSLATOR].

36. Cf. Baudelaire, "L'horloge," lines 3–4: "Les *vibrantes* / Douleurs dans ton coeur plein d'effroi / Se planteront bientôt comme dans une cible" [The vibrating pains in your fear-filled heart will soon be fixed in a target]. Also cf. Gautier, *España*, "L'Horloge": "Et dans nos coeurs criblés, comme dans une cible, *Tremblent* les traits lancés par l'archer invisible" [And in our hearts riddled with holes, as in a target, the arrows shot by the invisible archer *tremble*].

37. For example: *comme* → *ainsi que*, *flèche* [arrow] → *dard* [arrow], and ø → *qui tremble*. This verb is perceived in contrast to the microcontext of vibrant [vibrating] and thus can also be interpreted as a marker of lofty style (*variatio*).

38. The adjective *voluptueuse* is the revealing detail in Balzac, *La Recherche de l'absolu* (Paris: Pléiade, 1951–65), 9:497 (which should be contrasted with p. 476).

39. Proust, *A la Recherche du temps perdu*, 3:249 [*Remembrance of Things Past*, 3:251].

40. Cf. Marceline Desbordes-Valmore, "Les roses de Saadi": "J'ai voulu, ce matin, te rapporter des roses; / Mais j'en avais tant pris dans mes ceintures closes / Que les noeuds trop serrés n'ont pu les contenir" [I wanted, this morning, to bring you back some roses, but I had taken so many in my tied sashes that the too-tight knots could not hold them].

41. It is also an ironic commonplace that the ringing of clocks should be the guilty party here. Mark Twain described a sleepless night during which the carillons of a German church ring every hour, half-hour, and quarter-hour, and keep a tourist from getting even a monent's sleep (*A Tramp Abroad*, 1879, chs. 12 and 13). Cf. Proust, *Pastiches et mélanges*, p. 236: "L'église sonne pour toute la ville les heures d'insomnie des mourants et des amoureux" [The church rings for the whole city the sleepless hours of the dying and of lovers].

42. Hugo, *France et Belgique*, 18 août 1837, *En voyage* (Paris: Imprimerie nationale, 1910) 2:87–88. *Chanson chinoise* stresses the fantasy and whimsy of the melody. (It also develops the notion of the music of bells in an "ethnic" code. The music defines *carillon*, but it also corresponds to certain commonplaces about Chinese music and to the way it is represented in Western music.) It consequently accentuates the opposition with nonfantasy, which is to say with the boredom that envelops the sleepers. (Cf. *Le Rhin* 4:47, the "babillage moqueur, ironique et spirituel d'un carillon . . . reprochait à mes deux lourds voisins leur stupide bavardage" [mocking, ironic, and witty chatter of a carillon . . . reproached my two heavy neighbors for their stupid gossip].)

43. André Chénier, *Iambes*, poem IX, in *Oeuvres complètes* (Paris: Pléiade, 1940), p. 193: "Peut-être avant que l'heure en cercle promenée / Ait posé sur l'émail brillant, / Dans les soixante pas où sa course est bornés, / Son pied sonore et vigilant, / Le sommeil du tombeau pressera ma paupière" [Before the hour, on

its circular walk, has placed its resonant and watchful foot on the sixty steps in the bright enamel to which its course is confined, perhaps the sleep of the grave will weigh down on my eyelid]. Also see Hugo, *La Légende des siècles*, p. 200.

44. Of course, a relationship of inferiority represented by a polarity along the vertical axis can exist outside the bell theme. For instance, it can be actualized by a voice. Cf. *Chants du crépuscule*, poem IX, (1:847): "Seule au pied de la tour d'où sort la voix du maître" [Alone at the foot of the tower from which the master's voice is calling]. The relationship is so powerful, however, that it can make the listeners morally "inferior" even when the bell they are listening to is "benevolent" and friendly (since it represents the poet): men, "prosternés sous la tour, / Ecoutent, effrayés et ravis tour à tour . . . / La grande âme d'airain qui là-haut se lamente" [lying prostrate beneath the tower, alternately frightened and delighted, listen . . . to the immense bronze soul lamenting above]. (*Chants du crépuscule*, poem XXXII, part 4 (1:894). Cf. *Les Contemplations*, "A celle qui est restée en France," line 16: the church "Dont la *tour* sonne l'heure à mon *néant*" [whose *tower* tolls the hours for my *nothingness*].

45. Hugo, *Les Contemplations*, book V, poem VIII "A Jules J.," lines 13–16. I have italicized the words corresponding to the functions of the invariant: a threat from on high, implacable regularity, negative valorization. The victim's despondency is, moreover, actualized later on in the poem: cf. line 46, "L'abandon à chaque heure et l'ombre à chaque instant" [Every hour abandonment, every moment shadows], with *chaque* a variation on the *X to X* in *de moments en moments*.

46. *Ibid.*, book VI, poem XIV, lines 2–3. Here we notice the structural role of the syntagm */X/ à (par) /X/* [*X by (after) X*], which expresses the uninterrupted erosion of life with each minute that goes by. Cf. Baudelaire, "L'horloge": "Chaque instant te dévore un morceau du délice / A chaque homme accordé pour toute sa saison" [Every second eats up a morsel of the delight granted to every man for his entire season]; *ibid.*, book VI, poem VI, lines 516–517: "Et toute notre vie, en fuite heure par heure / S'en va derrière nous" [And all our life, escaping hour after hour, goes away behind us]; book VI, poem IX, line 11: [man] "tombe heure par heure" [falls hour after hour]; book V, poem XX, lines 5–6: "La vie auguste, goutte à goutte, / S'épand sur ce qui passe et sur ce qui demeure" [August life spreads, drop by drop, over that which ends and that which remains]; *Quatre vents de l'esprit*, book III, poem XXVII, lines 83–84: "L'homme est fait pour mourir heure par heure, hélas! / Les pleurs, pour tomber goutte à goutte!" [Man is made to die hour by hour, alas!, and tears to fall drop by drop!]. (The parallelism in this last example points to the syntagm's negative valorization.) "All-consuming Time" is signified not by the reality of the minutes and drops, but by the verbal geometry (a succession interrupted at regular intervals). See, too, the mimesis of the erosion of rock over the millennia in *Dieu, Seuil du gouffre*, XII (pp. 84ff). After synonyms of "acharnement" [relentlessness, fierce determination] are repeated (lines 51–53), we have "zone à zone" [from zone to zone] (line 55), "d'une lame percée allant à l'autre lame" [from one eroded strip going to another strip] (line 71), and "Du haut en bas, de bloc en bloc, de banc en banc" [From top to bottom, from block to block, from bed

to bed] (lines 84–85). See also this representation of ruins that "laissent tomber le passé *pierre à pierre* dans le Rhin, et *date à date* dans l'oubli" [drop the past *stone by stone* into the Rhine, and *date by date* into oblivion] (*Le Rhin*, letter xxv).

47. Hugo, *Toute la lyre*, section III, poem LVI (Paris: Imprimerie nationale, 1935), 1:258.

48. This negative coloration also spreads onto another component in the lexical field of *horloge*, the *pendulum*: "L'horloge de vos jours, ténébreuse sourdine, / Qui dans votre néant, *stupide, se dandine*" [The clock of your days, that dark mute which, in your nothingness, *stupidly swings*].

49. See Hugo, *Les Contemplations*, section III, poem II, lines 116–118. When the context does not give the descriptive system a negative orientation, the slave will be replaced by a worker. Cf. *Dieu, Le Seuil du gouffre*, poem XII, lines 369–370: "Le temps, cet ouvrier mystérieux qui court, / Au cabestan du ciel va donc s'arrêter court" [Time, that mysterious worker running round, will stop short at heaven's capstan].

50. *Toute la lyre*, section III, poem XLV, "Umbra," 1:226. For other examples, see Charles Baudouin, *Psychanalyse de Victor Hugo* (Paris: Colin, 1972), pp. 63–64.

51. *Chants du crépuscule*, poem XXXII (1:890). See the orchestra in *Les Rayons et les Ombres*, poem XXXV, ii (1:1099): "Les gammes, chastes soeurs dans la vapeur cachées, / Vidant et remplissant leurs amphores penchées" [The scales, chaste sisters hiding in the haze, emptying and filling their tilting amphoras] and "l'archet d'où les notes dégouttent" [the bow the notes are dripping from] (1:1100; cf. 1:836, where *épancher* [to pour forth] is used in reference to music). This image belongs to an allegorical subsystem in which the deity's attribute is an urn which she is emptying. This is the equivalent of a sentence expressing a cause–effect relationship. Gautier contrasts Peace emptying her horn of plenty and War, pouring "De son urne d'airain une grêle de balles, / Une grêle de mort" [out of her urn a hail of bullets, a hail of death] (*España*, poem IV, lines 10–11); the "original" image at the end is simply a transformation of the cliché that precedes it.

52. The *torturer/victim* relation is caricatured here. A different context would direct it toward a sadistic description—such as, for instance, that of a flaming liquid being poured over the victims of the Inquisition (*Torquemada*, I, I, vi and II, II, v).

53. *Les Contemplations*, VI, vi, lines 76 and 79–84.

54. Even though oblong shields and octagonal clockfaces (not to mention the original square ones), do exist in reality.

55. Gautier adopts the same code with the equivalences: *clockface* "combat area" and *hands of the clock* "spears" (*España*, poem III, lines 27–28).

56. There is no question that, until very recently, Tarpeia was part of the French public's mythology. The story in Livy (I, xi) was studied in school, and the allusions to her in Ovid and Propertius were well known. Her story was an *exemplum* used for moral edification (see the *De Viris*), and its bizarre details were hard to forget. All this proves to us that the strange use of the shield belongs

to a common code, and guarantees that the allusion will be understood—provided, however, that the text is indeed read. That seems elementary, but philological commentaries sometimes forget it. To read a text in its literariness is to read it in all its literalness, that is, to give in obediently to the *combinations* of the words. Indeed, the minimal style unit is the phrase, and not the isolated word as some commentators continue to believe: for this reason, their commentaries tend inevitably to confuse meaning in context with dictionary meaning. Vianey, for instance, in his edition of the *Contemplations* (Paris: Machette, 1922), 3:211, says that "The hour is an enemy who strikes and kills us; the clockface is its shield." He does not see that *bouclier* [shield] is the subject of the verb, and that its symbolic role stems from its grammatical role. Instead of reading *bouclier* within the syntagm, he reduces it to a generality whose pertinence has been negated by that syntagm; he reduces it to its normal use in language and war.

57. On the erroneousness of the concept of latent structures, see the third part of my *Essais de stylistique structurale* (Paris: Flammarion, 1971). Anomalies are sensed first as stylistic features, since they contrast with the context, and then they are identified as variants of a single invariant because of their relations by analogy to other anomalies in other contexts.

58. We could possibly attempt to come up with a literary classification of words according to whether or not they are able to generate a system, and according to their role in that system. A word like *plafond* [ceiling] generates a system that is more or less limited to terms like *plafond bas* [low ceiling] or *enfumé* [smokey]. Perhaps *lambris dorés* [gilded panels] should be placed in another system, in opposition to chaumière [thatched-roof (cottage)], for example. The descriptive system is therefore not as extensive as the semantic field, as it has been conceived of since Trier. Nor is it even as extensive as Bally's associative field, which embraces different levels of style as well as sequences that would never be found in the same context.

59. These prefabricated syntagms, by definition, lend themselves to *bricolage*: when they are rearranged on a thematic structure or superimposed on another system, they become codes.

60. Tautological and oxymoronic sequences are not limited to the noun-adjective group. A seme of the word triggering such a sequence can be made explicit with a verb and represent an action. Take the case of *castor* [beaver]: among its stock epithets we find *castor industrieux* or *laborieux* [busy beaver; literally: hardworking beaver]. The first theme in Rimbaud's prose poem "Après le déluge" is that of the resumption of life after a great flood, as if nothing had happened. It is hardly surprising that the structure corresponding to this return to normality is realized in the utterance *les castors bâtirent* [the beavers built]. The transformation of the adjective into a verb makes the difference between description and narrative.

12. The Extended Metaphor in Surrealist Poetry

1. This is precisely how André Breton defines this arbitrariness. As he puts it, the "strongest" image is "the one that displays the highest degree of arbi-

trariness . . .the one that takes the longest to translate into practical language." So it is arbitrary only in relation to usage. "[Premier] Manifeste du Surréalisme," in *Manifestes du surréalisme* (Paris: Pauvert, 1962), p. 53.

2. Studies of metaphor neglect the extended metaphor. The specialists say only that it is a continued metaphor, or if they do comment on it, they condemn it. See, for example, F. Brunot, *Histoire de la langue française* (Paris: Armand Colin, 1917–1953), vol. 3, part 1, 246–261. For this reason, it is well worth our while to undertake a formal analysis of the extended metaphor: see Philippe Dubois, "La Métaphore filée et le fonctionnement du texte," *Le Français moderne* (1975), 43:202–213.

3. Sainte-Beuve, *Vie, poésies et pensées de Joseph Delorme*, poem XI, Gérald Antoine, ed. (Paris: Nouvelles éditions latines, 1956), p. 145. Sainte-Beuve's contemporaries found this metaphor affected and precious (see Antoine's footnote 620).

4. This sequence is highly determined by clichés in French. It is commonplace to think of an elegy as a flow of tears, and lyric poets are known for their emotional outpourings. Furthermore, one of the most famous poems of the Romantic Lamartine was "Le Lac" (1820).—TRANSLATOR.

5. Desportes, *Diane* (1573); quoted in F. Brunot, *Histoire de la langue française*, vol. 3 part 1, p. 247.

6. Balzac, *Pierrette*, in *La Comédie humaine*, Marcel Bouteron, ed. (Paris: Pléiade, 1951), 3:670. Balzac is talking about Catholic milliners who want to retire far away from Paris.

7. The terms *tenor* and *vehicle* have been borrowed from I. A. Richards' theory of metaphor, *The Philosphy of Rhetoric* (New York and London: Oxford University Press, 1936), chs. 5–6, and as later refined by Max Black in *Models and Metaphors* (Ithaca: Cornell University Press, 1962), pp. 25–47.

8. See Roman Jakobson, "Closing Statements: Linguistics and Poetics," in *Style in Language*, T. A. Sebeok, ed. (Cambridge: MIT Press, 1960), pp. 350–377.

9. Breton, *Le Revolver à cheveux blancs*, "Sans connaissance," in *Poèmes* (Paris: Gallimard, 1966), p. 107.

10. *Ibid.*, p. 89. This is the title of one of the poems in *Le Revolver à cheveux blancs*.

11. By *slot*, I mean the position occupied by a word or phrase within one context or structure.

12. In a simple metaphor, either these systems remain implicit or else only the vehicle system is actualized in the text.

13. Black was the first to define the fundamental role of interaction in simple metaphors (*Models and Metaphors*, pp. 41–42).

14. I am well aware that Breton defined automatic writing as *automatisme psychique pur*, or "purely psychic automatism," but even the most unconscious associations are still expressed by verbal associations. In any case, my analysis will be confined to word associations, which are the only kind visible in poems. On these problems, see Michel Foucault, *Raymond Roussel* (Paris: Gallimard,

1963); Jean-Claude Chevalier, "Apollinaire et le calembour," *Europe* (1966), 451/452:56–76; A. H. Greet, *Jacques Prévert's Word-Games* (Berkeley: University of California Press, 1968); and my own *Essais de stylistique structurale* (Paris: Flammarion, 1971), pp. 161–181. These examples are intended only as illustrations of automatic writing; (VII) and (X) belong to extended metaphors.

15. René Char, *Le Marteau sans maître*, quoted in H. Jones, "L'écriture automatique," *Dialogue* (Montreal) (1963), 2:187. André Breton, *Poisson soluble*, prose poem 23, in *Manifestes du surréalisme*, p. 110.

16. Pierre Reverdy, *Les Ardoises du toit*, "Ciel étoilé," in *Plupart du temps* (Paris: Gallimard, 1969), p. 189.

17. Paul Eluard, *Capitale de la douleur*, "A la flamme des fouets," in *Oeuvres complètes*, M. Dumas and L. Scheler, eds. (Paris: Pléiade, 1968), 1:388. [The third-person singular, present tense, form of the verb *nuire*, "to harm," is *nuit*, which is the homonym of the noun *la nuit*, "night." *Métal* is metonymic of a weapon.—TRANSLATOR.]

18. Eluard, *La Vie immédiate*, "Le bâillon . . ." in *Oeuvres complètes*, 1:388. [In a theater context, the French *pièce* is a play. The compound expression *pièce d'eau* does not belong in that context: it designates an ornamental pond or lake.—TRANSLATOR.]

19. Breton, in Eluard and Breton, *L'Immaculée Conception*, in Eluard, *Oeuvres complètes*, 1:354. [The French *dorer la pilule* is the equivalent of our *to sugarcoat the pill*.—TRANSLATOR.]

20. Breton, *Poisson soluble*, 24, in *Manifestes du surréalisme*, p. 111. [The verb *tapir* signifies a very special kind of hiding: lurking and lying in wait before an ambush. It evokes stories à la James Fenimore Cooper with Indians and adventures.—TRANSLATOR.]

21. Connectives transpose the semantic parallelism of the two systems as a predication onto the unilinearity of the sentence.

22. They are more daring in their Surrealist variety, but they are not different: (IV) *train rond*, which is so shocking, is similar to Baudelaire's "Le *cantique muet* que chante le plaisir" [The silent hymn sung by pleasure] ("Femmes damnées," line 22). Harald Weinrich has attempted to analyze these degrees of boldness in "Semantik der kühnen Metapher," *Deutsche Vierteljahrsschrift für Literaturwissenschaft und Geistesgeschichte* (1963), 37:325ff.; see, in particular, pp. 333–335.

23. This is also true of precious extended metaphors like (II), whether or not they are ridiculous (with the exception of gratuitous parallelisms where the primary metaphor is unacceptable). From certain aesthetic viewpoints, overly systematic comparisons or comparisons of realities belonging to overly different social levels or aesthetics would be deemed improper or in poor taste, but that in no way alters the semantic working of the image. Consider, for example, Harlequin's extended metaphor in Marivaux's *Le Jeu de l'amour et du hasard*, act 2, scene 3: *amour grandissant/bébé* → *grand garçon* [growing love/baby → big boy]. Also see Trissotin's extended metaphor in Molière's *Les Femmes savantes*, act 3, scene 1.

24. Eluard, *La Rose publique*, "Le crépuscule . . ." in *Oeuvres complètes*, 1:431. I have quoted only the first derived metaphor.

25. See Georges Mounin, *Les Problèmes théoriques de la traduction* (Paris: Gallimard, 1963), pp. 230–231. C. F. Hockett, in *A Course in Modern Linguistics* (New York: Macmillan, 1958), pp. 261–265, has improved on the presentation of C. C. Fries, who is quoted by Mounin.

26. Breton, *La Clé des champs*, p. 113.

27. Eluard, *La Rose publique*, "La lumière éteinte . . ." in *Oeuvres complètes*, 1:425.

28. Cf. Eluard, *Facile*, "L'Entente," *ibid.*, 1:460: "tu bois au soleil" [you drink from the sun]. (The allegorical character to whom this is addressed is later called "tranquille sève nue" [tranquil, naked sap].) Cf. also Eluard, *Capitale de la douleur*, "Première du monde," *ibid.*, 1:179: "Un soleil tournoyant ruisselle sous l'écorce" [A whirling sun streams beneath the bark].

29. *Leurs* [their] is produced according to the rule in section 1.4 (Verb or adjective constructed with a noun from the vehicle). On the possessive as a connective, see Christine Brooke-Rose, *A Grammar of Metaphor* (London: Secker and Warburg, 1958), pp. 46–51, 186–191.

30. *Branches = streams*, however, still belongs to traditional, language-respecting poetics: the terms of the equation are not defined by a relationship of opposition. All there is between them is a contrast, which, moreover, is offset by their frequent contiguity in reality and frequent association in descriptions of nature. The *air/water* opposition accounts for the tension that can still be felt in compounds like *flying fish* (but is not felt in *sea dog*, for example), and even more so in an oxymoron like *scaphandrier de l'air* [air diver]. Eluard, *Les Nécessités de la vie*, "Le Grand jour," in *Oeuvres complètes*, 1:84. Cf. Gérard Genette, *Figures*, pp. 19–20, on the Baroque theme of the topsy-turvy world.

31. In *L'Image végétale dans la poésie d'Eluard* (Paris: Minard, 1966), p. 73, M. Meurand revealingly classified this line under symbols, the least accessible images, and she explained it in terms of dreams.

32. Other transpositions of the excellence paradigm can be found in Eluard: for instance, "Leurs lions en barre et leurs aigles d'eau pure" [Their golden lions and their eagles of pure water]. *La Rose publique*, "Ce que dit l'homme de peine . . ." *Oeuvres complètes*, 1:429.

33. Eluard, *La Rose publique*, "Le baiser," 1:442; see Hans Arp, *Jours effeuillés* (Paris: Gallimard, 1966), p. 257.

34. Witness La Fontaine, who calls the rooster a *réveille-matin*, or matins ringer, in the fable of "La Vieille et les deux servantes."

35. The complication of this image is most likely due to the automatic association: *porte* → [*battant de*] *porte* → *battant de cloche* [door → (flap of a) door → bell clapper]. In it, the intermediate link remains unconscious and acts despite the totally different meanings of *battant* in a door context and of *battant* in a bell context. This cannot be proved, but at least one example of this association exists: "La cloche n'a qu'un seul battant . . . [la porte] s'ouvre enfin, son battant claque" [The bell has only one *clapper* . . . (the door) finally opens; its *flap* slams]. Robert Desnos, *Contrée*, "La Peste," in *Calixto* (Paris: Gallimard, 1962), p. 51, lines 1–2, 12. [This punning association utterly defies translation.—TRANSLATOR.]

36. Leiris, "Les Aruspices," published in *La Révolution surréaliste* (1926), vol. 8.

37. Cf. Eluard, *La Rose publique*, "L'objectivité poétique . . . ," *Oeuvres complètes*, 1:422: "Matin brisé dans les bras endormis / Matin qui ne reviendra pas" [Morning crushed in sleeping arms, morning that will not return].

38. Cf. La Fontaine, "La Vieille et les deux servantes," line 11: "Un misérable coq à point nommé chantait" [A wretched cock crowed right on time]; Eluard, *La Vie immédiate*, "Récitation," *Oeuvres complètes*, 1:380: "Le réveille-matin qui fait des copeaux du dormeur / Et ne lui laisse que le temps de ne pas s'habiller" [The alarm clock which makes shavings out of the sleeper and only leaves him time not to get dressed].

39. *Briser* is generated here by the bell, which can itself be struck, rather than being swung. Taken literally, this gives us: "Maniant les battants comme des heurtoirs, ding, ding, ding, ding, ils frappent l'airain avec une rapidité frénétique" [Handling the clappers like door-knockers, ding, ding, ding, ding, they strike the bronze with frenzied speed]. Pierre Loti, *Figures et choses* (Paris: Calmann-Lévy, 1899), p. 109. And figuratively, "Qu'est-ce que ce marteau, la cloche, forge sur cette enclume, la pensée?" [What is this hammer, the bell, forging on this anvil, thought?] Hugo, *L'Homme qui rit* (Paris: Imprimerie nationale, 1907), p. 403.

40. Cf. Rainer Maria Rilke, *Sonnets to Orpheus*, part 2, sonnet 12: "Warte, ein Härtestes warnt aus der Ferne das Harte," quoted in Gaston Bachelard, *La Terre et les rêveries de la volonté* (Paris: Corti, 1958), p. 63. See also Bachelard's quotations from Knut Hamsun (pp. 160 and 190) and Ruskin (p. 198); cf. Hugo's line in note 39.

41. This is also precisely what happens in Rimbaud's "Fêtes de la faim," in which the hyperbole of inedible hardness and, consequently, the symbolic food of hunger is either stone or metal. This hardness is first emphasized by its role as an anvil in the onomatopoetic "Dinn! dinn! dinn! dinn!" and then by the series: "Mangez / Les *cailloux* qu'un pauvre *brise*, / Les vieilles pierres d'église, / Les *galets*, fils des déluges" [Eat the *gravel crushed* by a poor fellow, the old church stones, the pebbles, those children of the floods]. Also cf. Proust's pun in *Sodome et Gomorrhe* (Paris: Gallimard, 1954), 10:68: "galette . . . dure comme un galet" [a cake hard as a pebble], and Antonin Artaud, "Héloïse et Abélard," in *Oeuvres complètes* (Paris: Gallimard, 1970), 1:129: "sexes . . . durs comme des galets" [genitals hard as pebbles]; cf. pp. 132, 135. The place of *galet* in the French lexicon and its importance in the imagination have been amply demonstrated by Francis Ponge in his prose poem, "Le galet" (*Le Parti pris des choses*). See also R. Murier, "Prologue," *Courrier du Centre international d'études poétiques* (1966), 58:12–13; and Raymond Queneau, *Fendre les flots* (Paris: Gallimard, 1969), p. 35. In the seventeenth century, musings on etymology significantly accounted for the word *galet* by tracing it to a supposed Celtic root meaning "hard." This hypothesis was rejected by Ménage, but later on, in the nineteenth century, Larousse's *Grand dictionnaire* was still unwilling to give it up completely.

42. André Breton, "[Premier] manifeste du surréalisme," in *Manifestes du surréalisme*, p. 45. See Michel Carrouges, *André Breton et les Données fondamentales du surréalisme* (Paris: Gallimard, 1967), pp. 173ff.

43. Ghérasim Luca, *Héros-limite*, "L'écho du coeur," in J.-L. Bédouin, *La Poésie surréaliste* (Paris: Seghers, 1964), p. 106. Furthermore, in a case such as this it is impossible to distinguish the primary metaphor from its derivatives other than by their position. [Luca's punning is untranslatable. The French word for the border of a country is *frontière*, which happens to contain *front*, the word for "forehead"; similarly, *visage* [face] and *visa*.—TRANSLATOR.]

44. Breton, *Oubliés*, "Ecoute au coquillage," in *Poèmes*, p. 262.

45. Breton, *Le Revolver à cheveux blancs*, "La Forêt dans la hache," in *Poèmes*, p. 89.

46. See Breton, *Clair de terre*, "Au Regard des divinités," in *Poèmes*, p. 41. In it a similar image represents Truth *sub specie aeternitatis*: "le clocher du village des couleurs fondues / Te servira de point de repère" [the belltower of the village of the blended colors will be your landmark].

47. The animation, mythification, or personification of a noun is a common way to translate an abstract utterance into a narrative full of imagery. Consider, for example, *Poisson soluble*, prose poem 23 (*Manifestes du surréalisme*, p. 110): "Je ne suis pas perdu pour toi: je suis seulement à l'écart de ce qui te ressemble, là où l'oiseau nommé Crève-coeur pousse son cri" [I am not lost for you. I am just far away from what resembles you, where the bird called heartbreak is crying out].

48. Everything happens as if the special code set forth the translation rule *A* = "*A*". Cf. Hugo's coinage in "Booz endormi" (*La Légende des siècles*, I, vi): *Jérimadeth*. [When pronounced, the name of this nonexistent biblical land cannot be distinquished from the statement "j'ai rime à deth" (I have a [de] rhyme).—TRANSLATOR] In Breton's own work, we can find such neologisms as *oumyoblisoettiste*, a compound of *oubli* [forgetting], *myosotis* [forget-me-not], and the *-ettiste* suffix found in *clarinettiste* [clarinetist] (*Mot à mante*, part 2, in *Poèmes*, p. 209). We also find explanatory statements in which a comparison simply goes from one like term to another: "elle était en grand deuil. . . . Cette femme ressemblait à s'y méprendre à l'oiseau qu'on appelle veuve" [she was in deep mourning. . . . This woman could be mistaken for the bird that is called the widow] (*Poisson soluble*, prose poem 22, in *Manifestes du surréalisme*, p. 107).

49. Paul Eluard, *La Vie immédiate* (1932), "Le Bâillon sur la table" (*Oeuvres complètes*, 1:388).

50. Cf. *La Vie immédiate*, "Confections," poem XXX. The entire poem is based on the equivalence between *night* and *blindness*, as for example when sleep is called "honte d'être aveugle dans un si grand silence" [shame of being blind in so great a silence].

51. Over the expression of color, of course, but of shape as well, since the horizon forms a red *line*. See, for example, Lamartine, *Recueillements*, "L'Immatérialité de Dieu," IV: "D'une *bande de feu* l'horizon se colore" [The horizon is colored with a *strip of fire*]. Through a kind of trigonometry, the verbal

associations form the coordinates *red* and (*line* →) *bar*, which intersect at the point (*barre de) fer, fer (rouge)* [iron (bar), (red-hot) iron].

52. "Blason dédoré de mes rêves," *Oeuvres complètes*, 2:687. The manuscript reads: "rompu par le fer rouge / De la lumière et de la nuit" [broken by the red iron of light and night] (2:1205), so it is possible that the association was made in the opposite direction, from torture to the image of light. The extending of *fer rouge* to *nuit* underscores just how quickly the referential function can be altered. See also *ibid.*, 1:402: "une barre de fer rougie à blanc attise l'aubépine" [an iron bar reddened white stirs up the flame of the hawthorn].

53. For this reason, a critic with a "classical" bent can admire the image only if he does away with the incompatibility. Significantly enough, K. H. Schmitz translated it as "das zarte Rot des Eisens" [the iron's soft red], thereby disregarding "red-hot iron" and retaining nothing but the resultant color. *Die Sprache der Farben in der Lyrik Eluards* (Nuremberg: Erlangen, 1961), p. 33.

54. In an episode in Jules Verne's *Michel Strogoff* (II, v), the hero, whose adventures are familiar to all French schoolchildren, has been taken prisoner by the Tarters and is about to be blinded by a "lame ardente" [burning sword] moving back and forth before his eyes. According to the entry under *aveugler* [to blind] in the *Larousse du dix-neuvième siècle*, this Oriental torture was reserved for fallen princes. Because of the importance of the episode in Jules Verne, we can be sure that few French readers would fail to understand the exact meaning of this *fer rouge*. (Cf. Breton's obscure allusion to it in *Arcane 17*, p. 93, and in *Les Pas perdus*, p. 68.) In order to understand the essential, however, we really do not need any definite representation or specific historical knowledge.

55. Another is the spear that relieves pain in *Parsifal*.

56. *Poisson soluble*, prose poem 24, (*Manifestes du surréalisme*, pp. 112–113).

57. Cf. Breton, "[Premier] manifeste du surréalisme," *ibid.*, p. 55: "L'esprit qui plonge dans le surréalisme revit avec exaltation la meilleure part de son enfance" [A mind that dives into Surrealism exaltedly relives the best part of its childhood].

58. *Poisson soluble*, prose poem 7 (*ibid*, p. 81). [The word *parterre* has two meanings in French: (a) the orchestra section in a theater or concert hall; and (b) a flowerbed. If we take the word apart, however, it gives us *par* + *terre* [(on the) + earth]. From this, Breton derives *parciels* [par-skies].—TRANSLATOR.]

59. *Ibid.*, p. 81.

60. Breton, *La Clé des champs*, p. 79. On the difference between autonomy and nonsense, see Victor Erlich, *Russian Formalism*, p. 158.

13. Semantic Incompatibilities in Automatic Writing

1. See, among others, Anna Balakian, *André Breton* (New York: Oxford University Press, 1971), pp. 65ff.; Claude Vigée, "L'Invention poétique et l'automatisme mental," *Modern Language Notes* (1960), 75:143–154; Julien Gracq, "Spectre du Poisson soluble" in M. Eigeldinger, ed., *André Breton* (Neuchâtel: La Baconnière, 1970), pp. 207–220; and as a corrective: Jean-Louis Houdebine,

"Le Concept d'écriture automatique," in *Littérature et idéologie*, special issue of *La Nouvelle Critique* (1970), 39 (*bis*):*178–185*.

2. Attempts at a grammatical analysis yield little—e.g., Gerald Mead, "A Syntactic Model in Surrealist Style," *Dada-Surrealism* (1972), pp. 33–37. See also the more radical approach of Per Aage Brandt, "The White-Haired Generator," *Poetics* (1972), 6:77–83.

3. Quotations from *Poisson soluble* (1924) are taken from *Manifestes du surréalisme* (Paris: Pauvert, 1962).

4. I am concerned here not with the morphology of the tale, which could be reached with an analysis à la Propp, but rather with the awareness of such a pattern that a reader immersed in a language and its literary forms can actually acquire empirically. See also the initiatory adventures in Marie de France's lais: Jean Frappier, "Remarques sur la structure du lai," in *La Littérature narrative d'imagination: Colloque de Strasbourg, 1959* (Paris: Presses Universitaires de France, 1961), pp. 22–39.

5. On expansion, see chapter 3.

6. Not to mention the fact that, from the earliest grades in school on, French children learn to recognize the phrase as a stylistic marker of the medieval epic, or at least of the ideology of that epic, the best-known example of which is *La Chanson de Roland.*

7. The *lyre* was so popular a lighting fixture that Pierre Larousse's first *Grand dictionnaire* lists "lighting fixture" as one of the word's literal meanings: see the entry under "lyre," dated 1873.

8. On the other hand, Tristan Tzara's *coeur à gaz* [gas heart] involves an incompatibility at the referential level. The term, which was Tzara's own invention, suggests an impossible mechanization of the physiological. The signifiers are affected insofar as the distance between *gaz* and the emotions represented by the heart is particularly great.

9. Huysmans, *Les Soeurs Vatard* (Paris: Charpentier, 1879), ch. 8, p. 100. Breton alludes to this passage in *Entretiens 1913–1925*, pp. 11 and 143.

10. *Poisson soluble*, pp. 98 and 133. There is another animated lyre on p. 155.

11. *Oiseau* does not reappear in the text until the periphrasis is finished.

12. See chapter 3.

13. The first line of Mallarmé's "Sonnet en -yx."

14. We should also note the intertext in Rimbaud: "L'étoile a pleuré rose" [the star cried pink].

15. Germain Nouveau, "Les Mains," line 8. There is even a cliché, now fallen into disuse, about blood under one's nails, to the tip of one's nails, indicating generosity and strength.

16. See Baudelaire, "A une Passante": "je buvais . . . / Dans son oeil, ciel livide où germe l'ouragan, / La douceur qui fascine et le plaisir qui tue. / Un éclair . . . puis la nuit!—Fugitive beauté / Dont le regard m'a fait soudainement renaître, / Ne te verrais-je plus que dans l'éternité?" [I drank from her eyes, that livid sky where storms brew, the sweetness that fascinates and the pleasure that kills. A flash of lightning . . . then night! O, beautiful fugitive, your glance

made me suddenly be reborn. Shall I never see you again until eternity?]. Baudelaire's sonnet also contains *en grand deuil* and is clearly part of Breton's intertext.

17. Victor Hugo, *Les Misérables*, II, III, ix; (Paris: Pléiade, 1956, p. 462): "une petite fille tout en deuil qui portait une grande poupée rose" [a little girl dressed all in mourning and who was carrying a big, pink doll]; II, III, xi (p. 468): "son premier soin avait été d'acheter des habits de deuil pour une petite fille" [his first concern had been to buy mourning attire for a little girl]; II, IV, iii (pp. 478–479): "en prenant les mots dans leur sens le plus compréhensif et le plus absolu . . . Jean Valjean était le Veuf comme Cosette était l'Orpheline. . . . Cosette n'était plus en guenilles, elle était en deuil" [taking the words in their most comprehensive and absolute sense . . . Jean Valjean was the Widower just as Cosette was the Orphan. . . .Cosette was no longer in rags; she was in mourning].

18. *Ibid.*, II, III, xi (p. 469).

19. *Ibid.*, II, v, iv (p. 495).

20. Cf. Jean Valjean's topcoat with a secret pocket in its lining (*Les Misérables*, II, IV, iv and v (pp. 482 and 485), which is alluded to in *Poisson soluble*, p. 138. As with *oiseau* in *oiseau-lyre*, the automatic text obliterates the essential word and metonymically circles around the significant void: clothes make the man.

21. If further proof were needed that this is not a mere coincidence, Hugo uses *grelot* rather than *clochette*. [Both words refer to little bells, but whereas *clochette*, the diminutive of *cloche*, evokes a bell-shaped bell, *grelot* can only be a small round, jingle-bell.—TRANSLATOR.] *Les Misérables*, II, v, viii (p. 505): "Il entendait depuis quelque tempts un bruit singulier. C'était comme un grelot qu'on agitait. Ce bruit était dans le jardin. . . . Cela ressemblait à la petite musique vague que font les clarines des bestiaux la nuit dans les pâturages. . . . Il paraissait évident que le grelot était attaché à cet homme; mais alors qu'est-ce que cela pouvait signifier?" [For some time he had been hearing a very strange noise. It was like a little bell someone was shaking. The noise was in the garden. . . . It sounded like the vague little music made by cowbells at night in the pastures. . . . It seemed obvious that the little bell was attached to the man, but what could that mean?]. The Hugo intertext extends to other prose poems in *Poisson soluble* as well: the village Cosette comes from is mentioned by name on page 129, and Jean Valjean is referred to on page 131; cf. *Les Misérables*, II, II, iii (pp. 405ff.).

22. "Situation surréaliste de l'objet," in *Manifestes du surréalisme*, p. 327.

23. Quoted by Jean Starobinski, *Words Upon Words: The Anagrams of Ferdinand de Saussure*, Olivia Emmet, trans. (New Haven: Yale University Press, 1979), p. 7.

24. As we know, critics have wasted a great deal of time in suspecting the Surrealists of cleverly concocting false automatic effects. This reflects the age-old tendency to confuse what comes before the text with the text itself.

14. Overdetermination in the Prose Poem (I): Julien Gracq

1. Quotations refer to Julien Gracq, *Liberté grande* (Paris: Corti, 1958). Collected under this title are: *Liberté grande* (1947), *La Terre habitable* (1951), *Gomorrhe* (1957), and *La Sieste en Flandre hollandaise*.

2. Julien Gracq, *André Breton* (Paris: Corti, 1948), p. 194.
3. Gracq, *Liberté grande*, pp. 41–52.
4. On the theme of morbid sensations as an instrument in the mimesis of reality, see J.-L. Leutrat's excellent remarks in *Gracq* (Paris: Editions Universitaires, 1966), pp. 76–77. He quotes a passage similar to this one.
5. Even more so than the bedroom. The bedroom is, of course, more private and secret, but the *salon*, as both drawing room and living room, is what most fully encompasses the functions of the home as both a place of retreat and of privacy, as opposed to the outside.
6. Jean Giraudoux, *Provinciales* (Paris: Grasset, 1922), pp. 159–160. Cf. Rimbaud, *Une Saison en Enfer*, "Mauvais sang": "l'horloge ne sera pas arrivée à ne plus sonner que l'heure de la pure douleur" [the clock will never reach the point of ringing only the hour of pure pain]. *Oeuvres*, Suzanne Bernard, ed. (Paris: Garnier, 1960), p. 217.
7. This antiphrasis is overdetermined by the hypogram *wagon-salon* [parlor-car]. The same overdetermination generates the daydream of cosiness on the rails in Verlaine's "Maline," *Romances sans paroles*, in *Oeuvres poétiques complètes* (Paris: Pléiade, 1973), p. 131.
8. Jean Tardieu, *Le Témoin invisible*, "Personne," in *Le Fleuve caché* (Paris: Gallimard, "Poésie," 1968), p. 37.
9. Gracq, *Liberté grande*, p. 36.
10. *Rain* has two descriptive systems, depending on whether the weather is hot or cold. If the context does not specify otherwise, the word will trigger only the system for "rain in cold weather."
11. Cf. Charles Baudelaire, *Les Fleurs du Mal*, "Le couvercle" [The Lid], lines 9–14.
12. Cf. the inversion *ce qui faisait vivre tue* [that which gave life kills]. See, for instance, Baudelaire, *Les Fleurs du Mal*, "Au lecteur," lines 23–24: "Et quand nous respirons, la Mort dans nos poumons / Descend, fleuve invisible" [And when we breathe, Death, an invisible river, flows down into our lungs].
13. On these mechanisms, see chapter 12.
14. Gracq thus conforms in his poetic practice to the reservations that he voiced about automatic writing in his *André Breton*, pp. 171–180. When I speak of *conscious* justification, I am not hypothesizing about the author's intentions in hopes of explaining the text. I am simply noting the existence of an *encoded* intention in the sentence.
15. Paul Eluard, *Oeuvres complètes* (Paris: Pléiade, 1968), 1:588 and 725. A word on the difficult phrase "toute coïncidante à une idée d'elle-même" (and here, as a footnote, because that phrase does not belong to the sequence generated by *couvertures*): I believe it is the result of a crossing of *pur*—which also belongs to the tenor's descriptive system (the pureness of the air), since *pur* is "motivated" on the level of the vehicle—with a metalinguistic wordplay. This wordplay turns the very comparative structure into a tautology and emphasizes the fact that the element of comparison is taken, literally, from what is compared to it (thereby indicating how the poem should be read and understood). It also underscores,

through a semantic sliding from *idea* to *idea*, the pureness of *pur*. Cf. Giraudoux, *Elpénor* (Paris: Grasset, 1938), p. 110: "Aucune métaphore ne pouvait s'ajouter aux pensées ni aux mots et les alléger. Le soleil étincelait, semblable seulement au soleil. La lune semblable seulement à la lune, brillait" [No metaphor could be added to either the thoughts or the words to soften them. The sun sparkled, similar only to the sun. The moon, similar only to the moon, shone].

16. *Lianes* does not transform the downpour into a tropical rain. In spite of its tenor, the word is derived from *embrasse* [curtain loop], because it is the only term in vegetal code that can represent a link or loop. Similarly, amongst the fantastic flora of the Romantics, the bell-shaped flowers of digitalis were transformed into little bells.

17. See exactly the same derivation in "Villes hanséatiques" (*Liberté grande*, p. 40). It is based on an initial resemblance, which is confirmed as an erotic cliché: "approfondir sur le foin coupé l'arôme d'une chevelure étouffante, et ourler un pied et une main nue dont les doigts jouent sur les cordes compliqées de l'air" [deepening the aroma of suffocating tresses on cut hay, and hemming a foot and a bare hand, whose fingers are playing the air's complicated strings]. The woman playing the aeolian harp results from the crossing of the "aroma" system with the "air" system.

18. *Ibid.*, pp. 69–70.

19. *Caniche* is so purely formal that we end up with its nonsensical *absence frétillante*. This is not a hypallage of *caniche frétillante*, but a simple change from a + sign to a − sign. "On s'étonnait de son absence frétillante" is a transformation of "on ne s'étonnait pas de sa présence frétillante" [one was not surprised by its frisky presence]. Reality is of so little importance that the negation slided from the verb to the noun.

20. Gracq, *Liberté grande*: *La Terre habitable*, "Intimité," p. 99.

21. Gracq, *Liberté grande*, pp. 22–23. Cf. Charles Leconte de Lisle, *Poésies complètes*, vol. 2: *Poèmes barbares* (Paris: Lemerre, 1893), pp. 244–245.

22. Simple allusions are, of course, frequent. "Gomorrhe" (p. 107) begins by echoing Nerval. "La Vallée de Joséphat" (p. 86) takes certain details in the description of its inn from Verlaine's *L'Espoir luit comme un brin de paille* and perhaps borrows the inn itself from Baudelaire's "La Mort des pauvres," and so on. When they are recognized, these allusions give added value to the poem, just as clichés do.

23. Gracq, *Liberté grande*: *La Terre habitable*, p. 92.

24. *Ibid.*, pp. 58–59.

25. Rimbaud, *Une Saison en Enfer*, "Délires II," *Oeuvres*, pp. 229–230. (The title appears only in the version in the *Derniers vers*, *ibid.*, p. 155.) "Villes" (*ibid.*, p. 277) contains a similar image: "Et une heure je suis descendu dans le mouvement d'un boulevard de Bagdad où des compagnons ont chanté la joie du travail nouveau" [And for one hour I went down into the bustle of a Bagdad boulevard where journeymen sang hymns to the joy of new work]. It is all the easier to identify the Rimbaud intertext for the fact that the texts in *Liberté grande* are saturated through and through with Rimbaud: "Grand Hôtel" (p. 26) echoes

"Marine," "Pour galvaniser l'urbanisme" (p. 11) quotes "Dévotion," and so on. Of course, the themes of morning and the return to work are linked by many other poets as well: see, for instance, "Eclaircie" in Hugo's *Contemplations* and Baudelaire's "Crépuscle du matin."

26. Charles Cros, *Le Coffret de santal*, "Fantaisies en prose," in *Oeuvres complètes*, Louis Forestier and Pascal Pia, eds. (Paris: Pauvert, 1964), pp. 123–125: "C'est un meuble de marqueterie et voilà tout . . . [mais] quand le meuble est fermé, quand l'oreille des importuns est bouchée par le sommeil ou remplie des bruits extérieurs, quand la pensée des hommes s'appesantit sur quelque objet positif [ou] aussitôt le regard détourné . . . les girandoles s'allument. Au milieu de la salle, pendu au plafond, qui n'existe pas, resplendit un lustre" [It's an inlaid piece of furniture and that's all. But when it is closed up, when the ears of intruders are plugged by sleep or filled with outside noises, when men's thoughts settle on some positive object, or as soon as they have looked away . . . the candleholders light up. In the middle of the room, hanging from the nonexistent ceiling, a chandelier glows]—and on with the ball.

27. Gracq, *Liberté grande*, "Scandales mondains," pp. 54–55. "C'est du joli" is the equivalent of our poem's "rien, n'est-ce pas, ne s'était passé."

28. Not to mention the settings in *Argol*, in *Liberté grande* we find "villes hypnotisées" [hypnotized cities] which will be liberated by a sound (p. 15), forests as motionless and silent as "deux armées avant le chant de la trompette" [two armies before the trumpet call] (p. 60), and deserted neighborhoods "dans un silence plus prenant que celui d'une émeute avant le premier coup de feu" [in a silence more compelling than that of a rioting mob before the first shot] (p. 65).

29. The frequency of a form plays a part here. That the paving stones return to "leur place dans leurs alvéoles" is linguistic proof that the scene is fantastic since, in almost all cases, *alvéole* appears in constructions like *arracher de* [to pull out of]. The fantastic here is simply the verbal reversal of a cliché that cannot be reversed.

30. Here I am thinking of texts such as "La Fête chez Thérèse" in Hugo's *Contemplations* and, in *Les Illuminations*, of poems like "Nocturne vulgaire," where the countryside changes scenery like the stage of an opera house, as well as "Scènes" and "Fête d'hiver." There are even humorous versions of this: in Alphonse Daudet's *Tartarin sur les Alpes* (1885), for instance, a teller of tall tales imagines that the Swiss Alps are rigged out for the pleasure and safety of tourists.

31. Rimbaud, *Les Illuminations*, "*Villes*: Ce sont des villes!" *Oeuvres*, p. 276. (We should note that, like Gracq's poem, Rimbaud's text also contains processions [*cortèges*] and even the word *orphéonique*.) Hong Kong is depicted as the backstage of a theater in Jean Cocteau's *Mon premier voyage* (Paris: Gallimard, 1936), pp. 134–135.

32. In "Paris à l'aube" (*Liberté grande*, pp. 89–93), the same poetic experience is translated into a reasoned style—almost that of a sociological case study—which frames metaphors of a secret life and of the suspense of the twilight hours.

33. The secret, which was already expressed by *Coulisses* and *dissimulation*, as well as by the entire ruin, is once again briefly underscored in erotic code. The

onlooker becomes a voyeur and the clandestine activities become *scandales* [scandals] (p. 59), with "l'envol dans le chien et loup de l'aurore d'un jupon de dentelles" [the twilight flight of a lace petticoat] (see *La Basilique de Pythagore*, p. 62).

34. Cf. this highly revealing word group: *bestioles minuscules, ingénues* [miniscule, naive, little beasties] (*Un Beau ténébreux*, p. 161).

35. From the perspective of the text's genesis, this interference can be explained by the meeting of the cliché I have quoted and the cliché "dissiper les brumes de l'ivresse (l'alcool)" [to dissipate the fogs of drunkenness (alcohol)] belonging to the descriptive system of "drinker." (Drinkers are themselves a consequence of *orphéon*, which summons up an atmosphere of a municipal festival and drinking.)

36. Gracq, *André Breton*, p. 191.

37. *Ibid.*, p. 186.

38. These are the criteria that Gracq applied to André Breton in *Préférences* (Paris: Corti, 1961), p. 137.

15. Overdetermination in the Prose Poem (II): Francis Ponge

1. Francis Ponge, *Entretiens de Francis Ponge avec Philippe Sollers* (Paris: Gallimard-Seuil, 1970), pp. 111–112. Ponge's entire demonstration should be read, sentence by sentence, all the way to the end of this selection from *Le Parti pris des choses*.

2. Ponge, *Entretiens*, pp. 190–191. Like any structural invariant, the matrix sentence remains implicit, and it is the analyst's job to actualize it in its simplest form (as Ponge does when he says: "la beauté est la beauté"). It is, however, also possible to find the matrix sentence in the text, barely hidden by the scattering of the paragram, as is the case here in the sonnet's incipit.

3. See chapters 3, 5, and 11.

4. Ponge, *Pour un Malherbe* (Paris: Gallimard, 1965), p. 275.

5. *Idem*, "Des Cristaux naturels," in *Le Grand recueil*, vol. 2: *Méthodes* (Paris: Gallimard, 1961), p. 200.

6. In hypothesizing a transformation, I am making every effort to keep to word groups that actually exist in the language. Consider the following example of this transformation, which demonstrates the constraining nature of form all the more clearly since the verb *coffrer*, although derived from *coffre*, no longer has any relation to *trésor*: "[Mallarmé] a coffré le trésor de la justice, de la logique, de tout l'adjectif. Les magistrats de ces arts repasseront plus tard" [(Mallarmé) threw the treasure of justice, logic, and all adjectives into jail. The magistrates of these arts will have to wait to have their say.]. *Poèmes*, "Notes d'un poème," in *Tome premier* (Paris: Gallimard, 1965), p. 154.

7. Marcel Spada, *Francis Ponge* (Paris: Seghers, 1974), pp. 53–65; Gérard Genette, *Mimologiques* (Paris: Seuil, 1976), in particular pp. 377–381.

8. Ponge, *Entretiens*, pp. 189–190.

9. I have sketched out a poetics of humor in Ponge in my *Semiotics of Poetry* (Bloomington: Indiana University Press, 1978), pp. 124–138. See also chapter 10 of the present study.

10. I am thinking of Ogden Nash in the United States and, in France, of Audiberti, who, to give one example, turned *nuit* into the nonexistent *nouit* to make it rhyme with *oui* ("Chanson pour mourir un jour").

11. Ponge, *Le Grand recueil*, vol. 1: *Lyres* (Paris: Gallimard, 1961), p. 127. [The Marius referred to is Caius Marius, a Roman general who gained fame by crushing a massive army of Teuton invaders at Aix in 102 B.C. *Amadoué* (mollified) is, of course, a play on Mozart's latinate middle name, Amadeus—TRANSLATOR.]

12. In reference to *La Seine*, Marcel Spada similarly remarks that its "supposed [rhetorical] failure . . . saves the work from the banality of tourist guides and becomes a means of constructing a literary object with its own properties" (*Francis Ponge*, p. 37).

13. Ponge, *Fables logiques*, "De la bouche" (1924–1928), in *Le Grand recueil*, 2:181.

14. Grammatical in the broad sense of the term: here meaning that the description conforms to the distributional and semantic rules of the lexicon.

15. Ponge, *Le Grand recueil*, 2:200–202.

16. *Ibid.*, 2:202.

17. The paragram here is the genre itself. In other words, it is a system of what can be foreseen in the verbal sequence and, therefore, of the reader's expectations. The incompatibility may be limited to one of the meanings simultaneously proposed to the reader by a single word, or else it may involve the very phenomenon of wordplay and of tropes.

18. Ponge, "L'Asparagus," in *Nouveau recueil* (Paris: Gallimard, 1967), pp. 131–139; the above passage, p. 133.

19. *Ibid.*, p. 135.

20. This is very rare, but it is indeed the case: see the entry under *-ace* in Paul Imbs, *Trésor de la langue française* (Paris: Editions du CNRS, 1971), 1:485.

21. Ponge, "Interview sur les dispositions funèbres" (1953), in *Le Grand recueil*, 1:183. [In a context such as this, the reader cannot avoid seeing the maggot, or *asticot*, in the idiomatic verb *asticoter* meaning to pester or "bug" someone.—TRANSLATOR.]

22. Ponge, *Entretiens*, p. 170. Here Ponge confuses semantics with etymology when he says that "Best of all, for a text, would be for each of the words comprising it to be understood in each of the successive acceptations that the word has had in the course of its history." The pun *géné-analogie* [gene-analogy] happily replaces this rationalization à la Isidore of Seville with "associations of ideas" *hic et nunc*.

23. Ponge, *Pour un Malherbe*, p. 275.

24. On this emptiness of the *non-dit*, the unsaid, which is the very heart of the significance, see chapter 5.

25. Ponge, *Le Grand recueil*, 1:128–134. The text dates from 1956.

26. *Ibid.*, 1:129 and 130.

27. Ponge, "La Rage de l'expression," in *Tome premier*, p. 226.

28. Michelet, *L'Oiseau*, "L'Oeuf" (Paris: Hachette, 1856), p. 10. The play of parallels can be continued: Ponge calls the electric power plant feeding his "birds" the *Olympe de notre époque* [Olympus of our era], and he has it inhabited by fearsome gods [*dieux terribles*] and thunder [*tonnerre*]. See also his description of wasps as sparks shooting from a furnace (*Tome premier*, p. 168).

29. Ponge, "Notes prises pour un oiseau," *Tome premier*, p. 278.

30. Or rather, the *rules* of the title. Semantically, *illuminations* posits the invariant of the textual variants. Semiotically, its italics call for variation, since a word in italics plays at meaning something other than what it seems to mean.

31. Ponge, *Tome premier*, p. 283.

32. *Idem*, *Entretiens*, p. 171: "mort de l'objet du désir . . . du prétexte pour que puisse naître le texte" [death of the object of desire . . . of the pretext so that the text can arise].

33. *Idem*, *Le Grand recueil*, 1:25 (1932).

INDEX

Abstemius, 303*n*23
Acceptability, 108, 204, 205, 207, 209, 235, 253, 264, 307*n*20
Accumulation, 34–40, 143, 192, 216, 257, 287*n*26
Actualization, 10–11, 13, 16, 39, 44, 49–50, 53, 57, 60, 70, 76–78, 80–82, 86, 91, 95, 101, 106–7, 141, 146, 148–49, 152, 157–60, 173, 178, 186, 188, 192, 194–95, 205, 229, 231, 237, 241, 259, 266, 281
Adam, Antoine, 7–8, 295*n*15
Adynaton, 84
Albouy, Pierre, 284*n*17, 304*n*8
Alciatus, 119
Allegory, 33, 61, 97, 127, 178, 186, 192–93, 293*n*43
Ambiguity, 9–10, 26, 41, 264
Amphibology, 265
Analysis: formal or textual, 1–3, 6, 15, 24, 90, 99–100, 104, 106–8, 158, 185, 200; grammatical, 221
Anaphora, 34; *see also* Rhyme
Aneau, Barthélémy, 302*n*18
Anomaly, *see* Inappropriateness
Antithetical structure, 57, 114–17, 119–23, 218; *see also* Opposition, polar; Polarization
Apollinaire, Guillaume, 66–67, 70, 291*n*30, 302*n*14
Appropriateness, 82, 88, 117, 208, 212, 231, 234, 246, 249–50, 258, 265
Arbitrariness, 203, 241, 253, 263, 272, 317*n*1
Archaism, 101, 226, 249–50, 293*n*2, 294*n*6
Arp, Hans, 320*n*33
Artaud, Antonin, 321*n*41
Associative: probabilities, 41, 98, 199, 231; sequences, 39, 44, 47–48, 69–70, 91, 106, 120, 187–88, 202, 205, 209–12, 218, 222, 240, 245, 247–48, 257–58, 260–62, 264–65, 271, 273–74; *see also* Stereotype, stereotyped associations
Audiberti, Jacques, 330*n*10
Auerbach, Erich, 181
Author, 2, 4–5, 25, 43, 72, 90, 94, 102, 106, 125, 222, 226; author's intentions, 4–5, 27, 76, 90, 105, 159, 160, 170, 180, 236; author's voice, 142
Automatic writing, 202–3, 206–7, 214, 221–39, 247
Automatism effect, 222–23, 227, 234, 237

Bachelard, Gaston, 321*n*40
Baïf, Jean-Antoine de, 302*n*18
Balakian, Anna, 323*n*1
Baldensperger, Fernand, 299*n*25
Bally, Charles, 317*n*58
Balzac, Honoré de, 13, 21–22, 24, 55, 59, 159–67, 193, 203, 292*n*36, 297*n*3, 299*n*23, 300*n*27, 305*n*9
Baour-Lormian, Marie-François, 295*n*16
Bardèche, Maurice, 305*n*7, 307*n*16
Barineau, Elisabeth, 285*n*29, 299*n*18
Barrère, Jean-Bertrand, 184, 304*n*13, 306*n*2, 309*n*7, 310*n*12, 310*n*13
Barthes, Roland, 11, 299*n*23, 305*n*4
Baudelaire, Charles, 7–9, 16–17, 27–30, 39, 47–49, 53–61, 64, 78–79, 83–88, 90–93, 102–4, 107–8, 194, 233, 286*n*14, 289*n*11, 289*n*13, 289*n*14, 290*n*16, 290*n*18, 291*n*26, 292*n*36, 292*n*37, 294*n*5,

Baudelaire, Charles (*Continued*) 295*n*15, 296*n*6, 298*n*6, 298*n*15, 310*n*10, 311*n*21, 313*n*35, 314*n*36, 315*n*46, 319*n*22, 324*n*16, 326*n*12, 327*n*22
Baudouin, Charles, 316*n*50
Beaujour, Michel, 284*n*25
Bec, Pierre, 298*n*14
Bernard, Suzanne, 287*n*30, 298*n*10
Bersani, Leo, 292*n*34
Biography, of author, 94
Black, Max, 318*n*7, 318*n*13
Blason, 70; *see also Contreblason*
Blin, Georges, 8
Bornecque, Jacques Henry, 285*n*30
Brandt, Per Aage, 324*n*2
Bremond, Claude, 160, 304*n*1, 305*n*8
Breton, André, 2, 21, 24, 85, 203–7, 209–10, 215–16, 218–20, 221–39, 244, 302*n*19, 308*n*27, 314*n*35, 317*n*1, 318*n*14, 319*n*15, 319*n*19, 319*n*20, 322*n*42, 322*n*44, 322*n*45, 322*n*46, 322*n*47, 323*n*54, 323*n*56, 323*n*57, 323*n*58, 323*n*59, 323*n*60, 329*n*38
Bricolage, 41, 317*n*59
Brooke-Rose, Christine, 320*n*29
Brunot, Ferdinand, 318*n*2; and Charles Bruneau, 293*n*1
Buffon, Georges-Louis Leclerc, Comte de, 130, 275
Butor, Michel, 290*n*18
Byron, George Gordon, Lord, 131

Callot, Jacques, 92–93, 298*n*6
Cancellation, 34–35, 39, 190, 211, 225–26, 242–46, 148, 267, 281
Caricature, 18, 20
Carroll, Lewis, 209, 228
Carrouges, Michel, 322*n*42
Catachresis, 112, 115, 122, 159, 169, 265
Céard, Henry, 278
Cellier, Léon, 286
Chanson de Roland, La, 324*n*6
Char, René, 40, 206, 313*n*31, 319*n*15
Character(s), 174–79
Chateaubriand, François-René de, 49, 67–70, 72–73, 109, 125–56, 291*n*24, 291*n*27, 291*n*28, 294*n*9, 295*n*13, 295*n*23, 308*n*26
Chavée, Achille, 287*n*22
Chénier, André, 314*n*43
Chevalier, Jean-Claude, 291*n*30, 319*n*14
Chomsky, Noam, 283*n*8
Claudel, Paul, 299*n*25
Clausula, 52, 69, 84, 122, 280
Cliché, 7, 15–16, 30, 35, 37, 39, 41, 44–46, 48, 50, 52, 57, 64, 70, 72, 82, 91–92, 95–96, 103, 106, 108–9, 120, 127, 151, 167, 186, 189, 192–94, 197, 205, 207, 211, 223, 225, 229–31, 246, 254–55, 257, 261, 265, 274, 289*n*6, 290*n*16, 298*n*6
Cocteau, Jean, 77–82, 254, 328*n*31
Code, 4, 6, 11–12, 16, 35, 40–41, 43, 56, 64, 70, 72–73, 80, 83–84, 92–93, 99–100, 104–6, 108, 112, 116, 118–22, 127, 129–31, 146–47, 149, 161, 163–65, 171, 173–74, 185, 188, 190, 193, 197–200, 202, 207, 209–13, 217, 220, 227, 229, 247–49, 257. 266–68, 270–72, 290*n*22, 301*n*3, 317*n*59
Cohen, Jean, 30–31
Collocation, 41, 163, 185, 236, 266, 274
Comic, 20, 168
Commonplace, *see* Stereotype
Communication act, 283*n*7
Concretization of an abstraction, 213
Condensation, 67, 69, 71, 74, 76, 124, 167
Connective, 207–9, 211, 214–15, 217
Context, 31, 50, 60, 78, 100, 102, 105, 108–9, 120, 146, 162, 169, 188–90, 192, 198–200, 202, 204–5, 210, 214–15, 222, 230, 232, 234, 244, 246, 249, 263, 266, 268, 272, 280
Contiguity, 279
Contreblason, 97–98, 298*n*14
Convention, 103, 108, 131–32, 151, 186, 191, 204, 211–12, 219, 236, 249
Conversion, 43, 53–56, 84, 87, 97, 172, 179, 261, 265, 271, 291*n*31
Coppée, François, 67, 94–95, 294*n*8, 298*n*15
Corneille, Pierre, 81
Cottin, Madame Sophie, 307*n*20
Cratylism, 117
Crépet, Jacques, 8
Criticism, literary, 1, 10, 125
Cros, Charles, 253–54, 328*n*26

Daire, Père, 199
Daudet, Alphonse, 269, 328*n*30

Decoding, *see* Reading
Deictic: device, 165; feature, 12–13
Delille, Jacques, Abbé, 46, 289*n*25, 300*n*33
Demerson, Guy, 320*n*18
De Quincey, Thomas, 85
Derivation, 22, 44, 58, 63, 66, 68, 76–78, 80, 83–84, 114–15, 166, 179, 187–207, 209–14, 216–17, 220, 229–31, 234–35, 247–48, 261–64, 266–67, 270, 275–76; direct and indirect, 259; double, 265; multiple, 212–14; oxymoronic, 65, 68, 87; simple, 210–12; tautological, 65; *see also* Hypogram; Metaphor
Desbordes-Valmore, Marceline, 314*n*40
Description, 17, 24, 43, 52, 54, 56–58, 125, 127, 144, 161–63, 174, 180–201, 211, 226, 240, 255, 266, 281; parody of, 18
Descriptive: sentence, 67, 191; system, 13, 16, 19, 28, 39–40, 49–56, 68, 70, 72–73, 78, 80, 86, 92–93, 103, 106–7, 109, 113, 119, 189, 191, 193, 195, 200, 229–32, 235, 241, 244–46, 249, 251, 260, 265, 270, 276, 290*n*22, 291*n*27, 317*n*58
Desnos, Robert, 206, 229, 232, 320*n*35
Desportes, Philipe, 203
Detail(s), 12, 54, 92, 94–95, 103, 139, 144, 152–53, 161, 167, 175–76, 178, 182, 226, 228, 234–38, 241, 243, 254, 257, 280
Dialectic between text and reader, 114, 157–58, 182
Dickens, Charles, 175, 289*n*9
Diderot, Denis, 147
Digressions, 171–74, 180
Discrepancies: between form and content, 168; between text and reality, 27, 41, 240–41
Displacement, 76, 83, 86, 118, 169, 265, 281
Du Bellay, Joachim, 97, 111–24, 302*n*16
Dubois, Jacques, 295*n*19
Dubois, Philippe, 318*n*2
Dumarsais, César, 293*n*43
Dumas, Alexandre, père, 289*n*10
Du Perron, Jacques Davy, Cardinal, 303*n*29

Eluard, Paul, 36, 40, 203, 207–8, 210–12, 217, 247, 257, 294*n*10, 319*n*17, 319*n*24, 320*n*27, 320*n*28, 320*n*30, 320*n*32, 320*n*33, 321*n*37, 321*n*38, 322*n*49, 322*n*50, 323*n*52
Embedding, 57, 77, 231–32
Emblem, 79
Encoded, 91, 184, 193
Enigma, 115
Epigraph, 268
Equation, *see* Equivalence
Equivalence, 30, 46, 50, 55, 64, 66, 71, 78, 80, 88, 114, 144, 159, 173, 177, 200, 204–5, 207, 210, 248, 256, 267–68, 270, 279
Erlich, Victor, 283*n*1, 323*n*60
Evolution of a code, 16, 99–101, 104–5, 115, 227, 249, 300*n*6
Expansion, 43, 54, 56–61, 67, 76–77, 115, 166, 179, 225, 232–33, 259, 263–64, 267, 293*n*43
Explanation, 1–10, 23–25, 99, 283*n*6
Explication de texte, 2

Fantastic, 219, 226, 241, 328*n*29
Fénelon, François de Salignac de la Mothe, 303–22
Flaubert, Gustave, 223, 278, 300*n*26, 305*n*9, 308*n*25
Focusing, 167
Folktale, 222
Form, 46, 62, 75, 89–90, 100, 125–26, 141, 172, 206, 209, 217, 222, 258, 281
Formal: constant, 161; distortions 76
Formalists, 4
Foucault, Michel, 318*n*14
Frappier, Jean, 324*n*4
Freud, Sigmund, 180, 238
Fries, C. C., 320*n*25
Frohock, R. M., 298*n*15
Füglister, R. L., 297*n*6
Function, 95, 98, 120, 166, 168, 169, 174, 177, 179, 185, 191, 213, 217, 236, 244, 268, 280; narrative, 168–69; poetic, 209, 249; of structure, 141, stylistic, 127

Gadoffre, Gilbert, 301*n*5
Gary-Prieur, M.-N., 294*n*10
Gaudon, Jean, 284*n*17
Gautier, Théophile, 7–8, 53, 70–71, 96, 147, 169, 290*n*18, 290*n*20, 297*n*3, 314*n*36, 316*n*55

Gavarni, 7
Generation, 30, 32, 40, 43–44, 47–53, 56–57, 60–61, 65, 67, 73–74, 76, 78–79, 83, 89, 96, 106, 114, 116, 146, 158, 161, 164, 166, 172, 179, 187–88, 191–92, 196, 198–99, 201, 205, 219, 226, 228, 231, 241–42, 246–48, 254–55, 257, 265, 269–71, 275; oxymoronic, 70; rules of, 43–44, 56–67, 60–61; tautological, 70
Genesis of the text, 90–91, 106, 172, 184, 221
Genette, Gérard, 261, 293*n*42, 299*n*16, 305*n*2, 306*n*13, 321*n*30
Gengoux, Jacques, 298*n*10
Genre, 46, 67, 82, 90–91, 97–98, 112, 124, 168–69, 172, 174, 222, 226, 241, 265–67, 272, 281
Giraudoux, Jean, 244, 327*n*15
Given, 53, 63, 95, 222, 234, 248, 258, 261, 266–67, 275, 281
Glatigny, Albert, 94–96, 298*n*10, 198*n*11
Goethe, Johann Wolfgang von, 308*n*26
Goncourt, Jules and Edmond, 94
Gothic novel, 109
Gottschalk, W., 306*n*2
Gracq, Julien, 240–58, 323*n*1, 326*n*14, 329*n*38
Grammaticality, 266, 330*n*14
Grant, R. B., 307*n*15
Gray, Thomas, 295*n*15
Greimas, A. J., 158, 304*n*1, 305*n*3
Groupe μ, 289*n*3, 294*n*6
Guillemin, Henri, 306*n*2, 307*n*12
Guiraud, Pierre, 286*n*15, 293*n*1

Hamon, Philippe, 305*n*4
Hamsun, Knut, 321*n*40
Heine, Heinrich, 297*n*3
Hendricks, W. O., 283*n*3, 304*n*1
Henkel, Arthur, and Albrecht Schoene, 303*n*24, 303*n*25
Heredia, José-Maria de, 117, 286*n*11
Herodotus, 292*n*36
Hermeneutic feature, 12–13
Hieroglyphs, 238
Hockett, C. F., 320*n*25
Homer, 21
Homologue, 109, 179
Homophony, 236
Horace, 135–36, 153, 194
Houdebine, Jean-Louis, 323*n*1
Hubaux, J., and M. Leroy, 303*n*28
Hugo, Victor, 12–15, 22, 28–29, 32–33, 38, 40–41, 53, 71–72, 100–2, 147, 169–80, 182–201, 223, 226, 236–38, 254–55, 286*n*10, 286*n*11, 310*n*10, 310*n*13, 311*n*20, 311*n*21, 311*n*22, 312*n*24, 312*n*26, 312*n*29, 313*n*31, 314*n*42, 315*n*44, 315*n*45, 315*n*46, 316*n*49, 321*n*39, 322*n*48, 328*n*25, 328*n*30
Huguet, Edmond, 185, 294*n*12
Humor, 168–80, 262, 264, 272–73, 277–80, 295*n*20, 330*n*9
Hunt, H. J., 305*n*7
Huysmans, Joris-Karl, 94, 169, 227–28
Hyperbole, 9, 16–17, 21, 33–35, 45, 50, 55, 60, 64, 67, 70, 84, 95, 113, 146, 163, 169, 179, 189–90, 195–96, 201, 211–13, 225, 231, 243–44, 246, 249, 254–57, 266, 275, 287*n*26, 294*n*11, 321*n*41
Hypogram, 63, 70, 76, 79–80, 86–88, 229, 280–82, 326*n*7
Hypogrammatization, 44–47, 72–73
Hypotaxis, 39

Icon, 68, 80, 105, 123, 235, 268, 272
Ideology, 3, 4, 22; *see also* Sociolect
Idiolect, 52–53, 61–62, 82, 146, 163, 209
Imbs, Paul, 330*n*20
Imitation, 133
Inappropriateness, 30, 62, 64, 77–78, 83, 89, 92, 118, 142, 145–46, 194, 199, 200, 207, 223, 228–29, 233, 237. 240, 247–48, 265, 271, 274, 317*n*57
Incompatibility, 217, 221–39, 244, 266–67
Influence, 91–92, 94, 98
Ingres, Dominique, 132
Intention, 180
Intentional fallacy, 4–5, 76, 90
Interaction, 206–7
Interference, *see* Overlapping
Interpretant, 124, 235
Interpretation, 159, 165–66, 199, 222, 235, 273
Intertext, 53, 60, 78, 83, 85–87, 112–13, 117, 119, 234–35, 237, 292*n*36, 325*n*16, 325*n*21, 327*n*25
Intertextuality, 120, 232, 237, 250–51, 281
Invariant, 10–13, 36, 80, 112, 114, 121–

24, 146, 166–67, 171, 194, 259, 329*n*2, 331*n*30
Irony, 5, 169

Jakobson, Roman, 28, 44, 161, 209, 308*n*1, 318*n*8
Janin, Jules, 310*n*11
Jarry, Alfred, 98
Joke, 97, 307*n*12
Jolloffe, J., and M. A. Screech, 300*n*2
Juvenal, 46, 289*n*11

Kristeva, Julia, 284*n*14, 284*n*20, 289*n*8, 296*n*4, 296*n*5
Krüdener, Madame de, 307*n*20

La Fontaine, Jean de, 120–21, 173, 320–34, 321*n*38
Laforgue, Jules, 300*n*33
Lamartine, Alphonse de, 51–53, 56, 297*n*33, 322*n*51
Larousse, Pierre, *Grand dictionnaire universel du XIXe siècle,* 150, 276, 286*n*9, 292*n*35, 295*n*16, 299*n*23, 300*n*30, 321*n*41, 323*n*54, 324*n*7
Lautréamont, 21, 45, 98, 109, 302*n*14, 312*n*24
Lebègue, Raymond, 308*n*26
Leconte de Lisle, Charles, 250–51, 327*n*21
Lefèvre-Deumier, Jules-Alexandre, 285*n*7
Le Hir, Yves, 9
Leiris, Michel, 34–36, 213, 244, 323*n*31
Leutrat, J.-L., 326*n*4
Levaillant, M., 309*n*8
Lévi-Strauss, Claude, 41
Lewis, Matthew Gregory, 13
Linguistics, 1
Literariness, 1–2, 31, 46, 51, 62, 65, 80, 89, 98, 114, 157–58, 180–81, 238, 260, 268, 288*n*1, 316*n*56
Literary: discourse, 3, 4, 6, 15, 43, 46, 62, 65, 76, 88, 112, 125, 158, 181, 201, 260; history, 90–110, 168, 298*n*11; phenomenon, 1–3, 5, 90, 105, 114, 157–58, 171, 174, 181–82, 282; sentence, 45–61, 63, 288*n*1; *see also* Verbal, game
Loti, Pierre, 321*n*39
Lotringer, Sylvère, 296*n*1, 296*n*2, 296*n*3
Luca, Ghérasim, 214

Malherbe, François de, 259–60, 273–74
Mallarmé, Stéphane, 30–31, 59, 227
Mandariargues, André Pieyre de, 49
Marchand, Hans, 293*n*1
Marichal, Robert, 18–19
Marie de France, 324*n*4
Marivaux, Pierre Carlet de Chamblain de, 319*n*23
Marker, 20–21, 35, 53–56, 65, 67, 74, 86, 104, 107, 118–19, 122, 165, 175–76, 179, 215, 230, 267, 272
Marking, 53–56, 65, 106, 166–67
Marot, Clément, 300*n*1
Matrix, 47, 53–54, 57–61, 65, 69, 77, 79, 86, 114, 116, 166–67, 259–61, 265, 267–78, 270–71, 273, 277, 293*n*43, 329*n*2
Maupassant, Guy de, 278
Maxim, 46, 168, 289*n*7
Meaning: nonliterary, 26, 75, 146; poetic, 26, 29–31, 33, 40, 42–43, 83, 95, 146
Mead, Gerald, 324*n*2
Meleuc, S., 289*n*7
Memory: affective, 137–140; meditative, 137, 140
Ménage, Gilles, 321*n*41
Menemencioglu, M., 297*n*5
Metaphor, 26, 31–32, 41, 46, 48, 60, 77–79, 84, 87, 103, 116, 119, 127, 144, 146, 149, 152, 158, 164–65, 167, 173, 187–88, 191–92, 195, 199–201, 227, 246, 255, 264–65, 268, 270, 275–77; derived, 205, 208–14, 216–17; extended, 202–20, 234, 245–46, 265; primary, 204, 208, 210–12, 214–17
Metonymy, 26, 40, 46, 50, 52, 55, 66, 68, 71, 77–78, 80, 83–84, 86, 89, 106, 116, 122, 144, 149, 161, 164–67, 178, 182, 186–88, 191, 195, 205, 211, 229, 231, 251, 277
Meurand, M., 320*n*31
Michaux, Henri, 288*n*33
Michelet, Henri, 288*n*33
Mimesis, 4, 7, 9, 12–13, 24, 45, 52, 54–57, 64, 70, 73, 114–18, 121, 146–47, 161, 165, 171, 174, 180–201, 207, 223, 229–30, 238, 262, 265, 267, 279; distortion of, 12–14, 27, 31, 87
Mirbeau, Octave, 212*n*22
Model, 16, 39, 63, 73, 86, 95–96, 111,

Model (*Continued*)
166, 201, 204, 243, 261–62, 265, 268; hermeneutic, 163; of literary sentence, 43–61; narrative, 161–62, 222; thematic, 106–7, 193
Molière, 319*n*23
Monumentality, 99, 260
Moreau, P., and J. Boudout, 309*n*8
Morhange-Bégué, Claude, 294*n*7
Morin, V., 307*n*12
Motivation, 43, 50, 52, 54, 56, 61, 65, 67, 70, 73–74, 109, 118, 163, 185, 261, 265, 293*n*42
Mounin, Georges, 288*n*38
Mourot, Jean, 295*n*23
Murier, R., 321*n*41
Musset, Alfred de, 286*n*9
Mythology, 3, 15–16, 72, 93, 103, 106, 108, 110, 158, 186, 193; *see also* Sociolect

Narrative, 24, 43, 45, 52, 57–58, 78, 86, 157–80, 222–23, 237–38, 255, 260, 281, 293*n*43
Narratology, 157–58, 160–61
Nash, Ogden, 330*n*10
Naturalism, 94, 279–80
Neologisms, 62–74, 101, 142, 216, 219, 264, 294*n*9, 295*n*20, 300*n*28, 322*n*48
Nerval, Gérard de, 22, 63, 96, 186, 226, 286*n*9, 299*n*25, 301*n*12, 327*n*22; and François Méry, 310*n*11
Neumeister, Sebastian, 291*n*32
Nonliterary communication, 3–6, 17, 19, 26, 30, 40, 84, 88, 99, 158–59, 181, 201–2, 211, 237, 260, 263, 273
Nonsense, 209, 211, 232
Nouveau, Germain, 231

Obscurity, 9–10, 26, 88, 118, 121, 181, 200, 202, 245
Opposition, polar, 16–17, 29, 33, 44, 48, 67, 69, 103, 109, 117, 141, 143–44, 146, 178, 194, 211, 219, 241–43, 254, 263, 267, 303*n*27; *see also* Polarization
Orphism, 93
Ossian, 102
Overdetermination, 39, 41, 43–52, 64, 67, 69, 73, 79, 86–87, 89, 118, 120, 186, 192–94, 240–82, 288*n*2, 326*n*7
Overlapping, 41–42, 50, 52, 192, 199–200, 246, 270–71, 288*n*2
Ovid, 119, 316*n*56
Oxymoron, 55, 59–60, 64, 73, 191, 266, 317*n*60

Palimpsest, 46
Paradigm, 20, 64–65, 67, 73, 116, 122, 170, 177, 189, 211, 213–16, 230, 275–76, 280
Paragram, 10, 75–89, 123, 296*n*4, 329*n*2; loss of, 87–88
Paraphrase, 75
Parataxis, 36, 38–40
Parnassians, 95, 250
Parody, 18, 45, 161, 170, 178, 243, 272, 280–81
Paronomasia, 9, 52, 68, 72, 81, 86, 116, 277, 297*n*10
Particularization, 187, 189
Peirce, Charles Sanders, 124
Perceptibility, 99, 182
Perception, reader's, 15, 51–52, 62, 65, 75, 84, 88, 105, 114, 116, 157, 166–67, 171, 186, 189, 200, 223, 263, 271–73, 280, 296*n*4
Performance of text, 4, 6, 21
Periphrasis, 33, 51, 60, 66, 68, 73, 76, 114–15, 119, 122–23, 162, 228–29, 265, 281
Personification, 46, 72, 173, 187, 192, 226, 322*n*47
Petrarch, 111–13, 123–24, 165, 303*n*30
Pichois, Claude, 306*n*1
Pindar, 67
Pléiade poets, 121
Plessen, Jacques, 298*n*9
Plutarch, 134
Poe, Edgar Allan, 105
Poem, 26–42; communication in, 26, 222, 268, 273, 281; definition of, 222; descriptive, 181–201; prose poem, 222–282
Poeticity, 266
Poetics, 2
Poirier, Alice, 304*n*8
Polarization, 47, 55, 69, 77, 88, 95–96, 113–16, 176–78, 196, 263, 294*n*11
Polysemy, 10, 41
Pommier, Jean, 298*n*7

Ponge, Francis, 259–82, 321*n*41
Portmanteau word, 63, 65, 228
Predictability, 167, 222, 234, 251
Prefix, 55, 70, 276
Presupposition, 41, 55, 60, 65, 78, 142, 165, 174, 190, 273, 281
Prévert, Jacques, 298*n*13
Prévost, Jean, 28
Programming of text, 112
Prolepsis, 165
Propertius, 316*n*56
Proust, Marcel, 137–38, 190, 193–94, 310*n*12, 312*n*24, 314*n*41, 321*n*41
Proverb, 46, 120, 166–67, 172
Propp, Vladimir, 300*n*29, 304*n*1, 324*n*4
Pun, 81, 172, 206, 212, 214, 261, 267, 272–73, 276–77, 307*n*12; *see also* Wordplay
Punctuation, 280

Queneau, Raymond, 321*n*41
Quotation, 46, 87, 120, 134–35, 207, 265, 275

Rabelais, François, 17–21, 24, 97, 295*n*21
Racine, Jean, 11, 17, 189
Radcliffe, Ann, 13
Rationalization, 2–5, 17, 22, 36, 46, 118, 182, 207, 210–11, 222, 226, 228, 237, 303*n*27
Reader, 2–6, 10–13, 15–16, 25, 28, 35, 38–39, 43–44, 46, 51–52, 62, 65–67, 71–72, 76, 82, 84, 88–90, 92–94, 98–99, 101, 107–8, 111–12, 118–20, 123–24, 142, 153, 157–58, 161–62, 164–65, 167, 170–71, 181, 185–86, 199, 201–2, 204–5, 207–11, 213, 217–29, 222–23, 225–26, 229, 232, 235, 237–39, 241, 246, 249, 251, 253, 256, 262, 264, 266, 271, 273, 277, 280; of today compared to original, 16, 87–88, 99–106, 114–15, 121, 227, 249, 301*n*6
Reading, 4–6, 11–12, 14–15, 20, 22, 42, 44, 62, 66, 75–76, 82, 84, 88, 93, 96, 98, 114, 158, 161–162, 164, 167, 178, 185, 204, 215–16, 233, 239, 246, 249, 251–52, 271–74; double, 45, 88, 95, 109, 112, 250–51; intertextual, 119, 173; retroactive, 35, 37, 44, 66, 115, 159, 280, 287*n*23; as ritual, 88, 111
Realism, 21, 94, 97, 101, 175, 181, 279, 281
Reality: factor in communication, 43; illusion of, 21–22, 38–39, 100, 118, 121, 299*n*18; reference to, 17, 23–24, 152, 223; text judged in relation to, 26–28, 30, 40–42, 88, 181, 200, 277
Referent (reference, referentiality), 15–22, 24, 26, 29, 44, 56, 71, 78, 84, 89, 204, 206, 208–9, 235, 261, 265–66, 270; changes in referential function, 30, 35, 65, 77, 181; verbal, 76, 83, 85, 191, 266, 277
Repetition, 34–35, 57, 68–69, 76, 114, 139, 143, 161–62, 167, 178, 230, 270–71, 279, 287*n*26
Representation, 15–19, 181–201, 211–12, 221
Reverdy, Pierre, 319*n*16
Reversal, 31, 82, 95–96, 179, 219, 246, 286*n*11, 326*n*12
Rheims, Maurice, 293*n*1
Rhetoric, 131, 133
Rhodiginus, 300*n*30
Rhyme, 206, 214, 262
Richard, Jean-Pierre, 150, 154–55, 291*n*27
Richards, I. A., 309*n*5, 318*n*7
Richer, Jean, 310*n*11
Rilke, Rainer Maria, 321*n*40
Rimbaud, Arthur, 37–38, 41, 63–64, 94–98, 219, 234, 252–53, 255, 268, 275, 293*n*4, 294*n*5, 294*n*10, 298*n*6,298*n*11, 317*n*60, 321*n*41, 324*n*14, 326*n*6, 327*n*25, 328*n*30, 328*n*31
Robertson, M. E. I., 309*n*6
Rochette, Auguste, 306*n*2
Roman à thèse, 176
Roman gai, 174–75
Ronsard, Pierre de, 267
Roucher, Jean-Antoine, 295*n*16
Rousseau, Jean-Jacques, 131, 295*n*16
Ruff, Marcel A., 297*n*4
Ruskin, John, 321*n*40

Sainte-Beuve, Charles-Augustin, 104, 203
Saint-John, Perce, 313*n*30
Sand, George, 290*n*23
Satire, 97, 169
Saulnier, V. L., 302*n*20, 303*n*28

Saussure, Ferdinand de, 75–77, 86, 88, 238, 284n14, 296n2, 296n4
Schiller, Friedrich von, 226
Schmitz, K. H., 323n53
Schreber, Daniel P., 311n22
Science fiction, 219
Segmentation, 6–8, 93
Semantic: field, 265; network, 13, 52, 78, 88–89, 163, 169, 188; nucleus, 76–78, 80, 82, 88–89; program, 85; structure, 10, 29, 31, 65, 75, 82, 180, 222, 255; *see also* Seme
Semantics of the poem, 26–42, 157
Seme, 9, 35, 37–39, 51–52, 55, 58, 60, 70, 77–78, 80–81, 83, 88–89, 91, 102, 115, 178–79, 186, 188, 190–92, 200, 213, 228–29, 241, 244–46, 256, 259, 261, 270–72, 277, 291n30
Sememe, 55, 64
Semiosis, 35, 55–56, 72, 82, 118–24, 163, 261, 331n30
Semiotization, 114, 196
Senancour, Etienne Pivert de, 133
Sequence: automatic, 237; narrative, 130, 158, 167, 213, 222, 224; verbal, 34–35, 46, 63, 74, 77, 88, 110, 116–17, 167, 192, 200, 208, 213, 223, 250, 258, 279; *see also* Associative, sequences
Setting, decor, 162
Sign, 26, 32, 55, 71–72, 121–23, 166, 231, 235–36, 272–73, 279, 285n1; dual, 64, 293n41
Significance, 29, 54–55, 60, 64–65, 75–77, 81, 88, 90, 93, 97, 107, 112, 118, 120, 123, 159, 166–67, 245, 250, 260, 268, 273
Signifier, 15–17, 22, 26, 29, 33, 35, 37, 39, 40, 44–45, 52, 68, 71, 74, 180, 188, 191, 195, 199, 201, 205–6, 213, 219, 247, 266, 285n1
Slot, 188, 205, 247, 318n11
Sociolect, 43, 55, 263, 275; *see also* Mythology
Source, *see* Influence
Souriau, Etienne, 293n1
Spada, Marcel, 261, 330n12
Spitzer, Leo, 11, 295n21
Spoonerism, 206
Staël, Germaine de, 49, 131, 141, 153, 290n23, 307n29, 308n26
Starobinski, Jean, 88, 284n14, 296n1, 325n23
Stendhal, 307n20
Stereotype, 15–17, 21, 28–29, 37, 39, 41, 43, 50, 55, 58, 60, 64, 70–71, 73, 84, 86–87, 117, 119, 150, 163, 165, 186–88, 193–94, 201, 230–31, 235, 253, 260, 266, 276, 279; binary 47–49; stereotyped associations, 48, 207, 234, 276
Stock epithet, 9, 40, 58, 190–91, 199, 257, 295n16, 317n60
Structuralists, 6, 10
Structure, 34–36, 40–41, 53, 65, 75, 93, 95–96, 110, 113, 116, 124, 126, 144, 146–48, 150, 152, 157–58, 160, 169, 186, 195–96, 198–200, 205, 216, 219, 222, 232–33, 237, 239–40, 245, 247, 255
Style, 2, 6, 52, 75, 126, 129–30, 132, 170, 176, 213, 243, 272, 274
Stylistic: effect, 7–9, 12, 52, 62, 101, 175; feature, 7, 11, 114, 167, 201, 301n4; phenomena, 10–14; stylistic unit, 7, 15, 43, 52
Stylistics, 1
Substitution, 48, 51, 106, 131, 153, 162, 200, 215
Suffix, 68, 71, 322n48
Superimposition, 44, 46, 92, 109, 118, 122, 131, 138, 206, 243, 260
Surrealism (surrealists), 24, 98, 119–20, 202, 208–10, 214, 217, 220, 221–239, 244, 247, 302n19
Syllepsis, 205, 212
Symbol, 71, 80, 92, 117, 234, 238, 242
Symbolism, 40, 48, 53, 64, 72, 81, 107, 116, 120, 153, 159, 163, 173, 186, 208, 249–50
Symbolists, 54
Synonym (synonymy), 31, 36, 39, 44, 46, 58, 65, 73, 76, 78, 87, 97, 118, 124–25, 148–50, 153, 179, 188–89, 199, 201, 205, 208, 213, 215, 248, 250–51, 257, 261
Synecdoche, 182, 229, 238, 249, 270, 277

Tardieu, Jean, 245
Tasso, 125
Tautology, 18, 65, 72–73, 115–16, 201, 250, 261, 268, 271, 277, 317n60

Technicism, 38, 73, 101–2, 214, 266, 275–76, 295*n*16
Tenor and vehicle, metaphoric, 32, 204, 206, 217, 268
Text, 2–6, 10, 15, 17, 25–26, 31, 34, 43, 62, 70, 74–79, 81, 90–91, 98–99, 105–8, 110, 118, 121, 171, 180, 260–61, 271–74, 281; functioning of, 273; as monument, 2, 6, 8, 90, 99, 260; production, 267, 276, 282; self-reference of, 76, 271–72, 282
Textor, Ravisius, 300*n*30
Textuality, 2, 65, 184
Thematology, 106–7
Theme, 71, 93, 103, 106, 108, 110, 153, 165–66, 182, 204, 210, 217, 231, 233, 256–57, 276, 309*n*3
Theme-word, Saussurian, 75–76, *see also* Paragram
Thomson, James, 16
Tibullus, Albius, 135–36
Tieck, Ludwig, 223
Title, 37, 82–84, 112, 169–71, 180, 250, 266, 331*n*30
Todorov, Tzvetan, 305*n*2, 309*n*11
Topos, 222–23
Topsy-turvy world, 29, 97, 299*n*16
Toulouse-Lautrec, Henri de, 95
Transcoding, 69, 230, 232, 235, 262, 268
Transference, semantic, 159
Transformation, 29, 31–32, 35–37, 45–46, 50–61, 69–70, 76, 79, 84, 86, 96–97, 121–22, 164–65, 172, 179–80, 205, 217–19, 226, 254, 263, 271, 329*n*6; *see also* Conversion; Expansion
Transposition, 45, 61, 66, 129–30, 186–87, 199, 215–16, 279
Trier, Jost, 317*n*58
Trope, 168, 178
Twain, Mark, 314*n*41
Tzara, Tristan, 324*n*8

Ungrammaticality, 51, 62, 64–65, 79, 88, 200, 225, 239, 267, 292*n*36
Unsaid, 116, 120, 123, 301*n*9
Utterance, 283*n*6

Valéry, Paul, 2, 293*n*4
Valorization, 188–89, 191–92, 201, 250, 275, 288*n*37; *see also* Marking
Variant, 10–12, 14, 17, 21, 36, 40, 45–46, 53, 59–60, 66, 69–71, 75–76, 79–80, 84, 89, 93, 112–17, 124, 131, 146, 149–50, 152, 166–67, 171, 177–78, 182, 188, 194, 196, 222–23, 231, 253, 259, 262, 267–68, 296*n*5, 331*n*30
Verbal: game, 4, 17, 24, 215, 273, 281; logic, 247, 256, 262, 274, 280
Vergil, 87–88, 135–36, 139, 155, 189, 197*n*10
Verisimilitude, 24, 27, 40, 44, 54, 57, 61, 97, 103, 117, 130–32, 173, 185, 201, 221, 223, 232, 255, 260, 270, 279
Verlaine, Paul, 22, 326*n*7, 327*n*22
Verne, Jules, 323*n*54
Versification, 250; *see also* Rhyme
Vigée, Claude, 323*n*1
Villiers de l'Isle-Adam, Philippe de, 57
Visibility, 98, 261–62, 273, 280
Vitrac, Roger, 206
Vivier, Robert, 8
Voltaire (François Marie Arouet), 131, 264–65, 303*n*22

Weinrich, Harald, 319*n*22
Word(s): 100, 158, 178–79; compound, 227–28; foreign, 100–1, 104, 189; initial, 188, 201, 206, 280; nuclear, 39, 51–52, 77, 229, 241, 259, 261, 296*n*5; relationship among, 90–91, 125, 146, 156, 185–86, 204, 216; satellite, 105, 210; *see also* Archaism, Neologism, Portmanteau word, Technicism
Wordplay, 45, 70, 205, 261–62, 267–68, 271–73, 275, 277, 280, 297*n*10; *see also,* Pun

Young, Edward, 126

Zimbacca, Michel, 302*n*19
Zola, Emile, 23–24, 94, 299*n*23